KNOW IT ALL,
FIND IT FAST

KNOW IT ALL, FIND IT FAST

An A–Z source guide for the enquiry desk

Third edition

Bob Duckett
Peter Walker
Christinea Donnelly

facet publishing

Published by Facet Publishing ,
7 Ridgmount Street, London WC1E 7AE
www.facetpublishing.co.uk

Facet Publishing is wholly owned by CILIP: the Chartered Institute of
Library and Information Professionals

First published 2002
Second edition 2004
This third edition 2008
Reprinted digitally

British Library Cataloguing in Publication Data
A catalogue record for this book is available from the British Library.

ISBN 978-1-85604-652-7

Text printed on FSC accredited material.

Mixed Sources
Product group from well-managed
forests and other controlled sources
www.fsc.org Cert no. SA-COC-1565
© 1996 Forest Stewardship Council
FSC

Typeset in 10/14 pt Aldine 721BT and Nimbus by Facet Publishing.
Printed and made in Great Britain by MPG Books Group, UK.

Contents

CONTENTS

CONTENTS

Introduction to the first edition

Answering questions from its users is one of the most important services undertaken by a library's staff. Yet it is also one of the most difficult, least understood, and most neglected of subjects. Despite years of working in reference libraries, information units and subject departments, the lack of help we frontline staff get to assist people with their enquiries is a constant source of amazement and irritation. And puzzlement. How *do* you train staff to answer questions? Manuals on question-answering techniques – the social and psychological aspects – there are a-plenty. Lists of recommended reference books are also common. Courses on government publications, law reports, online searching and other specialist literatures and search techniques exist. These can help, of course they can, but all too frequently the questions fired at us out of the blue have not been covered on a course. And the majority of staff on enquiry desks do not have formal library qualifications and have not been on courses. And there is a queue, the phone is ringing unanswered, the photocopier has jammed, and your inquisitor is waiting impatiently for an answer. You are stressed and you can feel the panic rising. Few outsiders can understand the terror experienced by staff newly placed on public enquiry counters. Few of us who have been there will ever forget those early experiences.

What is needed is a guide that staff can use to know where to find the answers, and quickly! Hence this book. We hope it will help.

This book is intended as a first point of reference for library staff unfamiliar with the subject of the enquiry. It is aimed at general library staff and no prior knowledge is assumed. It is an A to Z because this is the quickest way to find a subject. Some typical questions are given to indicate the nature of the subject. Then follow a few background comments that will assist the member of staff to clarify the nature of the enquiry; before one can find an answer it is important to have asked the right follow-up question or questions to make sure the questioner and the questioned understand each other. Then come a few of the more commonly available sources that may help to answer the question. These include printed sources, electronic sources (mostly free websites), and some useful contacts for referral purposes. Finally we include some of the more common tips and pitfalls. A general, non-specialist service is assumed. This is not a book for the specialist.

The sources that can be used to find information are vast; the ones listed in this book are merely a few that the compilers have, themselves, found useful. Your own library will have others, and maybe better ones. The volumes of *Walford's guide to reference material*, published by Library Association Publishing (shortly to be superseded by *The new Walford: guide to reference resources* published by Facet Publishing), are an annotated guide to resources compiled for librarians and researchers seeking further sources, and there are other guides similar in character. An important tip is to get to know and use the sources that you *already* have to hand. It is amazing how many enquiries can be answered by an intelligent use of the local telephone directory, *Whitaker's almanack*, a dictionary and an encyclopedia.

Our aim is to provide a handbook that will help the hard-pressed member of staff serving the public to find a source that may contain the answer, or at least go some of the way to finding it. No book can ever provide the answer to everything, and obviously specialist or more experienced help will often be needed, but we hope that this little guide will help some of the time. All of us, the compilers, spend most of our time on enquiry counters and work with others who do likewise. We have tried to avoid jargon and to base this book on the reality of everyday enquiries. We hope you find it useful. We wish we had had such a guide when we started!

Our thanks go to our many colleagues who have helped us answer enquiries over the years, and to the publisher's reader who gave much useful advice and positive support.

Bob Duckett, Peter Walker and Christinea Donnelly

Introduction to the second edition

We were gratified by the enthusiastic reception given to *Know It All, Find It Fast* by reviewers, users, and those who purchased copies. We were not surprised though: all of us who work on the front line of enquiry service know how difficult it is to help new staff. There is a need for a quick guide to places where questions can be answered. The *Reference Reviews* award for the Best General Reference Work of 2003 was, though, a very welcome surprise.

What was intended to be a leisurely revision during this year was not to be. Stocks were running out and rather than go for another reprint we decided to go for a full revision. The basic structure and layouts remain although there has been some revision of headings and content. A 'General Sources' section has been introduced to pick up those almanacs, encyclopedias and websites that have a wide application, and our experiment of relying exclusively on 'see also' references has been abandoned in favour of providing an index as well – librarians seem to want an index!

Bob Duckett, Peter Walker and Christinea Donnelly

Introduction to the third edition

The need for information, and the need for a guide for those whose job it is to find information, or to help others to find it, continues unabated. This, the third edition of 'KIAFIF', is a thorough revision of the second edition of 2004. More than ever we find how rapidly the familiar landmark reference books have disappeared or become websites, sometimes free, sometimes only available on subscription, sometimes tricky to use. Websites appear and disappear with confusing rapidity; publishers and information producers change their names; sponsors and advertisers intrude; and the increasing dependence on computers and communications technology add further pressure on frontline staff.

Our focus remains on these frontline staff working with the general public on library enquiry desks. As a consequence we have generally ignored the more specialist, academic and expensive resources, though some of the classic reference works to be found in our larger libraries, which are often cited, are included: Joseph Wright's *English dialect dictionary* (1898–1905) and the *Victoria county histories* are two such examples.

In earlier editions we generally excluded subscription websites and CD-ROMs on the ground that most staff and members of the public would not have access to them, but now that most libraries subscribe to services such as *Britannica, Infotrac, Credo, Ancestry* and *EBSCO*, indeed often enabling library members to use them on their home computers, such exclusion no longer seems necessary. We have also continued to loosen the earlier tripartite division of resources into 'Printed', 'Electronic' and 'Organizations'. Such a division seems increasingly artificial and unsustainable. Some new headings have been introduced (e.g. Death, Funerals & Bereavement; Police & Security), some ditched (e.g. Textiles) and many modified (e.g. Books & Bibliographies; Tourism & Travel).

We would like to acknowledge the valuable information to be found in *Reference Reviews* (Emerald) and *Refer: Journal of the ISG* (Information Services Group of the

Chartered Institute of Library and Information Professionals). We also acknowledge the useful titles found on the shelves in many library reading rooms and bookshops, and suggestions from colleagues and members of the public.

Finally, we re-iterate the point that the titles, websites and organizations listed are just some of many; those we know about and have found useful. Maybe you know of others.

Bob Duckett, Peter Walker and Christinea Donnelly

GENERAL SOURCES

Typical questions

- I'm doing a quiz. Where would be a good place to start?
- I'm stuck with my homework. Are there any good websites that would help?
- Can you recommend some good reference books to buy for use at home?
- Is there a directory of websites?

Considerations

Many single resources, printed and electronic, cover a large number of subjects. These will often be the first places to seek answers, especially if they are near to hand. The information may be brief and you may need to go on to more specialized and detailed sources, but it is surprising how often brief information, quickly obtained, satisfies most enquiries. Keep things simple and go for the obvious are two lessons quickly learned. Many of the following sources should be on the Enquiry Desk or on nearby shelves.

Where to look

Guides to reference sources

Owen, T. B. (2006) *Success at the enquiry desk*, Facet Publishing
> As well as being an excellent introductory guide on how to deal with people making enquiries, this popular booklet has notes on the most useful reference works.

Bopp, R. G. (2008) *Reference and information services: an introduction*, 3rd edn, Libraries Unlimited
> Gives background to reference work and resources; US emphasis.

Dixon, D. et al. (2005) *Basic reference resources for the public library*, CILIP Information Services Group

Guides to information sources is the title of a series of books published by K. G. Saur (previously Butterworth) which currently covers 25 subjects. They give more detail than is usually needed by staff in general libraries, but they provide a valuable guide for those who need to go into some depth, including the sophisticated library user.

Walford's *Guide to reference materials* (Library Association) is being replaced by

The new Walford: guide to reference resources (Facet Publishing), general editor R. Lester.

This three-volume work is the standard UK guide to reference resources and provides a useful recourse should other approaches, such as direct appeal to library shelves, fail. Vol. 1, *Science, technology and medicine*, (2003), covers 8000 resources under 1000 subject headings. Vol. 2, *The Social Sciences*, was published in 2007; vol. 3 is in preparation, and will replace *Generalia, language, literature, the arts* (1998), 7th edn, Library Association.

Yakov, J. (ed.) (2004) *Public library catalog: guide to reference books and adult nonfiction*, 12th edn, H. W. Wilson.

A classified listing of over 8000 books regarded as 'core' to US public libraries.

Pinakes **www.hw.ac.uk/libwww/irn/pinakes/pinakes.html**

A free guide to information about reference sources. (The 'Pinakes' was the annotated catalogue of the great library at Alexandria.)

Almanacs and factbooks

Originally, an almanac was a book or chart containing a calendar of a given year with a record of various astronomical phenomena, predictions and other information. Nowadays almanacs tend to be annual compendia of facts. Unlike encyclopedias, almanacs and their modern equivalent, factbooks, are characterized by charts, tables, lists and diagrams rather than prose descriptions. Arrangement is generally thematic and some have an A–Z index.

The following are some of the best from this crowded market. Do get to know one or two of them well, for their arrangements are complex and not to be understood in a hurry.

Whitaker's almanack, A&C Black. Annual

A compendium of information on current affairs from a UK perspective.

Whitaker's Scottish almanack, A&C Black. Annual

Northern Ireland yearbook, The Stationery Office. Annual

A comprehensive reference guide to the political, economic and social life of Northern Ireland.

Montague, T. (2007) *The A to Z of almost everything: a compendium of general knowledge*, 4th edn, Little Brown

The Cambridge factfinder (2000) 4th edn, Cambridge University Press

Chambers book of facts (2007) 6th edn, ChambersHarrap

Financial Times (2005) *World desk reference*, 6th edn, Dorling Kindersley
25,000 facts and statistics, 600 maps, 5000 charts and diagrams.

Guinness book of answers: the complete reference handbook (1995) 10th edn,
Guinness Records Ltd

The Hutchinson factfinder (2000) 3rd edn, Helicon

Information please almanac, Houghton Mifflin. Annual
A US equivalent of *Whitaker's*.

The new Penguin factfinder, edited by D. Crystal (2005), Penguin

Pears cyclopaedia, Penguin. Annual

Reader's Digest (2003) *Facts at your fingertips*, Reader's Digest Associates

Schott, B. (2002) *Schott's original miscellany*, Bloomsbury
This is updated by *Schott's almanac*, Bloomsbury. Annual

Statesman's yearbook, Palgrave Macmillan. Annual
Describes the political, social and economic life of each country of the
world, with details of main institutions.

World almanac and book of facts, World Almanac Books. Annual
US equivalent of *Whitaker's*.

World factbook, CIA (Central Intelligence Agency). Annual
Also available as a free website: **www.cia-gov/library/publications/
the-world-factbook**

Electronic sources

Electronic versions of factbooks include:

www.about.com
www.ask.com (the successor to *Ask Jeeves*)
www.fact.index.com
This is an offshoot of Wikipedia (see under ENCYCLOPEDIAS below).
www.nationmaster.com
A popular version of the CIA *World factbook*, which allows users to compile
their own graphs, etc.

◼ GENERAL SOURCES

Encyclopedias

Encyclopedias have been the bedrock of reference and information work for over a century. They still are, though the large multivolume titles have tended to migrate to subscription websites or are obtainable as CD-ROMs and DVDs. There are now, in addition, many one-volume 'concise' encyclopedias on the market. Encyclopedias are exhaustively researched and well written. They should always be an early source in which to seek information.

Encyclopaedia Britannica (continuous revision) (32 vols) and *World book encyclopedia* (annual), World Book, Inc. (24 vols) are two English-language multivolume encyclopedias that remain in printed form. *World book* is perhaps more suited to a general readership as *Britannica* has, at least in its main 'Macropedia' volumes, a higher readership level. The longer articles of *Britannica* will be appropriate for more detailed information, although the more regular updating of *World book* and its two-volume Britain & Ireland supplement is a balancing factor. Use *Britannica*'s 'Micropaedia' for quick reference. Do use the indexes when the initial 'dive-in' approach to the main alphabetical sequence fails. CD-ROM and subscription websites are available for both titles (**www.britannica.com**; **www.worldbook.com**). Britannica has both concise and school editions.

Some of the older encyclopedias, such as *Chambers* and *Everyman's* and older editions of *Britannica*, are still useful for some topics (the 9th edn of *Britannica*, 1875–89, is known as the scholar's edition because of its essay-length articles by famous authorities).

Some excellent one-volume encyclopedias are:

Crystal, D. (ed.) (2000) *The Cambridge encyclopedia*, 4th edn, Cambridge University Press

Crystal, D. (ed.) (2007) *The Penguin concise encyclopedia*, 2nd edn, Penguin

Oxford English reference dictionary (2002) 2nd edn, Oxford University Press

Philip's encyclopedia, comprehensive edition (2002) George Philip

All Refer **www.allrefer.com**
Free online basic encyclopedia for general reference sources based on a number of reference books and the *Columbia Electronic Encyclopedia* (**www.columbia.edu/cu/cee/cee.html**).

Wikipedia **http://en.wikipedia.org/**
   A free online encyclopedia of over 1.5 million articles that allows users to input material.

Issues (18 issues per year), Independence Educational Publishers
   Not quite an encyclopedia, but useful for a wide range of topics, especially for school and college project work, is this series of booklets, which contain previously published information from magazines, newspapers and government sources on a wide variety contemporary issues. Material can be photocopied and is constantly updated. Over 60 titles are available covering over 1000 articles. There is an annual index. Some libraries provide the full set and/or online access (**www.independence.co.uk**).

The internet

Most libraries now provide public access to the internet. In many cases it will be appropriate to log the enquirer on to the internet and suggest that they search for the answer to their question themselves, either by giving them some recommended websites, or by using a search engine. Obviously it will be necessary to ascertain if they are familiar with using the internet and sometimes some light coaching may be necessary. As with printed sources, check from time to time that the enquirer is coping. Many libraries provide user guides to searching the internet. As well as freeing up your own time, it will provide the user with useful experience of using the internet for further enquiries.

   Many guides to the internet are available. Some good ones are:

Bradley, P. (2004) *The advanced internet searcher's handbook*, 3rd edn, Facet Publishing
   Covers search engines, weblogs, search toolbars, bookmark managers, free text searching, gateways, etc.

Cooke, A. (2001) *Guide to finding quality information on the internet*, 2nd edn, Library Association Publishing

Criddle, S. and others (2000) *The public librarian's guide to the internet*, Library Association Publishing

Poulter, A., Hiom, D. and McMenemy, D. (2005) *The library and information professional's internet companion*, Facet Publishing

Sauers, M. (2001) *Using the internet as a reference tool*, Facet Publishing

Websites

Websites are the basic sources of information obtained through the internet. Search engines and web directories are a useful way of identifying them (see below), though librarians will soon find a number of the more useful ones. Most will have links to related websites.

Among the most comprehensive free websites are:

About **www.about.com**

Ask **www.ask.com** (previously *Ask Jeeves*)

CIA World Factbook **www.cia.gov/cia/publications/factbook**

Direct.gov **www.direct.gov.uk**
    The focus for government information on a wide range of subjects.

Fact Index **www.fact-index.com**
    A general online encyclopedia.

Home Work Elephant **www.homeworkelephant.co.uk**

The Internet Public Library **www.ipl.org**

Nation Master **www.nationmaster.com**

Refdesk **www.refdesk.com**

There are many websites that help with local enquiries, for example about forthcoming events. The local newspapers, local authorities, radio and TV companies often have good ones. Many libraries themselves have sites with useful information and good links. Get to know them.

Web search services (search engines)

'Why have reference libraries when we now have search engines?' is a question people sometimes ask. Search engines are now an essential weapon in the librarian's armoury of question-answering techniques. For specific topics they are excellent, though searching for wider terms and complex enquiries can be difficult. Do learn to be clever about search strategies. You will probably have your own favourites but here are some of the more popular ones:

www.google.com
www.altavista.com
www.ask.com

www.excite.co.uk
www.hotbot.com
www.lycos.co.uk
www.yahoo.com

A useful listing of country-based search engines is **www.philb.com/countryse.htm.** This includes more than 4000 search engines covering 220 countries.

Metasearch services

Although generally slower than search engines, recourse to a meta search service can be useful if a search seems to be failing. These services search several search engines at once. Examples are:

www.dogpile.com
www.mamma.com
www.metacrawler.com

ChaCha Search **http://chacha.com**
> This is a search engine that offers a (human) guide who looks at the results of other search engines to produce tailored results.

Mahalo **www.mahalo.com**
> This is a human-mediated search engine that provides selected websites to the top 10,000 most commonly asked questions.

Web directories

Good Web Guide **www.thegoodwebguide.co.uk**
> Reviews the best websites on all subjects.

Sproose **http://sproose.com**
> A search engine which uses user feedback to evaluate sites.

Virtual Library **http://vlib.org**
> A catalogue of websites monitored by independent authorities.

Two printed guides are:

Tips & Advice: Internet. Fortnightly. Online subscription service available
> A popular periodical service giving information on useful websites.

Zakalik, J. (ed.) (1995) *Gale guide to internet databases*, Gale Research

Regional search services

It can be useful to limit a search to a region, for example, a country, by using a country domain, though this will miss websites using the international '.com' suffix. Examples are:

Euro Search **www.eurosearch.co.uk**
Search UK **www.searchuk.com**

Portals

Portals are websites that lead to recommended and mediated websites on specific topics. An excellent one that covers academic subjects arranged by the Dewey Decimal Classification is **http://bubl.ac.uk**

Aggregators

These are websites that give access to electronic versions of reference books, often searching across all titles using keywords. Usually they are subscription sites, though many libraries now subscribe to one or more and allow users access to them, sometimes through their home computers. Check to see if your library subscribes to any of them and if any passwords are necessary. Examples are:

Cambridge Companions Online **www.cambridge.org/online/ccol**
> An online collection of over 220 reference works published by Cambridge University Press.

Greenwood Digital Collection **http://ebooks.greenwood.com**
> 3000 titles from Praeger, Greenwood, Libraries Unlimited and other publishers.

Oxford Reference Online (ORO) **www.oxfordreference.com**
> Online 'library' of over 100 reference books from 26 reference publishers, including Oxford University Press, on a wide range of subjects. Oxford U.P. also offer e-versions of some 80 of their encyclopedias and dictionaries in their subscription Oxford Digital Reference Shelf (**www.oxford-digitalreference.com**). Again, many libraries subscribe.

Credo (formerly XRefer) **www.credoreference.com**
> Provides access to the content of over 270 reference titles from established publishers.

Gale Virtual Reference Library **http://gale.cengage.com/**

Online access to selected reference books published by Gale, Macmillan Reference, Scribners, St James Press, etc.

Know UK **www.knowuk.co.uk**
An online library of UK information covering over 100 titles.

For services giving access to e-books, not necessarily reference books, see chapter on LIBRARY & INFORMATION SERVICES, section on e-libraries.

Online enquiry services

There are several online enquiry services where one can ask a question that will be answered, usually by a librarian. These may work in real-time, or with a delayed response, usually within 24 hours. The main UK-based one is:

Enquire (formerly Ask A Librarian) **www.peoplesnetwork.gov.uk/enquire**
A 24/7 real-time free information service provided by UK public libraries.

Ask.Cymru **www.askcymru.org.uk**
A bilingual Welsh equivalent to Enquire.

Telephone directories

After *Whitaker's almanack*, a dictionary and an encyclopedia, the local telephone directory is probably the fourth most useful reference source. It is such an obvious source that it may embarrass enquirers who realize they have it at home! Do learn how people of the same name are arranged and also how the local authority and other utilities are styled (i.e. where you find them in the A–Z sequence). The preliminary pages include much useful local information such as national helplines (BT) and street maps (Thompson).

Note that numbers beginning 08 are free to the enquirer.

Other sources

Colleagues The collective knowledge of fellow staff and regular library users is massive. Use it! And even if not massive enough, colleagues may have experienced the same enquiry, or enquirer, before, and may know where to find the answer. Some organizations compile a database of staff expertise exactly for this sort of need. Foreign languages and the ability to read music are two areas of knowledge sometimes needed where colleagues can help.

Referral 'Asking around' can extend to other libraries and organizations, such as local authority departments. Again, it can be useful to make a record of such sources for future reference.

Leaflets The wide range of leaflets provided by public and voluntary bodies give essential information. Most libraries get free supplies, though keeping the collection up to date can be a problem.

A noteworthy service is the *Frills leaflet service*, a fee-based service to subscribers managed by Camden Libraries, which provides details and updates of over 700 free leaflets from some 400 government, charity and other public sector organizations. See **www.camden.gov.uk/frills**. There is a listing of suppliers: *FRILLS directory of leaflet suppliers* (2007), 19th edn, London Borough of Camden.

Fugitive files Many library and information units keep a record of answers to questions that have caused difficulty in the past and that are regularly asked. The information itself may be recorded, for example, 'how to set a barometer', 'the names of Santa's reindeer', or just the source to consult (e.g. wedding anniversaries; Roman numerals).

Newspapers and journals Much useful information is contained in feature articles in newspapers and magazines. See chapters on NEWSPAPERS & MAGAZINES and ARTICLES IN JOURNALS. The Clover Indexes are particularly good for general interest information.

Notes & Queries This is the title of a long-running journal in which contributors requested, and answered, many queries. Published by Oxford University Press, it is available online, full-text, from 2000. The title was taken up by the *Guardian* newspaper in a regular column. Many of the enquiries featured have been put on the *Guardian* website (**www.guardian.co.uk/notesandqueries/**) and published in a series of books edited by Brian Whitaker and published by Fourth Estate. There is a recent compendium: Harker, J. (2000) *The ultimate book of notes & queries*. Typically, these queries are the recondite or the 'funky', e.g. What is the origin of the tooth fairy? Do animals worry? For popular 'imponderables', both these sources may help.

Tips and pitfalls

- Always go for the obvious. Many users over-elaborate.
- With the internet, be aware of how many sites are compiled by companies with a commercial interest and which may be selective over what they contain. The same goes for pressure groups. Be aware also of bogus text

messages claiming to be from authoritative sources: the Citizens Advice Bureau has trouble with these.

- Get really familiar with a few good sources. Often the answer is there if you know how to use the book or website. (The annual quiz provided with new editions of *Whitaker's almanack* is useful training!) This also applies to search engines.
- Understand how *Encyclopaedia Britannica* works: Propaedia, Micropaedia, Macropaedia, index and yearbooks.
- Call 'time' on open-ended searches. Sometimes there *is* no answer. Sometimes the question is wrongly phrased.
- When using telephone directories, don't forget that most have three sequences: classified by subject, business and private.
- Watch out for the quiz addict, particularly over the phone. Do try to get them to do their own searching. We recommend having a limit on the time spent helping them.
- Related to this, have a 'rescue strategy' for colleagues who are getting too drawn into an enquiry. The bogus phone call is useful.
- Be sceptical over the words: 'encyclopedia', 'dictionary', 'handbook' and 'companion', since publishers tend to blur meanings; likewise be wary of 'comprehensive', 'complete' and, of course, 'up to date'.
- Always check the dates of your sources, or the date consulted in the case of websites.
- Always quote the source of your information.

ABBREVIATIONS & ACRONYMS

See also Dictionaries

Typical questions
* What do the letters NACRO stand for?
* What does *ibid.* mean?

Considerations
Abbreviations are shortened forms of a word or phrase, such as 'tel' for telephone, or 'fax' for facsimile. *Ibid.* is short for *ibidem* (Latin for 'in the same place'). Acronyms are groups of letters made up of some or all of the first letters of a name such as BL for British Library, NACRO for the National Association for the Care and Resettlement of Offenders, or CAMRA for the CAMpaign for Real Ale. Both abbreviations and acronyms are common in text and speech but they do cause difficulty for people unfamiliar with them. They are particularly common in technical or specialist writing where they are useful as a form of shorthand.

Where to look
Printed sources
Most general dictionaries include the more common abbreviations and acronyms, either in the main alphabetical sequence or in appendices. Specialist subject dictionaries and handbooks often contain them, though obviously the subject area needs to be known first.

Specialist dictionaries of abbreviations and acronyms include the following examples. They are usually shelved with general language dictionaries.

Acronyms, initialisms & abbreviations dictionary (2008) 38th edn, Gale. 4 vols

Fergusson, R. (2004) *Alphabet soup: an A to Z of abbreviations*, Bloomsbury

Fioretta, B. M. (2003) *Elsevier's dictionary of acronyms, initialisms, abbreviations and symbols*, 2nd edn, Elsevier

Oxford dictionary of abbreviations, (1998) 2nd edn, Oxford University Press

Paxton, J. (2002) *Everyman dictionary of abbreviations*, Dent

Subject dictionaries may be found with the subject itself. Some examples are:

Buttress's world guide to abbreviations of organizations (1996) 11th edn, Springer

Ramsay, A. (2001) *Eurojargon: a dictionary of European Union acronyms, abbreviations and sobriquets*, Fitzroy Dearborn

Electronic sources

Two good websites are:

The Internet Acronym Server **www.ucc.ie/info/net/acronyms/acro.html**
Acronym Finder **www.acronymfinder.com** (180,000 definitions)

Tips and pitfalls

Ask the enquirer for the context in which the abbreviation or acronym was heard or read. This will help narrow the search. Is it in current use? Was it in a newspaper or a book? If so, what was the subject? Is it a technical term? Or a literary one?

Beware the many abbreviations and acronyms that have more than one meaning. JSC can stand for Joint Stock Company and Joint Staff Council; 'p' for 'page' or 'pence'.

This is one of the areas where just asking colleagues may result in the answer.

In searching for abbreviations and acronyms, the spaces or full stops between letters may affect the exact placing of the term in an alphabetical sequence. Sometimes abbreviations come before full words. Always double check – it may be hiding!

ACCOUNTS, AUDITING & BOOKKEEPING

See also Companies – Accounts

Typical questions

- Have you got any information on keeping accounts?
- Can you give me details of a local accountant?
- What does . . . mean in accountancy?

Where to look
Books

French, D. (1991) *Dictionary of accounting terms*, Croner Publications

Beattie, V., Brandt, R. and Fearnley, S. (2001) *Behind closed doors: what company audit is really about*, Palgrave

Collis, J. and Hussey, R. (2006) *Business accounting: an introduction to financial and management accounting,* Palgrave

This covers financial and management accounting in a non-technical style and is particularly suitable for the non-specialist. It includes accounting principles and rules, the accounting system and a very useful section on financial statements of a sole trader, partnership and limited company.

Jeter, D. C. and Chaney, P. K. (2003) *Advanced accounting,* 2nd edn, John Wiley

Directories

Association of Chartered Certified Accountants directory of members
www.accaglobal.com
This has a searchable 'find an accountant' section. This can be found under the ACCA directory of business advisers.

Institute of Chartered Accountants of England and Wales list of members and firms,
Waterlow Specialist Information Publishing on behalf of ICAEW
www.icaewfirms.co.uk
This has a free searchable directory of chartered accountants by location, specialism or sector. Its excellent coverage and ease of use make it well worth a try.

Journals

There are a number of journals that are excellent for keeping up to date with accountancy practice. These are only a selection; it is best to check *Willings press guide* for further titles (see PUBLISHING).

Accountancy
Wolters Kluwer
Tel: 020 8547 3333; Fax: 020 8547 3637
Monthly
Covers everything to do with accountancy and auditing.

The Accountant
VRL Publishing
Tel: 020 7563 5631; Fax: 020 7563 5702
Monthly
Looks at the development of accountancy standards and practices worldwide.

Associations and websites

There are numerous associations dealing with accountancy and auditing. Refer to *Directory of British associations and associations in Ireland*. See ASSOCIATIONS & ORGANIZATIONS.

Accountancy Glossary **www.bized.co.uk/glossary**
> An excellent online glossary offering clear definitions, diagrams and acronyms. It is aimed primarily at students but it would be suitable for anyone to clarify accounting terminology.

Association of Chartered Certified Accountants **www.accaglobal.com**

Audit Commission
> 1st Floor, Millbank Tower, Millbank, London SW1P 4HQ
> Tel: 0844 798 1212
> **www.audit-commission.gov.uk**
> Concerned with ensuring that public money is spent well.

Business Bureau UK: Small Business Information Resource
> **www.businessbureau-uk.co.uk/accounting/book-keeping/index.htm**
> Offers a simple guide to what records to keep and defines the important accountancy terms.

Chartered Institute of Public Finance and Accountancy (CIPFA)
> **www.cipfa.org.uk**
> This organization is the authority on accountancy and financial management for the public services. It has an excellent website that includes the annual report, accounting issues and CIPFA for the regions. Each region has its own web pages full of news, jobs, events and information.

Institute of Chartered Accountants of England and Wales **www.icaew.co.uk**

Institute of Chartered Accountants of Scotland **www.icas.org.uk**

International Accounting Standards Board **www.iasb.org**
> This provides details of standards in force and current projects designed to develop an understandable and clear global accounting standards. It also gives details of publications.

National Audit Office
> 157–197 Buckingham Palace Road, London SW1W 9SP
> Tel: 020 7798 7000

www.nao.gov.uk

The NAO scrutinizes public spending on behalf of Parliament. It audits the accounts of all central government departments, agencies and other public bodies and reports the result to Parliament. Excellent site, packed with useful information on an extensive range of topics. Well worth a visit by students and the public alike.

ACTORS & ACTRESSES

See also Awards & Prizes; Films & Cinema; Television & Radio; Theatre & Acting

Typical questions

- Who starred as Barry in the TV series *Auf Wiedersehen Pet*?
- What films has Johnny Depp starred in?
- Have you a biography of Brad Pitt?
- Where and when was Emmanuelle Béart born?
- Which character did Nicholas Cage play in the film *Leaving Las Vegas*?

Considerations

Questions in this category can cover film, theatre and television, so a wide variety of sources can be used. There can also be many types of questions, as can be seen from the examples above.

Where to look
Printed sources

Walker, J. (ed.) (2006) *Halliwell's who's who in the movies*, 4th rev. edn, HarperCollins
This covers actors, directors, producers and writers involved in film making.

Lewis, J. E. and Stempel, P. (2001) *Ultimate TV guide*, 2nd rev. edn, Orion
Thousands of TV programmes from 1946 to the present day are covered. The Halliwell's of TV! Sadly not updated since 2001.

For general biographies, check your library catalogue.

If your library holds copies of the *TV Times* and/or *Radio Times*, remember that they can sometimes come in useful for recent TV films or programmes. Both magazines usually list casts.

For the actors' union Equity contact:

Equity

Guild House, Upper St Martin's Lane, London WC2H 9EG

Tel: 020 7379 6000

www.equity.org.uk

Electronic sources

A useful site on the internet is the *Internet Movie Database* (**www.imdb.com**). This includes cast listings for every imaginable film and television programme.

If you are searching for an actor or actress on the internet, simply type their name into a good search engine.

ACTS & REGULATIONS

See also Law

Typical questions

- Have you got the Pensions Act 2007?
- When did the Human Rights Act come into force?

Considerations

All major libraries should have copies of Acts. Most will keep statutory instruments and command papers, too. The arrival of the internet has made these available to everyone, even the smallest library. A 'statute' is an alternative name for an 'Act'. A 'green paper' is a discussion document; while a 'white paper', which usually follows a green paper, contains the Government's proposed legislation (i.e. to become an 'Act' of law).

Where to look
Printed sources

Halsbury's statutes, Butterworths

A multivolume publication that groups statutes by subject, with one or more subjects per volume. Volumes are updated at regular intervals. Loose-leaf updating service.

Halsbury's statutory instruments, Butterworths

A multivolume publication that groups statutory instruments by subject. Updated by replacement volumes.

Electronic sources

For government Acts from 1988 (and some prior to this date) go to:

www.opsi.gov.uk/acts.htm
www.opsi.gov.uk/legislation/scotland/s-acts.htm (Scottish Acts)
www.opsi.gov.uk/legislation/northernireland/ni-acts.htm (Northern Ireland)

For statutory instruments from 1987, go to the following site:

www.opsi.gov.uk/stat.htm

For green and white papers try:

www.opsi.gov.uk/official-publications/command-papers/index.htm

For bills before Parliament try:

http://services.parliament.uk/bills

For debates on Acts try *Hansard*:

www.parliament.uk/publications/index.cfm

Tips and pitfalls

The word 'regulations' applies both to statutory instruments (the 'instrument' by which a statute (or Act) is applied) and to regulations produced by government departments. The latter are 'published' or 'issued' in a bewildering variety of ways. Also, be aware that government and parliamentary sites are constantly changing. If you are stuck, type what you are looking for into a good search engine.

ADDRESSES & POSTCODES

See also Telephone Directories

Typical questions

- I want to find the address of Mr . . . in Saltash.
- What is the postcode for . . . Street in Wishaw?
- Who lives at no. 12 . . . Street in Tilehurst, Reading?

Considerations

Finding addresses can be tricky, especially ones that are out of your local area. Finding postcodes, though, could not be easier.

A ADDRESSES & POSTCODES

Where to look
Printed sources

One of the first places you should look is in the telephone directory. If you have a full set then you can search the whole of the country. Obviously, if a person is ex-directory, then this is no use. You could also check the electoral register for your local area. However, you can only check addresses with these and not people's names.

For postcodes, see if you have a local postcode directory, where you can look up an address and find its postcode.

Postcode atlas of Great Britain and Northern Ireland (2006) Collins
> This work contains main maps, presented on a scale of 1:263,000, 4.15 miles to 1 inch. An essential business tool, this atlas, which has been updated for 2007, clearly shows the postcode boundaries (down to district level) for the whole country on detailed colour mapping.

Electronic sources

Using the internet can save you mounds of time when looking for addresses. You can search telephone directories worldwide, check electoral registers in other parts of the country, and check postcodes at the touch of a button.

To look at the UK telephone directories, try:

www.thephonebook.bt.com

or for yellow pages:

www.yell.com

For telephone directories around the world:

www.infobel.com/en/world

To combine a telephone directory and electoral register search in the UK try:

www.192.com
> This service lets you search by name or address in a particular area. You do have to register and there is a charge if your search becomes wider. If you are simply trying to find Mr Smith in Brighouse then you should not have a problem.

The Royal Mail postcode finder lets you type in a street name and town and gives you the postcode. Alternatively, type in a postcode and it will give you the house number and street name. The service is free but you are limited to 15 searches per day!

http://pol.royalmail.com/

AGRICULTURE & FARMING

See also Food & Drink

Typical questions

* How many farms are there in the UK?
* What is the present Government's agricultural policy?
* What does diversified farming mean?

Where to look
Dictionary

For general terms and definitions try:

Dictionary of agriculture (2006) 3rd edn, A&C Black

> This has 7000 terms relating to agriculture, horticulture and veterinary science. Jargon-free entries make this particularly suitable to those without a background in agriculture.

Journals

There are numerous journals covering agriculture and farming, details of which can be found in *Willings press guide*. See JOURNALS & PERIODICALS.

Farmers Weekly

> Reed Business Information
> Tel: 0845 077 7744; Fax: 08456 760030
> **www.fwi.co.uk**
> Weekly
> Contains news, advice and research.

Market research

Key Note reports, Key Note

> For free executive summaries of report titles listed under agriculture visit **www.keynote.co.uk**. For details of obtaining full reports, contact Key Note (Tel: 020 8481 8750; Fax: 020 8783 0049).

Statistics

Agriculture in the UK, 2007, Department for Environment, Food and Rural
Affairs
This is freely available to download at
http://statistics.defra.gov.uk/esg/publications/auk/default.asp
Excellent annual report from DEFRA covering the farming industry, the
food chain, key events of the year, prices, animal health and welfare, rural
development and lots more.

Agriculture statistics in your pocket, Department for Environment, Food and
Rural Affairs, The Stationery Office

Farms Incomes in the UK, 2001-2002, Department for Environment, Food and
Rural Affairs
This is freely available to download at
http://statistics.defra.gov.uk/esg/publications/auk/default.asp

Economic position of the farming industry (Feb 2005), DEFRA
This is freely available to download at
http://defra.gov.uk/esg/reports/repfi.pdf

Farm diversification (2008), DEFRA
This is freely available to download at
http://statistics.defra.gov.uk/esg/publications/diversification.asp

Agricultural prices (2000–2007), Food and Drink Federation
Available to download at **www.fdf.org.uk**

Many of the statistics mentioned under Food & Drink will be suitable to use.

Organizations and websites

British Agricultural and Garden Machinery Association **www.bagma.com**

Compassion in World Farming Trust
River Court, Mill Lane, Godalming, Surrey GU7 1EZ
Tel: 01483 521950
www.ciwf.co.uk
Available to download freely Strategic Plan 2006–2011

Department for Environment, Food and Rural Affairs **www.defra.gov.uk**

This is an excellent site that has a wealth of information available to download. Well worth a visit.

Farming Futures **www.farmingfutures.co.uk**
This has an excellent set of downloadable fact sheets.

Farming Online **www.farmline.com**
Lots of links.

Food and Agriculture Organization of the United Nations **www.fao.org**

National Dairy Council **www.milk.co.uk**

National Farmers Union **www.nfuonline.com**

Sustain – The Alliance for Better Food and Farming **www.sustainweb.org**
Excellent for downloadable publications.

AIRCRAFT & AIRLINES

Typical questions

- What is the national airline of the Netherlands?
- What speed can a Boeing 757 reach?
- Can you give me the telephone number for Ryanair?
- I would like to know times of flights from Blackpool to London.

Considerations

There are several types of questions you could receive when dealing with this subject. Some may be about aircraft and their specifications. Others may be about flight schedules. The range is quite large. It is probably worth splitting airlines and aircraft into two separate sections in order to answer questions more effectively.

There are many sources of information for identifying aircraft and looking at their specifications: *Jane's* is the world leader in this subject. Larger reference libraries should have a copy of this.

As regards airlines and schedules, most major carriers are now represented on the world wide web and the information there is likely to be more up to date than any directories you may have.

A AIRCRAFT & AIRLINES

Where to look
Printed sources – aircraft

Jane's all the world's aircraft, Jane's Information Group. Annual

> This is the guide to both civil and military aircraft of the world. Every country with air potential is considered. It is now available online. There is a subscription fee.
>
> Your library may have some books about individual aircraft, such as Concorde or Spitfire. These 'in-depth' histories will be useful for more serious research.
>
> If you receive any enquiries about aircraft terminology, the following are good references:

Gunston, B. (1989) *Jane's aerospace dictionary*, Jane's Information Group

Crocker, D. (2007) *Dictionary of aviation*, A&C Black

Printed sources – airlines

When dealing with queries regarding airlines, the following publications are essential:

Pooleys 2008 United Kingdom Flight Guide, Pooleys

> Definitive information on more than 355 UK aerodromes, over 300 landing charts and multicoloured area charts, private airfields and farm strips, helicopter landing sites, microlight sites, glider sites, parascending sites.

World Airlines Directory, Flight International

> Provides a comprehensive listing of both scheduled and charter airline services, as well as cargo, non-jet commuter and regional operators. Company overviews, their basic fleet and route information, their maintenance and engineering capability and finally contact details, are all contained in this directory.

OAG Flight Guide, OAG

> This is the complete guide to air travel. It gives flight schedules, airline codes and information, airport codes and websites of operators.

Top world airlines, Avinar Data Ltd

> This gives details of the main airline companies, along with brief histories.

Electronic sources

Most of the world's major airlines now have a presence on the internet. You can find them simply by typing their name into a search engine. There is also a useful listing of airlines, with schedules, prices and online booking facilities at:

www.flyaow.com

Also try:

www.kls2.com/airlines

Other sources

Civil Aviation Authority
CAA House, 45–49 Kingsway, London WC2B 6TE
Tel: 020 7379 7311
www.caa.co.uk

Tips and pitfalls

When dealing with enquiries about airline schedules and prices, it would be prudent to direct the enquirer to a travel agent, especially if you do not have any up-to-date information at your disposal.

ALPHABETS & SCRIPTS

See also Languages & Translating; Signs & Symbols

Typical questions

- Have you got a copy of the Russian alphabet?
- I'm trying to read an old document, but having difficulty with some of the letters.
- Should I look under 'The', or 'B' for the address 'The Beeches'?
- I can't find this word in the index!

Considerations

Much will depend on how much the enquirer knows. Most enquiries about alphabets come from people who do not realize how complex scripts can be. A particular difficulty, especially with languages from the Middle East, India and Pakistan, is that a single language can be written in more than one script. Another difficulty can be that a single letter, or combination of letters, can be pronounced differently in different languages (think of the difficulty that Welsh presents to non-Welsh speakers). Some languages do not have vowels in their printed form; some scripts are read right to left, or even alternately upwards and downwards! Other languages do not use letters but pictograms and ideographs.

Old print can cause difficulty. In English, 'ss' was printed 'f', and the letters 'j' and 'u' did not exist before printing developed in the 16th century. (Be careful when using old indexes and catalogues: even the 1965 version of the British Museum catalogue often uses 'i' and 'v' for 'j' and 'u'.) In German, the ß is still commonly used for 'ss'.

Old handwriting (manu-script) is a more difficult problem, and the enquirer is best referred to someone with archival skills, or to a book on the subject.

Where to look
Alphabets

Brief descriptions of alphabets, often with a tabular presentation, can be found in the larger encyclopedias, dictionaries and teach-yourself-type grammars of the language concerned. Many general books on languages such as the *Dictionary of languages: the definitive reference to more than 400 languages*, Bloomsbury (1998) also have tables. Probably best is volume 2 of Diringer, D. (1968) *The alphabet: a key to the history of mankind*, 3rd edn, Hutchinson. This volume consists entirely of plates.

Calligraphy

For calligraphy, the art of fine writing, see, for example:

Harris, D. (1995) *The art of calligraphy: a practical guide to the skills and techniques*, Dorling Kindersley

Wilson, D. (1991) *The encyclopedia of calligraphy techniques*, Headline Press
Calligraphy is a subject sometimes taught at evening classes, or even features in kits that can be purchased at the bigger stationers or craft shops. Local Asian communities often teach calligraphy.

Old writing (palaeography)

Avrin, L. (1991) *Scribes, script and books: the book arts from antiquity to the Renaissance*, American Library Association/British Library.
A good all-round account.

Hector, D. (1991) *The handwriting of English documents*, 2nd edn, Edward Arnold

Munby, L., Hoble, S. and Crosby, A.. (1993) *Reading Tudor and Stuart handwriting*, British Association of Local History

Archivists have training in reading old scripts and deciphering old documents. They may be able to help.

Society of Archivists
> 40 Northampton Road, London EC1R 0HB
> Tel: 020 7278 8630; Fax: 020 7278 2107
> E-mail: societyofarchivists@archives.org.uk
> **www.archives.org.uk**

Filing and indexes

Filing, or the order in which letters and words are arranged, is a seriously underrated topic! Does 'Social Work' file before or after 'Socialism', for example? Users of indexes and directories need to be aware how such things as hyphenated names are presented (by first or second element of the name?), how names that are the same but have different meanings are distinguished, and whether or not the definite and indefinite articles ('the', 'a', 'an') are used to influence order. Sophisticated filing rules do exist but are frequently ignored, particularly in computer-generated lists. When someone complains they can't find something in an index, it may be that they are not aware of alternative methods of filing.

Two British Standards are:

BS 1749: 1985 (1991) *Recommendations for alphabetical arrangement and the filing of numbers and symbols*

BS 6478: 1984 (1990) *Guide to filing bibliographic information in libraries and documentation*

Indexing

Wellisch, H. H. (1996) *Indexing from A to Z*, 2nd edn, H. W. Wilson
> Just one of many books on indexing.

Society of Indexers
> Globe Centre, Penistone Road, Sheffield S6 3A
> Tel: 0114 281 3060; Fax: 0114 281 3061

E-mail: admin@socind.demon.co.uk

www.socind.demon.co.uk

The Society runs courses on indexing and provides practical advice to indexers and those who want to contact them.

Tips and pitfalls

Beware non-Roman scripts that have been put into a Roman script phonetically. Many of the older dictionaries use systems of transliteration (correspondences between sounds and letters, or one system of letters into another) no longer understood by those whose languages are being transliterated. Russian and Chinese are two that can cause confusion. Thus Tchaikovsky can also be spelt Chaikovskii, and Peking is now generally spelt Beijing ('Pinyin' characters replaced the 'Wade-Giles' system in the mid-1950s, though both use the Roman alphabet). Beware classic and modern versions of the same language, e.g. Arabic and Greek.

ANIMALS, PETS & VETS

See also Birds; Natural History

Typical questions

- I think my pet is ill. Have you a book that will help?
- Where can I find a vet?
- What are the qualities to look for in a pedigree dog?
- What is the difference between a stoat and a badger?

Considerations

Pets, and animals in general, often mean a great deal to people, and library staff have to be particularly sensitive when dealing with queries about them. Although there are many good cheap books about pets, there are occasions when the resources of the library are sought.

Be careful not to be give advice about pets, that's a job for vets. All staff can do is to refer people to sources.

Where to look
General sources

Most general encyclopedias will have useful articles on animals. Other good books include:

Allaby, M. (ed.) (1997) *The dictionary of zoology*, 2nd edn, Oxford University Press

Black's veterinary dictionary (2005) 21st edn, A&C Black
Black's is a standard reference dictionary for vets, students and journalists, and is frequently revised. It covers topical issues such as BSE and foot and mouth disease.

Coke, F. (ed.) (2004) *The encylopedia of animals*, University of California Press

Macdonald, D. W. (ed.) (2006) *Encyclopedia of mammals*, 2nd edn, Oxford University Press

My Pet Stop **www.mypetstop.com**
Gives information and health advice.

UKPets **www.ukpets.co.uk**
Directory of pet shops and suppliers; advice.

Individual animals

HarperCollins produces an excellent series of field guides on a wide range of animals.

Cats

Fogle, B. (2001) *The new encyclopedia of the cat*, 2nd edn, Dorling Kindersley

Morris, D. (1996) *Cat world: a feline dictionary*, Ebury Press

Cats Protection **www.cats.org.uk**
Advice, news and archive of cat photos.

Dogs

Kennel Club (1998) *The Kennel Club's illustrated breed standards*, 3rd edn, Ebury Press

Fogle, B. (2000) *The new encyclopedia of the dog*, 2nd edn, Dorling Kindersley

The Kennel Club
1 Clarges Street, London W1J 8AB
Tel: 0870 606 6750; Fax: 020 7518 1058
www.the-kennel-club.org.uk

A ANIMALS, PETS & VETS

Fish

Axelrod, H. R. (1997) *Atlas of freshwater aquarium fishes*, 9th edn, TFH
Over 3500 photographs.

Campbell, A. and Dawes, J. (eds) (2005) *Encyclopedia of underwater life: aquatic invertebrates and fishes*, Oxford University Press

Fishlink **www.fishlink.com**

Horses

Flade, J. E. (1987) *The complete horse*, David & Charles

Equiworld **www.equiworld.net**
A directory, magazine and advice service.

Horse passports
Every horse, pony and donkey in England and Wales must have its own passport as a control to prevent horses treated with certain drugs from being sold as horsemeat. The following organisations will help:

DEFRA Helpline, Tel: 08459 335577, **www.defra.gov.uk**

British Horse Society **www.bhs.org.uk**

Other animals

House Rabbit Society **www.rabbit.org**

Bat Conservation Trust, Tel: 0845 1300 228, **www.bats.org.uk**

People's Trust for Endangered Species **www.ptes.org**
Has information on a wide range of species.

Animal rights

Clough, C. and Kew, B. (1993) *Animal welfare handbook*, Fourth Estate

Donnellan, C. (ed.) *Animal rights*, Independence Publishing.
Recent news articles.

Kistler, J. M. (2000) *Animal rights: a subject guide, bibliography and internet companion*, Greenwood Press

Animal Life (quarterly) is the official journal of the RSPCA.

Animal Aid

> The Old Chapel, Bradford Street, Tonbridge, Kent TN9 1AW
>
> Tel: 01732 364546; Fax: 01732 366533
>
> E-mail: info@animalaid.org.uk
>
> **www.animalaid.org.uk**
>
> Aims to expose and campaign peacefully against the abuse of animals in all its forms and to promote a cruelty-free lifestyle.

League Against Cruel Sports

> 83–87 Union Street, London SE1 1SG
>
> Tel: 020 7403 6155; Fax: 020 7403 4532
>
> **www.league.org.uk**

Vets (Veterinary surgeons) and animal welfare

Black's veterinary dictionary (see section on general sources above) provides information about vets.

Merck Veterinary manual online, 8th edn

> **www.merkvetmanual.com/mvm/index.jsp**
>
> More technical than Black's. Free.

PDSA (People's Dispensary for Sick Animals)

> The PDSA have local surgeries providing basic veterinary care in return for donations.
>
> Headquarters: PDSA, Priorside, Telford, Shropshire TF2 9PO
>
> Tel: 01952 290999
>
> **www.pdsa.org.uk**

The Royal College of Veterinary Surgeons

> Belgravia House, 62–64 Horseferry Road, London SW1P 2AF
>
> Tel: 020 7222 2001 Fax: 020 7222 2004
>
> **www.rcvs.org.uk**
>
> The RCVS publish: *Directory of veterinary practices* (Annual), which is also on their website.

RSPCA (Royal Society for the Prevention of Cruelty to Animals)

> Wilberforce Way, Southwater, Horsham, West Sussex RH12 9RS
>
> Tel: 0870 3355999; Fax: 0870 7530284
>
> **www.rspca.org.uk**

The world's oldest animal welfare charity. Check phone directories for local centres or consult their website.

DEFRA www.defra.gov.uk/animalh/quarantine/index.htm
Animal quarantine regulations and advice on overseas travel and the Pet Travel Scheme.

To find vets, try the Yellow Pages or the RCVS directory.

Tips and pitfalls

Sometimes people bring in their pets; this can make for interesting anecdotes! Have the contact details of the local RSPCA close to hand.

ANTIQUES & COLLECTIBLES

See **also** Medals & Decorations

Typical questions

- I have some old porcelain vases. How much are they worth?
- Have you any information on old Corgi toys?
- I have a collection of old cigarette cards. Are they worth anything?

Considerations

There are several points to consider here. Is the enquirer simply wanting to know how much an item is worth, or are they wanting more detailed information about a particular piece? Some enquirers may be wanting to read up about collecting as a hobby. Whatever the scenario, if you do get a lot of enquiries regarding antiques, it may be worth subscribing to a journal or magazine on the subject. They can keep you up to date with prices, auctions and fairs, and will be more 'current' than many books.

Where to look
Printed sources

One of the best journals is *Antique Dealer and Collectors Guide*, Statuscourt Ltd (bimonthly). This magazine is excellent for listing countrywide auctions and antique fairs. It also includes features on different types of antiques and is up to date with its prices.

There are so many books about antiques and collectibles that you could probably start your own collection! Books may date and prices may be years out of date, but descriptive information should still be good. Ensure that you have a current price guide though. These can be invaluable.

Norfolk, E., *Miller's antiques price guide*, Octopus. Annual
This annual guide lists prices for thousands of different types of antiques.

Miller's do a number of useful popular guides, off-shoots of their price guides. Examples are:

Marsh, M. (2004) *Miller's collecting the 1960s*, Octopus

Marsh, M. (2004) *Miller's collecting the 1950s*, Octopus

Bishop, C. (2000) *Miller's collecting kitchenware*, Octopus

Another similar title is:

Curtis, T. (ed.) *Lyle antiques price guide*, Lyle Publications. Annual

These are two of the most popular price guides. There are also guides to different categories of antiques and collectibles, e.g. toys, porcelain, watches. Check your shelves for availability.

If you are looking for antique shops, check the Yellow Pages or see if you have the following publication:

Adams, C. (2005) *Guide to the antique shops of Britain*, Antique Collectors Club

Sotheby's and Christie's produce auction catalogues which can be useful guides to prices if you have any of them.

Care of antiques
Miller, J. (2008) *Care and repair of antiques and collectables: a step-by-step guide*, Mitchell Beazley

Electronic sources
An excellent gateway site to the subject is

LAPADA
535 Kings Road, Chelsea, London SW10 0SZ
Tel: 020 7823 3522; Fax: 020 7823 3511
www.lapada.co.uk

The website of the Association of Art & Antiques Dealers (LAPADA) gives useful advice and links.

Tips and pitfalls

Never tell an enquirer whether an item is worth anything. Simply guide them in the direction of an antique specialist. Also, be careful not to endorse a particular antique specialist as this can also cause problems.

Local museums can be useful contacts, especially as regards objects relevant to the locality.

ARCHAEOLOGY

See also History; Local History

Typical questions

- Where can I take part in a 'dig'?
- What is the difference between archaeology and pre-history?

Considerations

In the previous edition of this book, archaeology and history were treated together, but with the growing interest in archaeology, and especially industrial archaeology, we decided it was time to treat then separately. 'History' is the narrative of events based on written, oral and material evidence, whereas 'archaeology' is the study of that material evidence, the artifacts, and the techniques of locating, excavating, and studying them.

Where to look
General

Two of many general large-format illustrated guides are:

Bahn, P. (ed.) *The illustrated world encyclopedia of archaeology*, Lorenz Books

Cremin, A. (2007) *Archaeologica: the world's most significant sites and cultural treasures*, Frances Lincoln

Some good dictionaries and encyclopedias are:

Jones, W. (2006) *Dictionary of industrial archaeology*, 2nd edn, Sutton

Kipfer, B. A. (2007) *Dictionary of artifacts*, Blackwell

Murray, T. (ed.) (2001) *Encyclopedia of archaeology*, 3 vols, ABC Clio

Orser, C. E. (ed.) (2002) *Encyclopedia of historical archaeology*, Routledge

Specialist sources
UK sites

Taylor, T. (2005) *The Time Team guide to the archaeological sites of Britain and Ireland*, Channel 4 Books.
Illustrated regional guide to sites, ancient and modern.

Techniques and interpretation

Cookson, N. (2000) *Archaelogical heritage law*, Countryside Press
A 900-page handbook.

Evan-Hart, J. and Stuckey, D. (2004) *Beginner's guide to metal detecting*, Greenlight Press

Kipfer, B. A. (2007) *The archaeologist's fieldwork companion*, Blackwell

Renfrew, C. and Bahn, P. (2004) *Archaeology: theories, methods and practice*, 4th edn, Thames & Hudson

Wilkinson, P. (2007) *Archaeology: what it is, where it is, and how to do it*, Archaeopress
A popular, slim, introductory work.

Excavations

Archaeology handbook
Gives information on excavations ('digs'), societies, education, careers, etc.

Current Archaeology (6 p.a.) **www.archaeology.co.uk**
Reports latest excavations and discoveries, UK focus.

Society

The Society of Antiquaries of London **www.sal.org.uk**
The Society of Antiquaries of London has the UK's leading specialist collection on archaeology, antiquaries and related subjects.

Tips and pitfalls

Keep the distinction between history and archaeology clearly in mind.

ARCHITECTURE & PLANNING

See also Construction; Historic Houses & Castles

Typical questions

- How can I find out if a particular building is listed?
- Where can I find a plan of my house?
- How do I get planning permission?
- What's a corbel? And dressed stone?

Considerations

Architecture and building design is a huge subject and users are best referred to specialist libraries, but many of the more common practical questions can be dealt with in smaller libraries. Local planning matters should be referred to the local authority planning departments, but local planning applications may be filed in local libraries.

Where to look

Architecture

There are numerous dictionaries of architectural features; most general encyclopedias will give information. Use their indexes. Three useful books are:

Maliszewski-Pickart, M. (1998) *Architecture and ornament: an illustrated dictionary*, McFarland

Curl, J. S. (2006) *A dictionary of architecture and landscape architecture*, 2nd edn, Oxford University Press

Speaight, A. and Stone, G. (2000) *Architect's legal handbook: the law for architects*, 7th edn, Architectural Press

Royal Institute of British Architects (RIBA)
66 Portland Place, London W1B 1AD
Tel: 020 7580 5533
www.architecture.com
The RIBA website has information on all aspects of architecture.

Lists of buildings

The fullest list of descriptions of architectually important buildings is the *Buildings of England* series of books (Yale University Press) by Nikolaus Pevsner. The *Victoria County History* series is also important, especially for older buildings. Most libraries will have these, or at least the volumes for their locality. There are several other popular sources, e.g.:

Orback, J. (1987) *Blue guide to Victorian architecture in Britain*, A&C Black

Tjack, G. and Brundle, S. (1994) *Country houses of England*, Blue Guides, A&C Black

Clifton-Taylor, A. (1974) *English parish churches as works of art*, Batsford.

Useful websites are:

English Heritage **www.english-heritage.org.uk**
English Heritage (the successor to the Royal Commission on Historic Monuments) is the UK government statutory adviser on England's built heritage, concerned with every building, monument and site in England that is of architectural significance. The website contains information on conservation, obtaining grants and other heritage issues.

Images of England **www.imagesofengland.org.uk**
Photographs every one of England's 370,000 listed buildings.

Great Buildings **www.greatbuildings.com**
Over 1000 buildings searchable by architect, building or location. Photos and 3D models.

National Monuments Record **www.english-heritage.org.uk**
Kemble Drive, Swindon SN2 2GZ
Tel: 01793 414600
The public archive of English Heritage. Holds more than 10 million photographs.

Most tourist offices will have information and handouts on historically and architecturally important buildings. Local history societies and local publications can also be helpful.

Listed buildings and conservation

Lists of protected buildings in a particular area may be consulted in local authority planning departments. Library local studies departments may also have lists. The full English national list is kept (in some 300 folders) by English Heritage at the National Monuments Record, Kemble Drive, Swindon SN2 2GZ.

The standard text on the law of listed buildings is:

Suddards, R. W. and Hargreaves, J. H. (1996) *Listed buildings: the law and practice of historic buildings, ancient monuments and conservation areas*, Sweet & Maxwell

English Heritage **www.heritage.co.uk/apavilions/glstb.html**
This website features frequently asked questions such as the grading criteria, advice on listing, and grants and loans.

English Heritage also publishes *Conservation principles, policies and guidance* (2008).
The Listed Buildings Information Service (Tel: 020 7208 8221) will fax a copy of the listing for one particular building.

See also: **www.icon.org.uk**, the website of the Institute of Conservation.

Planning

Moore, V. (2000) *A practical approach to planning law*, 7th edn, Blackstone Press

Planning policy guidelines ('PPGs')
The Government produce a series of guidelines for local architects and planning departments and developers. These are frequently asked for. Do check if, and where, your library keeps them. The full texts are available at **www.communities.gov.uk/planningandbuilding/planning/ planningpolicyguidance.**

Willman, J. (1990) *The Which? guide to planning and conservation*, Consumers' Association and Hodder & Stoughton

Armour, M. (1988) *Home plans*, 4th edn, PRISM Press
Standard plans and fittings for the home builder.

Plans of local houses rarely exist, but local large-scale maps will give outlines to property for most areas. Try the local studies library or planning department. Old Ordnance Survey maps can be of value for highlighting unusual features.

Local planning applications are often kept in local libraries and council offices for public consultation.

Tips and pitfalls

Local tourist offices may have information and free leaflets on architecturally important buildings in their area.

Caution! Members of the public may ask for copies of large-scale local maps for use in planning applications. Local planning offices may not accept these – so check what the local regulations are.

ARCHIVES

See also Family History & Genealogy; Local History

Typical questions

- Where are your archives? I want to trace my family tree
- Where can I find original records of a firm?

Considerations

'Archives' is a word that is often used loosely. It is popularly used to refer to old documents, particularly if handwritten (manu-script), but it is also used of modern typed and printed records which are the result of the work of an organization such as memos, reports, letters, minutes of meetings, even e-mails and computer discs. ('Records' is a phrase used in this context.) A rule of thumb is that an archive is any document that has not been published, that is to say, not produced in quantities for public use. It is necessary to ask exactly what the enquirer has in mind. Many of the enquiries for archives may well be answered by using printed, microfilmed and electronic alternatives.

Warn readers that archives, being unique documents, are subject to strict rules of access and use. Archive departments and record offices often work on an appointment system, and material is located through indexes and 'calendars' and needs to be fetched from stores rather than being made openly available on public shelves. Some archives may be 'embargoed' or have restrictions on their use. Users need to be precise in what they want and to give themselves plenty of time, both for the material to be fetched, and to consult it.

Where to look
Directories

Archon Directory **www.nationalarchives.gov.uk/archon**
   Online directory of UK record depositories and archives services.

Forster, J. and Sheppard, J. (eds) (2002) *British archives: a guide to archive*

resources in the United Kingdom, 4th edn, Palgrave.
Some 1500 locations are described.

Aldridge, T. M. (1993) *Directory of registers and records*, 5th edn, Longman
Particularly strong on current social records.

Melferty, S and Refausse, R. (eds) (1999) *Directory of Irish archives*, 3rd edn,
Irish Academic Press

O'Neill, R. K. (2002) *Irish libraries, archives, museums and genealogical centres:
a visitors' guide*, Ulster Historical Foundation

Catalogues and indexes

A2A (Access to Archives) **www.a2a.org.uk** (transferring to
www.nationalarchives.gov.uk/a2a during 2008).
A database containing over 10 million catalogue entries drawn from over
400 record offices in England of catalogues describing archives in various
organizations in England and Wales.

National Register of Archives **www.nationalarchives.gov.uk/nra/default.asp**
The National Register of Archives contains information on the nature and
location of manuscripts and historical records that relate to British history.
Over 40,000 collection lists of archives held in UK repositories.

Archives Network Wales **www.archivesnetworkwales.info**
Collection summaries only.

Scan **www.scan.org.uk**
Collection summaries for Scottish record repositories plus access to digital
images.

Archives Hub **www.archiveshub.ac.uk**
Collection summaries for archives held by UK universities and colleges.

*National Inventory of Documentary Sources in the United Kingdom and Ireland
(NIDS)*
NIDS is a reference work that reproduces on microfiche the finding aids to
thousands of archive and manuscript collections in over 120 libraries and
record offices, museums and private collections throughout the UK and
Ireland. Published in eight units per year, accompanied by cumulative
index. The index is also available on CD-ROM and there is an occasional

newsletter. Contact: Proquest, The Quorum, Barnwell Road, Cambridge CB5 8SW, Tel: 01223 215512.

www.proquest.com/products_umi/descriptions/National-Inventory-187. shtml

Many record offices have their own websites, often with catalogues and indexes. These are usually linked to local authority websites. Thus Manchester's 'Past Finder' (**www.gmcro.co.uk/gmpf/index.htm**) lists over 4000 archives collections held by local government services in Greater Manchester.

Organizations

Historical Manuscripts Commission
The HMC was amalgamated with the Public Record Office in 2004 to become The National Archives.

The National Archives (TNA)
The National Archives was created in 2004 by the amalgamation of the Public Record Office (PRO) and the Historical Manuscripts Commission (HMC). There are public search rooms for public using the collections.

The TNA website has a huge amount of information. The 'Research' link includes useful guides, which can be printed out, and the 'Search Archives' feature has links to the National Archives catalogue (A2A) and other websites listing collections not in the TNA collection.

The National Archives, Kew, Richmond, London TW9 4DU
Tel: 020 8876 3444
www.nationalarchives.gov.uk

National Sound Archive (NSA; British Library) **www.bl.uk/soundarchive**
The NSA is the national collection of sound recordings.

Public Record Office (PRO)
The PRO was amalgamated with the Historical Manuscripts Commission in 2004 to become The National Archives; see above.

Society of Archivists
40 Northampton Road, London EC1R 0HB
Tel: 020 7278 8630; Fax: 020 7278 2107
E-mail: societyofarchivists@archives.org.uk
www.archives.org.uk

National Council on Archives (NCA) **www.ncaonline.org.uk**
   The over-arching body representing archive services.

UK Web Archiving Consortium (UKWAC) **www.webarchive.org.uk**
   Information on preserving websites.

Many firms and other organizations keep their own archives and records and may even have their own archivist. Apply direct to the organization to find out.

Churches and cathedrals are often in people's minds when they use the term archives, but it is usually best to refer the enquirer to the local archive or record office first. Even if the office does not have the original, it may have a copy.

Tips and pitfalls

Since most archives have not been published, it is necessary to warn the enquirer to check about copyright conditions in case they want to make copies.

Do beware of the vague idea that people have of what an 'archive' is and the loose way in which the word is used. In particular, beware the school child who insists on consulting 'archives' or 'primary sources' (as the National Curriculum asks him or her to do!). 'Primary sources' can be published sources such as newspapers, but archives, being unique and often fragile, are unsuitable for heavy use.

Alert users of archives that they may have to put their bags in lockers, use only pencils for writing, and book in advance.

ARMED FORCES

See also Battles & Battlefields; Medals & Decorations; Uniforms

Typical questions

* How many aeroplanes do the RAF have?
* I want a book about the history of the RAF.
* How many soldiers does Britain have?
* What are the names of Britain's aircraft carriers?

Where to look
Printed sources

Both *Whitaker's almanack* and the *Statesman's yearbook* have statistics for different countries' air forces, armies and navies, listing numbers of aircraft, naval vessels, armoured vehicles, personnel, etc. *Whitaker's* has a more detailed section on all three armed forces, including the number and type of aircraft and naval vessels owned, numbers of officers, names of ships, and army divisions. The *Statesman's yearbook* goes into more detail for countries other than the UK. The *NATO yearbook* is the best for NATO armies.

The following publications are both useful and list the major military- and security-related events of the year:

Brassey's defence yearbook, Centre for Defence Studies. Annual

International Institute for Strategic Studies, *Strategic survey annual*, Oxford University Press

Air Force

For more detail on the Royal Air Force (RAF), its history and its squadrons try:

Jefford, C. G. (2001) *RAF squadrons*, 2nd rev. edn, Crowood Press
There is a more detailed description of all the world's air forces in:

Taylor, M. J. H. (1990) *Encyclopedia of the world's air forces*, Facts on File
This lists all the major air forces, showing all their aircraft, the air force symbol and its history.

Army

Chandler, D. (ed.) (1994) *Oxford illustrated history of the British army*, Oxford University Press
Covers British armed forces from 1485 to the present day. Excellently illustrated.

Makepeace-Warne, A. (1998) *Brassey's companion to the British army*, Brassey's
An essential reference book for anyone seeking information on any matter relating to the British army since 1660.

Heyman, C. (2008) *The British Army: a pocket guide 2008–2009*, Pen and Sword
A guide to the organization, equipment and tactics of today's British Army.

Navy

Thomas, D. A. (1998) *A companion to the Royal Navy*, Harrap
Covers the development of the Royal Navy for over three centuries to the present day.

History

Usher, G. (2004) *Dictionary of British military history*, 2nd edn, Bloomsbury

Messenger, C. (ed.) (2001) *Reader's guide to military history*, Fitzroy Dearborn

Personnel

The Stationery Office brings out a list of all armed forces personnel every year. These can be useful for tracing records of former personnel.

Websites

Army **www.army.mod.uk/**
Royal Navy **www.royal-navy.mod.uk/**
Royal Air Force **www.raf.mod.uk/rafhome.html**
NATO **www.nato.int**

ART & DESIGN, THE ARTS

See also Museums & Galleries

Typical questions

* Who painted 'The Kiss'?
* I want some information about the artist Paul Delvaux.
* I have a painting by Atkinson Grimshaw. What is it worth?
* What is the Pont Aven School?

Considerations

This is a huge and often troublesome area, but it can frequently be broken down into more manageable concepts like sculpture, graphic art, design, etc. Enquirers often expect libraries to have information about every artist that ever lived, famous or otherwise! The range of art-related questions can be mind-boggling. This section aims to help you find your way around this minefield.

Where to look
General

Bubl Link **http://bubl.ac.uk**
   Includes a selection of internet resources on the arts.

Intute **www.intute.ac.uk/artsandhumanities**

A free online 'gateway' providing access to the best websites on the arts and creative industries on the internet.

Jones, L. S. (1999) *Art information and the internet: how to find it, how to use it*, Fitzroy Dearborn

Oxford Reference Online **www.oxfordreference.com**
Many libraries subscribe to this service which contains the text of many reference books on the arts.

Encyclopedias and dictionaries

Art cyclopedia **www.artcyclopedia.com**
Free website.

The Grove dictionary of art (1996) Oxford University Press
The 34-volume classic resource.

Grove Art Online **www.oxfordartonline.com**
The online subscription version, which includes the *Oxford companion to art*. Includes 2500 images and links.

Osborne, H. (2001) *Oxford companion to art*, Oxford University Press

Chilvers, I. (ed.) (2004) *Oxford dictionary of art*, 3rd edn, Oxford University Press

Murray, P. and Murray, L. (1997) *Penguin dictionary of art and artists*, 7th edn, Penguin

Lucie-Smith, E. (2003) *The Thames & Hudson dictionary of art*, 2nd edn, Thames & Hudson

Who's who in art (2002), 13th edn, Art Trade Press.
3000 names and 400 signatures, British and Commonwealth.

Timeline of art history **www.metmuseum.org/toah/splash.htm**
Free online encyclopedia of art information from the Metropolitan Museum of Art. Includes essays and a chronology.

Artlex art dictionary **www.artlex.com** Free.
3600 terms used in discussing art and visual culture. Includes images, pronunciation notes and quotations.

A ART & DESIGN, THE ARTS

Art movements and genres

Examples are:

Richard, L. (1978) *Concise encyclopedia of expressionism*, Chartwell

Alexandrian, S. (1985) *Surrealist art*, Thames & Hudson

Materials and techniques

Mayer, R. (1969) *A dictionary of art terms and techniques*, 2nd edn, HarperCollins

Fuga, A. (2006) *Artists' techniques and materials*, Getty Publications

Design

Byars, M. (2004) *The design encyclopedia*, 2nd edn, Laurence King/Museum of Modern Art

Erlhoff, M. and Marshall, Y. (eds) (2008) *Design dictionary*, Birkhäuser Verlag

Julier, G. (2004) *The Thames and Hudson dictionary of design since 1900*, 2nd edn, Thames & Hudson

Livingston, A. and I. (2003) *Dictionary of graphic design and designers*, 3rd edn, Thames & Hudson

Woodham, J. M. (2004) *A dictionary of modern design*, Oxford University Press

Bibliographies and indexes

Bibliographies and indexes can cover many different subjects and are useful in finding books and articles on a subject. Check for bibliographies in individual books or biographical works. The *British humanities index* lists journal articles, and newspaper indexes like *The Times* or *Clover* list articles in newspapers (see ARTICLES IN JOURNALS). See also:

Design and applied arts index, Design Documentation. Print and CD-ROM versions

You may have books on individual artists or on the artists of a specific period, country, style or movement. Check your library catalogue.

Finding a painting

If you are searching for information on a specific painting but the artist or title is unknown, there are several sources you could use. One of the best is:

Monro, I. S. and Monro, K. (1956) *Index to reproductions of European paintings*, H. W. Wilson

Valuations

Hislop, D. (ed.) *Art Sales Index*, Art Sales Index Ltd. Annual
Contains price and details of oil paintings, watercolours, drawings, miniatures, photographs, prints and sculptures sold at public auction throughout the year.

Locations of works

Wright, C. (1976) *Old master paintings in Britain*, Philip Wilson
Lists Continental old master paintings in British public collections.

Many of the major galleries around the world have good websites which include catalogues of their paintings. In Great Britain these include the National Gallery, National Portrait Gallery and the Tate. See MUSEUMS & GALLERIES for more information.

The Public Catalogue Foundation publishes a series of county catalogues with colour images of every oil painting in public ownership; 80 catalogues are planned. Contact The Public Catalogue Foundation, 9 Silchester Court, Penenden Heath, Maidstone, Kent ME14 2DF; Tel: 0870 128 3566; **www.thepcf. org.uk**.

Sculpture

Boström, A. (ed.) *Encyclopedia of sculpture*, Fitzroy Dearborn

National Recording Project of the British Public Monument and Sculpture Association **http://pmsa.courtauld.ac.uk/home/dtbfrm.html**
Online database free via the internet. An ongoing project to catalogue all public sculpture and monuments in the UK.

Directories

Artists' yearbook, Thames & Hudson. Annual
Guide to some 3000 visual art businesses and organizations.

Art Libraries Society, UK & Ireland, *Annual directory*, ARLIS.
Useful list of personal and institutional members.

Marcan, P. (2001) *The Marcan handbook of arts organisations*, 5th edn, Peter
   Marcan Publications
   Information on some 2290 UK and international arts and cultural
   organizations.

Art & Design directory, ISCO Careerscope. Annual
   Detailed guide to further education courses in the UK.

Collections in museums, galleries and historic houses, Tomorrow's Guides Ltd.
   Annual
   Details of art in over 1600 buildings in the UK..

Tips and pitfalls

Don't panic if you get an enquiry you cannot deal with. You may be able to pass
it on to your local art gallery or even to an expert association. Check the *Directory
of British associations* to see if there are any relevant bodies. Examples include art
societies, art libraries, art galleries and museums, even government bodies.

ARTICLES IN JOURNALS

See also Research & Study

Typical questions

- Have any articles been published on . . .?
- Where can I get this journal article?

Considerations

Sometimes somebody may have details of a particular article from a magazine or
journal they want to read. More usually they want information on something and
suggest that there might be something in a journal. Often a librarian suggests there
may be an article of relevance, particularly when they have failed to find a book
on a subject. It is often the case that an article in a journal, magazine or newspaper
may exist when no book has been written on a topic. Millions of articles are written
every year: one of the skills of the librarian is to trace them.

   This skill is more applicable to queries in academic and research libraries and
there will often come a point at which it will be sensible to refer the enquirer to
such a library, which may have large holdings of journals and indexing and
abstracting sources.

An important preliminary point is to be aware that unless an article can be obtained online, getting it from another source, such as the British Library, will often incur expense and take time. There may be local policy guidelines on this matter. It is best to treat such enquiries in two stages: 1) to seek articles the library has in stock and that the enquirer can consult or photocopy immediately; 2) to broaden the search using published or online indexes to journals the enquirer will have to consult elsewhere, pay for a download, or obtain through interlibrary lending.

The availability of journals on the internet (usually via subscription) is changing the way in which librarians access material. Do check your local resources.

Where to look
Printed sources

Some journals have their own indexes. Examples are *New Scientist*, *New Statesman* and *Nation*. Newspapers such as *The Times* and the *Guardian* also have printed indexes (as well as indexes on the internet). Check which of these your library has, and where they are located. Are they with the journal, or filed in a separate index sequence?

British Humanities Index, Bowker. Monthly and annual cumulations
> This easy-to-use A–Z index, available in most large libraries, indexes articles in 360 journals and periodicals. Articles are indexed by subject, source, author and title. Includes economics and politics as well as the traditional humanities. About 15,000 articles a year. A useful general source. CD-ROM and web versions are available.

Applied Social Sciences Index, Bowker. Monthly and annual cumulations
> Includes sociology and psychology. 600 journals indexed. CD-ROM and web versions also available.

Clover Information Index, Clover Publications. Fortnightly with annual volumes
> Indexes articles in some hundred popular British magazines. CD-ROM and web versions are also available.

Clover Newspaper Index, Clover Publications
> Indexes news items and feature articles published in UK newspapers.

For older journals see:

The Wellesley Index to Victorian Periodicals, 1824–1900 (1989), 5 vols, University of Toronto Press. Volumes 1–4 give contents pages of 43 UK journals. Volume 5 is the index.

Poole, W. F. (1882–1908) *Index to periodical literature 1802–1906*, 6 vols, Osgood (Boston), Turner (London)

Humanities and Social Science Index Retrospective: 1907–1984
www.hwwilson.com/Databases/ssi_hum_retr.htm Subscription service
Has citations to 1.3 million articles with indexing for 1000 journals.

Subject indexes

Note that all the following services are subscription-based, but many libraries do have them:

Educational Research Abstracts Online, Subscription website **www.tandf.co.uk/era**
700 journals scanned, 70,000 abstracts from 1995.

Humanities Index, H. W. Wilson

Social Sciences Index, H. W. Wilson

MLA International Bibliography (Modern Language Association), Gale
www.mla.org
Information on articles from over 4000 journals published regularly. Print and online versions.

Electronic abstracting and indexing services

The following are some of the many subscription-based services that may be available in local libraries which provide information about articles:

Current Abstracts (EBSCO) **http://search.ebscohost.com**

Google Scholar **http://scholar.google.com**

Journal Seek **www.journalseek.net**

Link @ Ovid **www.ovid.com**

OCLC Article First **www.oclc.org/services/databases**

Swets Wise **www.swetswise.com**

Wilson Web **http://vnweb.hwwilsonweb.com/hww/login**

Zetoc (British Library) **http://zetoc.mimas.ac.uk/www.bl.uk**
  Contents lists to 20,000 current journals and 16,000 conference proceedings.

Article supply

Many subscription-based online services provide the full text of articles. These may include a journal-specific website site, a publisher's website, a commercial service which covers many publishers (an 'aggregator'), or even a library-based service. In addition there are some journals that are wholly electronic ('e-journals'). Use a good search engine to find these. The downside to these databases is that they tend to lack files going back many years. The following are some of the online subscription services that may be available locally:

British Library Direct **http://direct.bl.uk**
  Pay-as-you-go service providing access to 20,000 international research journals.

Emerald **www.emeraldinsight.com**

Ingentia **www.ingentia.com**

OCLC First Search **www.oclc.org/firstsearch**

Ovid Online **www.ovid.com/site/products/content/index**

Swets Wise **www.swetswise.com**

Tips and pitfalls

If possible, get the enquirer to search the indexes for themselves. Not only can such searches become time-consuming and open-ended, but it is often best for the enquirer to decide for themselves whether or not items are worth pursuing. Guidance may be needed to interpret the cryptic references, and advice given on where to locate the journals.

  Note the difference between indexes (which give only bibliographic details and maybe a subject indicator), abstracts (which give, in addition, an indication of what an article is about) and full text. These differences are particularly important in electronic databases. Some users will want the full text of an article while others will just want an idea if the article is worth reading at all.

ASSOCIATIONS & ORGANIZATIONS

Typical questions

• Is there an organization that deals with . . .?
• Is there a professional body responsible for . . .?
• What's the address of . . .?

Considerations

It is important to ask the enquirer whether they believe the association/organization is local, national or international. Local associations/organizations are often the hardest to locate. Your library may keep a list of local societies and associations/organizations; if it does, it is essential to keep this up to date. It is worth also checking telephone directories for local contacts in professional or trade associations/organizations. If the search for a local organization is proving difficult another idea would be to look at possibilities in the next town, city or county. Many local authorities are now putting their local societies/organizations databases on the internet. It is worth looking via local government websites.

Where to look

Directories

Directory of British associations and associations in Ireland, CBD Research
> With coverage of over 7000 associations this publication provides information on national associations, societies and institutes that have a voluntary membership. It also includes regional and local organizations concerned with industries and trades. In addition, it has chambers of commerce and county agricultural, archaeological, historical, natural history and sports bodies. It is arranged alphabetically by group name. There is a subject index at the back, providing a list of relevant groups. There is also an abbreviations index. Also available on CD-ROM from CBD Research (Tel: 0871 222 3440; Fax: 020 8650 0768).

It is worth trying also:

Adams, R. (ed.) *Centres, bureaux & research institutes: UK concentrations of effort, information and expertise*, CBD Research
> The majority of the 4350 centres listed in this directory are associated with universities and their constituent colleges. It is arranged alphabetically by

centre name. There is a subject index, an abbreviations index and a sponsors index.

Councils, committees and boards including government agencies and authorities, CBD Research
An A–Z guide to 1700 councils, committees, boards, commissions, government agencies, national training organisations and tribunals. It is arranged alphabetically. There is a subject index, an abbreviations index and an officials index.

Key organizations, Carel Press
This has an A–Z listing of 3000 organizations and groups throughout the UK. In addition, it has a thematic guide to organizations, which is useful for those looking for a particular subject. It is also available on CD-ROM and online; for details contact Carel Press (Tel: 01228 538928; **www.carelpress.co.uk**).

ASK Hollis – The directory of UK associations, Hollis Publishing. Annual
This covers 6000 organizations, including, among others, pressure groups, institutes, unions, medical support groups, trade bodies and societies. It has an A–Z list of organizations, a keyword index, an activity index, a location index and a master index. (A.S.K. = Associations, Sources, Knowledge.)

Trade associations and professional bodies of the UK and Eire, Gale
Provides contact details for over 3500 associations and bodies in the UK and Eire.

Whitaker's almanack, A&C Black
This has details of some named associations/organizations. Try also the website **www.acblack.com**.

International organizations

World directory of trade and business associations, Euromonitor
This has 5000 industry bodies and named contacts. It has extensive country and sector coverage.

World guide to trade associations, vol. 1 (2002), K. G. Saur

Try also:

Encyclopedia of associations: international organizations, Gale Group. Annual

A ASSOCIATIONS & ORGANIZATIONS

Pan-European associations, CBD Research

Yearbook of international organisations, Bowker
Gives contact details and activities of organizations worldwide.

Directory of European professional and learned societies (2008), CBD Research
This has over 6000 European professional, academic, scientific and technical societies. It covers all countries in Europe, not just in the EU. However, Great Britain and the Republic of Ireland are excluded.

The London diplomatic list, Foreign and Commonwealth Office. Bi-annual
This incorporates the *Directory of international organizations*. This is available to download at **www.fco.gov.uk**. Go to Directory.

Many trade directories will include details of trade and professional associations, including international ones.
For European groups try:

Europa directory of international organizations, Europa

Directory of 9300 trade and professional associations in the European Union, Blue Book, The Stationery Office

Trade associations and professional bodies of continental Europe, Graham & Whiteside
Provides information on 6500 trade and professional associations in each country of continental Europe.

For the USA try:

National trade and professional associations of the US (2003) Hoover
Includes 7400 US trade associations, professional societies and labour organizations.

Websites
Trade Association Forum **www.taforum.org.uk**

Tips and pitfalls
Most larger associations/organizations have websites (addresses can be found in the above directories) which may have information or links to related associations/organizations, including international groups. This can often help when looking for some of the smaller or more obscure groups.

ASTRONOMY & SPACE TRAVEL

Typical questions
- How can I recognize the 'Great Bear'?
- What is 'The Procession of the Equinoxes'?
- When did man first land on the moon?

Considerations
There is an increasing interest in cosmology and space travel. Much of it comes from the younger generation doing school projects. General encyclopedias are usually the best place to start, but atlases of the moon and pictures of a star-filled night sky require more sophisticated resources.

Where to look
General

Angelo, J. A. (2002) *The Facts on File space and astronomy handbook*, Facts on File

Darling, D. *The encylopedia of astrobiology, astronomy, and spaceflight: an alphabetical guide to the living universe*, Darling
Online version (free): **www.daviddarling.info/encyclopedia/ETEmain.html**

Darling, D. (2003) *The universal book of astronomy*, Wiley

Freedman, R. A. and Kaufmann, W. J. (2004) *Universe*, 7th edn, Palgrave Macmillan
Also available in two volumes: *Stars and galaxies* and *The solar system.*

Dunlop, S. (2006) *Practical astronomy*, Philips

Kitchin, C. (2000) *Illustrated dictionary of practical astronomy*, Springer-Verlag

Moore, P. (ed.) *Yearbook of astronomy*, Macmillan

Old Farmer's Almanac **www.almanac.com**
Good for astronomical information as well as weather forecasts. Has a US focus.

Rees, M. (2007) *Universe: the definitive virtual guide*, Dorling Kindersley

Ridpath, I. (2007) *A dictionary of astronomy*, 3rd edn, Oxford University Press

Ridpath, I. and Tirion, W. (2007) *Stars and planets*, 4th edn, Collins

Star guides

Ridpath, I. (ed.) (2000) *Norton's star atlas*, 20th edn, Pi Press

Sparrow, G. (2007) *The stargazer's handbook: an atlas of the night sky*, Quercus

Philips also publish a number of atlases to the stars.

Space travel

Angelo, J. A. (2000) *Encyclopedia of space exploration*, Facts on File

Darling, D. (2002) *The complete book of spaceflight*, Wiley

Tips and pitfalls

Watch out for the confusion between astrology and astronomy.

ATLASES & GAZETTEERS

See also Maps

Typical Questions

- Where is Ansdell?
- There is a town called Coudes in France. Where is it exactly?
- What is the OS grid reference for St Ives?

Considerations

This subject area should not cause too many problems. Most enquirers will simply be asking where specific places are, or planning routes in an atlas. Every reference library should have an atlas of the United Kingdom. Most will have one of Europe and the world too. All these atlases will have indexes.

Gazetteers provide more in-depth coverage. They are simply a list of place names and locations, some with grid references.

Do learn how the various atlases are arranged.

Where to look
Printed sources

There are many good atlases available. Your library should have some of them.

The Times produce a very good range of atlases, e.g.:

The Times comprehensive atlas of the world (2008) Times Books

For gazetteers, these are two 'essentials':

Ordnance Survey gazetteer of Great Britain (1999) MacMillan Reference
Every name from the 1:50,000 landranger map series is included here. Ordnance Survey sheet numbers are included, as well as grid references and longitude and latitudes.

For world coverage, the *Columbia gazetteer* is by far the best:

Cohen, S. B. (2008*) Columbia gazetteer of the world*, Columbia University Press

Electronic sources

There are many maps and atlases available on the internet. These range from town plans to suggested route plans.
For UK maps, try the following:

www.multimap.com
www.streetmap.co.uk

For Europe:

www.mappy.com

and for route plans:

www.theaa.co.uk
www.rac.co.uk
www.mappy.com

For gazetteers, the *Getty thesaurus of geographic names* is worth a look:

www.getty.edu/research/conducting_research/vocabularies/tgn

Tips and pitfalls

Make sure you have a current atlas. The changes in the post-Soviet world have made immense differences to countries and you should have an atlas that covers these. Do learn how to use longitude and latitude.

AUCTIONS

Typical questions

* Can you give me a list of local auctions?

◼ A AUCTIONS

- When is the next auction for antique furniture?
- Do you know of any X machinery sales?

Considerations

It is not always easy to track down where and when an auction is going to be held. The Yellow Pages can provide lists of the local auction houses, which the enquirer can ring to find out their next sale date. Many of the large auction houses operate catalogue-only sales that require either a subscription or purchase of the catalogue before the sale takes place. Your local paper may have a day for advertising auctions, usually listed in the classified section; it is worth making a note of this. These will probably be mostly of a general nature such as household items, antiques and paintings; sometimes they may include industry equipment, car and property sales. Auctions can also be known as liquidation sales and disposal of stock. In addition to local newspapers, many of the national daily and Sunday newspapers advertise auctions. For details of auctions taking place abroad take a look at some of the established auction house websites, which are listed below.

Where to look
Printed sources

Guide to the antique shops of Britain, Antiques Collectors' Club
    This has a very good chapter on auctioneers arranged by area.

Household items

National and local newspapers, trade and industry journals.

Industry equipment

National and local newspapers, trade and industry journals.

For cars

National and local newspapers.

For property

National and local newspapers, and *Estates Gazette*.

National Association of Estate Agents **www.naea.co.uk**
    Lists auctions of residential, commercial property and land.

Journals

Government Auction News
Wentworth Publishing
Tel: 020 7353 7300; Fax: 020 7353 6533
www.ganews.co.uk
Monthly
Provides auction news and UK listings.

Electronic sources

AuctionGuide.com **www.auctionguide.com**
A directory of auctions and auctioneers worldwide.

Best-of-the-best-auctions **www.start-page.org/uk**
Select auctions from the BOTB contents list. This has an extensive listing of auction websites and addresses. Excellent.

Car & Van Auctions UK **www.carandvanauctions.co.uk**

Christie's **www.christies.com**

eBay **www.ebay.co.uk**

Government Auctions **www.government-auctions.co.uk**

Motor Auctions **www.rmif.co.uk**

National Association of Estate Agents **www.naea.co.uk**
Lists auctions of residential, commercial property and land.

Phillips **www.phillips-auctions.com**

Sotheby's **www.sothebys.com**

UK Classic Car Online Auctions **www.classic-car-auctions.co.uk**

www.yell.com
For auction houses.

Tips and pitfalls

Don't try to give advice on whether goods are acceptable for auction or a likely price they would fetch; neither can you advise on a buying price. It is best to refer the enquirer to one of the many price guides available. See the relevant subject sections in this directory.

AWARDS & PRIZES

See also Grants & Funding

Typical questions

- Who won last year's Man Booker Prize?
- Have you a list of Nobel Prize winners?
- What is The Alan Ball Award given for?

Considerations

Awards and prizes are a feature of everyday life. Unfortunately they are not always easy to find out about. If you unfamiliar with the award, find out from the enquirer what the subject of the award is (literature? civil service?), the country it is awarded in, and the date for which the information is required. If they know any of these it will make finding easier. If a specific subject is known, it may be quicker to go to a subject source rather than a general one.

Where to look
Printed sources

For recent awards, newspapers and news services are a good source. Some books to consult for previous winners are:

Cook, C. (ed.) (1994) *Pears book of winners and champions*, Pelham Books

Marshall, A. (1994) *The Guinness book of winners*, Guinness Publications

Siegman, G. (ed.) (1990) *World of winners: a current and historical perspective on awards and their winners*, Gale Research

Good general reference books will list the main prizes, e.g. Oscars, Booker, Nobel, etc. Try:

Crystal, D. (ed.) (1998) *Cambridge factfinder*, Cambridge University Press

Whitaker's almanack lists current holders only but covers a wide range of awards, e.g. BAFTAs, Pulitzer Prize.

The *London Gazette* covers Honours Lists and military awards.

Electronic sources

Previous Oscar winners:

www.filmsite.org/oscars.html

For current Oscars, BAFTAs, Brits, Emmys, Golden Globes, etc.:

www.niata.net/awards/index.html

There is a useful site for literature awards, with links to sites giving previous winners:

www.literature-awards.com

For Nobel prizes:

http://almaz.com/nobel/nobel.html

This site has various awards listed:

www.library.ucsb.edu/subjects/awards.html

The homepage for the British honours system is here:

www.honours.gov.uk

If you would like to nominate somebody for an honour, you can contact the Prime Minister's Office:

http://petitions.pm.gov.uk

Tips and pitfalls

It is sometimes quickest to simply type in the name of the award you are looking for into a good search engine.

BANKS & BANKING

See also Accounts, Auditing & Bookkeeping; Companies

Typical questions

- I need to know the address for a bank in Spain.
- I have a complaint against my bank; who do I write to?
- Where's the nearest branch of Lloyds TSB?

Considerations

The majority of enquiries about banks and building societies will relate to contact details both home and abroad. Most of these can be answered using the excellent *Bankers almanac* or the *Building societies yearbook*. The disgruntled bank user is best contacting the Financial Ombudsman Service. Finally, there are those who want to know more about their bank or the banking industry in general. For these you can't beat the bank's own annual report. If your library doesn't keep annual reports you could look at Carol (Company Annual Reports OnLine). In addition you can use one of the banking websites now available (see below). These can also be useful for those going for job interviews or for students with projects covering the banking industry.

Where to look
Printed sources
Directories

Bankers almanac, 5 vols, Reed Business Information
Information on 4000 major international banks of the world and details of 19,000 other authorized banks. Published twice yearly – in January and July.

Also available is the *Bankers almanac (BANKbase) CD-ROM* or, via the internet, **www.bankersalmanac.com**, which is a subscription service from Bankers Almanac (Tel: 01342 335889).

World bank directory, 2 vols, Accuity
www.accuitysolutions.com

Building societies yearbook, Building Societies Association. Annual
Provides a complete alphabetical listing of building societies' details and balance sheets. This includes branch details.

Tracing dormant accounts

The British Bankers Association (BBA; **www.bba.org.uk**), the Building Societies Association (BSA; **www.bsa.org.uk**) and National Savings and Investments (NS&I) offer a free tracing service for people who have lost track of accounts. Also there is a free downloadable booklet called *Dormant savings accounts*. Claim forms are available from all banks and building societies or via the associations' websites. For web-based tracing, the BSA, BBA and NS&I offer a joint service called **mylostaccount.org.uk**. There is also a downloadable leaflet called *Lost savings?*

Electronic sources
Market research

Bank for International Settlements **www.bis.org/cbanks.htm**
    This gives a list of world central banks' websites. Excellent.

Bank of England **www.bankofengland.co.uk**
    Excellent site for banking statistics, financial reports and much more. Loads available to download.

British Bankers Association **www.bankfacts.org.uk**

Building Societies Association **www.bsa.org.uk**
    Excellent website offering a huge amount of consumer information, statistics and studies, publications and reports, and consultation responses.

Building Societies Association
    www.bsa.org.uk/generalpages/whereismybsnow.htm
    Provides a comprehensive list of mergers, transfers and changes of names since 1937.

Banks and annual reports

Barclays Bank **www.barclays.co.uk**

Halifax **www.halifax:co.uk**

HSBC **www.hsbc.co.uk**

Lloyds TSB **www.lloydstsb.com**

National Westminster Bank **www.natwest.com**

Royal Bank of Scotland **www.rbs.co.uk**

Carol (Company Annual Reports OnLine) **www.carol.co.uk**
Once you have registered you have unlimited free access to annual reports online, including those from banks.

Associations

British Bankers' Association
Pinners Hall, 105–108 Old Broad Street, London EC2N 1EX
www.bba.org.uk

Building Societies Association
6th Floor, York House, 23 Kingsway, London WC2B 6UJ
Tel: 020 7216 8830
www.bsa.org.uk

Association of Foreign Banks
1 Bengal Court, London EC3V 9DD
Tel: 020 7283 8300
www.foreignbanks.org.uk
Excellent for further links to other banking and finance associations.

Association of Friendly Societies
P.O. Box 21, Altrincham, Cheshire WA14 4PD
Tel: 0161 952 5051
www.afs.org.uk

Financial Ombudsman Service
South Quay Plaza, 183 Marsh Wall, London E14 9SR
Consumer helpline: Tel: 0845 080 1800

Tips and pitfalls

Avoid comment on the merits or problems of individual banks or building societies. Don't be drawn into calculations of overcharging, etc. Suggest the enquirer contacts the Financial Ombudsman Service if the issue cannot be resolved with the bank or building society itself.

BATTLES & BATTLEFIELDS

Typical questions

• I am doing a project on the Battle of Waterloo. Have you any information?

- How many lives were lost at the Battle of Marston Moor?
- Where is Stamford Bridge, the site of the famous battle?

Considerations

This subject is always very popular, especially the battlefield's area. Relations often want to know about where their loved ones fought or perished. Many even want to visit the battlegrounds.

Where to look
Printed sources

There may be detailed histories of certain battles available on your shelves, but for quick enquiries, encyclopedias and the following reference books should be sufficient:

Laffin, J. (1986) *Brassey's battles: 3500 years of conflict, campaigns and wars, from A–Z*, Pergamon

An encyclopedia of battles: accounts of over 1560 battles from 1479 BC to the present (1985) Dover Publications

For more recent battles:

Snow, P. and Snow, D. (2007) *The world's greatest twentieth century battlefields*, BBC Books

Other useful sources of information include the Imperial War Museum and the Ministry of Defence.

Imperial War Museum
Lambeth Road, London SE1 6HZ
www.iwm.org.uk

Ministry of Defence
Tel: 0870 607 4455
www.mod.uk

Battlefields

If you are trying to find battlefields in the UK, try the excellent:

Smurthwaite, D. (ed.) (1984) *Ordnance Survey complete guide to the battlefields of Britain*, Webb and Bower

There are useful guides to the more recent battlefields of World Wars 1 and 2 in Northern Europe:

Holmes, R. (1995) *Army battlefield guide: Belgium and Northern France*, HMSO

Snow, P. and Snow, D. (2004) *Battlefield Britain*, BBC Books

Electronic sources

The Commonwealth War Graves Commission publishes lists of the burial places of the war dead of World Wars 1 and 2, as well as other items relating to battles and battlefields. You can get more information, as well as free access to their huge database of war dead, at **www.cwgc.org**.

Again, there are good histories of battles online. Simply type the name into a good search engine.

BEERS & BREWING

Typical questions

- Who brews a certain brand of lager?
- Can you give me a list of breweries?
- What is the most popular beer?
- I'm doing a project on the beer industry.

Considerations

Questions on this subject area fall into two categories: those that are asking about brands and company information which require contact details, and those that are asking about the industry itself, which requires market research and statistical information. A number of directories will give you company and product details (listed below) and there is a plethora of market research available. For those without access to market reports there are some great sources on the internet. This is an area where there has been a growth in the number of good websites, particularly those listing types of beer and breweries. The websites listed offer some of the best available to a wealth of information.

Where to look
Dictionary

Rabin, D. and Forget, C. (1998) *The dictionary of beer and brewing*, 2nd edn, Brewers Publications

Specialist publications

Brewers Publications **www.gazellebooks.co.uk**
Has many specialist publications.

Directories

Yeo, A. (ed.) *The brewery manual*, PJB Publications. Annual
An invaluable and extensive directory, which provides analysis of the UK alcoholic drinks market. It provides listings of beer brands, brewing companies, industry related contacts, importers and wholesalers and a who's who.

The Grocer directory of manufacturers and suppliers (2008) William Reed
Publishing. Annual UK edition
This provides information on 9000 companies, 300 products and over 16,000 brand names. It covers primary producers, agents and brokers, export and import, wholesalers and distributors.

The Grocer directory of manufacturers and suppliers – European information online
www.william-reed.co.uk
This provides information on 9000 food and drink manufacturers and suppliers across Europe and 11,000 contacts.

The BFBI directory, Brewing, Food and Beverage Industry Suppliers Association
Provides details of products and services, UK brewers, smaller independent brewers and pub operating groups, and a directory of trade names.

CAMRA (Campaign for Real Ale) good beer guide, Camra Books. Annual

Modern Brewery Age Blue Book – International (2007) Business Journals Inc.
Guide to the global brewing industry with listings of brewers by country, importing companies, names of brands imported and trade associations.

Modern Brewery Age Blue Book – North America (2007) Business Journals Inc.
Guide to the North American brewing industry with listings of US brewers, importing companies, wholesalers and non-beer producers and marketers. Also gives statistical information on US beer and alcohol market.

Brewing and Distilling Directory, Institute and Guild of Brewing
Guide to the brewing industry with listings of worldwide brewing contacts, pub groups and distilling companies.

Journals

Brewers' Guardian
   Advantage Publishing
   Tel: 01737 735018; Fax: 01737 735195
   Monthly
   An international journal covering technological developments and market trends.

Market intelligence

Key Note reports, Key Note
   For free executive summaries of report titles listed under drinks and tobacco visit **www.keynote.co.uk**. For details of obtaining full reports, contact Key Note (Tel: 020 8481 8750; Fax: 020 8783 0049).

British Beer and Pub Association statistical handbook, Brewing Publications.
   Annual
   www.beerandpub.com
   This provides a wealth of information on the industry and beer.

Websites

BDI Brewing and Distilling International (includes a buyers guide)
   www.bdinews.com

Beer Info Source **www.beerinfo.com**

Beermad **www.beermad.org.uk**
   Extensive database containing details of every beer known to have been produced in the British Isles since 1976. Also has links to 2000 beer-related sites.

British Beer and Pub Association **www.beerandpub.com**
   This includes information about the history and different types of beer, brewing, sales and export statistics (for the UK and the rest of Europe), UK beer exporters, the brewing process and visits to breweries. Also links to websites covering careers in brewing and relevant press releases.

Brewing, Food and Beverage Industry Suppliers Association **www.bfbi.org.uk**

CAMRA (Campaign for Real Ale) **www.camra.org.uk**

Cask-Marque **www.cask-marque.co.uk**

Great British Beer **www.greatbritishbeer.co.uk**
  Includes the beer database.

Independent Family Brewers of Britain **www.familybrewers.co.uk**
  Gives statistics relating to independent family brewers and to British beer market. Also provides links to members' websites.

Institute of Brewing and Distilling **www.ibd.org.uk**

Society of Independent Brewers (SIBA) **www.siba.co.uk**

BENEFITS

See also Social Welfare

Typical questions

- Have you details on the Jobseekers Allowance?
- I've just been made redundant; what benefits am I entitled to?
- What's the social services office?

Considerations

Enquiries about benefits can be difficult and distressing. Difficult, not because benefit regulations are complex and difficult to understand, although they are, but because you are dealing with a socially, politically and psychologically charged topic. Sometimes the enquirer will be calm and objective and used to using library materials; but often the enquirer will be emotional and demanding, asking, insisting even, that you give them advice and tell them what to do. Other people will be shy, diffident, and have poor language skills. It requires considerable skill on the part of the librarian to remain calm and objective.

  As with all such legal and financial enquiries, one must be careful not to give advice on interpreting regulations. To do so could invite all sort of complications, from being sued for losing someone benefits to inviting crowds of other benefit seekers wanting free advice!

  The role of the librarian here is twofold. First, to provide text- or web-based sources giving the statutory and legal regulations and related commentary. Second, to provide details of places the enquirer can go to get advice and further information. A complication may be that the enquirer *has* tried the Benefits Office or Citizens Advice Bureau and *they* have been unhelpful (or so the enquirer says). One can only stick to one's job, which is to provide information, not to give legal advice.

B BENEFITS

A point worth making here, and which is something relatively new, is that many, and probably most, workers in this field no longer use printed sources and turn first to websites. Since they can then print out the information there is less need to carry large stocks of leaflets. Chances are they have the same resources as you do – just more experience in using them!

Where to look
General sources

Advice guide **www.adviceguide.org.uk**
> The online CAB (Citizens Advice Bureaux) service that provides independent advice on people's rights. Gives practical, up-to-date information on a wide range of topics, including benefits and housing, employment rights and discrimination, debt and tax issues; has links to local CAB offices; information in a range of languages; a wide selection of fact sheets to print off; and details of other reliable sources of information.

Benefits Agency **www.dwp.gov.uk**
> The Benefits Agency is part of the Department of Work and Pensions. The website covers benefits, pensions, tax credits, and all related topics for workers, pensioners, children and disabled people.

CANS digest of social legislation, CANS Trust. [CANS = Citizens Advice Notes Service]
> Available in a three-volume loose-leaf publication or as a CD-ROM. Provides legal information on all the social legislation of Great Britain written in plain English. Includes nationality, consumer protection, employment, housing, discrimination and social security. An electronic version is available on subscription at **www.cans.org.uk**.

Directgov **www.direct.gov.uk**
> Probably the quickest and most comprehensive guide to benefits available. It is the source that many benefits workers use first.

Social services year book, Pearson Education
> Over 50,000 contact details for all social services related organizations in the UK. Includes voluntary, charitable and private organizations. Also available on CD-ROM.

Welfare benefits handbook & tax credits, CPAG (Child Poverty Action Group).

Annual
Information on all social security benefits.

Welfare rights bulletin, CPAG. 6 times a year
Most of the information needed is likely to be on free leaflets and most libraries will have a selection of these – though see note about printing from websites above. Most can be obtained from local Benefits and Council information offices.

Frills leaflet service **http://frills.camden.gov.uk/frills**
The Frills leaflet service website lists some 700 practical leaflets covering health, money, education, housing, law and travel. All the leaflets are free in large quantities, and are written for the general public. Many libraries subscribe to the service.

Particular subjects
Care

Paying for care handbook (2008) 6th edn, CPAG

Carer's Allowance Unit (DWP) Tel: 01253 856123

Carers Association
Tel: 0345 573 369
Advice-line regarding benefits.

Nursing Care in Nursing Homes
Tel: 0870 1555 455 (England); 029 2082 5191 (Wales)
Phone for free leaflet about NHS funding care in nursing homes.

Children

Child support handbook, CPAG. Annual

Child Benefit Office (HM Revenue and Customs)
Tel: 0945 302 1444

Child Poverty Action Group (CPAG)
94 White Lion Street, London N1 9PF
Tel: 020 7837 7979 Fax: 020 7837 6414
E-mail: staff@cpag.demon.co.uk
www.cpag.org.uk
A campaigning group with an active publishing programme.

Child Support Agency (DWP) **www.csa.gov.uk**
Covers all aspects of child maintenance with leaflets and application forms that can be downloaded.

Debt

Debt advice handbook (2008), 8th edn, CPAG

Disability

Disability rights handbook, CPAG. Annual

Disabled Living Foundation (UK national charity)
380 Harrow Road, London W9 2VU
Tel: 020 7289 611; Helpline: 0845 130 9177
www.dlf.org.uk

Disability Benefits Enquiry Line
Tel: 0800 88 22 00 (freephone)

Disability Living Allowance Helpline
Tel: 0845 712 3456
For advice and information on benefits for disabled people and their carers.

Disability Benefits Helpline
Tel: 0345 123 456

Invalid Care Allowance
Tel: 01253 856 123

Attendance Allowance (for disabled pensioners and carers)
Tel: 0800 88 22 00

Fares

Local councils (or The Transport Executive in metropolitan areas) must provide reduced fares for people over 60 years old. Fares on local bus services are free for pensioners throughout England provided they have a valid pass, and there are reductions on train services in many areas. See local telephone directories for details.

Fuel

Fuel rights handbook (2008) 14th edn, CPAG

Winter Fuel Payments
Leaflet WFP1 *Winter Fuel Payments* or phone helpline, Tel: 08459 15 15 15

Home Energy Efficiency Scheme
For grants to the elderly and those on income-related benefits, Tel: 0800 952 0600 (England); 0800 316 2815 (Wales).

Health

Health Cost Advice Line
Tel: 0800 917 7711

Invalid Care Allowance (for cases of severely disabled persons)
Tel: 01253 856 123

Help with health costs
Leaflet HC 11 *Are you entitled to help with health care?* Or phone Health Literature Line: Tel: 088 555 777 or write to the Department of Heath, PO Box 777, London SE1 6XH.

Housing and council tax

Zebedee, J. and Ward, M. (annual) *Guide to housing benefit and council tax benefit*, Shelter
An authoritative overview of the rules in Great Britain.

Findlay and others (annual) *CPAG's housing benefit and council tax benefit legislation, 2001–2002*, CPAG

Catholic Housing Aid Society (CHAS)
National Office, 209 Old Marylebone Road, London NW1 5QT
Tel: 020 7723 5928
www.chascl.org.uk
CHAS give advice and practical help to homeless people and those with associated debt or benefit problems. There are local offices. Website has FAQs and links to other sites.

Housing rights guide 2008–9 (2007) Shelter.

Council tax handbook (2007) 7th edn, CPAG

Shelter (the national campaign for homeless people)
88 Old Street, London EC1V 9HU

Tel: 020 7505 2000; Fax: 020 7505 2169
www.shelter.org.uk

Income support

Minimum Income Guarantee claim line (paid on Income Support)
Tel: 0800 028 1111 to apply for Minimum Income Guarantee.

Income tax

For income tax benefits such as the Married Couple's Allowance contact the local tax office.

Tax Credit Helpline (Pensions Service)
Tel: 0945 300 3900

Pensions

The Pensions Service has a network of local centres, issues numerous informational leaflets, and can give advice. Its website **www.pensions.gov.uk** has the texts of leaflets that may be printed out. The Pension Service (part of the Department of Work and Pensions) publishes an annual leaflet *Pensioner's Guide*.

International Pension Centre
Tel: 0191 218 7777
For advice and information from the DWP on benefits for people who live overseas. See also Leaflet GL29, *Going abroad and social security benefits.*

Pensions Advisory Service Helpline
Tel: 0845 6012923
An independent non-profit organization that provides information and guidance on pensions.

British Pensioners and Trade Unions Action Association
Tel: 024 7650 2429 for advice on welfare rights.

Veterans Welfare Service (previously the War Pensioners' Welfare Service)
Helpline: 0800 269 2277
www.veterans.uk/info/welfare.html

Tax and pensions living abroad
Leaflet IP 121 *Income tax and pensioners* from Inland Revenue Enquiry Centre and tax offices (see phone book) or **www.inlandrevenue.gov.uk** or Tel: 0151 472 61892.

Pensions and Overseas Benefits Directorate
Room TB228, Tyneview Park, Whitley Road, Benton, Newcastle-upon-Tyne, NE98 1BA
Tel: 0191 218 2756

Teachers' Pension Agency
Mowden Hall, Darlington, DL3 9FE

Personal Investment Authority
Pensions helpline: Tel: 020 7417 7001

Society of Pension Consultants
Tel: 020 7353 1688

Pensions Ombudsman
Tel: 020 7828 9794

OPAS (Occupational Pensions Advisory Service)
11 Belgrave Road, London SW1V 1RB.
Tel: 020 7233 8080; Fax: 020 7233 8016

Association of Retired and Persons Over 50
ARP/050 Freepost, London SW1P 1YY
Tel: 020 7828 0500
E-mail: info@arp.org.uk
www.arp.org.uk
A campaigning and social membership organization with numerous helplines available on subscription. Regional co-ordinators.

Young people

Student support and benefits handbook, CPAG and National Union of Students. Annual

Other sources

Referral is often the best option for benefits issues. The local DWP (Department for Work and Pensions) Benefit Office and the Citizens' Advice Bureaux are obvious places. See telephone directories for local offices.

There are numerous leaflets available giving information about a whole range of benefits obtainable from local agencies. Libraries generally make these freely available.

National Association of Citizens Advice Bureaux (NACAB)
> Myddleton House, 115–123 Pentonville Road, Camden, London
> **www.citizensadvice.org.uk**
> The CAB provides confidential and independent advice from over 3000
> locations. See **www.adviceguide.org.uk**.

Tips and pitfalls

Never underestimate the amount of knowledge about state benefits that seemingly unsophisticated enquirers may have. They have probably spent a lot more of their life reading the leaflets, talking to experts, and sharing experiences with other seekers than you have. And they are probably better motivated.

Be aware, in the most tactful way possible of course, if any of your colleagues has experience of benefits. Answering enquiries is all about shared experience and teamwork. Many of your regular users might volunteer their expertise. If they should not be giving advice, they may, at least, understand the question!

Although some enquirers will be demanding and intrusive, others may be shy and embarrassed. Make sure there is plenty of relevant material on open access and notices giving the addresses of local offices.

Many libraries have formal links to appropriate advisory bodies – these are worth cultivating. A list of emergency contacts to the DWP local offices, shelters and social services is worth having and keeping up to date. Currency of publications is essential.

Do check for out-of-date leaflets.

BIOGRAPHIES

Typical questions

- Can you tell me something about Lord Healey of Riddlesden?
- I'm trying to find out about the life of Humphrey Lyttleton.

Considerations

This section concentrates mainly on general British biographies and lists some of the more valuable resources. Biographies of individuals in specific subjects will appear in other chapters in this book, e.g. SPORTS.

Where to look
Printed sources

First stop if you are looking for a brief biography should be a general biographical dictionary or even an encyclopedia:

Crystal, D. (ed.) (1999) *Cambridge biographical encyclopedia*, Cambridge University Press
This gives basic information for over 16,000 people, describing their life and achievements. Obviously, this is not suitable for detailed research, but it can be an ideal starting point. For more detailed information, the *Oxford dictionary of national biography* is a must.

Oxford dictionary of national biography (2004) 60 vols, Oxford University Press
This covers British notables from earliest times to 2000, though only if they have died. Many libraries now subscribe to this online too. Check your own service.

Who's who (1849–) A&C Black. Annual
This covers prominent living people, principally British. Also available online via subscription.

Debrett's people of today, Debrett's. Annual
Some 32,000 leading figures in British society.

Who was who (1897–2000) A&C Black, 10 vols plus index
This is a companion to *Who's who* and contains biographies of those who have died during this period. It is published every ten years.

Current biography (1940–) H. W. Wilson
This has articles about living leaders in all fields of human accomplishment the world over.

Dictionary of international biography, Melrose Press. Bi-annual
Over 5000 men and women in all professions and fields of interest worldwide. Back-files now cover 200,000 people.

There are also numerous specialist biographical dictionaries covering specific subjects or areas of the world, e.g.:

Who's who in international affairs (2007) Europa Publications

Crockfords clerical directory, Church House Publishing. Annual

Marshall, C. (2002) *Cricketer's who's who*, Queen Anne Press

Watkins, B. (2002) *The book of saints*, 7th edn, A&C Black

Books covering the history of a subject, or giving an introduction to a subject, may also contain information about people associated with that subject.

Obituaries are also useful. If you have newspaper indexes (e.g. of *The Times*, *Telegraph*), check them to see if you can find the date of an obituary for the person you are interested in.

Electronic sources

The excellent biography.com is worth a look:

www.biography.com

Or type in the name of the individual into a search engine.

Tips and pitfalls

Some local studies or local history libraries keep cuttings from local newspapers and publications about local worthies. These can be incredibly useful.

BIRDS

See also Animals, Pets & Vets; Natural History

Typical questions
- What is the average wingspan of a golden eagle?
- Have you got any books for identifying birds?

Considerations

The most common questions about birds concern the identification of certain species. Make sure your library has some guides.

Where to look
General sources

Perrins, C. H. (ed.) (2003) *The New Encyclopedia of Birds*, Oxford University Press

Recognition

Cramp, S. et al. (eds) (1977–) *Handbook of the birds of Europe, the Middle East and North Africa*, Oxford University Press
This nine-volume set describes all the species of birds in this area and shows habitats, populations, movement, voices, plumage, etc. Also available on CD-ROM.

More concise are:

Hume, R. (2007) *RSPB complete birds of Britain and Europe*, 2nd edn, Dorling Kindersley

Snow, D. N. and Perrins, C. M. (1997) *The Birds of the Western Palearctic, concise edition*, Oxford University Press, 2 vols

Svensson, L. et al. (2000) *Collins bird guide: the most complete guide to the birds of Britain and Europe*, HarperCollins.

For birds worldwide, the premier reference is:

Dickinson, E. C. (ed.) (2003) *The Howard and Moore complete checklist of the birds of the world*, 3rd edn, Christopher Helm

Hoyo, J. D. et al. (1992–) *Handbook of the birds of the world*, Lynx Editions
HBW is intended to be the definitive handbook on all the world's 9000-plus species of birds. To be in 16 volumes when complete.

Electronic sources

Sometimes the best way to find information about a specific bird is to simply use the internet. Type the bird's name into a good search engine. See also:

All About Birds **www.birds.cornell.edu/programs/allaboutbirds**

RSPB **www.rspb.org.uk**

Organization

Royal Society for the Protection of Birds (RSPB)
UK Headquarters: The Lodge, Sandy, Bedfordshire SG19 2DL; Tel: 01767 680551
Northern Ireland: Belvoir Park Forest, Belfast BT8 7QT; Tel: 028 9049 1547
Scotland: 25 Ravelston Terrace, Edinburgh EH4 3TP; Tel: 0131 311 6500

Wales: Sutherland House, Castlebridge, Cowbridge Road East, Cardiff CF11 9AB; Tel: 029 2035 3000

Tips and pitfalls

Ornithology is a complex subject, but you should get by in most cases with a good book for identifying birds. For more information about specific types of bird, the internet can often help with queries.

Refer enthusiasts to local naturalist societies or branches of the RSPB.

BOOKS & BIBLIOGRAPHIES

See also Copyright & Legal Deposit; ISBNs & ISSNs; Journals & Periodicals; Libraries & Information Services; Media & The Press; Newspapers & Magazines; Publishing; Writers & Writing

Typical questions

- Has a book been published on . . .?
- Where can I get this book?
- I have an old book. Is it valuable?
- Can you give me advice on looking after old books?
- My tutor has asked me to prepare a bibliography. How do I do that?
- I've been given this reference, but I don't understand it.
- How should this report be cited?
- What is the Harvard system?

Considerations

Tens of thousands of books are published every year. Millions of different books exist. And the public expect librarians to know them all!

Although some library users are book experts, the majority are not, so library staff will generally have the advantage of experience. One problem is that the field is vast and complex, yet the public will not appreciate this. So, as always, progress carefully, step by step, taking nothing for granted. Another problem encountered is that many people have a touching faith in the value of books, both monetary and content-wise, and often we have to deflate high expectations, particularly of the monetary variety!

As librarians, we are used to how books are described in catalogues and we groan when someone hands us incomplete or garbled details about a book they want.

Accuracy about book details is something we soon learn, but people who are not bookish do not always realize the need for such precise details. And which details?

Where to look
Books in general

Feather, J. (1986) *A Dictionary of Book History*, Croom Helm

Peters, J. (ed.) (1983) *The bookman's glossary*, 6th edn, Bowker

Cambridge history of the book in Britain (in progess), Cambridge University Press.
To be in seven volumes.

Books in print

For books in print, that is, available in standard bookshops and by mail order see: *Books in print* (for US books); *Whitaker's British books in print*; *International books in print* and other national trade bibliographies. Many of these services are available in fiche, CD-ROM and online formats on subscription. Check with your library's Bibliographical Department for these.

Amazon.com **www.amazon.com**
Generally the first place to look for new and recent books. Free.

Bookseller, Whitaker. Weekly
A good source of information about new and forthcoming publications. Indexed.

Google Books **http://books.google.com**

Publisher's Weekly, Publisher's Weekly
Similar magazine to *The Bookseller* for the USA.

British National Bibliography, British Library. Weekly, with cumulations
This national bibliography records all books and new serials deposited at the Legal Deposit Office of the British Library since 1950. Also published monthly on CD-ROM. BNB is usually available in larger public libraries. **www.bl.uk/services/bibliography/natbib.html**

Bowker/Whitaker Global Books in Print Plus on CD-ROM (Subscription)
The largest database. Available in most library headquarters.

Nielsen Book Data **www.nielsenbookdataonline.com**

Subscription service taken by many libraries listing newly published books giving price and availability. Some 7 million titles.

Most bookshop chains have their stock holdings online, and often on their (free) websites. Examples are:

WH Smith International Bookshop **www.whsmith.co.uk**

Waterstones **www.waterstones.co.uk**

Blackwells **www.blackwell.co.uk**

Foyles **www.foyles.co.uk**

There are also online 'bookshops' offering books, music, DVD and video:

Amazon Books **www.amazon.com**
    Has the largest listing.

These are free services and a good first place to look, but the detail may need to be supplemented by other sources.
    Similarly, most publishers have details of their books on their websites. Often these will give more information about the books than is available in bibliographies. Examples are:

www.galegroup.com
www.macmillan.com
www.butterworths.co.uk

A directory of online publications, though somewhat dated, is:

Nobari, N. (ed.) *Books and periodicals online*, Library Technology Alliance.
    Annual

Book reviews

Some bookshop websites contain book reviews. Others are:

Times Literary Supplement **www.the-tls.co.uk**

Independent **www.independent.co.uk/books**

Yahoo! **www.yahoo.co.uk/Arts/Humanities/Literature/Reviews**

Amazon Bookshop **www.amazon.co.uk**

A standard US guide for good non-fiction titles is Yaakov, J. (ed.) (2004) *Public library catalog: a guide to reference books and adult non fiction*, 12th edn, H. W. Wilson.

This aims to provide a core collection for public libraries. Useful as a general readers' advisory and general reference tool. North American focus.

Bibliographies and library catalogues

(see also LIBRARIES & INFORMATION SERVICES)

A 'bibliography' is a list of books; a 'catalogue' is a list of books in the stock of a library.

Copac **www.jisc.ac.uk**

Access to the merged catalogue of 24 major university research libraries in the UK plus the British Library and the national libraries of Scotland and Wales. Free.

Google Book Search **http://book.google.com**

Free. Provides a listing, with extracts, of books: 'an online card catalogue'.

Library Thing **www.librarything.com**

Free. Library Thing is designed as a catalogue tool with access to records of 20 million books from over 100 major libraries. Access is by author, title, ISBN, etc. Registration needed.

New Cambridge bibliography of English Literature, 5 vols, Cambridge University Press

Good for books on authors and types of literature.

Online Books Page **http://onlinebooks-library.upenn.edu**

Over 20,000 online books. Complete texts available free of charge.

Ovid **www.ovid.com**

Access to databases of books and journals. Subscription service.

Oxford Scholarship Online

www.oxfordscholarship.com/oso/public/index.html

'OSO' has the full text of over 2215 titles from the Oxford University Press, plus others added annually. Subscription to the full texts, but free access to view abstracts and keywords.

ESTC (English Short Title Catalogue) **http://estc.bl.uk**

Lists over 460,000 items published before 1800 held in some 2,000 libraries worldwide.

National catalogues such as the *National union catalog* and the *British Library catalogue* have comprehensive listings of books. See chapter on LIBRARIES & INFORMATION SERVICES.

Bookshops

See telephone directories for local bookshops, or contact:

Booksellers Association
272 Vauxhall Bridge Road, London SW1V 1BA.
Tel: 020 7802 0802
www.booksellers.org.uk
Over 4000 bookselling outlets in the UK and Ireland.

Amazon (**www.amazon.com**) is the largest online bookseller.

Citations and references

References and citations mean the same thing and refer to how details of a book or other source of information is described. Sometimes, especially in technical and specialist subjects, it is difficult to understand citations. Law is one such common area of confusion. Most books on how to write dissertations and reports (see chapter on WRITERS & WRITING) have a section on preparing a bibliography. If compiling a bibliography, it is important to seek the preferences of the tutor or publishers since there are so many styles of citing. Many publishers have their own style manuals.

In the Numeric or Vancouver style of citing, sources quoted or referred to in the text are indicated by a running number. Full details are given in numerical order in the bibliography at the end of the article or chapter.

The Harvard or Short Author style of citing indicates the source referred to in the text by using the author's surname followed by the date of publication. Full details are given in the bibliography in alphabetical order of surname.

Two style guides in popular use are:

Modern Humanities Research Association (2002) *MHRA style guide: a handbook for authors, editors and writers of theses*, 6th edn, Maney Publishing

Butcher, J., Drake, C. and Leach, M. (2006) *Butcher's copy-editing: the Cambridge handbook for editors, copy-editors and proofreaders*, 4th edn, Cambridge University Press. A popular and detailed handbook.

BS 5605: 1990 *Recommendations for citing and referencing published material.*

It may seem obvious but do check the prefatory matter of a book or index for information on how the author has set out his or her listings. Sometimes numbers refer to columns not pages, for example in *Halsbury's laws of England*; sometimes letters are used to indicate columns, and sometimes parts of a page, for example in the *Index to the Times*. Often abbreviations have been used that are not obvious.

Government publications

UKOP (United Kingdom Official Publications), The Stationery Office and Proquest
  A comprehensive and up-to-date catalogue of UK official government publications since 1980. A resource held by larger public and academic libraries. There are fiche, CD-ROM and internet versions.

Old books

A distinction needs to be made between 'remainders' (books which a publisher decides to dump cheaply); second-hand books (books discarded or sold off cheaply by their owners); antiquarian books (old books of value); and rare books (which can be scarce though not necessarily valuable).

Bernard, P. (ed.) (1994) *Antiquarian Books: a companion for booksellers, librarians and collectors*, Scholar Press.

Carter, J. and Barker, N. (2004) *ABC for Book Collectors*, 8th edn, Oak Knoll Press/The British Library

Ellis, I. C. (2006) *Bookfinds: how to find, buy, and sell used and rare books*, Perigee Books

Porter, C. (2003) *Miller's collecting modern books*, Millers Collectables

Sheppard's British Isles: a directory of antiquarian and secondhand book dealers in the United Kingdom, Richard Joseph Publishers. Annual
  www.sheppardsworld.co.uk

For book values, see, for example:
Connolly, J. (1993) *Modern first editions: their value to collectors*, 4th edn, Little, Brown and Co.
  An A–Z author guide.

Jackson, C. (2001) *Collecting children's books*, Book and Magazine Collector

12,000 titles by the most collectable authors with current values of all first editions.

Russell, R. B. (Annual) *Guide to first edition prices*, Tartarus Press
35,000 titles and 600 colour illustrations.

Book auction records (1924–) Dawson. Annual
This is useful for the more valuable books and will give an idea of top prices fetched at auction.

Annual register of book values, The Clique. Annual
This selects details from booksellers' catalogues.

Rare books in libraries

Bloomfield, B. C. (ed.) (1997) *A directory of rare book and special collections in the United Kingdom and the Republic of Ireland*, 2nd edn, Library Association Publishing
Many dealers produce their own printed catalogues, with the larger dealers and booksellers having their own websites. Get to know your local booksellers so you can redirect enquiries if appropriate.

Electronic resources

The internet has seen a revolution in the marketing of antiquarian books, thus:

AbeBooks **www.abebooks.com**

Alibris **www.alibris.com**
This provides free searching for the old and out-of-print books from over 1550 secondhand and antiquarian booksellers.

Bibliofind **www.bibliofind.com**
Lists some 20 million used, rare and out-of-print books, periodicals and ephemera offered for sale by booksellers around the world.

Biblion **http://biblion.co.uk**
An online stocklist of a large number of dealers in out-of-print books.

UK Book World **www.ukbookworld.com**
This lists 2.5 million books, old, rare and out of print, from 450 British bookshops and booksellers.

Directories relating to old books are:

The Book Fair Calendar **www.inprint.co.uk/thebookguide/fairs/index.php**

The Bookshop Guide **www.inprint.co.uk/thebookguide/shops/index.shtmal**
Lists some 275 UK bookshops selling old, rare and secondhand books.

The Register of British Internet Bookdealers **www.clique.co.uk/bibfind.htm**
Gives the contact details of some 2100 British internet bookdealers
handling old and out-of-print books, with links to individual bookdealer
websites and their holdings.

Journals

Antiquarian Book Review. Monthly
Gives news of book auctions and feature articles, and has a regular selection
of bookdealers' websites, multi-dealer databases and auction house
websites.

Book and Magazine Collector. Monthly
Gives useful price lists.

Organizations

Two useful organizations in this area are:

PBFA (Provincial Booksellers Fair Association)
The Old Coach House, 16 Melbourn Street, Royston, Herts SG8 7BZ
Tel: 01763 248400; Fax: 01763 248920
www.pbfa.org
The PBFA organizes bookfairs and publishes a directory of members.

Antiquarian Booksellers' Association
Sackville House, 40 Piccadilly, London W1J 0DR
Tel: 020 7439 3118; Fax: 020 7439 3119
www.aba.org.uk

Description of book details

In the antiquarian book world very precise descriptions of books are needed. A
standard work is:

Bowers, F. (1994) *Principles of bibliographical description*, Oak Knoll

Care of books

Barnes-Cope, A. D. (1989) *Caring for books and documents*, 2nd edn, British Library
A brief layman's guide.

Greenfield, J. (1988) *The care of fine books*, Lyons & Burford

National Preservation Office
E-mail: npo@bl.uk
www.bl.uk/services/npo/publicationsleaf.html
NPO issues leaflets, free of charge and downloadable.

Shep, R. L. (1991) *Cleaning, repairing and caring for books: a practical manual*, 4th edn, Richard Joseph

Other sources

Seek assistance from your library's bibliographic, cataloguing and ordering departments. Many of the sources that are useful for answering book enquiries are also those which are the tools of the librarian's job and may be sitting on the desks of colleagues! They may also have online subscription tie-ins with library suppliers.

Many library colleagues will be knowledgeable about books. Seek their help. Do refer people to the specialist bookshops and dealers – they are the experts – but be careful when recommending particular ones as this may be seen as promotion. It is useful to have a free list of local bookshops to give enquirers.

Tips and pitfalls

It may seem obvious, and librarians are sometimes ashamed to be seen doing so, but do check the prefatory matter of a book or index to see how the author has arranged the listings. Often abbreviations have been used that are not obvious. This is particualrly true of antiquarian booksellers' catalogues.

The book market can be volatile and printed sources, in particular, may be out of date, although out-of-date websites can also be a pitfall. With older material, most (non-bookish) enquirers will have an inflated idea of the value of their books. Most books that are brought into libraries have little or no value. Be prepared to let the enquirer down gently. You will be doing them, and your colleagues, a favour. The condition of a book influences its value. Prices quoted in the price guides tend to be for books with dust wrappers and in good condition.

Never give a judgement on a book's monetary value. This is a job for experts, and even they will be cautious. Get it wrong and you could be sued! Just give advice on general points such as condition, whether it could be a first edition (surprisingly few people look at the back of a title page or can understand Roman numerals) and give the location of the nearest specialists. *Whitaker's almanack* has a good section on Roman numerals.

BRITISH STANDARDS

Typical questions
* Which British Standard do I need to look at for . . .?

Considerations

'A standard is defined as a document, established by consensus and approved by a recognized body, that provides, for common and repeated use, rules, guidelines or characteristics for activities or their results.' This is the basic definition taken from the British Standards website under 'What are standards?' (**www.bsi-global.com**). Visit the site for a more detailed definition, but also to view the wealth of information available to help in understanding standards.

You may not be lucky enough to have the full collection of British Standards at your disposal but the *British Standards catalogue* and British Standards Institution website allow you to look up any British Standard by subject or BS number. For those trying to set up in business use *Business opportunities profile*, Cobweb Information Ltd, to find out the British Standards that need to be consulted:

www.cobwebinfo.com

Where to look
Directories

British Standards catalogue BSI
Available to download at **www.bsi-global.com**.

Websites

British Standards Institution **www.bsi-global.com**
This has an excellent site with an explanation of what a standard is. It includes a whole section devoted to education, divided into age groups, and it is an excellent resource for teachers and children. In addition, it includes a search facility to find out a BS number using a keyword or vice versa. It

includes both European and international standards. British Standards can be purchased online.

BUSINESS – SETTING UP

Typical questions

- I want to start a business and need help preparing my business plan.
- Are there any organizations who can help me start a business?
- Who can help me finance my new business?

Considerations

There is so much to consider when starting a new business, from the initial idea to putting together a business plan. Normally, the idea bit is easy; the hard part is demonstrating on paper how the business could work. It is easier to break the business plan down into small parts. The main part, which you, as an information worker, will find yourself involved in, is probably providing statistics and market research that will back up the idea. There are numerous sources of information that can be used, many of which are listed below. It is also an area in which a little bit of lateral thinking goes a long way.

Where to look

Directories

Cobweb Information for Business
> **www.cobwebinfo.com**
> Tel: 0191 461 8000
> Excellent subscription-based small business adviser information service.

Market research

A full guide to market research resources can be found under Market Research. See also Statistics.

Refining the business idea and developing the unique selling point (USP)

Use trade directories to find suppliers, competitors or business-to-business customers within the industry on both a regional and national basis. See Companies for general directories.

Trade journals can provide overviews of the industry, providing statistics on the latest trends and developments. They can highlight the need for a service or help to refine the unique selling point. Although most will be national in coverage, many of these journals are important sources of industry/service information and will be widely read.

Most industries and services will have associations and professional bodies. See ASSOCIATIONS AND ORGANIZATIONS for relevant directories. Some offer information on the market and include relevant statistics, trends and developments. Increasingly you will find this information available on the internet.

Local market research information

Whereas the above provide excellent coverage of the national market, in reality it will be research using local information that will give the best support to any business idea and/or indicate whether or not it is viable.

Local sources

Local newspapers provide a wealth of information for market research. One of the best places to find out about local competitors is in the advertisements section. As well as the names of local businesses, information relating to services and products offered may be available, including in some cases prices. This type of information will enable identification of major competitors. As well as competitors, local newspapers can be used to locate suppliers and potential business-to-business customers.

Local directories provide local company information (see COMPANIES).

Statistics and Census data

Not only are statistics useful to show trends and developments in the market sector but they also provide a valuable source of local information with regard to the local population, age groups and ethnic mix. This type of information is useful for planning the location of a business and to build up a profile of potential customers. The best source of local statistical data is the Census. Most libraries will keep Census data for the local area. However, if you do require local data for outside your area, use the Neighbourhood Statistics site from National Statistics **www.statistics.gov.uk/neighbourhood**.

Books

There are simply hundreds of books published that deal with setting up in business. Here are a few recommended titles:

Williams, S. *Financial Times guide to business start up*, Financial Times/Prentice Hall, 2005, 19th edn

Barrow, C. (2005) *The complete small business guide: sources of information for new and small businesses*, 8th edn, Capstone Publishing
This is a useful guide for anyone thinking of starting a business. It is packed with useful advice and considerations, and details of contacts and where to get help.

Good small business guide: how to start and grow your own business, A&C Black Publishers, 2006

Business Plan websites

www.bplans.com
www.myownbusiness.org

Organizations and websites

Barclays Small Business Site **www.smallbusiness.barclays.co.uk**

Business Link **www.businesslink.gov.uk**
Select Starting Up.

British Chambers of Commerce **www.britishchambers.org.uk**
Excellent for business advice, guides, exporting and much more. It has a section to find your nearest chamber. Well worth a visit.

British Franchise Association **www.thebfa.org/**

Business Gateway **www.bgateway.com**
Select Starting Up

Department for Business Enterprise & Regulatory Reform **www.berr.gov.uk**

Enterprise Zone **www.enterprisezone.org.uk**
A gateway to business information that includes business start-up.

Federation of Small Business (FSB) **www.fsb.org.uk**

H M Revenue & Customs **www.hmrc.gov.uk/startingup/**

Institute of Directors **www.iod.com**

Prince's Trust **www.princes-trust.org.uk**

Shell LiveWIRE
    Unit 3, Ground Floor,
    7 – 15 Pink Lane
    Newcastle NE1 5DW
    Tel:0845 757 3252
    www.shell-livewire.org
    Provides lots of free publications on setting up in business.

Small Business Research Portal **www.smallbusinessportal.co.uk**
    Excellent for a wide range of resources.

Small Business Research Trust **www.sbrt.co.uk**

Small Enterprise Research Team **www.serteam.co.uk**
    Produces some useful priced publications and have a free summary
    download of the Quarterly Survey of Small Business in Britain

Start Ups **www.startups.co.uk**
    This has information on starting a business, a franchise and much more.

Tips and pitfalls

Use a variety of sources. Try to instil in the enquirer that time taken to do desk research is well worth while for producing a good business plan. If you can take the time yourself to know exactly what needs to go into a business plan and other considerations for starting a business, then you will be in a better position to advise and assist.

CANALS & WATERWAYS

See also Tourism & Travel

Typical questions

- Can anyone use a canal?
- Are towpaths public rights of way?
- Who owns rivers?
- What's a 'navigation'?

Considerations

After decades of decline and disuse, canals and inland waterways are seeing increasing leisure use (and some commercial use as well). Cruising in owned or hired narrowboats, and walking the large network of towpaths, are popular occupations. For the librarian this translates into enquiries about using the canals, their history, and perhaps even volunteering to help in restoration work. A 'navigation' is a river that has been made navigable, often by making a new 'cut' to avoid rapids, etc.

Where to look
History

The standard history of the canals of the UK are the eight regional volumes by Charles Hadfield, published by David & Charles.

An excellent historical encyclopedia is:

Paget-Tomlinson, E. (2006) *The illustrated history of canal and river navigation*, 3rd edn, Landmark

General

Waterscape **www.waterscape.com**
    Gives information about waterside areas and the national waterway network.

Edwards, L. A. (1985) *Inland Waterways of Great Britain*, 6th edn, Imray Laurie Norie & Wilson
    A detailed account of every canal and navigable river, giving history and detailed technical information.

Towpath (monthly). Mortons Media Group **www.towpathtalk.co.uk**
    Newspaper for waterways users.

Maps and guides

Inland Waterways Map of Great Britain (2006) Nicholson/HarperCollins
Full colour map.

Nicholson guides to the waterways, Nicholson/Collins, 7 vols
Nicholson's detailed regional guides to the canals and navigable waterways of the UK, with maps based on the Ordnance Survey showing locks and towpaths, and giving information on navigation, boatyards, services and local information, are the canal user's 'Bible'.

Pearson's canal companions, J. M. Pearson & Sons
Less detailed than Nicholson, but adequate for the water user. The candid observations of places covered are a feature.

Organizations

British Waterways
Customer Service Centre, Willow Grange, Church Road, Watford WD17 4QA
Tel: 01923 201120; Fax: 01923 201102
E-mail: enquiries.hq@britishwaterways.co.uk
www.british-waterways.org
British Waterways manage a network of two thousand miles of canals and navigable rivers. It has regional offices.

Inland Waterways Association
3 Norfolk Court, Norfolk Road, Rickmansworth WD3 1LT
www.waterways.org.uk
The campaigning group for the use, maintenance and restoration of Britain's inland waterways.

Tips and pitfalls

Like most hobbyists and enthusiasts, the user will often know far more about the subject than the librarian. Access to Hadfield's histories and the local *Nicholson guides* will usually suffice, plus the phone number of local tourist information centres. Note, however, that towpaths and paths on riverside embankments, unless they are also a public right of way, tend not to be indicated on Ordnance Survey maps.

CAREERS & QUALIFICATIONS

See also Employment – Rights & Statistics; Jobs

Typical questions

- What qualifications do you need for nursing?
- I am interested retraining as a teacher.
- What GCSEs do I need for . . .?

Considerations

Many libraries have small careers sections, but more comprehensive information can be found at the local careers office. The specially trained staff there can offer better advice too.

Where to look
Printed sources

One of the best references available is:

Davies, K. (2003) *Occupations*, Careers and Occupational Information Centre
This book has entries for most careers and offers guidance on what qualifications you may need to enter the profession, the work involved, pay and conditions, training courses and addresses for further information. Slightly dated but still a good starting point.

Jobfile – the essential careers handbook, VT Careers Management
Covers 830 jobs and 1435 job titles in alphabetical order.

There are also specialist directories such as:

Careers in food and drink directory (2008) William Reed Business Media

For more information on careers education use:

Careers education and guidance in England: a national framework 11–19
Available to download from **http://publications.teachernet.gov.uk**

Websites

Careers Education
www.teachernet.gov.uk/techingandlearning/14to19/careereducation

Careers Europe: The UK Euro Guidance Centre **www.careerseurope.co.uk**

This is the UK national resource centre for international careers information. It provides resources to career services, Connexions services and other information and advisory services throughout the UK.

Career Transition Partnership **www.ctp.org.uk/ctp/**
For personnel leaving the armed forces.

Connexions Direct **www.connexions-direct.com**
Information and advice for young people. Select Careers. Excellent.

Skill **www.skill.org**.uk
National bureau for students with disabilities giving information on training and careers.

Qualifications

To check which qualification is which use:

British Qualifications (2007) 38th rev. edn, Kogan Page
This is a complete guide to professional, vocational and academic qualifications in the UK.

Websites

City and Guilds **www.cityandguilds.com**

Council for the Curriculum Examinations and Assessment in Northern Ireland **www.ccea.org.uk**

Ofqual Office of the Qualifications and Examinations Regulator **www.ofqual.gov**.uk
Provides definitions on types of qualifications.

National Database of Accredited Qualifications **www.accreditedqualifications.org.uk**

Qualifications and Curriculum Authority **www.qca.org.uk**

Qualifications in Wales **http://wales.gov.uk/topics/educationandskills**

Scottish Qualifications Authority **www.sqa.org.uk**

UK National Reference Point for Qualifications **www.uknrp.org.uk**
Covers international and UK vocational qualifications.

Tips and pitfalls

Never offer any careers advice to enquirers. Suggest that they visit their local careers office or job centre for more information and specialist advice.

CARS & THE MOTOR INDUSTRY

See also DIY & Repair Manuals

Typical questions

- I want to know how much my old car is worth.
- Can you give me the address of . . . car manufacturer?
- How many cars are produced in the UK per year?
- I'm doing an assignment on the car industry.
- How many people own a car in the UK?

Considerations

Queries about used car prices can be quickly answered using *Parkers*, now only available freely on the internet (**www.parkers.co.uk**). For queries relating to car manufacturers either use *Kompass* or *Key British enterprises* (see COMPANIES) or one of the more specialized directories listed below. Local car dealers can be tracked down using Yellow Pages or **www.yell.com**. If it's the motor industry you are searching for, it is best to home in on exactly what the enquirer wants: it is a huge industry. Listed below are some useful sites for statistics and market research.

Where to look
Directories

The UK motor industry directory, Society of Motor Manufacturers and Traders
This directory is invaluable for answering queries related to manufacturers of car parts and accessories. It includes details of 4000 companies supplying products and services to the motor industry. It provides an A–Z listing of companies with contact details. In addition it has a supplier list arranged by category such as passenger vehicles, motor goods vehicles, special purpose vehicles and trailers. Also available is the *The UK motor industry directory CD-ROM* from SMMT (Tel: 020 7344 1612/1661).

European vehicle manufacturers, IMS Ltd
This provides detailed company profiles of the major European vehicle

manufacturers arranged alphabetically. The data includes vehicle sales and market share.

Motor Trader buyers' guide, Reed Business Information
An excellent directory providing four sections of information: wholesalers and distributors by county, wholesalers and distributors A–Z, buyers' guide (divided into 400 categories of products and services) and a company A–Z listing.

Worldwide automotive supplier directory, Automotive Engineering International
This covers the Americas, Europe and the Pacific. It has both a supplier index and a product index.

Beaulieu encyclopaedia of automobile coachbuilding, The Stationery Office
An excellent reference work on the automobile.

Beaulieu encyclopaedia of the automobile, The Stationery Office
A comprehensive book covering the history and social significance of private motoring. Gives details on every make and type of car ever built.

For motorcycles try:

Motorcycle trader directory 2000, Seven Kings Publications
This provides an alphabetical listing of all organizations supplying goods and services to the trade. These are cross-referenced with detailed product locators. There is also an alphabetical listing of nearly 1000 brand names of clothing, accessories and spare parts.

Journals

Motor Trader
Highbury Business Communications
Tel: 020 8722 6000; Fax: 020 8722 6025
www.motortrader.com
47 issues per year
Covers news and information on the latest developments within the automotive industry.

What Car?
Haymarket Autosports and Classic Publications
Tel: 020 8267 5629; Fax: 020 8267 5750
www.whatcar.com

13 issues per year

News and specifications on latest cars, advice on purchasing secondhand and new cars. Road tests, safety and security tips and information on used cars.

Market intelligence

Key Note reports, Key Note

For free executive summaries of report titles listed under transport and motor goods visit **www.keynote.co.uk**. For details of obtaining full reports contact Key Note (Tel: 020 8481 8750; Fax: 020 8783 0049).

Mintel reports, Mintel International Group

For details visit **www.mintel.co.uk**

Refer also to sources and websites mentioned in Market Research.

Statistics

World automotive statistics, Society of Motor Manufacturers and Traders (SMMT)

This looks at car and commercial vehicle production in the UK and overseas. Also provides a survey of motor-producing countries.

Mitchell, K. and Lawson, S. (1998) *The great British motorist*, Automobile Association

Websites
Used car prices

Parkers OnLine **www.parkers.co.uk**

This replaces the monthly publication from Emap. The website is updated daily. It offers advice on buying a car and includes prices, reviews and road test reports.

Glass's Information Service **www.glass.co.uk**

Includes a range of Glass's Guides. One of the most popular is *Glass's guide to part-exchange values and purchase prices*.

Automobile Association (car data check) **www.theaa.com**

Autohit **www.autohit.co.uk**

Autotrader **www.autotrader.co.uk**

Direct Line (car-buying site) **www.jamjar.com**

Hoot **www.hoot-uk.com/index2.html**

Market research

Association of Car Fleet Operators (ACFO) **www.bizjet.com/fleet**

Society of Motor Manufacturers and Traders **www.smmt.co.uk**

Technical information

Society of Automotive Engineering **www.sae.org**

> An international one-stop resource for technical information used in designing, building, maintaining and operating self-propelled vehicles for use on land or sea, in air or space. It offers access to SAE standards to purchase. Details and content of standards offered free. Also available is *Ground vehicles standards on CD-ROM*. Price on application to SAE (sales rep e-mail: elecpubs@sae.org).

Road Tax Calculator **www.theaa.com/allaboutcars/index.html**

Tips and pitfalls

Don't be drawn into commenting on the value of someone's old car; once you have referred them to sources let the user make their own decision about how accurate it is.

CATERING & COOKERY

See also Food & Drink

Typical questions

- Are there any recommended restaurants in . . .?
- How much does the average person spend on eating out?
- Do you know the address of any catering schools?
- I want to find a recipe for bread making
- What recipes were popular during World War 2?

Considerations

The catering industry looks after the business of preparation and cooking of food for others through restaurants, sandwich bars, cafés, work canteens, hospitals and schools. The types of enquiries can range from restaurant recommendations and how much we spend on eating out to how to start a business in catering. For local restaurants and cookery schools you can use the Yellow Pages or **www.yell.com**. Your library or local tourist office may also produce local eating-out guides. For cookery courses in your local area check adult education classes; see EDUCATION – LIFELONG LEARNING & E-LEARNING for a list of websites.

Where to look
Catering
Directories

Caterer and hotelkeeper directory online, Reed Business Information
   www.caterer-directory.com
   This is an excellent dedicated catering search engine and database for the UK catering hospitality industry. It lists 11,000 catering suppliers in the UK and also has the facility to view online catalogues from industry suppliers.

Turvill, A. (2009) *The Which? good food guide*, Which? Books
   Lists 1200 establishments from top hotels to cafés and pubs. Main reviews provide information on new openings, prices, chefs' menus and wine lists. A directory in its 57th year must be worth consulting.

AA restaurants guide (2005) Automobile Association
   Lists 1800 restaurants in the UK with an AA rosette.

Journals

Caterer and Hotelkeeper
   Reed Business Information
   Tel: 01444 475 633; Fax: 01444 445 447
   www.caterer.com or **www.caterersearch.com** for even more information
   Weekly
   Covers all aspects of the hospitality industry.

Statistics

Consumer Trends, The Stationery Office. Quarterly
   www.statistics.gov.uk

Websites

British Hospitality Association (BHA) **www.bha-online.org.uk**

This provides a list of titles of surveys, statistics and journals that are useful to the hotel and catering industry.

Cookery
Printed sources

Smith, D. (1992) *Delia Smith's complete cookery course*, BBC Consumer
Publishing
This book has become a modern classic and for many will answer most questions. But, like food, people's favourite chef or cook is all a matter of taste. Check your library shelves for other favourite chefs and cooks.

There is another classic:

Good Housekeeping Institute (2005) *'Good Housekeeping' cookery book (new edition): the cook's classic companion*, Ebury Press

There is also a wealth of specialized cookbooks. For example, there are books on regional cookery, cooking for special occasions, cooking with specific appliances (e.g. microwave ovens, food processors, etc.), and cooking for different diets or medical conditions. Check the library shelves for availability.
There is an excellent book that concentrates on the English and their food:

Drummond, J. C. and Wilbraham, A. (1991) *The Englishman's food: five centuries of English diet*, rev. edn, Pimlico
This shows in great detail what we have eaten from Tudor times to the 20th century. There are no recipes, but the book provides a fascinating history.

The following titles are also useful and/or interesting:

Davidson, A. (2006) *Oxford companion to food*, Oxford University Press
A huge and authorative dictionary of 2650 entries on just about every foodstuff available.

McGee, H. (1988) *On food and cooking: the science and lore of the kitchen*, Scribner

Hall, C., Hayes, J. and Pratt, J. (2003) *The nation's favourite food: Britain's top 100 dishes*, BBC Consumer Publishing

Paston-Williams, S. (1999) *The art of dining: a history of cooking and eating*, National Trust
The National Trust publishes a range of historically themed cookery books.

Labensky. S. et al. (1998) *On cooking: techniques for expert chefs*, (1998), 2nd edn, Prentice Hall

Lebensky. S. et al. (2006) *On cooking: textbook of culinary fundamentals*, (2006), 4th edn, Prentice Hall

Electronic sources

There are thousands of cookery sites on the web. The best way to find them is to use a popular search engine and type in your key words or to bookmark the following:

www.bbc.co.uk/food
Excellent for recipes, information, a food glossary and a fantastic back-to-basics section. Well worth a visit.

Or try:

UK Cookery Websites **www.UK250.co.uk/cookery**
Excellent and well worth a visit.

Cooking.com **www.cooking.com**

Directory of Cooking **http://dmoz.org/Home/Cooking**
Includes cooking tips, encyclopedia of terms and ingredients and searchable recipe database. Excellent and totally addictive.

CHARITABLE ORGANIZATIONS

See also Associations & Organizations; Volunteering

Typical questions
- Can you give me a list of childrens' charities?
- Can you tell me which charities offer grants for . . .?
- How does my group/organization gain charitable status?
- I would like to know more about the financial status of . . . charity.

Considerations

Many people associate charities with names they have seen on high street charity shops or collection days; however, there are thousands of charitable organizations and they come in many shapes and sizes. When people are referring to charities they can also mean voluntary groups, trusts and foundations. The directories listed below will define each of these. However, before embarking on an enquiry try to clarify what the 'charity' does and where. National and international organizations are, of course, easier to find than local ones and many produce annual reports. These are excellent for financial information. The internet can also be a great help, especially as more and more local charities have web pages.

With regard to the term 'charitable status', the *Charities digest* has a section on setting up a charity which should answer this query, or you can refer to:

Phillips A. (2008) *Charitable status: a practical handbook*, Directory of Social Change

Blake J. (2008) *Charitable status*, Directory of Social Change

Cairns E. (1996) *Charities: law and practice*, 3rd edn, Sweet & Maxwell

In addition, there is a section on registering a charity on the Charity Commission website **www.charity-commission.gov.uk.**

Where to look
Directories
Charities digest: selected charities and voluntary organizations, Waterlow Professional Publishing
An excellent source of information providing an alphabetical list of over 5000 national and regional charities and key independent organizations. Information given includes name, date of foundation, charity registration number, contact details and the type of activities of the organization. There is a subject index. In addition, it is excellent for providing a list of Citizens Advice and volunteer bureaux, community foundations and adoption societies.

Charities Choice United Kingdom 2008, CaritasData Ltd
This is an encyclopaedia of 8500 charitable and voluntary organizations within the UK.

Charities Choice Scotland 2007, CaritasData Ltd
Provides details on 3000 charitable and voluntary organizations.

Charities Choice Northern Ireland 2008, CaritasData Ltd
Provides details of 1500 charitable and voluntary organizations.

Who's who in charities, CaritasData Ltd

This provides information on over 90,000 charity staff with contact details and biographies.

Top 1000 charities in Scotland, CaritasData Ltd

French, A., Johnston, S., Lillya, D. and Smyth, J. (eds) *Directory of grant making trusts*, Directory of Social Change
An invaluable reference source for details of charitable grant makers in the UK covering 2500 grant-making trusts.

RCM top 3000 charities, CaritasData Ltd
This publication is not only excellent for listing details of charities but very useful for charity trends and data. Includes the latest financial accounts of the top charities, league tables, charity sector statistics, grantmaking charities and corporate donors. Also available online from CaritasData Ltd (Tel: 020 7324 2362; Fax: 020 7549 8677).

Traynor, T. and Lillya, D. *Guide to the major trusts, vol. 1, 2007–08*, Directory of Social Change.
Covers the top 400 UK trusts.

French, A. and Smyth, J. *Guide to the major trusts, vol. 2, 2007–08*, Directory of Social Change.
Covers the next 1200 trusts.

Dyer, P. (2003) *Good trustee guide*, 4th edn, NCVO

French, A. (2006/2007) *A guide to local trusts in London*, Directory of Social Change

Smyth, J. (2006/2007) *A guide to local trusts in the Midlands*, Directory of Social Change

Rylands, R. (2008) *A guide to local trusts north*, Directory of Social Change

Lynch, G. (2006/2007) *A guide to local trusts south*, Directory of Social Change

Traynor, T. (2006/2007) *A guide to Scottish trusts*, Directory of Social Change

French, A., Smyth, J. and Traynor, T. (2005) *Welsh Funding Guide*, 2nd edn, Directory of Social Change

Holly, K. (2005) *Directory of European grantmakers 2006–2007*, Chapel and York
This provides details of 1000 private trusts and foundations that fund charities, non-profit companies and individuals.

Directory of American grantmakers 2008–2009 (2007) Chapel and York
This provides details of 700 American foundations offering grants to charities and individuals working outside the USA.

Holly, K. (2007) *Directory of Asia Pacific grantmakers 2007*, Chapel and York
This provides details of 900 independent grantmakers.

Voluntary agencies directory, National Council for Voluntary Organizations
An alphabetical listing of 3000 organizations, providing contact details and descriptions for each. There is a classified index at the back. In addition it has a section of useful addresses, which includes some European contacts.

Pybus, V., *International directory of voluntary work*, Vacation Work
This covers organizations worldwide in need of volunteers with a wide range of skills. It provides contact details and a description of the work and organization.

International foundation directory, Europa Publications
This directory, covers over 2500 institutions worldwide.

International directory of corporate philanthropy, Europa Publications
A guide to the 1200 national and international corporations in 100 countries that make charitable donations internationally.

Anheier, H. K. (2005) *A dictionary of civil society, philanthropy and the nonprofit sector*, Routledge

Journals

Charity Times
Perspective Publishing Ltd
Tel: 020 7562 2402; Fax: 020 7374 2703
www.charitytimes.com
Eight issues per year

Third Sector
Haymarket Marketing and Media Publications
174 Hammersmith Road, London W6 7JP
Tel: 020 8267 4929
www.haymarketgroup.com
Weekly

Charity Finance
  Plaza Publishing
  3 Rectory Grove, London SW4 0DX
  Tel: 020 7819 1200; Fax: 020 7819 1201
  www.charityfinance.co.uk
  Looks at recent financial news in the third sector.

Market research

Key Note reports, Key Note
  For free executive summaries of report titles listed under financial services
  (charity funding), visit **www.keynote.co.uk**. For details of obtaining full
  reports contact Key Note (Tel: 020 8481 8750; Fax: 020 8783 0049).

Statistics

For key facts, figures, analysis and trends:

Charity trends 2007, CaritasData Ltd with Charities Aid Foundation
  Annual analysis of charities finance. Excellent.

Awareness days

Count me in **www.countmeincalendar.info**
  Awareness campaigns, charity events, national days etc. are all listed.

Websites and associations

Charities Aid Foundation (CAF) **www.cafonline.org**
  Advice on setting up trusts and legacies. Includes CharityNet.

Charity Choice **www.charitychoice.co.uk**
  Provides a listing of registered charities in the UK and their objectives.

Charity Commission
  Harmsworth House, 13–15 Bouverie Street, London EC4Y 8DP
  Tel: 0870 333 0123 (contact centre); Fax: 020 7674 2300
  www.charitycommission.gov.uk
  This is the official watchdog of the charities. The website is packed with
  information and downloadable guides. Well worth a visit.

Directory of Social Change **www.dsc.org.uk**

Voluntary Services Overseas (VSO) **www.vso.org.uk**

Tips and pitfalls

All registered charities will have their registration number on their official documents and letters, which can prove useful when searching for information.

CHEMICALS & THE CHEMICAL INDUSTRY

See also Medicines & Drugs

Typical questions

- I need the chemical formula for . . . .
- I have an assignment on the chemical industry.
- Can you tell me the manufacturer of . . .?

Considerations

The chemical industry and the pharmaceutical industry are often confused. The chemical industry relates to the raw chemical materials used in drug making and other industries such as fertilizers. It also includes equipment used within the industry. It is necessary, therefore, to think around this subject area when answering enquiries and establish exactly what the user wants. Directories can be used to find both company details and/or product and service information. Don't rule out using some general directories such as *Kompass* or *Dun & Bradstreet's key British enterprises*. *See* COMPANIES.

Where to look
Chemical data

Lide, D. R. (ed.) (2007) *CRC handbook of chemistry and physics: a ready reference book of chemical and physical data*, 88th edn, CRC Press
Excellent reference book covering the whole subject area. Also available as a special students' edition and online.

Speight, J. (2005) *Lange's handbook of chemistry*, 16th edn, McGraw-Hill
This is a comprehensive handbook of chemistry and chemical data.

Directories

James, S., Porter, H., Scott, M. and Ward, S. (eds) *Major chemical and petrochemical companies of the world*, 10th edn, Graham and Whitehead Ltd
Includes details of 7000 companies connected to the chemical and petrochemical industry worldwide.

Market intelligence

Key Note reports, Key Note

For free executive summaries of report titles listed under market sector listing visit **www.keynote.co.uk**. For details of obtaining full reports, contact Key Note (Tel: 020 8481 8750; Fax: 020 8783 0049).

Statistics

PRODCOM quarterly industry reports, Office for National Statistics

Excellent source of UK manufacturer sales, imports and exports statistics. Available to download free of charge from **www.statistics.gov.uk/OnlineProducts/default.asp**

Journals

Chemical Week

Chemical Week Associates

Tel: 020 7436 7676; Fax: 020 7436 3749

www.chemweek.com

Weekly

Worldwide coverage of the global chemical industry.

Websites

Chemical Industries Association **www.cia.org.uk**

European Chemical Industry Council **www.cefic.org**

Excellent for downloadable facts and figures.

Royal Society of Chemistry **www.rsc.org**

Links for chemists **www.liv.ac.uk/Chemistry/Links/links.html**

Offering a wealth of links to chemistry resources, this is well worth a visit.

CRC Press Periodic Table Online **www.chemnetbase.com/periodic-table/per-table.html**

Use to download periodic table.

CHILDCARE

See also Benefits; Social Welfare

Typical questions

• Have you a list of childminders and nurseries?
• How do I set up a nursery or day care centre, etc.?

Considerations

It is usually the case that the local council maintains lists of registered childminders and nurseries. It is best to suggest that the user talks to the relevant department for this type of information because of the strict checks that are carried out on people included on their lists. You will find the number in your local telephone book or contact details may be available on the council's website. You may want to keep a copy of the list for your library, but remember to keep it up to date. Nurseries, day-care and childminders are inspected by Ofsted; these inspection reports can be found at **www.ofsted.gov.uk**. Ofsted does not provide names and addresses of childminders; reports are accessed through unique identifications numbers. For details of childminders try using **www.childcarelink.gov.uk**. You can also get a copy of *Looking for childcare?: a SureStart guide to help you make the right choice* free of charge by contacting the Department for Children, Schools and Families (Tel: 0845 602 2260).

Where to look

General

British opportunity profiles, Cobweb Information
    Tel: 0191 461 8000; Fax: 0191 461 8001
    www.cobwebinfo.com
    These are very good for those thinking of setting up a childcare service. They provide an introduction to the market, its potential customers and possible competitors. They indicate start-up costs and legal considerations. They also include further reading and useful addresses of relevant associations and organizations. Titles listed are Childcare, Childminding and Children's Day Nursery. Information available via online subscription.

Market intelligence

Mintel reports (childcare facilities and children's holiday clubs), Mintel
    International Group
    For details of reports visit **www.mintel.co.uk** or contact Mintel
    International Group (Tel: 020 7606 4533; Fax: 020 7606 5932).

Key Note reports, Key Note

For free executive summaries of report titles visit **www.keynote.co.uk**. Titles to use are Childcare and Working Women. For details of obtaining full reports, contact Key Note (Tel: 020 8481 8750; Fax: 020 8783 0049).

Organizations

Daycare Trust

21 St George's Road, London SE1 6ES

Tel: 020 7840 3350; Fax: 020 7840 3355

www.daycaretrust.org.uk

The *Childwise Newsletter* (the Daycare Trust quarterly publication) can also be downloaded. Look under Information for parents.

4Children

City Reach 5, Greenwich View Place, London E14 9NN

Tel: 020 7512 2112; Fax: 020 7537 6012

www.4children.org.uk

Excellent website covering a wide range of child issues, including childcare.

National Childminding Association

Royal Court, 81 Tweedy Road, Bromley, Kent BR1 1TG

Tel: 0845 880 0044

www.ncma.org.uk

Includes free download of *How to become a registered childminder*

National Family and Parenting Institute

430 Highgate Studios, 53–79 Highgate Road, London NW5 1TL

Tel: 020 7424 3460; Fax: 020 7485 3590

www.nfpi.org

An excellent website with a huge quantity of freely downloadable publications, one of which is *Is it legal? a parents' guide to the law*. Well worth a visit.

National Day Nurseries Association

National Early Years Enterprise Centre, Longbow Close, Huddersfield, West Yorkshire HD2 1GQ

Tel: 01484 407070; Fax: 01484 407060

Websites

Barnado's **www.barnardos.org.uk**

BBCi Parenting **www.bbc.co.uk/parenting**
   Includes advice, tips and support for parents.

Childcare careers **www.childcarecareers.gov.uk/index.cfm**

Childcare Link **www.childcarelink.gov.uk**
   Lots of information available.

Childline **www.childline.org.uk**

Child Tax Credit and Working Tax Credit
   www.taxcredits.inlandrevenue.gov.uk

Nannies **www.nannyjob.co.uk**
   Excellent site for all sorts of information on childcare, salaries, employment
   and great for links. Includes a nanny agency directory.

Ofsted **www.ofsted.gov.uk**
   Responsible for the regulation and registering of all childminding and
   daycare providers.

SureStart **www.surestart.gov.uk**
   Excellent for publications and the SureStart magazine.

Tips and pitfalls

This is definitely an area in which to avoid giving your own advice or
recommendations, no matter what your experience. It is best to use tried and tested
resources and leave the decisions firmly in the hands of the carer.

CLOTHES & CLOTHING

See also Costume & Fashion

Typical questions
* I need to know who makes this brand of sportswear.
* Have you got a list of dress manufacturers?
* Can you tell me who makes . . .?

Considerations

Do not take for granted that the name given by the user is definitely a company
name: it could well be a brand (trade) name or vice versa. The clothing industry

is riddled with brand names. Most of the directories mentioned below are good for looking up both company names and/or brand names. Also bear in mind that some users may be interested in wholesalers as well as manufacturers. *Kompass*, *Kelly's* and *Dun & Bradstreet's key British enterprises* (see COMPANIES) are all good sources to use but for more details and a more comprehensive coverage of the clothing industry the directories listed below would be useful.

Where to look
Directories

Kemps British clothing industry yearbook, Kemps Publishing Ltd
> An excellent starting point for many queries. This directory provides an alphabetical list of companies, a classified list of products (product lists are provided in a number of European languages) and a trade names section. The products section is further subdivided within categories.

European clothing retailing handbook, Mintel in association with the International Apparel Federation

Market research

Mintel reports, Mintel International Group
> For details visit **www.mintel.co.uk** or Tel: 020 7606 4533; Fax: 020 7606 5932. There is a wide selection of clothing reports.

Key Note reports, Key Note
> For free executive summaries of report titles under clothing and personal goods visit **www.keynote.co.uk**. For details of obtaining full reports, contact Key Note (Tel: 020 8481 8750; Fax: 020 8783 0049).

History and collecting clothes

Harris, C. (2000) *Collecting fashion and accessories*, Miller's

Try also

Victoria & Albert Museum: fashion, jewellery and accessories collections
> **www.vam.ac.uk/collections/fashion/index.html**
> This is an excellent online resource for students and members of the public alike. Well worth a visit.

Journals

There are a number of journals that are excellent for keeping up to date with the world of fashion. These are a selection of the most useful, but it is best to check *Willings press guide* for further titles.

Company Clothing
> Hemming Group
> Tel: 020 7973 6404; Fax: 020 7973 5057
> **www.companyclothing.co.uk**
> Ten issues per year
> Covers all aspects of corporate and work clothing.

Drapers Record & Menswear
> Emap Fashion
> Tel: 020 7391 3378; Fax: 020 7391 3370
> **www.drapersrecord.co.uk**
> Weekly
> Covers all aspects of the clothing and fashion industry.

Try also **www.drapersonline.com/index.html**.

Fashion Forecast International
> Benjamin Dent and Co
> Tel: 020 7637 2211; Fax: 020 7637 2248
> Published in December and August.

FW
> Emap Fashion
> Tel: 020 7520 1500; Fax: 020 7520 1501
> Weekly
> Covers men and women's fashion.

Statistics

PRODCOM quarterly industry reports, Office for National Statistics
> Excellent source of UK manufacturer sales, imports and exports statistics. Available to download free of charge from **www.statistics.gov.uk/ OnlineProducts/default.asp**.

Organization

> British Fashion Council
> 5 Portland Place, London W1B 1PWT

Tel: 020 7636 7788; Fax: 020 7436 5924

Websites

www.londonfashionweek.co.uk

British Footwear Association **www.britfoot.com**
> This has a directory which gives information and contacts for those looking for non-standard footwear, e.g. made-to-measure.

Company Clothing Online **www.companyclothing.co.uk**
> This has free access on registration to 2500 contacts and 1300 companies across the clothing sector.

Children's Foot Health Register **www.shoe-shop.org.uk**

Independent Footwear Retailers Association **www.shoeshop.org.uk**

KFAT **www.poptel.org.uk/kfat/**

Shoeworld.com **www.shoeworld.com**

COINS & STAMPS

See also Medals & Decorations; Money

Typical questions

- How much is this old coin worth?
- Is this coin Roman?
- I have an old stamp album. Is it worth anything?
- What can I do with old stamps?

Considerations

Most questions regarding coins and stamps will be about their value and/or identification. Best to give enquirers the catalogues to consult themselves, else you may get 'dragged in' to passing opinions.

Identifying stamps is a skilled business that involves watermarks, perforation scales and colour charts. A magnifying glass and pair of tweezers are handy aids to keep at the counter. Have a large, draught-free table for the regulars!

Where to look
Coins

There are many books available on coins. Check your shelves to see what you have. The following texts, or ones similar to these, should help you answer most enquiries.

Krause, C. L. and Mishler, C. (eds) (2003) *Standard catalog of world coins*, Krause Publications
Provides full details of coins with current values and identification keys.

Spinks standard catalogue of British coins: coins of England and the United Kingdom, Spink. Annual **www.spink-online.com**
This lists coins from Celtic times to the present day. It is an invaluable publication for identifying British coins and finding their values.

Spink and Co. are the longstanding specialist publisher of books on coins and medals. Their website (**www.spink-online.com**) has details of their titles.

Royal Numismatic Society, c/o The British Museum, Department of Coins and Medals, Great Russell Street, London WC1B 3DG
www.numismatics.org.uk

Local museums can also be a useful source of information if they have coin collections.

Stamps

The stamp collector's 'bible' is the collection of Gibbons catalogues, e.g.:

Stamps of the world, 4 vols; *British Commonwealth*, 2 vols
These catalogues are annual and are published by Stanley Gibbons Ltd. There are simplified versions of these catalogues, but enthusiasts will want their main libraries to stock the expensive complete volumes which will beyond their pockets.

There is a useful 'gateway' site for stamp collectors at **www.ukphilately.org.uk**.

The national society for stamp enthusiasts is:

The Royal Philatelic Society, 41 Devonshire Place, London W1G 6JY
Tel: 020 7486 1044; Fax: 020 7486 0803
www.rpsl.org.uk

Tips and pitfalls

Avoid getting drawn in to assisting in identifying stamps or coins, just provide the books . . . and magnifying glass!

COMPANIES

See also Jobs

Typical questions

- Have you got the address of . . .?
- Who owns . . .?
- I'm going for an interview; have you got any information about this company?
- Can you give me a list of companies who make steel rods?

Considerations

It is certainly useful to know what constitutes the various types of registered company. The following are brief descriptions annotated from Company Law Club:

www.companylawclub.co.uk

(1) **Private Companies Limited by Shares** – These will have the word 'Limited' or 'Ltd' at the end of the name. They are usually small or medium-sized and therefore need only file 'small' accounts at Companies House. A private company cannot offer shares or debentures to the public.

(2) **Public Limited Companies** – Despite our familiarity with the term PLC, there are, in fact, only a small proportion of companies that are public companies. The company name will end in the words 'Public Limited Company' or 'PLC'. They are large businesses with shares available to the public. Public companies have greater legal requirements than private companies, filing full accounts at Companies House.

(3) **Property Management Companies** – This is a type of private limited company. It is set up to own the freehold of a property that is divided and owned in parts by individuals, e.g. flats.

(4) **Companies Limited by Guarantee** – A company limited by guarantee is a private company, very like a private company limited by shares, but it does not have a share capital. It is widely used for charities, clubs, community enterprises and some co-operatives. Such companies are registered at Companies House and are subject to the requirements of the Companies Acts.

There are no shares and therefore no shareholders but they do have members, who control each company through general meetings. The directors are often called a management committee but in law are still company directors and subject to the rules.

(5) **Unlimited Companies** – It is possible to register at Companies House a private company which is unlimited – the members accept complete liability for the company's debts. It is not required to register annual accounts at Companies House.

(6) **Community Interest Companies (CICs)** – are a fairly new type of company (from 2005) which can only be registered for objects that are for the good of the community. Assets and profits must be permanently retained within the CIC and used solely for community benefit (asset lock) or transferred to another organization which itself has an asset lock as a charity.

Sole traders and partnerships are not strictly companies.

For company information it is advisable to make sure you are familiar with at least two good directories. There are a number listed below. If you do not have any of these available in your library, you may want to bookmark a few of the excellent online directories listed below.

Where to look
Directories

Kompass, 3 vols, Reed Business Information
www.reedbusiness.com
This provides details of 46,000 products and services and 41,000 companies.

It is worth also trying:

Kompass OnLine **www.kompass.co.uk**
This is an excellent site that is free to search and provides product, service and company details for UK and international companies. Subscribers can view the full list of results; otherwise a selection is provided free.

Key British enterprises UK, 4 vols, Dun & Bradstreet
Provides contact, financial, operational and corporate details for the 50,000 companies covered.

Try also:

United Kingdom's 5000 largest companies 2008, ELC International
Available also on CD-ROM

Kelly's industrial directory, Reed Elsevier Business Publishing Group

Provides both company and products and services information. For each company the address, telephone, fax and business activity are given. Also use **www.kellysearch.co.uk**. This is one of the largest business search engine resources in the world. It can search by product, service or company. Excellent.

Sell's products and services directory, 2 vols, United Business Media

Who owns whom UK and Ireland, 2 vols, Dun & Bradstreet

This is indispensible for finding out company ownership.

Waterlow stock exchange yearbook, CaritasData

This provides information on all companies and securities listed on the London and Dublin stock exchanges and all those traded in the alternative investment market. Companies in administration, liquidation and receivership are also included as well as a section on dealing with government, corporation and provincial stocks and bonds.

Directory of directors, 2 vols, Hemscott

Volume 1 provides names of 50,000 directors of leading companies. Volume 2 covers all UK registered quoted companies, leading UK unquoted companies plus large quoted and unquoted Irish companies. Available free when subscribing to Directory of Directors online **www.hemscott.com**.

Dun & Bradstreet business registers, 32 vols, Dun & Bradstreet

This is a set of 30-plus regional directories. The listing includes businesses with five or more employees, or an annual sales turnover in excess of £250,000, and their branches.

LexisNexis corporate affiliations, 3 vols, Lexis Nexis

www.corporateaffiliations.com

Over 200,000 parent companies, affiliates, subsidiaries and divisions worldwide. Also available on CD-ROM.

Online services

Companies House **www.companieshouse.gov.uk**

Companies House provides information on 2 million registered companies. Information available includes company reports, company director details, dissolved companies and disqualified directors, document images. The basic company and director details are free. The other information can be paid for either by credit card or by subscription.

ICC – Juniper

For more details contact **www.icc.co.uk** or Tel: 020 7426 8506. ICC covers credit and business information for 6.5 million UK companies. Juniper is an internet subscription-based service providing access to financial information, directors and major shareholders for all 1.4 million limited companies in the UK. It is updated daily. The service also provides credit risk scores and access to an image bank of all director reports, accounts and annual returns since March 1995. There is also a database of unincorporated businesses.

Finding out more about a company

International directory of company histories, St James Press, Gale Group

A multi-volume work that provides histories of more than 4550 of the major and influential companies of the world.

Websites

Annual Reports Library **www.global-reports.com**

Annual reports and documents for 30,000 companies worldwide. Subscription site.

Applegate Company Information **www.applegate.co.uk**

Covers the following sectors: food and agribusiness, electronics, packaging, transport, textiles and clothing, construction, engineering, chemical oil and gas, plastics and rubber, and recruitment. This has information on 239,314 companies cross-referenced to 78,440 products.

Bized **www.bized.ac.uk**

Business Network **www.countyweb.co.uk**

Carol (Company Annual Reports OnLine) **www.carol.co.uk**

Users need to register, after which they can search for annual reports free of charge.

Companies House **www.companieshouse.gov.uk**

Corporate Information **www.corporateinformation.com**

Free company and industry reports.

Financial Times **www.ft.com**

Hemscott **www.hemscott.com**

Institute of Directors **www.iod.com**

Northcote: The LINK to annual reports and press releases
www.northcote.co.uk
Excellent.

The Times 100 **www.thetims100.co.uk**
A resource for business studies student. Useful for some company history of major companies.

Tips and pitfalls

Always check the spelling of companies with the enquirer. If they have a letter from the company, ask if you can look at it: it may well give you some leads. Company information is expensive but there is a lot of free information on the internet. Don't be frightened of searching, for example, **google.com** with a company name. Many companies will have websites which include company information and trade catalogues.

COMPANIES – ACCOUNTS

Typical questions

- Have you got the annual report for . . .?
- Can you tell me the turnover for . . .?
- Have you got a credit rating for . . .?

Considerations

In the main, company financial information does not come cheap, especially if further analysis has been carried out by the supplier. The best source of free company financials is the annual report. If your library does not keep annual reports, the enquirer can either contact the company directly for the annual report (see COMPANIES) or use one of the websites such as Carol (Company Annual Reports OnLine; **www.carol.co.uk**).

Where to look

Reid, W. and Myddelton, D. R. (2005) *The meaning of company accounts*, Gower

Online services

Companies House **www.companieshouse.gov.uk**

Companies House provides information on 2 million registered companies. Information available includes company reports, company director details, dissolved companies and disqualified directors, document images. Free search for registered office, incorporation date and date of accounts.

ICC – Juniper & Plum

For more details visit **www.icc.co.uk** or Tel: 020 8481 8847. ICC covers credit and business information for 6.5 million UK companies. Juniper is an internet subscription-based service providing access to financial information, directors and major shareholders for all 1.4 million limited companies in the UK. It is updated daily. The service also provides credit risk scores and access to an image bank of all director reports, accounts and annual returns since March 1995. There is also a database of unincorporated businesses.

Dun & Bradstreet's Company Information

Subscription based service. For more information visit **www.dnb.com**.

Websites

Carol (Company Annual Reports OnLine) **www.carol.co.uk**

User needs to register before searching for free annual reports.

Companies House **www.companieshouse.gov.uk**

Corporate Information **www.corporateinformation.com**

Provides free company snapshots which include brief financial information.

Northcote: The LINK to annual reports and press releases
www.northcote.co.uk
Requires free registration.

The Times 100 **www.thetimes100.co.uk**

COMPANIES – DEFUNCT

Typical questions

• Can you tell me if this company still exists?

- When did this company go into liquidation?

Considerations

Here are some definitions of what all these terms mean. 'Liquidation' (or 'winding up') means that the assets of a company are sold off and the money shared among its creditors according to their position in the payment queue. 'Voluntary liquidation' is the result of a resolution by the shareholders and 'compulsory liquidation' is the result of a court order. At the end of liquidation the company will be 'dissolved'. 'Administration' is a court-based procedure under which a company may be reorganized or its assets realized under the protection of statutory moratorium. 'Administrative receivership' and 'receivership' are not strictly insolvency proceedings but are available to a secured creditor (usually the bank) allowing realization of assets which are subject to security, e.g. the bank lends money, the company offered a warehouse as security, the bank then sends in receivers to get what is due. The difference between the receiver and the administrator is basically the 'receiver' looks after whoever appoints him, the 'administrator' looks after creditors.

In the majority of cases, enquirers don't know that the company they are looking for no longer exists. You may find you have to go through the full search process using the sources mentioned under COMPANIES before you actually find this out. When you are actually faced with someone who is trying to find out about a dissolved company you will probably be limited in the amount of information you can offer. The best advice is for the enquirer to contact Companies House.

Where to look

Companies that have gone into liquidation, amalgamated or changed their name can be traced using one of the following:

Companies House **www.companieshouse.gov.uk**
    Companies House provides information on 2 million registered companies. Information available includes company reports, company director details, dissolved companies and disqualified directors, and document images. It also provides company change of name with the date it took place or the date a company was dissolved. This service is also available via the telephone. The other information can be paid for either by credit card or by subscription.

Waterlow stock exchange yearbook, Waterlow Specialist Information Publishing

This provides lists of companies in administration, receivership and liquidation. Also has a register of defunct and other companies.

London Gazette **www.london-gazette.co.uk**

This daily publication lists petitions and resolutions for winding up, appointments of liquidators, meetings of creditors, final meetings and bankruptcies. Select Browse then Corporate Insolvency.

Websites

Companies House **www.companieshouse.gov.uk**

Insolvency Service (DTI) **www.insolvency.gov.uk**

Excellent website for providing information on what to do regarding insolvency.

COMPANIES – INTERNATIONAL

Typical questions

- Have you got the address of . . .?
- Who owns . . .?
- Have you got the telephone number for a company in Rome?
- Can you give me a list of companies who make clocks in Spain?

Considerations

Enquirers may not always know the nationality of a company and neither will you. It is difficult to offer assistance without having at least a few of the resources listed below. However, you could use one of the free internet databases.

Where to look
Directories

Try the following, all published by Graham & Whitehead:

Major companies of the Arab world
Major companies of the Africa south of the Sahara
Major companies of central and eastern Europe and the Commonwealth of Independent States
Major companies of Europe
Major companies of the Asia and Australasia

Major companies of Latin America and the Caribbean
Major companies of Scandinavia
Major companies of Southwest Asia
Ward's business directory of US private and public companies

Kompass **www.kompass.co.uk**
Kompass produces directories for a large number of countries. They are arranged and organized in a similar way to the UK Kompass. Try also Kompass Worldwide on the internet. Select country; use either product, service or company search.

Who owns whom continental Europe, Dun & Bradstreet
This directory provides corporate family trees of parent companies registered in Austria, Belgium, Denmark, Finland, France, Germany, Greece, Italy, Luxembourg, Norway, Netherlands, Portugal, Spain, Sweden and Switzerland. In addition it provides parent companies worldwide with those of their subsidiaries or associates incorporated within continental Europe. The second volume provides an alphabetical index to subsidiaries and associates of parent companies listed in the first volume.

Who owns whom the Americas (also *Ireland, Australia, Asia, Middle East, Africa*), Dun & Bradstreet

Europe's 15,000 largest companies, ELC International
Lists the top companies in Europe ranked by turnover and, in the case of banks, assets. It provides tables on Europe's 500 largest companies, the largest industrial companies in Europe and the largest service companies in Europe along with an alphabetical index of all companies. This is also available as a CD-ROM.

Europages: the European business directory **www.europages.co.uk**
This covers 18 sectors of activity, listing companies for each of the 22 countries covered. It includes a market analysis of each sector. This can be very useful for an overview of the sector. There is an alphabetical index of suppliers at the back of the publication.

Websites

Carol (Company Annual Reports OnLine) **www.carol.co.uk**
User needs to register before searching for free annual reports.

Corporate Information **www.corporateinformation.com**
> This is the sort of site we all dream of. It offers free company and industry reports for the Americas, Europe and Oceania. The reports include financials, analysis and competitor comparisons. Well worth a visit and one to bookmark.

Tips and pitfalls

Don't rule out using the world telephone directories for basic contact details. Look at **www.infobel.com**.

COMPANIES – LAW

See also Employment – Law; Law

Typical questions

- What are the legal obligations of a company director?
- Can you give me a guide to the Companies Acts?

Considerations

This is a huge area and for many queries specialist help may be required. However, for information purposes there are a number of reference books that are excellent. Company law is constantly being updated and it is important to check the date of the information offered.

Where to look
General reference books

For a general reference book try:

Dine, J. (2007) *Company law*, Palgrave Law Masters, Palgrave
> This is an excellent publication, providing a concise yet comprehensive introduction to the subject without oversimplifying the complex issues involved. It is very readable.

Also:

Mayson, S., French, D. and Ryan, C. (2007) *Mayson, French and Ryan on company law*, Oxford University Press

French, D. (2007) *Statutes on company law*, Oxford University Press

This brings together statutes relating to company law in one volume. Primarily aimed at students, it is excellent for answering enquiries regarding this area.

Don't rule out using publications such as:

Rose, F. (2004) *Company law nutshells*, Nutshells, Sweet & Maxwell
This presents the essentials of law in clear and straightforward language.

Also, for a guide to the duties and liabilities of company directors:

Martin. D. (2007) *The company director's desktop guide*, Thorogood

Health and safety

This is an important aspect of company law.

Selwyn: the law of health and safety at work 2007/2008, Croner CCH Group

Hsedirect **www.hsedirect.com**
Hsedirect was developed by the Health and Safety Executive (in partnership with Butterworths) and provides health and safety legislation and guidance. It is also available on CD-ROM. Requires subscription, call Tel: 0845 300 3142.

Websites

Company Law Club **www.companylawclub.co.uk**
Excellent.

Delia Venables' site **www.venables.co.uk**
This is good for links.

Infolaw **www.infolaw.co.uk**

International Centre for Commercial Law **www.icclaw.com**

Law Commission **www.lawcom.gov.uk**

LegalPulse **www.legalpulse.com**
Provides free legal information for small businesses. After free registration you are given access to the Documents Library, which covers all aspects of business including forming a company, developing a business, employment matters, etc. There is also a legal dictionary.

Social Science Information Gateway (SOSIG) **www.sosig.ac.uk/law**

CONFERENCES & EXHIBITIONS

Typical questions

- Can you tell me the organizers of . . .?
- Where and when will the next . . . conference be held?

Considerations

When we talk about exhibitions we usually mean a show on a specific interest. These commonly fall into two categories: either trade and professional exhibitions or craft and special interest such as art. Details of exhibitions can be found in many professional and special interest journals. There are a few journals dedicated to listing exhibitions and these are listed below. This is a subject area well covered by the internet and most professional journals will give relevant conference details.

Where to look
Directories

Conference blue and green, CMP Information

These are the leading directories for the conference industry in the UK, distributed free of charge. They cover nearly 7700 companies and 3600 venues. They are available in hard copy, CD-ROM or at **www.venuefinder. com**. Excellent for links too.

The white book, Ocean Media Group

This is an essential reference book for event organizing with contact information for conferences and events both in the UK and overseas. It can also be searched online via **www.whitebook.co.uk**.

Journals

Conference Calendar

Fleming Information Services

Tel: 020 7237 9777

104 times per year

Listings of conferences, awards and affiliated exhibitions in the UK and overseas.

Exhibition Bulletin
    Mash Media
    Tel: 020 8971 8282; Fax: 020 8971 8283
    Monthly
    Provides details of trade exhibitions both in the UK and abroad.

Websites

Association of British Professional Conference Organisers **www.abpco.org.uk**

TSNN Global Network **www.tsnn.co.uk**
    The online companion to *Exhibition Bulletin*. Subscribers to the bulletin can
    have full access; others have limited period access.

Fine Art Trade Guild **www.fineart.co.uk**
    Lists artists' exhibitions, trade fairs and branch events.

FT Conferences **www.ftconferences.com**

Trade Fairs and Exhibitions UK **www.exhibitions.co.uk**
    The official website for the UK exhibition industry, sponsored by UK
    Trade & Investment, providing a free listing of all consumer and trade
    exhibitions. Highly recommended.

TSNN Global Network **tsnn.co.uk**
    Contains data on more than 16,000 exhibition suppliers.

Venuefinder **www.venuefinder.com**
    This is for meeting and event organizers and is particularly good for links.

Try also:

Art in Action **www.artinaction.org.uk**
    96 Sedlescombe Road, London SW6 1RB
    Tel: 020 7381 3192
    Holds annual exhibitions for artists and craftworkers.

Tips and pitfalls

Many art and craft exhibitions are held locally and it is worth checking your local
newspapers and newsletters, and with local groups. It is worth asking local art
groups where they advertise forthcoming exhibitions and making notes.

CONSTRUCTION

See also Architecture & Planning

Typical questions

- Can you give me the address of a housebuilding firm?
- Is there a list of specialist builders available?
- Where can I find a recommended builder?
- I'm interested in statistics related to the construction industry.
- Do I need building regulations for my loft conversion?

Considerations

There are numerous specialist directories for the construction industry but if you don't have access to any of the following don't rule out using *Kompass* or *Dun & Bradstreet's key British enterprises*. *See* COMPANIES. Contracts within the construction industry are listed in both *Building* and *Construction News* (see below).

Where to look

General

MacLean, J. H. and Scott, J. S. (1993) *The Penguin dictionary of building*, 4th edn, Penguin Books

Defects in buildings: symptoms, investigation, diagnosis and care (2001) 3rd edn, Carillion Series, The Stationery Office
Covers common defects in all the principal types of construction.

Directories

RIBA product selector, RIBA Information Services
An indispensable three-volume directory. It contains product and company information on 7800 manufacturers and suppliers of building products and services, 24,000 trade names and 1000 advisory organizations. It is worth also looking at the RIBA Information Service website **www.ribaenterprises.com**. This provides a link to Sweet's Product MarketplaceTM **www.sweets.com** for those involved in the European and/or American construction industry.

Barbour compendium – big red, Barbour Index PLC
This is a building product reference source of 7500 UK manufacturers. There is also the Barbour Compendium, a free database of building product

and supplier information, including contact details, product catalogues, images and case studies. See **www.barbour-index.co.uk**.

Spon's price books are invaluable guides to the construction industry. Titles available include:

Spon's architects and builders' price book
Spon's civil engineering and highway works price book
Spon's landscape and external works price book
Spon's mechanical and electrical services price book

All now available with free internet download. Other titles are available also. Spon also produce international price books. Titles available include:

Spon's African construction costs handbook
Spon's Asia and Pacific construction costs handbook
Spon's European construction costs handbook
Spon's Irish construction price book
Spon's Latin American construction costs handbook
Spon's Middle East construction costs handbook

For more details visit **www.pricebooks.co.uk**.

Building restoration and conservation

Building conservation directory: a guide to specialist suppliers, consultants and craftsmen in traditional building conservation, refurbishment and design (2007)
Cathedral Communications
Provides work specialists for historic buildings, their contents and surroundings, a starting point in the search for appropriate products and services and expert advice. It is also useful to look at the website **www.buildingconservation.com**, which provides a gateway to the building conservation and restoration industry.

Try also:

Conservation register **www.conservationregister.com/index.asp**
This includes a 'Find a local conservator-restorer' facility.

Institute of Conservation **www.icon.org.uk**
Includes a set of 'How to care for . . .' advice guides such as architectural ironwork.

Building regulations

Building regulations are government-approved specifications relating to health and safety, energy conservation, and the welfare and convenience of disabled people. As well as the suggestions given it is worth checking your library shelves for books such as Polley. S., *Understanding the building regulations*, Taylor and Francis Ltd.

For detailed information try:

Knight's building regulations, with approved documents, Lexis Nexis
A two-volume loose-leaf publication with two updates per year. Covers England and Wales.

Or the excellent:

Planning Portal **www.planningportal.gov.uk**, which is the government's online planning and building regulations resource for England and Wales. It covers planning and building regulations, applying for planning permission and much more.

Also useful is the Health and Safety Executive – Construction Information **www.hse.gov.uk/construction/information.htm**. This is packed with information on guidance, advice leaflets and risk assessment.

Construction – TSO Online Bookshop **www.tsoshop.com**
Choose Construction for a list of building and construction documents to purchase.

Market intelligence

Key note reports, Key Note
For free executive summaries of report titles listed under construction visit **www.keynote.co.uk**. For details of obtaining full reports, contact Key Note (Tel: 020 8481 8750; Fax: 020 8783 0049).

Journals

Building
CMP Information
Tel: 020 7921 5000
Weekly
Covers major developments in the industry.

C CONSTRUCTION

Construction News **www.cnplus.co.uk**
Schofield Publishing
Tel: 01603 274130; Fax: 01603 274131
Weekly
There are numerous journals for the construction industry, details of which can be found in *Willings press guide* (see JOURNALS & PERIODICALS).

Statistics

Construction statistics annual, Department for Business Enterprise and Regulatory Reform
Available to download free of charge or to view at **www.berr.gov.uk/sectors/construction/ConstructionStatistics/page16429.html**.

PRODCOM annual industry reports, Office for National Statistics
Excellent source of manufacturer sales, imports and exports statistics. Available to download free of charge from **www.statistics.gov.uk/OnlineProducts/PRODCOM2000_annual.asp**.

Quarterly State of Trade Survey, Federation of Master Builders **www.fmb.org.uk**
Free statistical publication. Look under Publications.

Websites

Automated Builder Magazine **www.automatedbuilder.com**

Online to the Built Environment **www.barbourexpert.com**

Building Conservation **www.buildingconservation.com**

Building Products Index Online **www.bpindex.co.uk**
Excellent.

Careers in Construction **www.careersinconstruction.com**

Chartered Building Company and Consultancy Scheme **www.cbcscheme.org.uk**

Chartered Institute of Building **www.ciob.org.uk**
Good for online publications, research and lists of construction books.

Construction Confederation **www.constructionconfederation.co.uk**

ConstructionNet **www.constructionnet.net/**

House Builders Federation **www.hbf.co.uk**

Institution of Civil Engineers **www.ice.org.uk**

International Council for Research and Innovation in Building and
Construction **www.cibworld.nl**

National Federation of Builders **www.builders.org.uk**
Includes a 'Find a Builder' facility.

RICS Online **www.rics.org.uk**

RUDI (Resource for Urban Design Information) **www.rudi.net**

UK Construction **www.ukconstruction.com/builders.html**

CONSUMER INFORMATION

See also Retailing & Consumer Spending; Rights

Typical questions
- Who do I complain to about a product/service?
- Have you got a guide to consumer law?
- Have you got a survey on the best kettle to buy?
- How do I contact the ombudsman for . . . ?

Considerations

The consumer is someone who buys a product or service. Consumers are either
seeking information because they want to purchase something or because they have
a grievance about a product or service, which they cannot resolve with the seller.
Advice on the purchase of goods can only be limited to providing good product
surveys such as those done by *Which?*. Consumers with a complaint in the main want
to know who can help with the problem. The *Which? Report on Ombudsmen* January
2008 is an excellent guide to using ombudsmen for your complaint, providing a
sample letter to use, a step-by-step guide on how to complain and consumer rights.

www.which.co.uk/reports_and_campaigns/consumer_rights/index.jsp

Where to look
Surveys
Which?
2 Marylebone Road, London NW1 4DF

Tel: 020 7770 7000; Fax: 020 7770 7600
www.which.co.uk
Titles include: *Computing which?*, *Gardening which?*, *Holiday which?* and *Which?* These contain product tests and campaigns for improvements in goods and services.

Legislation

A useful book to refer to is:

Lowe, R. and Woodruffe, G. (2003) *Consumer law and practice*, Sweet & Maxwell

Try also:

Miles, R. (2001) *Blackstone's sale and supply of goods and services*, Blackstone Press
This offers a one-volume guide to the legislation relating to the sale and supply of goods, together with a background to the law of contract.

Complaints

Wiseman, S. (2004) 2nd edn, *Leaves on the line: how to complain effectively*, Law Pack Publishing
www.howtocomplain.com

Ombudsman schemes

These deal with complaints against industry or sectors, privates companies and government organizations. They exist in different areas (see below).
   To find an ombudsman use:

British and Irish Ombudsman Association **www.bioa.org.uk**
This is an excellent website allowing the consumer to find out the correct ombudsman to complain to by entering one word. Also has useful links and information. Well worth a visit.

For government and NHS departments

Parliamentary & Health Service Ombudsman
   Millbank Tower, Millbank, London SW1P 4QP
   Tel: 0845 015 4033

For councils
Local Government Ombudsman
   PO Box 4771, Coventry CV4 0EH
   Tel: 0845 602 1983

For EU organizations
European Ombudsman
   1 Avenue du President Robert Schuman, CS 30403, FR-67001 Strasbourg
   Tel: 00 33 388 172313

For financial services
Financial Ombudsman Service
   South Quay Plaza, 183 Marsh Wall, London E14 9SR
   Tel: 020 7964 1000

For lawyers
Office of the Legal Services Ombudsman
   3rd Floor, Sunlight House, Quay Street, Manchester M3 3JZ
   Tel: 0845 601 0794

For telecommunications
Office of the Telecommunications Ombudsman
   Otelo, PO Box 730, Warrington WA4 6WU
   Tel: 0845 050 1614

For buyers, sellers, tenants and landlords of residential property
Ombudsman for Estate Agents
   Beckett House, 4 Bridge Street, Salisbury, Wiltshire SP1 2LX
   Tel: 01722 333306

For (complaints against) landlords, agents and other housing agents
Housing Ombudsman Service
   81 Aldwych, London WC2B 4HN
   Tel: 020 7421 3800

Journals

TS Today
> Trading Standards Institute
> Tel: 0845 608 9421
> **www.tsi.org.uk**
> Monthly
> Deals with trading standards and consumer protection.

Associations and organizations

Use your local telephone directory for your local Trading Standards Department or use Trading Standards Central **www.tradingstandards.gov.uk/consumers/ consumers.cfm**. Excellent for consumers; this has advice leaflets to download and allows you to enter your postcode to find your nearest trading standards office.

Department for Business Enterprise & Regulatory Reform (BERR)
> 1 Victoria Street, London SW1H 0ET
> Tel: 020 7215 5000
> **www.berr.gov.uk/consumers/index.html**
> Excellent site packed with publications and links.

Office of Fair Trading
> Fleetbank House, 2–6 Salisbury Square, London EC4Y 8JX
> Tel: 08454 040506 (Consumer Direct)
> **www.oft.gov.uk**
> Excellent site packed with information and advice.

National Consumer Council
> 20 Grosvenor Gardens, London SW1W 0DH
> Tel: 020 7730 3469; Fax: 020 7730 0191
> **www.ncc.org.uk**
> Excellent for publications and reports.

Websites

> Consumer Direct
> Tel: 08450 040506
> **www.consumerdirect.gov.uk**
> A government-funded telephone and online service offering information and advice on consumer issues.

Which? Online **www.which.co.uk**

E-zine covering consumer interest articles from *Which?* magazine.

Trading Standards Institute **www.tsi.org.uk**

Excellent site packed with information and publications for consumers and businesses.

Tips and pitfalls

Avoid comment on individual problems. Equally, you cannot recommend goods and services, merely present the information.

COPYRIGHT & LEGAL DEPOSIT

See also Inventions, Patents & Trade Marks; Publishing

Typical questions

- Can I photocopy this?
- How can I take out copyright on my work?
- Someone told me I've got to send a copy of a book I've written to the British Library. Is this true?
- Can I get money because people borrow my book from libraries?

Considerations

Concerns about copyright, particularly photocopying material, are frequent. It is important that library staff provide correct advice. This is particularly so since it is usually library material that is being copied, and on library equipment. It is an offence to infringe copyright, and unlike most of the other subjects covered in this book, this is one where library staff should be able to give clear advice. Guidelines, such as in the books listed below, and notices by copying equipment, should be readily available to the staff and public. The fact that libraries provide photocopiers and printers for the public to use for themselves obliges the library management to make sure that notices are up to date and clearly displayed; if not, library staff could be liable for any misuse of the machine.

Every library will have its own procedures and guidelines relating to copying and it is important that staff have access to those. Thus some subscription services will have licensing restrictions and many libraries will be registered with the Copyright Licensing Agency (see below). Despite the somewhat fraught, complex and often unclear law on copyright, the general principle is clear – that people copying in quantity or for a commercial purpose must have the permission of the author or copyright owner, and that proper acknowledgement is made. If in doubt, ask the person requesting the copies to get written permission from the publisher, or to sign a declaration that the material is to be used for the purposes of private study. Better to say 'No' than break the law.

Visual, audio and digital material, as well as printed, is covered by copyright.

We concentrate here on copyright and copying, but copyright extends into other areas such as patent and design law, intellectual property and designation. Refer to the library catalogue for these heavyweight subjects. See also INVENTIONS, PATENTS & TRADE MARKS.

As for taking out copyright, there are no special requirements needed apart from being able to prove that you did, in fact, produce the work when you claimed you did.

Where to look
Printed sources

Cornish, G. P. (2004) *Copyright: interpreting the law for libraries, archives and information services*, 4th edn, Facet Publishing
A popular guide by the former copyright officer of the British Library.

Holt, T. and others (2006) *Intellectual property law*, 4th edn, Palgrave Macmillan

Norman, S. (2004) *Practical copyright for information professionals: the CILIP handbook*, Facet Publishing
This replaces the sectoral guides by the same author published by Library Association Publishing.

Padfield, T. (2007) *Copyright for archivists and records managers*, 3rd edn, Facet Publishing

Pedley, P. (2008) *Copyright compliance: practical steps to stay within the law*, Facet Publishing

Pedley, P. (2007) *Digital copyright*, 2nd edn, Facet Publishing

Sharpe, C. C. (1999) *Patent, trademark and copyright searching on the Internet*, McFarland
US emphasis.

Wherry, T. L (2002) *The librarian's guide to intellectual property in the digital age: copyright, patents, and trademarks*, American Library Association

The following statutory instruments are basic to the subject:

SI 89/816 Copyright, Design and Patent Act 1988

SI 89/1212 The Copyright (Librarians and Archivists) (Copying of Copyright Material) Regulations 1989

SI 96/2967 The Copyright and Related Rights Regulations 1996

Electronic sources

Intellectual Property **www.intellectual-property.gov.uk**

A UK Intellectual Property Office website, which gives a wide range of copyright and intellectual property issues. There is an FAQ page.

US Copyright Office **www.loc.gov/copyright**

Other sources

Anti-Copying in Design (ACID)

150 Aldersgate Street, London EC1 4EJ

Tel: 020 7794 2173

www.acid.uk.com

Authors' Licensing and Collecting Society (ALCS)

Marlborough Court, 14–18 Holborn, London EC1N 2LE

Tel and fax: 020 7395 0600

E-mail: alcs@alcs.co.uk

www.clcs.co.uk

Copyright Licensing Agency(CLA)

100 Euston Street, London NW1 2HQ

Tel: 020 7436 5931; Fax: 020 7436 3986

E-mail: cla@cla.co.uk

www.cla.co.uk

The CLA licenses schools, colleges, universities, public bodies and commercial organizations to copy extracts from book, journals and periodicals.

Copywatch

2 Vyse Street, Birmingham B18 6LT

Tel: 0121 236 2657; Fax: 0121 237 1106

www.copywatch.org.uk

C COPYRIGHT & LEGAL DEPOSIT

HMSO Copyright Section
> St Clements, Colegate, Norwich NR3 1BQ
> Tel: 01603 521000; Fax 01603 723000
> **www.hmso.gov.uk/copy.htm**

KWTL (Keeping Within the Law) **www.kwtl.co.uk**
> A subscription site for librarians hosted by Facet Publishing.

Ordnance Survey
> Copyright Branch, Romsey Road, Maybush, Southampton SO9 4DH
> Tel: 01703 792706; Fax: 01703 792535
> **www.ordsvy.gov.uk**

MCPS-PRS Alliance (Musicians, Composers and Publishers Society;
Performing Right Society)
> 29–33 Berners Street, London W1P 4AA
> Tel: 020 7580 5544; Fax: 020 7306 4740
> **www.mcps-prs-alliance.co.uk**

Watch (Writers, Artists, and Their Copyright Holders) **www.watch-file.com**
> A database of copyright contacts for writers, artists and prominent figures
> in other creative fields.

Legal deposit

This is a legal requirement that every publisher in the UK and the Republic of Ireland
must send a copy of every publication to the British Library within one month of
publication, and further copies to the other copyright libraries on demand. Legal
deposit used to be a condition of copyright but is no longer. Contact:

The Legal Deposit Office
> British Library, Wetherby, West Yorkshire LS23 7BY
> Tel: 01937 546267; Fax: 01937 546176

Newspapers should be sent to:

The Newspaper Legal Deposit Office, The British Library, Unit 3, 120
> Colindale Avenue, London NW9 5LF
> Tel: 020 7412 7382

Agent for the Copyright Libraries
> 100 Euston Street, London NW1 2HQ

Tel: 020 7388 5061; Fax: 020 7383 3540

The Agent for the Copyright Libraries is responsible for acquiring legal deposit material for the other five copyright libraries (Bodleian Library, Oxford University; Cambridge University Library; National Library of Scotland; National Library of Wales; and Trinity College, Dublin).

Public Lending Right (PLR)

PLR is a scheme whereby an author can register his or her book and get paid for the estimated number of times that it is borrowed from public libraries. Contact:

The Registrar, PLR Office, Bayheath House, Prince Regent Street, Stockton
  on Tees TS18 1DE
  Tel: 01642 604699; Fax: 01642 615641
  www.plr.uk.com

Tips and pitfalls

The public are often lax and cavalier about copying material and may regard the library staff as ridiculously authoritarian and bureaucratic when they insist that regulations are observed. Tough!! Better unpopular than in prison! Make it clear that you are merely carrying out the law, not making it up. Besides, you wouldn't want *them* to get into trouble!

COSTUME & FASHION

See also Clothes & Clothing; Uniforms

Typical questions

- What did a policeman wear in Victorian times?
- I need a picture of a traditional Bulgarian folk costume.
- Which men's clothes were fashionable in the 1920s?

Considerations

Costume and fashion are two separate, but related subjects. Costume tends to deal with the clothing and dress of particular groups or occupations. Fashion deals with what type of dress is popular at a particular time. Most questions regarding these two subjects will be historical – what costumes used to be worn or what fashions used to be like. You may also receive enquiries about modern-day fashion, or fashion terms and types.

C COSTUME & FASHION

Where to look
Printed sources

An excellent source for costumes around the world is:

Yarwood, D. (1978) *The encyclopedia of world costume*, Batsford
This is in simple A–Z order with over 2000 line drawings and colour illustrations.

If you are looking for occupational or work costumes, the following book is useful:

Cunnington, P. and Lucas, C. (1976) *Occupational costume in England: from the eleventh century to 1914*, A&C Black

Fashions can be more difficult to pinpoint. A good starting point for recent fashions is:

Mendes, V. and de la Haye, A. (1999) *20th century fashion*, Thames and Hudson

Electronic sources

There is a useful costume gateway at:

http://members.aol.com/nebula5/costume.html

There is a great list of fashion designers, new and old, in:

http://nymag.com/fashion/fashionshows/designers/

Other sources

For the serious student of costume, the Gallery of Costume in Manchester is a great resource:

Gallery of Costume
Platt Hall, Rusholme, Manchester M14 5LL
Tel: 0161 224 5217
www.manchestergalleries.org/html/costume/goc_info.html

Tips and pitfalls

Find out from the enquirer exactly what they are looking for. They may ask for a book on Victorian costume and really they just want a picture of a Victorian policeman. It may be just as quick to find a book on the history of the police force as to check through all your costume books.

144

A useful place to check for fashions is in old magazines. Check to see if your library has back runs of any suitable titles, e.g. *Vogue* or *Cosmopolitan*. *Picture Post* and *Illustrated London News* can be useful for older fashions. Some libraries may even have copies of old mail order catalogues, and these can be most useful for looking at past fashions.

COUNTRIES

See also Atlases & Gazetteers; Flags; Geography, Geology & Earth Sciences; History; Maps; Statistics

Typical questions
- What is the population of Moldova?
- What is the capital of Sierra Leone?

Considerations

This is such a large subject area that you will need to quiz the enquirer to find out exactly what they are looking for. A typical scenario is the following: A member of the public comes to the enquiry desk and asks for some information on Bulgaria. This information alone is usually not sufficient. Are they intending to go on holiday there, to go on a business trip, doing a project, or simply answering a quiz question? Once you have found out what type of information they are looking for, your task should be easier. You may have to extend your search further by looking under other relevant headings in this guide, e.g. HISTORY, TIMETABLES & JOURNEY PLANNING.

Where to look
Printed sources

For general information, e.g. about capital cities, populations, areas, currency, etc., *Whitaker's almanack* is a good bet, as is any decent encyclopedia. For more detailed information, the *CIA world factbook* or *Statesman's yearbook* go into much more depth. They include sections on geography, people, government, economy, communications, transport and the military.

CIA world factbook, Central Intelligence Agency. Annual
　　This is a 700-page compendium of information. It is in A–Z order by country, and includes maps.

Statesman's yearbook, Macmillan Reference. Annual
    This is a useful and concise annual reference.

Europa world yearbook, Europa Publications. Annual
    This provides detailed facts and statistics giving a political and economic survey of over 200 countries. Also excellent are the Europa Regional Surveys, published bi-annually. These include:

Eastern Europe, Russia and Central Asia
Central and South Eastern Europe
The Middle East and North Africa
Africa, south of the Sahara
The Far East and Australia
South America, Central America and the Caribbean
The USA and Canada
Western Europe

These are all available online at **www.europaworld.com**.

Travel advice

    Contact:
    Foreign Office Travel Advice Unit
    Consular Division, Old Admiralty Building, London SW1A 2PA
    Tel: 020 7008 0232/3
    www.fco.gov.uk

Electronic sources

The *CIA world factbook* is also available online:

    https://www.cia.gov/library/publications/the-world-factbook/

Most countries have an official website. Simply type their name into a good search engine. Embassies and consulates can also be useful sources of information. For a full list try:

    www2.tagish.co.uk/Links/WesternEurope/UK/Embin.htm

Tips and pitfalls

Questions regarding countries should be quite straightforward once you have found out exactly what your customer wants.

CRAFTS

Typical questions

- Can you give me a list of craft fairs in the region?
- Have you got the address of a . . . manufacturer?
- I'm interested in rag rugs; are there any groups I can join?

Considerations

There are hundreds of crafts with hundreds more products. Craft also spills over into many other areas such as textiles, clothing, ceramics, jewellery, clock-making and metalwork to name but a few. The directory below is highly recommended for covering lots of products and services for the craft industry. However, depending on the area, you may want to use additional directories as well. Local newspapers can give details of local craft fairs to be held. Also use your local Yellow Pages or **www.yell.com** for local organizations.

The craft industry is also a popular one for start-up businesses. Not only will these people require directory information but market information too, especially when they are preparing their business plan.

Where to look
Directories

Craftworkers Yearbook, The Write Angle Press

This directory has three main sections of information. First, it lists craft shows, fairs, festivals and exhibitions, arranged chronologically by date. Second, it provides details of organizers. For each record the name of the company is given, address, telephone and fax, contact name, cost per day for event space and the selection policy. Third, it has a classified list of suppliers of products and services to the craft industry. In addition, there are contact details of craft associations, societies, guilds and other relevant organizations.

Richardson, S. (ed.) *The textile directory 2007*, 6th edn
www.thetextiledirectory.com
Includes details of courses, galleries and museums, publications, specialist holidays, textile artists who teach and specialist bookshops.

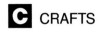

Journals

There are numerous journals on individual crafts, details of which can be found in *Willings press guide*, see JOURNALS & PERIODICALS.

Crafts
Crafts Council
Tel: 020 7806 2500; Fax: 020 7837 6891
www.craftscouncil.org.uk
Six issues per year
Includes an online directory, downloadable reports and surveys.

Craft & Design
PSB Design and Print Consultants
Tel: 01377 255213; Fax: 01377 255730
www.craftanddesign.net
Six issues per year
Information on every aspect of the UK craft industry. Includes craft supplies directory.

Exhibition Bulletin
Mash Media
Tel: 020 8971 8282; Fax: 020 8971 8283
www.tsnn.co.uk
Monthly
Provides details of exhibitions both in the UK and abroad.

Market intelligence

Mintel reports, Mintel International Group.
These provide in-depth research, looking at market factors, market segmentation, the consumer and the future. Also available on CD-ROM. For details, visit **www.mintel.co.uk** or Tel: 020 7606 4533; Fax: 020 7606 5932.

Business opportunity profiles, Cobweb Information
www.cobwebinfo.com
Tel: 0191 461 8000; Fax: 0191 461 8001
These provide an introduction to the market, its potential customers and possible competitors. They indicate start-up costs and legal considerations. They also include further reading and useful addresses of relevant associations and organizations. Information available via online subscription.

Websites and associations

Artists Information Company **www.a-n.co.uk**

Arts Council **www.artscouncil.org.uk**

Crafts Council **www.craftscouncil.org.uk**
   44a Pentonville Road, London N1 9BY
   Tel: 020 7806 2500

Craft Fairs **www.craft-fair.co.uk**

Handmadecrafts **www.handmadecrafts.co.uk**

Queen Elizabeth Scholarship Trust **www.qest.org.uk**
   Here you can find the directory of Queen Elizabeth Scholars, who offer
   specialist crafts and services and information about grants for craft training.

Wales Crafts Council **www.walescraftcouncil.co.uk/**

UK Craft Show Guide **www.craftshows.co.uk**

Tips and pitfalls

Don't rule out using the internet to search for specific crafts; searching for a named
craft in **google.com** will give good results.

CRIME & CRIMINALS

   See also Law; Police & Security; Prison & Probation

Typical questions

- How many crimes are reported each year in the UK?
- What is a crime of passion?
- Who was Ruth Ellis?

Considerations

This is always a popular subject. Enquirers may be looking for crime figures in
a particular area, or they may be researching, or merely interested in 'notorious'
criminals. As well as specialist sources, many of the encyclopaedias will be useful,
especially *Oxford Reference Online*.

Where to look
Legislation
Power, R., *The 1998 Crime and Disorder Act explained*, The Stationery Office

Or the excellent website:

Crime and Disorder Act 1998 **www.opsi.gov.uk**
> Select UK Legislation, then Acts, then 1998; then select Crime & Disorder from the alphabetical list.

Crime statistics
For crime statistics use:

> **www.statistics.gov.uk/onlineproducts/default.asp**
> Click on Crime and Justice and select 'Crime in England and Wales'.

or *British crime survey*, which is available to download from the Home Office:

> **www.homeoffice.gov.uk/rds**

Regional trends and *Social trends* have sections on crime and justice.

For local crime statistics use **www.statistics.gov.uk/neighbourhood**

Notorious crimes or criminals
If you are looking for notorious crimes or criminals, some of the following publications should be useful:

Green, J. (1980) *Directory of infamy: the best of the worst. An illustrated compendium of over 600 of the all time great crooks*, Mills and Boon

Rafter, N. H. (ed.) (2000) *Encyclopedia of women and crime*, Onyx Press

Symons, M. (1994) *The book of criminal records*, Headline
> Has lots of firsts, lasts and lists of obsolete offences. Useful for enquiries about capital punishment, etc.

Nash, J. R. (1992) *World encyclopedia of twentieth century murder*, Crime Books Inc.

Nash has also produced a very good dictionary of crime terminology:

Nash, J. R. (1992) *Dictionary of crime*, Crime Books Inc.

Or use:

Sifakis, C. (2003) *A dictionary of crime terms,* Facts on File Inc.
This has definitions and explanations for 2000 terms from crime lingo to Mafia jargon.

Websites

The following websites should cover most types of enquiries:

British Society of Criminology **www.britsoccrim.org**

Crime, Justice and the Law **www.direct.gov.uk**
Select Crime, Justice and the Law.

Criminal Records Bureau **www.crb.gov.uk**

Crime Stoppers **www.crimestoppers-uk.org**

Crimewatch **www.bbc.co.uk/crimewatch**

Restorative Justice Consortium **www.restorativejustice.org.uk**
Meets the need of victims and reduces offending.

Serious Organised Crime Agency (SOCA) **www.soca.gov.uk**
An executive non-departmental public body sponsored by, but operationally independent from, the Home Office.

Blacksheep Ancestors **www.blacksheepancestors.com/uk/blacksheep.shtml**
Allows searching for blacksheep ancestors in free prison and convict records, court records etc.

United Nations Crime and Justice Information Network **www.uncjin.org**
Includes the *Global report on crime and justice* to download. Excellent.

University of Leeds: Centre for Criminal Justice Studies **www.law.leeds.ac.uk**
Select Research, then Centre for Criminal Justice Studies. Fantastic for links both UK and international.

Youth Justice Board for England & Wales **www.yjb.gov.uk/en-gb**

Tips and pitfalls

Local newspapers are essential for looking at local crime. Your local police force should produce reports listing crime figures in your area.

CUSTOMS, FESTIVALS & FOLKLORE

See also Dates, Calendars & Anniversaries; Etiquette & Forms of Address; Myths & Mythology

Typical questions

- Where are well-dressing ceremonies held?
- When did Father Christmas become a feature of Christmas?
- Why is shaking with the left hand thought to be evil?

Considerations

Folklore covers a wide field with connections to most aspects of life, all age groups, and all parts of the world, urban and rural. It is as much a feature of the modern technological age as of times past. It includes characters such as Father Christmas and Robin Hood, calendar customs such as April Fool's Day and St Valentine's Day, superstitions (charms, crossing fingers), supernatural beliefs (fairy rings, devil's hoofprints), and performance customs such as morris dancing and well dressing.

Where to look
Printed sources
Customs

Hole, C. (1976) *British folk customs*, Hutchinson
A–Z with background.

Shuel, B. (1985) *The National Trust guide to traditional customs of Britain*, Webb & Bower
Background and illustrations.

Days

Debrett's guide to the Season (2000) Vine House
The 'Season' being Ascot, Chelsea Flower Show, Cowes Week, Goodwood, Glyndebourne, Henley, Wimbledon, etc.

Dunkling, L. (1988) *A dictionary of days*, Routledge
A–Z from Acadian Day and Advent to Yom Teruah and Yule Eve.

Roud, S. (2006) *The English years: a month-by-month guide to the nation's customs and festivals, from May Day to Mischief Night*, Penguin

Festivals

Festivals.com **http://festivals.com**
Lists c. 40,000 community events worldwide.

Dennis, M. (2000) *Encyclopedia of holidays and celebrations: a country-by-country guide*, 3 vols, Facts on File

Jeffries, B. (2008) *The Best of British Festivals*, Summerscale
Over 500 festivals arranged by region and indexed by month.

Travers, L. (ed.) (2006) *Encyclopedia of American holidays and national days*, 2 vols, Greenwood Press

Folklore

Briggs, K. M. (1970) *A dictionary of British folk-tales*, 4 vols, Routledge

Jones, A. (1995) *A dictionary of world folklore*, Larousse

McMahon, S. and O'Donoghue, J. (2004) *Brewer's dictionary of Irish phrase and fable*, Weidenfeld & Nicolson

Opie, I. and P. (eds) (1997) *The Oxford dictionary of nursery rhymes*, 2nd edn, Oxford University Press

Seal, G. (2002) *Encyclopedia of folk heroes*, ABC Clio

Simpson, J. and Round, S. (2000) *A dictionary of English folklore*, Oxford University Press

Vickery, R. (1997) *A dictionary of plant lore*, Oxford University Press

Zipes, J. (ed.) (2000) *The Oxford companion to fairy tales*, Oxford University Press

The Folklore Society
c/o The Warburg Institute, Woburn Square, London WC1H 0AB
Tel: 020 7862 8562
www.folklore-society.com

American Folklore Society **http://afsnet.org**

CUSTOMS, FESTIVALS & FOLKLORE

Superstitions

Caradeau, J.-L. and Donner, C. (1985) *Dictionary of superstitions*, Granada

Opie, I. and Tatem, M. (eds) (1992) *A dictionary of superstitions*, Oxford University Press

Pickering, D. (1995) *Dictionary of superstitions*, Cassell

Congratulations from the Queen

It is traditional to get a card (originally a telegram) from the Queen on someone's 100th birthday. A request has to be made on a form obtainable from the Anniversaries Office, Buckingham Palace, London SW1A 1AA. Cards are also sent for 105th birthday and yearly thereafter; 60th, 65th and 70th wedding anniversaries also qualify for a card from the Queen.

DATES, CALENDARS & ANNIVERSARIES

See also Customs, Festivals & Folklore; History

Typical questions

- Can you tell me what day of the week I was born on?
- What happened in the year of my birth?
- What are the dates of the Crimean War?
- When does the Chinese New Year start?
- What year is it in the Muslim calendar?
- What present should one give on a fifth wedding anniversary?

Where to look

General

Munby, L. M., *Dates and time: a handbook for local historians*, British Association of Local History.

> How people measured time, what dating systems they used, and how documents and other sources may be dated.

Calendars

Whitaker's Almanack (Annual), A&C Black, 1900–

> This has an excellent section on time measurement and calendars, including the useful 'Calendar for any year 1780–2040', in which the day of any week of any year can be identified.

Dates

There are many different ways of arranging dated information: by day of week, by event, by date within year (anniversary), chronological; by day within a year – arranged from 1 January to 31 December (calendar arrangement), giving events that happened on that day of the year.

Beal, G. (1992) *The Independent book of anniversaries*, Headline

Beeching, C. L. (1997) *A dictionary of dates*, 2nd edn, Oxford University Press

Fergusson, R. (2004) *Chambers book of days*, 2nd edn, ChambersHarrap

Frewin, A. (1979) *The book of days*, Collins

Marsh, W. B. and Carrick, B. (2005) *365: your date with history*, Totem Books

A–Z by event

General encyclopedias feature noteworthy events, as do newspaper indexes such as those to the *Guardian* and *The Times*.

Butler, A. (1995) *Dent's dictionary of dates*, 8th edn, Dent

By year divided by event; chronologies

The annual register: a record of world events. 1758 to the present, Keesings World
   Wide. Annual
   This year-by-year record of world events provides information with historical context, perspective and biographical information. Large libraries may have the full set. Also available as a subscription website from ProQuest.

Facts on file. Weekly with cumulating indexes and annual binders (1984–)
   World news digest with index. This major news service indexes events within each year.

Keesing's record of world events, Keesing's Worldwide
   Provides summaries of news from around the world. Weekly updates and subject indexes.

The Chronicle series of heavyweight books published by Chronicle Communications such as *Chronicle of the World, Chronicle of America, Chronicle of Britain*, etc. give newspaper-type accounts, with illustrations to events. They are very popular with children.

Very full is the four-volume series published by Helicon in 1999:

Mellersh, M. E. L., *The ancient world 10,000BC–AD799*

Storey, R. L., *The medieval world 800–1491*

Williams, N., *The expanding world 1492–1762*

Williams, N. and Waller, P., *The modern world 1763–1992*, 2nd edn

There are many other similar works.

Chronological tables

Cassell's chronology of world history: dates, events and ideas that made history (2005) Weidenfeld & Nicholson

Steinberg, S. H. (1991) *Historical tables 58 BC to AD 1990*, 12th edn, Macmillan
Columns by part of world.

By day of week

Dunkling, L. (1988) *A dictionary of days*, Routledge

Forthcoming events

What's on When **www.whatsonwhen.com**

Tsnn.com **www.tsnn.com**
Covers trade shows and similar events.

Weekahead **www.monitor.bbc.co.uk/weekahead.shtml**
The BBC's news diary.

Time zones

See 'Time zones' in *Whitaker's almanack*, desk diaries and many annuals. Websites include:

www.worldtimeserver.com
www.timeanddate/worldclock
www.greenwichmeantime.co.uk

Wedding anniversaries

Whitaker's almanack has a useful section on wedding anniversaries. Or try **www.hintsandthings.co.uk/library/anniversary.htm**. This also tells you what item is associated with a particular anniversary and has a useful section for birthstones.

Birthdays

The Birthday Calendar **www.paulsadowski.com/birthday.asp**
A fun site giving information about birthdays and events on birth years.

Tips and pitfalls

In 1753 the Gregorian Calendar was adopted in the UK by the loss of 11 days, 18 February being reckoned as 1 March. This change of calendar can catch out genealogists. In the same year the beginning of the new year also changed, from 25 March (Lady Day) to 1 January.

DEATH, FUNERALS & BEREAVEMENT

See also Parish Registers

Typical questions
- What do I do when someone dies?
- How do I make a will?
- Can I get help to pay for a funeral?

Considerations

The role of the librarian here is to make sure there is a plentiful supply of books and leaflets that can be readily issued.

Where to look
Wills

Fairweather, M. and Border, R. (2004) *Living wills and enduring powers of attorney*, 2nd edn, Cavendish Publishing

Public Guardianship Office **www.guardianship.gov.uk**
Provides downloadable information on the legal rights of people who are unable to look after their own affairs.

Bereavement

Bereavement Services Portal **www.bereavement-services.org**
An online resource for cemetery and crematorium professionals managed by the Institute of Cemetery and Crematorium Management (ICCM). Over 600 downloads including listings of over 1000 cemetery, crematorium and natural burial ground operators covering over 3500 burial grounds and crematoriums.

Donnellan, C. (ed.) (2006) *Grief and loss*, Independence Publishers
A collection of recent articles from newspapers and magazines.

Child Death Helpline
Freephone: 0800 282986

CRUSE Bereavement Care **www.crusebereavementcare.org.uk**
Tel: 0870 167 1677
Helpline for bereaved people and those caring for bereaved people. Local branches are listed in phone books under 'Counselling and advice'.

National Association of Bereavement Services
Tel: 020 7709 0505; Helpline: 020 7709 9090

Support Line **www.supportline.org.uk**
Helpline: 020 8554 9004
Confidential emotional support.

Death

Harris, P. (2006) *What to do when someone dies: from funeral planning to probate and finance*, 19th edn, Which? Books

If I Should Die **www.ifishoulddie.co.uk**
Independent practical advice.

Funerals

Private sector cemetery companies began to be established from the 1820s and by 1850 churches had lost their virtual monopoly of burial powers. Legislation was passed in the 1850s when private sector burials declined and local authorities were empowered to provide cemeteries. The first cremations occurred in 1885.

Baun, R. R. (ed.) (1999) *Funeral and memorial service readings, poems and tributes*, McFarland
A useful anthology for those difficult occasions.

Confederation of Burial Authorities (CBA), The Gatehouse, Kew Meadow Path, Richmond, Surrey TW9 4EN
Tel: and fax: 020 8392 2997
E-mail: ibcabob@aol.com

Davies, D. J. (2005) *Encyclopedia of cremation*, Ashgate

Gill, S. and Fox, J. (2004) *The dead good funerals book*, The Stationery Office
Wide coverage on funerals from their history to what to do after a death. Has practical suggestions and a list of organizations.

Rugg, J. (ed.) (2001) *The CBA directory of cemeteries and crematoria in the UK*, 2nd edn, Confederation of Burial Authorities.
Available free on the Bereavement Service portal
www.bereavementservices.org

Whitman, G. (1991) *The funeral guide and information book*, the author

Tips and pitfalls

Make sure you know where to find books on making wills and the occasion of death; neither the law nor public health classification in Dewey is straightforward. On death itself, doctors and funeral parlours (Yellow Pages) will provide the necessary information. You will, of course, know where the local Registrar of Births, Marriages and Deaths is located!

DENTISTS

Typical questions

- Have you got a list of local dentists?
- How do I complain about my dentist?

Considerations

As well as national directories your library should keep up-to-date local lists of dentists.

Where to look

Directories

Dental care professional register, General Dental Council
This lists alphabetically dentists in the UK giving professional qualifications and posts, but no contact telephone numbers are given. There is also an index by town. This directory is also available on the website of the General Dental Council **www.gdc-uk.org**.

Also use the 'Find a dentist' search from the NHS website **www.nhs.uk**. Enter place or postcode to find a list of nearest dentists.

Complaints against dentists

General Dental Council
37 Wimpole Street, London W1G 8DG

Tel: 0845 222 4141

www.gdc-uk.org

There is an excellent section for the general public.

Website

British Dental Association **www.bda-dentistry.org.uk**

Packed with information including about dental schools and becoming a dentist.

DICTIONARIES

See also Abbreviations & Acronyms; Languages & Translating; Quotations & Speeches

Typical questions

- How do you spell 'burocracy'?
- Which is the correct spelling: 'practice' or 'practise'?
- What other word can I use instead of 'dream'?
- What's the word for a group of lions?

Considerations

Without words we could neither talk nor write. Perhaps we could not even think. Words are the basis of communication, and hence of society and civilization. Or should it be spelled/spelt 'civilisation'?! Little wonder that dictionaries are one of the oldest and largest categories of reference works.

Sometimes unfamiliar words are foreign, sometimes technical, sometimes oddly abbreviated, sometimes special to a place, and sometimes used in strange ways for effect. There are so many kinds of dictionaries and uses that we can only indicate some of the main types. As with so much of reference work, know your stock, and how to use it. Many dictionaries are arranged in ways other than the obvious alphabetical (e.g. thesauruses) and most will have supplementary sequences or appendices. Yet again, librarians are often called on to help decipher cryptic abbreviations indicating parts of speech, pronunciation or origin.

One problem is that many people insist there is a 'correct' way to spell or use a word. Often there isn't, though books on usage and style may help. Don't waste time looking for the non-existent! Fashions change, as does language.

Not listed here are (1) age-related dictionaries, such as school dictionaries; (2)

dictionaries compiled for non-native English speakers: ESL (English as a Second Language) or EFL (English as a Foreign Language); and (3) illustrated dictionaries, typified by the pioneering Duden company. All have their place on library shelves.

Where to look
Books on dictionaries

Dalby, A. (1998) *A guide to world language dictionaries*, Facet Publishing

Kabdebo, T. and Armstrong, N. (1997) *Dictionary of dictionaries*, Bowker-Saur
Gives annotations on, and details of, dictionaries on subjects ranging from abbreviations and accounting to zoology and Zulu.

Oxford guide to the English language (1984, 1992 reprint), Guild Publishing
Combined dictionary, grammar and guide to usage.

Standard dictionaries

Dictionaries of a language (monolingual) range from the single volume, such as those published by Chambers, Longmans, Collins, Oxford, Bloomsbury and other publishers, to the multi-volume *Oxford English* and *Websters*.

The Oxford English dictionary (1989) 2nd edn, Oxford University Press, 20 vols, the 'OED'
The definitive guide to the meaning, history, and pronunciation of over half a million words, both present and past. Most large libraries will have this and although it is useful for old and obscure words, it is not a quick source to use. It is best regarded as a source of last resort, rather than the first place to look. It is also available as a subscription website (**www.oed.com**), on CD-ROM and in a two-volume micro-print version (requiring a magnifying glass).

The Shorter Oxford English dictionary (2007) 6th edn, Oxford University Press
The two-volume abridgement of the OED, which will cater for most needs.

Most libraries have a variety of one-volume English dictionaries. Take time to familiarize yourself with the characteristics of each, and what each is best for. Everyone will have their favourite. *The Concise Oxford English dictionary* (2006) 14th edn, Oxford University Press, or *Chambers dictionary* (2006) 10th edn, ChambersHarrap, are just two of many excellent dictionaries.

Web dictionaries

The American Dictionary of the English Language **www.bartleby.com/61**

Onelook **www.onelook.com**
> Online dictionary of more than five million words from over 900 online dictionaries; includes definitions and translations.

Word iq **www.wordiq.com**
> An extended dictionary.

Abbreviations and Acronyms

See separate chapter ABBREVIATIONS & ACRONYMS.

Anagrams

Anagrams are words or phrases formed by transposing the letters of another word or phrase.

Anagram Genius **www.anagramgemius.com**

Edwards, R. J. (1999) *Longman anagram dictionary*, Viking

Collectives

A very common enquiry, often generated by crossword puzzles and quizzes, is about the collective nouns used for a group of animals. Some useful titles are:

Collings, R. (1992) *A crash of rhinoceroses: a dictionary of collective nouns*, Bellew Publications

Sparkes, I. (ed.) (1985) *Dictionary of collective nouns and group terms*, 2nd edn, Gale

Confusables

For words which one does not know the exact spelling of try:

Exalead **www.exalead.com**
> This has approximate and phonetic spelling options.

Crosswords and games

Many dictionaries are published for enthusiasts of crosswords and word games such as Scrabble. They can be arranged by word length, last letter, etc. Examples are:

D DICTIONARIES

Bradford, A. R. (2007) *Bradford's crossword solver's dictinary*, 7th edn, Collins

One Across **www.oneacross.com**
  A crossword puzzle solver.

The Oxford crossword dictionary (2000) 2nd edn, Oxford University Press

Scrabble Words (2006) 2nd edn, Collins
  'The official word list.'

Dialect and jargon

Green, J. (1987) *Dictionary of jargon*, Routledge

Partridge, E. (1991) *Dictionary of slang and unconventional English*, 8th edn, Routledge

Wright, J. (1898–1905) *English dialect dictionary*, 6 vols, H. Frowde

Emoticons

Computer User
  www.computeruser.com/resources/dictionary/emoticons.html

Travis Carden **www.traviscarden.com/etc/dictionary-of-emoticons**

Foreign language dictionaries

Monolingual dictionaries are dictionaries that give meanings of words in the same language, e.g. French words defined in French. Only larger libraries are likely to have foreign (non-English) dictionaries in the foreign language. Most libraries will have bilingual (e.g. English–French, French–English) dictionaries for the more common languages such as French, German, Spanish and Russian. Caution! Some dictionaries will be a-symmetrical, translating only one way, e.g. French into English, but not English into French. Watch out for how dictionaries are arranged on library shelves: the library classification systems such as Dewey are very complex; some libraries simply arrange dictionaries alphabetically by language.

Multilingual dictionaries

Many technical dictionaries cover several languages. Watch out for how they are arranged on library shelves. They may be located with other books on the subject (textiles, electronics, etc.) or placed together in a dictionary section.

Names

See chapter on NAMES

Origins (etymologies)

Hoad, T. F. (ed.) (1993) *The concise Oxford dictionary of English etymology*, 2nd edn, Oxford University Press

Onions, C. T. (ed.) (1996) *The Oxford dictionary of English etymology*, Oxford University Press

Room, A. (1986) *Dictionary of changes in meaning*, Routledge

Word Wizard **www.wordwizard.com**
Includes origins, quotations and neologisms.

Phrases and idioms

Some of the best dictionaries are:

Room, A. (2005) *Brewer's dictionary of phrase and fable*, 17th edn, Weidenfeld & Nicolson
The classic first choice

Buchanan-Brown, J. (1991) *Le mot juste: a dictionary of classical foreign words and phrases* Kogan Page

Cambridge dictionary of American idioms (2003) Cambridge University Press

Cambridge idioms dictionary (2006) 2nd edn, Cambridge University Press

Cowe, P. and Mackin, R. (1975, 1983) *Oxford dictionary of current idiomatic English*, Oxford University Press.

Delahunty, A. et al. (2001) *Oxford dictionary of allusions*, Oxford University Press

Ehrlich, E. (1996) *Nil desperandum: a dictionary of Latin tags and phrases*, Hale

Farkass, A. (2002) *The Oxford dictionary of catchphrases*, Oxford University Press

Guinagh, K. (1983) *Dictionary of foreign phrases and abbreviations*, 3rd edn, H. W. Wilson

Knowles, E. (2005) *Oxford dictionary of phrase and fable*, 2nd edn, Oxford University Press
Gives background to over 20,000 phrases.

Siefring, J. and Speake, J. (2007) *Oxford dictionary of idioms*, 3rd edn, Oxford University Press

Spears, R. A. (2006) *Dictionary of American slang and colloquial expressions*, 4th edn, McGraw-Hill; paperback version entitled: *American slang dictionary*

Spears, R. A. (2005) *McGraw-Hill's dictionary of American idioms and phrases*, McGraw-Hill

Urdang, L. (1979) *Longman dictionary of English idioms*, Longman

Pronunciation

Jones, D. (2006) *Cambridge English pronouncing dictionary*, 17th edn, Cambridge University Press
A standard textbook; technical.

Olausson, L. and Sangster, C. (2006) *Oxford BBC guide to pronunciation*, Oxford University Press

Rhyming

Fergusson, R. (ed.) (1985) *The Penguin rhyming dictionary*, Penguin

Synonyms

Synonyms are words of similar meaning.

Roget's thesaurus
> There are numerous versions of this classic work, both in the original structured style, and in later alphabetical sequences. Some people will ask for a 'thesaurus' or even 'Roget's'. Do get to know how a thesaurus works.

Chambers synonyms and antonyms (2004) Chambers

Longman synonym dictionary (1986) Longman

Oxford dictionary of synonyms and antonyms (2007) Oxford University Press

Subject and technical dictionaries

All subjects have special terms and vocabularies, sometimes with meanings quite different from those in common use. These may be monolingual, bilingual or multilingual. Watch out for how these are arranged in the library. They may be arranged with books on the subject, or together as a group of technical dictionaries.

Many specialist words will be found in the larger language dictionaries, as well as in encyclopedias and textbook vocabularies, glossaries and indexes.

Examples are: *Words and phrases legally defined*; *German–English science dictionary*; and *Four-language technical dictionary of data processing, computers and office machines*.

Usage

For grammars see chapter on LANGUAGES & TRANSLATING

Ayto, J. and Simpson, J. (2005) *Oxford dictionary of modern slang*, Oxford University Press

Blamire, H. (1999) *The Cassell guide to common errors in English*, Cassell

Burt, A. (2000) *The A to Z of current English*, How to Books

The Cambridge guide to English usage (2003) Cambridge University Press
A–Z reference guide to US, UK, Canadian and Australian English usage.

Fowler, H. W. (1998) *A dictionary of modern English usage*, 4th edn, Oxford University Press

Good word guide (2003) 5th edn, Bloomsbury
A guide to English usage.

Gowers, E. (1986) *The complete plain words*, 3rd edn, HMSO
A classic.

Manser, M. H. (2007) *Good word guide: the fast way to correct English spelling, punctuation, grammar and usage*, 6th edn, A&C Black

Todd, L. and Hancock, I. (1990) *International English usage*, Routledge

Tips and pitfalls

Spellings vary from century to century and country to country. As do pronunciations. Most word-processing packages have spelling checkers. Watch out for differences between American and UK usage. Find a one-volume dictionary with a good typeface to put on the enquiry counter, and get to know it well.

DIY & REPAIR MANUALS

Typical questions

* Have you got the car manual for a Ford Escort?

- Have you got a circuit diagram for a Sony video recorder?
- I'm trying to repair our washing machine. Have you got a repair guide?
- What's the difference between an Enfield and a Croydon tap?

Considerations

Generally, enquiries about repairs fall into two categories: the DIY (do it yourself) and the technical data enquiry. The first category is best answered by the loan of a book (with the request not to get it wet or oily!). Reference departments may carry some of the large-format popular DIY guides, but the enquirer is best advised to photocopy the required pages.

It is the expensive technical data manual that will be most requested of the information librarian, and here there are difficulties. Either the librarian will not have a clue about the subject (let alone how to use the book), or no books will exist. Manufacturers of equipment rarely publish their manuals or specifications since they would far rather you bought more of their products instead. Against this, however, many of the enquirers will know exactly what they want and are technically literate. Many enquirers will be self-employed technicians unable to afford the high-priced technical manuals and thus look to the public library to have a stock.

Often the answer is to find contact details of the manufacturer, or refer the enquirer to a good DIY shop, which will have its own contacts and specialists. Specialist websites are also proliferating.

Where to look
General DIY

There are a number of useful books that cover all aspects of household repairs and copies should be available for the casual DIYer. Examples are:

Cassell, J. and Parham, P. (2006) *Know how with show how*, Dorling Kindersley

Jackson, A. and Day, D. (2007) *Collins complete DIY manual*, Collins

Lawrence, M. C. (1999) *Which? way to fix it*, 4th edn, Which? Books

Readers Digest DIY manual (2008) Readers Digest

You can do it! The complete B & Q step-by-step book of home improvement (2007) 3rd edn, Thames & Hudson

Among the many websites offering DIY advice are:

The Federation of Master Builders **www.fmb.org.uk/consumers**

This website covers most aspects of home maintenance and has a directory of reputable builders in the UK.

There are printed manuals and websites on specific topics, for example:

Jackson, A. and Day, D., who have authored *Planning and heating*; *Wiring and lighting*; *Energy saving*; and *Outdoor DIY* for Collins

Holloway, D. (2000) *The Which? book of plumbing and central heating*, Which? Books

Lawrence, M. C. (2000) *The Which? book of wiring and lighting*, 4th edn, Which? Books

Reader's Digest wiring and lighting manual (2007) Reader's Digest

The Plumber **www.theplumber.com/hillsplb.html**
   Online help. US orientated.

Many retail suppliers such as B & Q and Focus issue leaflets on a range of DIY activities and have hints on their own websites, e.g. **www.comet.co.uk**.
   Willings press guide lists several DIY magazines.

Car and motorcycle manuals

The large numbers of manuals published by the Haynes Publishing Group for each car and bike model serve most needs. See the list on **www.haynes.co.uk**.

Directories of repair specialists

Yellow Pages **www.yell.co.uk**

Thomson Directories **www.thomweb.co.uk**

Bigfoot (for US) **www.bigfoot.com**

Television and video

Trundle, E. (1988) *Newnes guide to TV and video technology*, Newnes

Television servicing, U-View Publishers. Annual
   Circuit wiring diagrams.

Video servicing, U-View Publishers. Annual
    Circuit wiring diagrams.

Tips and pitfalls

Beware differences between UK (Imperial) and US measurements, and between Imperial and metric. (See chapter on WEIGHTS & MEASURES.) A large number of manufacturers provide online help and advice on their websites. These can be found by using a search engine.

DOCTORS

Typical questions

- I'd like to check the name of a doctor.
- How do I find out this doctor's area of expertise?

Considerations

As well as national directories your library should keep up-to-date lists of local doctors.

Where to look
Directories

Medical directory, 2 vols, Informa Healthcare
    Lists alphabetically medical practitioners in the UK, giving professional qualifications and posts. There is also an index by town. Also available is the *Medical Directory on CD-ROM*; Tel: 020 7017 5375 or online **www.themeddirectory.co.uk**.

You can also use the 'Find a doctor' website from the NHS:

www.nhs.uk/ Pages.ServiceSearch.aspx

Enter place or postcode to find a list of nearest doctors, including whether they are accepting new patients.

Complaints against doctors

    General Medical Council
    178 Great Portland Street, London W1W 5JE
    Tel: 020 7580 7642; Fax: 020 7915 3641

www.gmc-uk.org

Look at 'Concerns about doctors' on the General Medical Council's website for advice and further information.

EDUCATION – GENERAL

Typical questions

- How many women are there in higher education?
- Can you give me the address of . . . education authority?
- Have you got any information on educating my child at home?

Considerations

It would be difficult to list all the types of questions you could possibly be asked about such a huge subject area, but suffice to say they usually fall into two categories; those relating to statistical or research information and those relating to contact details. In this book education has been divided into four chapters, on:

- general educational matters (includes statistics, law and research)
- schools and pre-school
- universities and colleges
- lifelong learning and e-learning.

Where to look

General

Education yearbook, Pearson

> Provides information and contact details of all those involved in education provision in the UK, including local education departments, central government, educational establishments and other educational organizations. There is also a section on overseas education.

World of learning (2008) 58th edn, Europa

> Covers 30,000 academic institutions and 200,000 staff and officials. These include universities, colleges and schools of art and music among other institutions. Also available via online subscription: **www.worldoflearning.com**.

Journals

Times Educational Supplement
> TSL Education
> Tel: 020 7782 3000; Fax: 020 7782 3100
> **www.tes.co.uk**
> Weekly

Times Higher Education Supplement
TSL Education
Tel: 020 7782 3000; Fax: 020 7782 3100
www.timeshighereducation.co.uk
Weekly

Statistics

For brief statistics on education use the chapters on education in *Social Trends* or *Annual Abstract of Statistics*, both published by the Office for National Statistics.

For more detailed statistics use the excellent website of the Department for Children, Schools and Families **www.dcsf.gov.uk**. Many statistical publications can be downloaded freely. Go to 'Tables and statistics' and select 'Research and statistics' or 'Local statistics about Education'. Highly recommended.

OECD (2007) *Education at a glance: OECD indicators*, OECD
400 pages of statistics and commentary. Available to download at **www.oecd.org**. Excellent.

For research

For research publications covering all aspects of education use the excellent website of the Department for Children, Schools and Families **www.dcsf.gov.uk**. Go to 'Resources' and select 'Publications' or use 'Tables and statistics' and select 'Research and statistics'.

Key Note Reports
For free executive summaries of report titles listed under Education and Training visit **www.keynote.co.uk**. For details of obtaining full reports contact Key Note Tel: 020 8481 8750; Fax: 020 8783 0049.

British Education Index
This is a subscription database of information about UK literature relating to educational research, policy and practice. It is available in various formats – print, CD-ROM and online. For details about the subscription, contact British Education Index, Tel: 0113 343 5525 or **www.leeds.ac.uk/bei**.

Chartered Institute of Public Finance and Accountancy – Children's Services Panel **www.cipfa.org.uk/panels/childrensservices**
Information on education finance.

For law

Try:

Booth, C. (con. ed.), Coleman, J., Widdrington, T. and Hancox, N. (eds),
The law of education, 7 looseleaf vols, Butterworth Lexis Nexis

Tottel's education law manual, Tottel looseleaf

Or use:

Guidance on the law **www.dcsf.gov.uk/publications/guidanceonthelaw**

Or look at:

www.teachernet.gov.uk/management

Websites and organizations

Advisory Centre for Education (ACE)
1c Aberdeen Studios, 22 Highbury Grove, London, N5 2DQ
Advice line: Tel: 0808 800 5793
www.ace-ed.org
This provides a wide range of publications, some of which are free to download. Excellent and well worth a visit.

British Council
General enquiries Tel: 0161 957 7755; Fax: 0161 957 7762
www.britishcouncil.org
Excellent website.

Department for Children, Schools and Families **www.dcsf.gov.uk**

Department of Education Northern Ireland **www.deni.gov.uk**

Education Guardian **http://education.guardian.co.uk/**
Excellent site.

Education Otherwise
PO Box 325, Kings Lynn, PE34 3XN
Tel: 0845 478 6345
www.education-otherwise.org
Provides support, advice and information for families considering home-based schooling. Some local groups.

General Teaching Council for England **www.gtce.org.uk**

National Curriculum online **www.nc.uk.net**

National Union of Teachers **www.teachers.org.uk**
Excellent website for education issues and more.

Qualifications and Curriculum Authority (QCA) **www.qca.org.uk**

Scottish Executive Education Department
www.scotland.gov.uk/Topics/Education

Welsh Assembly Government **http://new.wales.gov.uk**
Select 'Education and Skills'.

EDUCATION – LIFELONG LEARNING & E-LEARNING

Typical questions
- Have you any details of adult education courses?
- How do I get qualified in . . . ?
- I need help with reading, who do I contact?
- I have a new computer but can only plug it in, is there a local course?

Considerations
There is a lot of information regarding lifelong learning produced and it is hard to keep up to date with new initiatives and schemes. The websites below should keep you well informed and provide the right information and/or courses.

Where to look
Directories
Opportunity: a directory of sources of lifelong learning and career development information, 13th edn, 2007–2008, ADSET

Adult learning **www.direct.gov.uk**
Select 'Education & learning' then 'Adult Learning'. Excellent, packed with information.

Websites and organizations
Adult Learning **www.waytolearn.co.uk**

Excellent site covering courses, qualifications, funding, advice on learning and more.

BECTA www.becta.org.uk
BECTA is involved in the use of technology for learning.

E-skills UK www.e-skills.com

Learndirect www.learndirect-advice.co.uk

Learndirect (Scotland) www.learndirectscotland.com

Learning and Skills Council www.lsc.gov.uk
Responsible for funding and planning education and training for over 16 year olds in England.

National Institute of Adult Continuing Education (NIACE) www.niace.org.uk
This is the national organization for adult learning. It works with national and local government, educational institutions, Learning and Skills Councils and employers to promote equal opportunities of access to learning for all adults.

Open University www.open.ac.uk
The Open University is the only university where you can study without any prior qualifications. It has both degree and non-degree courses and students can learn over a period of years, taking breaks if necessary.

Tips and pitfalls

This can be a difficult subject to tackle and it is best to avoid giving advice but to direct enquiries to the relevant organizations, which can offer detailed information and courses. It would be wise to bookmark some, if not all, of the above websites. It would also be useful to keep up-to-date contact details of your local Learndirect centre, adult education service and the careers service. But most of all, when answering questions on this subject information professionals need to be just that, professional. Sometimes it may not be easy for an enquirer to ask about returning to education or developing basic skills; they require you to have patience, integrity and understanding. Handing a piece of paper and pen to someone who has just asked about improving their reading or writing skills is thoughtless and unnecessary; far better to suggest printing out the relevant page and highlighting details.

EDUCATION – SCHOOLS & PRE-SCHOOL

Typical questions

- Have you got the address and the name of the headteacher at . . . School?
- Are there any schools that specialize in education for children with dyslexia?
- Have you got the Ofsted report for . . .?

Where to look

Printed sources

Both the *Catholic directory of England and Wales* (Gabriel Communications) and the *Church of England directory* give details of their church-aided schools. Other religious denominations also have schools and it is best to check the relevant directories for details. If you don't have such specialist directories available, use one of these excellent sources:

Schoolswebdirectory **www.schoolswebdirectory.co.uk**
> Allows searching by county, local education authority, name of school or postcode.

Sunday Times best schools guide, Trotman. Annual

Findlay, R., *Choose the right primary school: a parent's guide to all primary schools of Britain*, The Stationery Office

Findlay, R., *Choose the right secondary school: a parent's guide to all state and independent secondary schools*, The Stationery Office

These are both slightly dated now but may give some pointers.

Travers, C. (2004) *Education @ 16*, John Catt Educational

Also visit **www.schoolsearch.co.uk**.

IB world schools yearbook, John Catt Educational
> The official guide to schools offering the International Baccalaureate.

Choosing a school

Parents can select 'Schools (Parents section)' for help choosing a school at **www.direct.gov.uk**

or use the

Good schools guide 2008, Lucas Publications **www.goodschoolsguide.co.uk**

Independent schools

Which school?: guide to independent schools, John Catt Educational
> A directory of 2000+ British independent schools, includes nursery, preparatory, junior and senior schools, day and boarding.

Try also

Hobsons UK boarding schools guide. Annual

Choosing a boarding school – a guide for parents, Department for Children,
> Schools and Families in conjunction with the Boarding Schools Association Free copies are available from the Boarding Schools Association **www.boarding.org.uk** under BSA Publications.

The independent schools guide, Kogan Page, 14th edn, Annual
> Gives detailed information on over 2000 schools. Excellent.

Special education and schools

Schools for special needs: a complete guide, 13th edn, Kogan Page
> This provides details of over 2000 establishments as well as a wealth of information for parents, carers and professionals dealing with education provision for children and young people.

Which school? for special needs, John Catt Educational
> This is a guide to independent and non-maintained schools and colleges of further education in Britain for pupils with special educational needs.

Websites and organizations

Department for Children, Schools and Families **www.dcsf.gov.uk**

Ofsted (Office for Standards in Education) **www.ofsted.gov.uk**

Online Publications for Schools **http://publications.teachernet.gov.uk**

Professional Council for Religious Education **www.retoday.org.uk**

Rathbone Special Education Advice **www.rathboneuk.org**
> A charitable service to support parents of children with special educational needs.

Schools **www.bbc.co.uk/schools**
> Learning resources for home and schools.

Schoolzone **www.schoolzone.co.uk**
> Includes organizations, events and materials.

Sex Education Forum **www.ncb.org.uk/sef**

Teacher Training Agency **www.tda.gov.uk**

EDUCATION – UNIVERSITIES & COLLEGES

See also Grants & Funding

Typical questions

- Can you tell me where I can study a course on . . .?
- Have you got a list of universities?
- How do I apply for university?
- Are there any local colleges that offer part-time courses?

Considerations

Many larger libraries may keep university and college prospectuses but increasingly libraries are using the web for this information. Most if not all universities and colleges have websites so most enquiries can probably be satisfied by simply finding the correct site. However, there are also some excellent guides which offer either additional or alternative information. A few are listed below.

Where to look
Printed sources

UCAS, the big guide. Annual
> The official guide to university and college entry in the UK. Also includes the *Big guide* CD-ROM.

Good university guide **www.thegooduniversityguide.org.uk**

The Times good university guide, **www.timesonline.co.uk/tol/life_and_style/ educationgood_university_guide**

Caprez, E. (2004) *The disabled students' guide to university 2005*, 3rd edn, Trotman

Hobson's postgraduate directory **www.postgrad.com**
Allows postgraduate course searches as well as information and news. Excellent. Lists over 20,000 postgraduate courses.

International Association of Universities, *International handbook of universities*, Palgrave
Covers 9200 university institutions worldwide.

Experience Erasmus: the UK guide to Socrates–Erasmus programmes, ISCO Careerscape. Annual **www.careerscope.info**

UK Socrates-Erasmus Council **www.erasmus.ac.uk**

Erasmus Student Network **www.esn.org**

Commonwealth universities yearbook: a directory to the universities of the Commonwealth, Association of Commonwealth Universities

For a more independent point of view try:

Dudgeon, P., *Virgin alternative guide to universities*, Virgin

Heap, B., *Choosing your degree course and university*, Trotman

Websites of organizations

Educational Grants Advisory Service (EGAS) **www.egas-online.org/fwa**
Offers guidance and advice on funding for those studying in post-16 education in the UK.

National Union of Students (NUS) **www.nusonline.co.uk**

National Unions of Students in Europe **www.esib.org**

Skill – National Bureau for Students with Disabilities **www.skill.org.uk**
Excellent site.

The Association of Commonwealth Universities **www.acu.ac.uk**

UK Council for International Student Affairs **www.ukcosa.org.uk**

Universities

For a list of all university and college websites try:

www.ucas.com/instit/index.html

and

AimHigher **www.aimhigher.ac.uk**
  Includes 'unifinder' and 'find a course'.

HERO official gateway to universities, colleges and research organizations in
  the UK:
  www.hero.ac.uk
  Includes university finder.

Tips and pitfalls

Avoid giving advice on courses or places of study; instead suggest the use of the
local careers centre. It is worth having their details and opening hours to hand.
It is worth having some of the above websites bookmarked. You can also suggest
that potential students look at some of the many guides produced, which you may
have in your non-fiction section.

ELECTION RESULTS

See also Members of Parliament

Typical questions

- I want to see the full list of candidates who stood for the Blackpool North
  constituency in 1997.
- I want to look at the election results from 2005.

Where to look
Printed sources

You can check newspapers for the election dates if you have them on microfilm
or fiche. All the results and candidates from the most recent general election are
available in *Whitaker's almanack*. For a more comprehensive round-up of British
general election results, a good source is:

E ELECTION RESULTS

Rallings, C. and Thrasher, M. (2007) *British electoral facts 1832–2006*, Ashgate
This gives easy access to a host of facts and figures on all general elections since 1832, as well as European Parliament elections and over 3700 by-elections.

Waller, R. and Criddle, B. (2007) *The almanac of British politics*, Routledge
This includes detailed accounts of every Parliamentary constituency in the UK.

The most recent general election results are listed in the:

Times guide to the House of Commons 2005 (2005) Times Publishing

For local elections try:

Local elections handbook, Local Government Chronicle. Annual
This covers every local authority ward.

You should also check local papers for local results.

For worldwide election figures, try:

Gorvin, I. (ed.) (1999) *Elections since 1945: a worldwide reference compendium*, Longman

Electronic sources

For recent local election results try:

www.localgov.co.uk

UKPolitics **www.ukpol.co.uk**
The most recent general election results, with summaries of previous elections, can be found on this website. There are over 10,000 pages about British politics and elections: biographies, past elections, manifestos, polls, constituency contacts and an excellent links section.

Elections and Electoral Systems Around the World
www.psr.keele.ac.uk/election.htm
An extensive list of general and country specific links about elections.

The electoral register

The electoral register lists the name and address of everyone who has registered to vote. By law, every local authority has to make the electoral register available for anyone to look at. The register is held at the local electoral registration office (or council office in England and Wales) and some public buildings, mainly libraries (however, this is not always possible as new regulations require that any viewing of the electoral register is supervised, and libraries do not always have the necessary resources).

Until recently, any company, organization or person could buy a copy of the register. But the government has changed the law so that now you have some choice about who can buy details of names and addresses. Under the changes there are two versions of the register: the *full* version and the *edited* version. When you fill in your electoral registration form, you will be able to choose whether you want your details to be included in the edited register.

- **The full register** has the names and addresses of everyone registered to vote and is updated every month. Anyone can look at it, but copies can only be supplied for certain purposes, such as elections and law enforcement. Credit reference agencies are also allowed to use the register, but only to check your name and address if you are applying for credit, and to help stop 'money laundering'. Anyone who has a copy of the register will be committing a criminal offence if they unlawfully pass on information from it. You do not have a choice about your name and address being on this register.

- **The edited register** is available for general sale and can be used for any purpose. You can choose not to be on it. It is kept separate from the full register and updated every month. The edited register can be bought by any person, company or organization and could be used for different purposes such as checking your identity and commercial activities such as marketing.

For more details go to the Electoral Commission website:

www.electoralcommission.org.uk

Tips and pitfalls

Local election results can sometimes be difficult to trace. Try and photocopy results from the local newspaper and keep them in a file for future use.

EMBASSIES & CONSULATES

Typical questions

- Can you give me the address of the embassy for . . .?
- Where is the UK embassy in Paris?

E EMBASSIES & CONSULATES

Considerations

Make sure you understand whether it is a specific country's embassy in the UK that is wanted or the UK embassy in another country. You may get asked about embassies in countries other than the UK; for these the best place to look is *Europa world year book*. The difference between an embassy and a consulate is one of size and importance.

Where to look
Directories

Europa world year book, 2 vols, Routledge
> Provides a list of diplomatic representation in each country.

London diplomatic list, Foreign and Commonwealth Office
> This is an alphabetical guide to all the representatives of foreign states and Commonwealth countries in London. In addition to outlining the composition of the foreign embassies and Commonwealth High Commissions in London, it provides their addresses and the telephone numbers of each department. Available to download from **www.fco.gov.uk**.

Turner, B. (ed.) *Statesman's Yearbook*, Palgrave Macmillan
> Provides an A–Z listing of every country. At the end of each country there is a list of diplomatic representatives.

Whitaker's almanack, A&C Black. Annual
> Provides an A–Z list of countries of the world; for each country it provides details of the UK embassy in the specific country and the country's embassy in the UK.

Yellow pages for central London
> Look under Embassies for telephone numbers. It includes consulates in its listing.

Websites

EmbassyWorld.com **www.embassyworld.com**
> Excellent site.

EMPLOYMENT – LAW

Typical questions

- What are my rights as a temporary worker?
- What is the law on payment for bank holidays?
- How much paternity leave am I entitled to?

Considerations

Employment law is a huge area and constantly changing as new legislation comes along. It is advisable to check the dates of the sources you are using and if possible to use sources that are updated frequently such as *Croner's employment law*. Failing this, many excellent organizations dealing with employment law now have websites.

Where to look

Books

Croners Employment Law, Wolters Kluwer
   This has everything you need to know about employment law. A loose-leaf handbook with six updates per year. Available also as a CD-ROM or online. Contact Croner 020 8547 3333

Try also:

Bowers, J. (2005) *A practical approach to employment law*, OUP

Selwyn, N. (2006) *Selwyn's law of employment*, 14th edn, OUP

Butterworths employment law handbook (2008) 16th edn, Tolleys Butterworth

Tolley's employment handbook, (2008), 22nd edn, Tolleys Butterworth
   Two excellent handbooks that cover every aspect of employment law.

Websites

Advisory, Conciliation and Arbitration Service (ACAS) **www.acas.org.uk**
   Includes guidance publications to download.

British Employment Law **www.emplaw.co.uk**
   The employment law super portal. Excellent and probably all you need. It includes codes of practice for a range of employment situations, offers a

huge number of links to useful organizations, free information from lawyers and links to employment law publishers.

Employment Matters **www.berr.gov.uk/employment/index.html**
Select Employment Policy & Legislation

EMPLOYMENT – RIGHTS & STATISTICS

See also Careers & Qualifications; Employment – Law; Equal Opportunities; Jobs

Typical questions

- Can you give me the number of people employed by sector?
- What is the current unemployment figure?
- I have a grievance against my employer; who can help me?

Considerations

The world of employment is full of statistics, rights and issues, law, and organizations. It is best to be familiar with a few good reference sources that are reputable and updated frequently and to bookmark some of the suggested websites. For trickier queries refer to the Citizens Advice Bureau or suggest a consultation with a solicitor, most offer free advice for the preliminary enquiry.

Where to look

As well as using the handbooks listed in Employment – Law the following are useful.

Croner employment:key rates and data 2007–2008, Croner

Business information factsheets, Cobweb Information
www.cobwebinfo.com
A looseleaf publication which offers one-page factsheets on many employment issues especially for the new or small business.

Statistics

Economic and labour market review, The Stationery Office
This is a monthly publication, which provides news, articles and statistics for the UK's labour market.

Incomes Data Services **www.incomesdata.co.uk**
Excellent for statistics, surveys and employment issues. Most of which are priced publications or subscriptions.

Annual abstract of statistics, The Stationery Office
Provides labour market statistics.

Social trends, The Stationery Office. Annual
Contains data on employment.

Monthly digest of statistics, The Stationery Office
Contains data on employment. Available to freely download at www.statisitcs.gov.uk

Regional trends, The Stationery Office. Annual
This includes regional employment figures.

Manpower employment outlook survey, Manpower PLC
www.manpower.co.uk
A free downloadable quarterly survey looking at employment prospects. Excellent, highly respected report, well worth using.

Graduate market trends **www.prospects.ac.uk**
A quarterly review of the graduate labour market, available to freely download.

Employment rights and issues

There are a huge number of issues surrounding employment, requiring the latest information. It is best to stick to reliable sources that are updated regularly. One such resource is the excellent government website www.directgov. uk/en/Employment/index.htm This provides user-friendly guidance through employment law, rights and issues.

Websites and organizations

Advisory, Conciliation and Arbitration Service (ACAS)
Helpline 08457 47 47 47
www.acas.org.uk

Department of Work and Pensions **www.dwp.gov.uk**

Government Equalities Office **www.equalities.gov.uk**

Institute of Employment Rights
  The People's Centre,
  50 – 54 Mount Pleasant,
  Liverpool. L3 5SD
  Tel: 0151 702 6925
  www.ier.org.uk

Jobcentre Plus **www.jobcentreplus.gov.uk**

Manpower **www.manpower.co.uk**
  Quarterly employment survey available, great for links

People Management OnLine, Chartered Institute of Personnel and Development
  www.peoplemanagement.co.uk
  This gives in-depth analysis of key issues for employers.

TUC **www.tuc.org.uk**
  Excellent site for research publications.

ENERGY

See also Utilities

Typical questions
- Who is the main supplier of coal?
- Do you have a contact for wind power?
- What is renewable energy?
- How much oil is produced worldwide?

Considerations

Energy and energy issues have taken centre stage over the past few years, so you could find a surge in enquiries relating to various aspects of energy. Information on alternative energy has always been popular and even more so now as its potential and realistic use becomes more apparent. There are some excellent websites available, which should offer a range of information.

Where to look
Terms and definitions
Dictionary of energy and fuels (2007) Whittles Publishing

Directories
Major energy companies of the world (2008) 11th edn, Graham & Whiteside
Profiles the 4000 top players in all sections of the industry including coal
mining, electricity, fuel distribution, natural gas, nuclear engineering, oil
and gas exploration and services and oil refining.

Major chemical and petrochemical companies of the world (2008) Graham &
Whiteside.

Power plants in Western Europe directory (2001) Marketing Communications
Media

Global energy contacts directory (2000) Marketing Communications Media

Global coal directory (2001) Marketing Communications Media

These provide corporate and financial data for the world energy industries.
Although slightly dated now they are still useful as a starting point to further
research.

Other directories include:

International guide to the coalfields (2008) Tradelink Publications
A country by country profile with extensive details of operating companies
and mines.

Global oil and gas directory (2002) Marketing Communications Media
This directory provides details of over 350 oil and gas producers and 700
specialist oil and gas service companies and equipment suppliers. In
addition it has a who's who of the international oil and gas industry.

Global power directory (2001) Marketing Communications Media
This directory provides details of 300 global power distributors and 900
suppliers of equipment and services to the power industry. In addition it
has a who's who of the international power industry.

Oil and gas directory – Middle East (2008), Dar Al Fajr Group
www.oilandgasdirectory.com
Allows searching by company name, brand and classification.

■ E ENERGY

Statistics

UK energy statistics, DTI
UK energy in brief, DTI
Quarterly energy prices
Energy trends. Quarterly
UK energy consumption
UK energy indicators

All available free to download from:

www.berr.gov.uk/energy/statistics/publications/index.html

For international energy statistics use:

Annual energy and transport review, European Commission & D-G for Energy
and Transport
This looks at the current energy situations worldwide. Available to
download at **http://ec.europa.eu**. Select publications.

Energy statistics yearbook 2005 (released 2008), United Nations, Department of
Economic & Social Affairs

Journals

There are numerous journals for the energy industry, details of which can
be found in *Willings press guide* (see JOURNALS & PERIODICALS).

Websites

Association for the Conservation of Energy **www.ukace.org**

Centre for Alternative Technology **www.cat.org.uk**
Excellent for factsheets, booklets and resource guides.

Coal International **www.coalinternational.co.uk**

Confederation of British Industry **www.cbi.org.uk**
Select 'Energy' under PDF downloads and policy mini-sites.

Department of Business Enterprise & Regulatory Reform
www. berr.gov.uk/energy
Excellent site and provides lots of free downloadable information, statistics
and publications.

190

European Commission **http://ec.europa.eu**

Select publications by theme. Packed with documents on energy to download.

Fuel Cell Today **www.fuelcelltoday.com**

Fuel cells, which generate electricity by combining hydrogen and oxygen, are poised to become the leading energy source of the 21st century. This is a global internet portal for companies and individuals.

Ofgem **www.ofgem.gov.uk**

Regulates the electric and gas industry in Great Britain

Petroleum Institute **www.petroleum.co.uk**

Packed with links for oil and gas companies and information worldwide.

ENGINEERING

Typical questions

- Can you tell me the manufacturer of . . .?
- Can you give me the contact details of . . .?
- Who makes . . .?

Considerations

Often users confuse company names with trade names. In most cases it is best to check under both company and trade. If you do not have specialized trade directories such as the ones listed, some of the more general directories such as *Kompass*, *Kelly's* or *Key British enterprises* are excellent. See COMPANIES for details.

Where to look
General information

For general information on engineering terms, definitions and fundamentals try:

Kempe's engineers yearbook, Miller Freeman Information Services

Now in its 105th year of publication, this reference work is the authority on a whole range of engineering disciplines. It has excellent chapters on materials, manufacturing, electrical engineering, environmental engineering, energy and railway engineering. It has a detailed index.

Try also:

Dictionary of engineering (2008) McGraw-Hill.

Keller, H. and Uwe, E. (1994) *Dictionary of engineering acronyms and abbreviations*, 2nd edn, Neal-Schuman Publishers

Vernon, J. (2003) *Introduction to engineering materials*, 3rd edn, Palgrave Macmillan

Tapley, B. D. (ed.) (2005) *Eshbach's handbook of engineering fundamentals*, Muse Inc.

Hicks, T. G. (1995) *Standard handbook of engineering calculation*, 3rd edn, McGraw-Hill

Engineering Council UK Annual Reveiw, Engineering Council
www.engc.org.uk

Directories

Engineering industry buyers guide, CMP Information
An excellent directory providing an alphabetical listing of companies, products and services, and brand and trade names. Most useful is the list of overseas manufacturers and their UK agents.

Journals

There are numerous journals for the engineering industry, details of which can be found in *Willings press guide* (see JOURNALS & PERIODICALS). The following is particularly useful:

Engineer
Centaur Publishing
Tel: 020 7970 4000; Fax: 020 7970 4189
www.theengineer.co.uk
25 issues per year
News, comment and analysis on the engineering industry.

Market research

Key Note reports, Key Note
For free executive summaries of report titles listed under engineering and heavy industries visit **www.keynote.co.uk**. For details of obtaining full reports, contact Key Note (Tel: 020 8481 8750; Fax: 020 8733 0049).

Mintel industrial reports, Mintel International Group
> For details visit **www.mintel.co.uk** or Tel: 020 7606 4533; Fax: 020 7606 5932.

Statistics

Economic and labour market trends, Office for National Statistics
> A monthly publication that includes engineering and construction, output and orders. Available to download at **www.statistics.gov.uk/elmr/**.

PRODCOM quarterly industry reports, Office for National Statistics
> Excellent source of UK manufacturer sales, imports and exports statistics. Available to download free of charge from **www.statistics.gov.uk/OnlineProducts/default.asp**.

Organizations and websites

Engineering Council UK
246 High Holborn, London WC1V 7EX
Tel: 020 3206 0500
www.engc.org.uk

Engineering Employers' Federation **www.eef.org.uk**
> The voice of engineering and manufacturing in the UK. Excellent for publications.

There are numerous professional bodies and organizations covering all aspects of the engineering industry. For details use the *Directory of British associations*, CBD Research Publications.

Tips and pitfalls

Engineering is the generic term for a whole host of industries involving mechanics, robotics, electronics and electricals. Ask as many questions as you can about products to try to ascertain their use and consequently work out which bit of engineering you are dealing with. Don't be afraid to check terms in an engineering dictionary.

ENVIRONMENT & GREEN ISSUES

See also Geography; Geology & Earth Sciences

Typical questions
- What is the government's environmental policy?
- Can you give me the address of some environment groups?

Considerations
When people talk about the environment they can mean a whole variety of things from the urban environment in which they live, to recycling. It is important to ascertain what the enquirer really is referring to. In this section the term environment is used to refer mainly to environmental concerns such as pollution control and quality of air, materials reclamation and recycling, ecological sustainability and energy saving, to name but a few. There are loads of great websites, which should give you much of the information you require. Some of the best are listed below. For queries such as times of opening of local tips contact the relevant department of your local authority. It is good practice to keep contact details and to keep them up to date or to bookmark the relevant section from your local council web pages.

Where to look
Terms and definitions:
Dictionary of environmental science and technology (2008), 4th edn, Wiley Blackwell

Goodie. A. and Cuff, D. (eds) *Encyclopedia of global change: environmental change and human society*, OUP

Directories
Environment industry yearbook, Waterlow Specialist Information Publishing
A comprehensive directory giving details of UK companies involved in the waste, water and environment industry. Includes an extensive buyers' guide covering ten primary industry areas, which is cross-referenced to the A–Z company listing. Available to search online at **www.eiy.co**.uk.

There is a section on waste management in the *Municipal yearbook*; see GOVERNMENT.

Air quality guidelines for Europe, 2nd edn, World Health Organization
These guidelines provide background information and guidance to international, national and local authorities on a number of air pollutants.

Curran, S. (2001) *The environment: confronting the issues*, 2nd rev. edn, The Stationery Office
Key facts about the environment; handbook style.

Environmental protection yearbook **www.nsca.org.uk**

Environmental regulation and your business, Stationery Office
Looks at current legislation and regulation for the small to medium-sized company.

Lorton, R. (2003) *A–Z of countryside law*, The Stationery Office

Pollution handbook (2006) National Society for Clean Air and Environmental Protection supported by Environment Agency **www.nsca.org.uk**.
This provides a comprehensive overview of pollution control legislation in force or pending as at December 2005.

Reduce, reuse, recycle and your business, The Stationery Office

Journals

There are numerous journals covering the environment and green issues, details of which can be found in *Willings press guide* (see JOURNALS & PERIODICALS).

CIWM: the Journal for Waste & Resource Management Professionals
Chartered Institute of Waste Management
Tel: 01604 620426; Fax: 01604 604467
www.ciwm.co.uk
Monthly

Recycling & Waste World
A & D Media Ltd
Tel: 01722 716997; Fax: 01722 716926
Weekly
Covers developments and news in the waste and recycling industry.

Market research

Key Note reports, Key Note

For free executive summaries of report titles under Environment visit **www.keynote.co.uk**. For details of obtaining full reports, contact Key Note (Tel: 020 8481 8750; Fax: 020 8783 0049).

Statistics

e-digest of environmental statistics, Department for Environment, Food and Rural Affairs and *The environment in your pocket*, DEFRA

Both are available to download from **www.defra.gov.uk/environment/statistics/index.htm**.

Organizations and websites

Aluminium Can Recycling Association **www.alupro.org.uk**

BBC **www.bbc.co.uk/nature**

British Trust for Conservation Volunteers **www2.btcv.org.uk**

Department for Environment, Food and Rural Affairs **www.defra.gov.uk**

Excellent for statistics and surveys.

Earthscan **www.earthscan.co.uk**

A specialist publisher on environment and sustainable development.

Ends Environmental Consultancy Directory **www.ends.co.uk**

The Green Providers Directory **www.search-for-me.co.uk**

Natural England **www.naturalengland.org.uk**

Excellent site for research publications, maps, science and technology papers and lists reserves and much more.

ARKive **www.arkive.org.uk**

An initiative of The Wildscreen Trust, ARKive will be the world's electronic archive of photographs, moving images and sounds of endangered species and habitats.

Carbon Trust **www.carbontrust.co.uk**

Envirolink **www.envirolink.org**

A huge site including animal rights and reference information.

Friends of the Earth **www.foe.co.uk**
Subjects include food, pollution, transport, green power, protection of wildlife and FOE campaign news.

Nature Net **www.naturenet.net**
Covers law, nature reserves, voluntary work and news.

Wild Life Trusts **www.wildlifetrusts.org**

World Wide Fund For Nature **www.panda.org**

Environment Council
212 High Holborn, London WC1V 7BF
Tel: 020 7836 2626
www.the-environment-council.org.uk

European Environment Agency **www.eea.eu.int**

Envirowise: Practical Environmental Advice for Business
www.envirowise.gov.uk
An excellent site packed with information and free publications to download.

Green Party for England and Wales
1a Waterlow Road, London N19 5NJ
Tel: 020 7272 4474
www.greenparty.org.uk

Greenpeace
Canonbury Villas, London N1 2PN
Tel: 020 7865 8100
www.greenpeace.org.uk

Industry Council for Packaging and the Environment **www.incpen.org**

Natural Environment Research Council (NERC) **www.nerc.ac.uk**

Plantlife International – The Wild Plant Conservation Charity
www.plantlife.org.uk

Sustrans **www.sustrans.org.uk**
The sustainable transport charity.

Woodland Trust **www.woodland-trust.org.uk**

Young People's Trust for the Environment **www.ypte.org.uk**

EQUAL OPPORTUNITIES

See also Employment – Law; Employment – Rights & Statistics

Typical questions
- Can you provide an equal opportunities policy?
- What is meant by equal pay?

Considerations
There is a mass of information on the subject of equal opportunities. How much you want to offer the enquirer will depend on the level of the enquiry and the accessible resources that you have. Hopefully, some of the resources below will provide good free information. Some of the general resources mentioned in Employment will also cover equal opportunities. In addition, some of the newspaper indexes will be useful for articles. A great place to start is about equal opportunities, **www.aboutequalopportunities.co.uk**, which is excellent and probably all you will need in most cases.

Where to look
Bourne, C. (2000) *The Discrimination Acts explained*, The Stationery Office
    Excellent publication that covers the Sex Discrimination Act, Race Relations Act and Disability Discrimination Act. Now slightly dated but still a good starting point.

Organizations
Equality and Human Rights Commission
    3 More London, Riverside, Tooley Street, London SE1 2RG
    Tel: 020 3117 0235
    www.equalityhumanrights.com
    This is an excellent site for news and information. It provides free publications, some of which can be downloaded from the internet.

Cabinet Office **www.cabinet-office.gov.uk**
    Provides equal opportunity publications.

Equality and Human Rights Commission in Scotland
    The Optima Building, 58 Robertson Street, Glasgow G2 8DU
    Tel: 0141 228 5912

Equality and Human Rights Commission in Wales
3rd Floor, 3 Callaghan Square, Cardiff CF10 5BT
Tel: 029 2044 7710

Home Office **www.homeoffice.gov.uk**

Race Relations Employment Advisory Service (RREAS)
4th Floor, 2 Duchess Place, Hagley Road, Birmingham B16 8NH
Tel: 0121 452 5447/8/9
E-mail: hq.rreas@dfes.gsi.gov.uk
RREAS will provide free strategic advice on policies and practices for racial equality in the workforce.

ETIQUETTE & FORMS OF ADDRESS

See also Death, Funerals & Bereavement

Typical questions

- How do I address a letter to a bishop?
- How should I greet and introduce a baroness?
- When should I use 'Yours faithfully' and when 'Yours sincerely'?
- What are the duties of a bridesmaid?

Considerations

Etiquette refers to the customs or rules governing social behaviour regarded as correct: standard or conventional behaviour. Although some people can get over-obsessed with correct form, it is important to be aware of standard practice.

Where to look
General

Axtell, R. E. (ed.) (1993) *Do's and taboos around the world*, 3rd edn, J. Wiley

Bremner, M. (1992) *Enquire within upon modern etiquette and successful behaviour for today*, Hutchinson
Includes work situations.

Morgan, J. (1999) *Debrett's new guide to etiquette and modern manners*, Headline

Russell, H. (2006) *Etiquette: a guide to modern manners*, Cassell

Forms of address

Titles and forms of address: a guide to correct use (2002) 21st edn, A&C Black
Covers formal invitations and addressing letters, listings of ranks, honours and official appointments, as well as the correct way of addressing people in both speech and correspondence. Establishment orientated.

Debrett's people of today, Debrett's Peerage Ltd. Annual
Although used particularly for personal details of famous people, each entry usefully concludes with the person's preferred style of address.

Montague-Smith, P. (1999) *Debrett's correct form*, 4th edn, Headline
Over 400 pages.

Letters

Kurth, R. (1999) *Debrett's guide to correspondence*, Debrett's Peerage Ltd
Covers stationery, forms of address, particular types of letter, and style.

Webster, J. (1988) *Forms of address for correspondence and conversation*, Ward Lock

Meetings

McKenzie, C. (1994) *Debrett's guide to speaking in public*, Headline

Walker, G. (1987) *Points of order for those in public life*, 4th edn, Shaw & Sons
A pocket guide to public speaking, conducting meetings and etiquette in simple language.

Cordes, M., Pugh-Smith, J. and Keene, A. R. (2008) *Shackleton on the law and practice of meetings*, 11th edn, Sweet & Maxwell
The standard heavyweight on points of order, etc.

The season

Noel, C. (2000) *Debrett's guide to the season*, Debrett's Peerage Ltd
Covers the main social events from Ascot and Cowes Week to Glyndebourne and Wimbledon.

Weddings

Llewellyn, J. (2007) *Debrett's wedding guide*, Debrett's

www.net-weddings.co.uk/Etiquette/etiquettemenu.shtml

Tips and pitfalls

Have a copy of A&C Black's *Titles and forms of address: a guide to correct use*, or similar small volume, by the phone. It is surprising how often the need to 'do the right thing' occurs. Etiquette can be very important to people; always treat questions on the subject seriously whatever your own feelings.

EUROPEAN INFORMATION

See also Companies – International

Typical questions

- What is the Single European Market?
- How do I find out about European legislation?

Considerations

There are huge amounts of information produced about Europe and from Europe. Keeping up to date is the difficulty most library workers have. It is probably best to get familiar with a few good sources rather than to try to know them all. The internet is an excellent tool for providing and finding European information. The websites given below should cover most enquiries.

Where to look
Directories

Eurosource 2009, Vacher Dod. Annual
   The definite guide to the EU. Excellent.

Guide to EU information sources on the internet, Routledge
   This is a one-stop source for finding EU information on the internet. All the sites listed have been checked and indexed.

Directory of EU information sources, Routledge
   The 'Red Book' contains information on all EU institutions and lists key personnel, databases, publications, information networks and libraries specific to each institution. This is an excellent sourcebook for all European information.

Directory of Community legislation in force 01/03/2008 **http://eur-lex.europa.eu/ en/index.htm**

Select 'Legislation in Force' then 'Directory of Community Legislation in Force'. Chapters can be downloaded.

Who's who in the EU?, Office for Official Publications of the European Communties, Europa Publications
The official directory of the European Union. Available at **http://europa.eu/whoiswho/public/index.cfm?lang=en**

Statistics

Eurostat, the Statistical Office of the European Commission **www.eustatistics. gov.uk**, produces statistics for the EU members. One of the main publications is:

Eurostat regional yearbook 2007, European Commission Eurostat
An excellent publication for statistics on people, land and environment, national income and expenditure, enterprises and activities in Europe and the European Union. Available as a pdf. Go into 'Bookshop' then select 'Statistics'.

The Office also publishes:

Statistical portrait of the European Union, *Key figures on Europe* and *Key facts and figures about Europe and the Europeans*, which are also available as pdfs.

Journals

Official Journal
If your library does not subscribe to the hard copy, you can access it via **http://publications.europe.eu/official/index_en.htm**.

Organizations

Corbett, R. et al. (2007) *The European Parliament*, 7th edn, John Harper

European Information Centres (EICs)

These provide information on European issues, directives and regulations and help to small and medium-sized businesses. To find your nearest centre use **www.euro.info.org.uk**.

European Documentation Centres (EDCs)

These are situated in university libraries. Most hold one copy of all official publications of the European Communities. It is possible to contact your nearest

EDC to clarify or assist with an enquiry or to arrange for an enquirer to use the resources for reference only. A list can be found at 'Europe' in the UK **www.europe.org.uk/info**.

From 'Information Network' select 'European Documentation Centres'.

European Public Information Centres (EPICs)

These are based in public libraries. They provide a large amount of free literature from the EU to help explain many of the differences and benefits that membership of the EU has made to the lives of people. A list can be found at 'Europe' in the UK **www.europe.org.uk/info**.

From 'Information Network' select 'European Public Information Centres'.

Websites

Britain and the EU **www.fco.gov.uk/en/fco-in-action/institutions/britain-in-the-european-union**

Community Research and Development Information Service (CORDIS) **http://cordis.europa.eu**

Department for Business Enterprise & Regulatory Reform **www.berr.gov.uk/europeanandtrade/index.html**

Europages: the European Business Directory **www.europages.net**

European Central Bank **www.ecb.int**

European Commission Representation in the UK **http://ec.europe.eu/unitedkingdom**

European Industrial Relations Observatory On-Line **www.eiro.eurofound.ie**

European Information Association **www.eia.org.uk**
Excellent. Packed with information and links.

European Information Network in the UK **www.europe.org.uk**

European Investment Bank **www.eib.org**

European Parliament **www.europarl.eu.int**

European Parliament UK Office **www.europarl.org.uk**

Europa **www.europa.eu.int**

Gateway to the European Union. An excellent starting point for basic information on the EU with links to other sites. It also has access to legal texts, publications, databases, statistics and EU grants and loans. In addition, there is a link to EUR-Lex for EU legal texts.

European Union **http://europa.eu**

EU in the United Kingdom **http://ec.europa.eu/unitedkingdom**
Excellent.

Tips and pitfalls

Make a point of finding out which European information units are in your area or region. Then make contact to ascertain what sources of information they have and can offer. It would be sensible to have a contact list for your library and to be sure of their referral procedure. It would also be useful to bookmark some of the websites above for use in the library.

EXAMINATIONS

See also Careers & Qualifications

Typical questions

- Have you got the syllabus for GCSE maths?
- Have you got copies of past exam papers?
- Which local schools take the EdExcel syllabuses?

Considerations

There are frequently queries from people who want to check course syllabuses and to consult past examination papers. Students, parents and teachers are the likely enquirers. Since there are many different examining boards, many different levels of examinations, often several alternative syllabuses, and schools and colleges can change the examination authorities from year to year, the librarian must tread carefully. As always, try to clarify the enquiry as much as possible. Which examination board? What year? Which syllabus, exactly? And, as is often the case, critical details will be missing. You can then suggest that the enquirer needs to get more information. Often it will be appropriate that the enquirer, particularly if the enquiry relates to school examinations, should check with his or her school. (Schools will usually stock copies of both syllabuses and past papers.)

Examination boards sell copies of past papers. Some libraries stock the syllabuses of the examination boards that are in use locally, and some, probably fewer, stock copies of past papers. Check to see what your local practice is.

Most colleges and universities set their own examinations. The same goes for professional bodies; contact these directly for latest information.

Where to look
General

Education authorities directory and yearbook, The School Government
  Publication Co.
  This has a section on examination organizations.

See also the *Education year book*, Prentice Hall.

The government website, gov.direct, has useful information:

**www.direct.gov.uk/en/EducationAndLearning/QualificationsExplained/
  index.htm**

Organizations

AQA (The Assessment and Qualifications Alliance)
  Devas Street, Manchester M15 6EX
  Tel: 0161 953 1180; Fax: 0161 273 7572
  www.aqa.org.uk
  AQA was formed from the amalgamation of the Associated Examining Board and the Northern Examination Assessment Board.

Edexcel Foundation
  Stewart House, 32 Russell Square, London WC1B 5DN
  Tel: 0870 240 9800; Fax: 020 7758 6960
  E-mail: enquiries@edexcel.org.uk
  www.edexcel.org.uk

Joint Examining Board
  30a Dyer Street, Cirencester, Gloucestershire GL7 2PH
  Tel: 01285 641747; Fax: 01285 650449
  www.jeb.co.uk
  For teacher training qualifications and continuing professional development (CPD).

E EXAMINATIONS

OCR (Oxford, Cambridge and RSA Examinations)
  1 Regent Street, Cambridge CB2 1GG
  Tel: 01223 553998; Fax: 01223 552553
  E-mail:helpdesk@ocr.org.uk
  www.ocr.org.uk

Scottish Qualification Authority
  Hanover House, 24 Douglas Street, Glasgow G2 7NQ
  Tel: 0141 242 2214; Fax: 0141 242 2244
  E-mail: helpdesk@sqa.org.uk
  www.sqa.org.uk

City & Guilds
  1 Giltspur Street, London EC1A 9DD
  Tel: 020 7294 2800; Fax: 020 7294 2405
  www.city-and-guilds.co.uk

Northern Ireland Council for the Curriculum, Examinations and Assessment (CCEA)
  29 Clarendon Road, Belfast BT1 3BG
  Tel: 028 9026 1200; Fax: 028 9026 1234
  www.ccea.org.uk

Welsh Joint Education Committee
  245 Western Avenue, Cardiff CF5 2YX
  Tel: 029 2026 5000
  E-mail: exams@wjec.co.uk
  www.wjec.co.uk

Qualifications and Curriculum Authority
  29 Bolton Street, London W1Y 7PD
  Tel: 020 7509 5555
  www.qca.org.uk
  The regulatory body for public examinations and publicly funded qualifications.

Tips and pitfalls

The organization of examinations and examination organizations is changing rapidly. Don't assume that what is true one year will be so the next. Check the datedness of your sources, then check (or get the enquirer to check) with the organization setting the examinations. Schools and colleges change their examination boards from time to time. Always check with the institution for the latest situation.

Work colleagues who are parents of children at school can be useful.

EXPORTS & IMPORTS

Typical questions

- Can you give me a list of companies who export . . . to France?
- How do I import from India?
- What percentage of . . . does the UK (or another country) export?

Considerations

First, let's clarify the terms 'exports' and 'imports'. Goods or services that are produced in one country and then sold or traded to another are known as exports. Goods or services that are brought into a country are known as imports. Enquiries relating to exports or imports are on the whole quite specialized and for many it is probably best to offer contacts to organizations that can provide specialist advice. Your local Chambers of Commerce will offer help and advice and the Department of Trade and Industry **www.dti.gov.uk** produces information on trading with numerous countries. The British Standards Institution has a very useful section on its website **www.bsi-global.com** called 'Satisfying technical requirements of world markets', which is of value to anyone thinking of exporting.

Where to look
Directories

H.M. Customs and Excise tariffs, The Stationery Office
Volume 1 provides general information. Volume 2 covers the schedule of duty and trade statistical descriptions, codes and rates. Volume 3 covers customs freight procedures.

Also available are:

British exports **www.kompass.com**
A free searchable database of UK companies involved in import–export.

Directory of UK importers, 2 vols, Newman Books

International directory of importers, 9 vols, Coble International
This directory can either be purchased as a nine-volume set or by

individual regions. The full directory would provide details of 150,000 international importers. It is also available on CD-ROM. For more detail, take a look at **www.importexporthelp.com.**

Croner's reference book for exporters, Croner CCH Group. Monthly
A looseleaf reference service with monthly updates, covering the documentary and official requirements affecting the export of goods to overseas countries.

Croner's reference book for importers, Croner CCH Group. Monthly
A looseleaf reference service with monthly updates, covering the documentary and official requirements affecting the importation of goods.

Journals

Croner's Export Digest
Croner CCH Group
Tel: 020 8547 3333; Fax: 020 8547 2637
Monthly

Export Times
Nexus Media
Tel: 01322 660070; Fax: 01322 667633
Ten issues per year

Importing Today
Hemming Group
Tel: 020 7973 6404; Fax: 020 7233 5053
Six issues per year

International Trade Today
Hemming Group
Tel: 020 7973 6404; Fax: 020 7233 5053
Ten issues per year
Concentrates on opportunities for importers and exporters.

Statistics

International trade statistics, World Trade Organization
These statistics are available in English, French and Spanish, in hard copy, CD-ROM or on the World Trade Organization website **www.wto.org.**

Websites

British Chambers of Commerce **www.britishchambers.org.uk**
> This includes 'Find your chamber'. It is excellent for information, economic surveys, publications, events, exports, and news and policy.

Export Control Organisation **www.dti.gov.uk/exportcontrol**

Export Credit Agency **www.ecgd.gov.uk**

HM Customs and Excise **www.hmce.gov.uk**
> Import and export statistics from HM Customs and Excise.

Official Trade Statistics **www.trade-statistics.com**
> This has the Pathfinder database, which has contact details of 135,000 importers in the UK. It is updated monthly, from official data supplied by HM Customs and Excise.

Trade Partners UK **www.tradepartners.gov.uk**
> A government network dedicated to helping British businesses build success overseas. It includes country and sector information.

Market and country profiles for exporters **www.link2exports.co.uk**

Office of the US Trade Representative **www.ustr.gov**

World Trade Organization **www.wto.org**
> Excellent site for publications on world trade policy and statistics, including the *International trade statistics*, which are available free to download.

FAIRY TALES & NURSERY RHYMES

Typical questions

- Can you help me find a few Irish fairy tales?
- What is the origin of *Goosey Goosey Gander*?
- Who wrote xxxx?

Considerations

There should be at least some classic fairy tales and nursery rhymes in your children's library. Check what is available on the catalogue. However, finding the historical origin of, and studies about, fairy tales and nursery rhymes can be a bit trickier. Some of the excellent websites below should help.

Where to look
Printed sources
Fairy tales

There is quite a comprehensive index to fairy tales:

Eastman, M. H. (1926) *Index to fairy tales, myths and legend*, Faxon
This provides about 30,000 references in an alphabetical, as well as geographical, sequence. Further supplements have been produced in this index.

Zipes, J. (ed.) (2000) *Oxford companion to fairy tales*, Oxford University Press

Nursery rhymes

For nursery rhymes use:

Opie, I. and Opie, P. (eds) (1952) *The Oxford dictionary of nursery rhymes*, Clarendon Press
This book is indexed by first line and by notable figures.

Websites
Fairy tales

This is a selection of some of the best, however, it is certainly not definitive:

Fairy Tales **www.bestoflegends.org**
A huge selection of fairy tales.

Fairy Tale Resources **www.myweb.dal.ca/barkerb/fairies/resource.html**
A guide to fairy tale resources on the web.

Grimm's Fairy Tales **www.nationalgeographic.com/grimm/index2.html**
Grimm's fairy tales based upon a 1914 translation.

Brothers Grimm Fairy Tales **www.grimmfairytales.com**
Folk and fairytales by the Brothers Grimm – interactive and animated stories.

Hans Andersen Fairy Tales **www.andersenfairytales.com**
Hans Andersen fairy stories – interactive and animated stories.

Fairy Tale and Folklore Studies **www.surlalunefairytales.com**
Fairy tale and folklore studies featuring annotated stories. Includes discussions and illustrations.

Aesop's Fables **www.aesopfables.com**

DLTK's Fairy Tales and Nursery Rhymes **www.dltk-teach.com/rhymes/index.htm**

Nursery rhymes

Mother Goose Nursery Rhymes **www.zero.com/family/nursery/**
Nursery Rhymes – Lyrics and Origins **www.rhymes.org.uk**

Tips and pitfalls

Check with the enquirer whether they want the original fairy tale or if an abridged version will do. Childrens' libraries contain many picture books and anthologies with abridged versions of these tales. It might be useful to keep a checklist of some of the more popular fairy tales and to keep a note of which anthologies they can be found in.

FAMILY HISTORY & GENEALOGY

See also Archives; Heraldry & Coats of Arms; Local History; Parish Registers

Typical questions

- How can I trace my family tree?
- Have you got the IGI? Mormon index? St Catherine's House index?

- Where can I see old wills?

Considerations

The ever-increasingly popular activity of tracing ancestors produces a great deal of work for librarians. Many enquiries come from people who know very little about the complexities and hard work involved in tracing ancestors. In this case the role of the librarian is to indicate that the task is complex, that it will involve a lot of research and time, and that the first step is to read up about the subject. Referral to the lending shelves is a sensible response! Other enquirers may be experienced in the subject and have requests for specific library materials. Unless staff have experience or training in the subject it is best to refer the enquirer to the local studies or archive staff.

Staff need to beware three dangers. The *first* is of getting involved too deeply in the enquiry. Before help can be given, staff will need to know how far the enquirer has progressed and what he or she knows. This can take time and carries the danger of getting carried along with the enquiry beyond the call of duty. Family history is research and staff need to 'disengage' at a fairly early stage. *Second*, other people's ancestors can be incredibly boring and 'family tree-ers' amazingly garrulous. Be careful not to yawn! Have some 'rescue' strategies in place! *Third*, newcomers think tracing your ancestors is easy and may not take kindly to what they regard as your unhelpful bureaucratic response. The overseas visitor who flies in on Friday night, visits the library on a busy Saturday, and expects to have 'found their folks' by closing time, is all too familiar.

'Genealogy' refers to the records of descent and ancestry whereas the term 'family history' has a wider connotation, involving the social context of a family.

Do warn enquirers that tracing family history will almost certainly involve a lot of time, visits to many different libraries and record offices, and . . . expense!

One particular problem for staff is that genealogical research involves the use of databases in a wide variety of mediums, both new and old. Card and paper indexes, microfilm, microfiche, computers, CD-ROMS and print. This will entail giving assistance to many people unfamiliar with using the various items of equipment needed to access these resources, and the need for print-outs and copies. The subject is heavily technology-dependent, for which staff need training and constant familiarization.

Where to look
Introductory sources

The journals *Family Tree Magazine* (monthly), *Ancestors* (6 p.a.) and *Genealogist's Magazine* (quarterly) carry advertisements and news giving information, tips for using the internet and best websites, with articles and research advice.

Bevan, A. (2006) *Tracing your ancestors in the National Archives: the website and beyond*, 7th edn, The National Archives

Christian, P. (2005) *The genealogist's internet*, 3rd edn, The National Archives

Currer-Briggs, N. and Gambier, R. (1991) *Debrett's family historian: a guide to tracing your ancestry*, Debrett and Webb & Bower

Davis, B. (2001) *Irish ancestry: a beginner's guide*, 3rd edn, Federation of Family History Societies

Family and local history handbook (2008) 11th edn, Robert Blatchford
Includes a guide to resources.

Fitzhugh T. V. H. (1998) *The dictionary of genealogy*, 5th edn, A&C Black
A standard reference work for family historians, providing information on archives, the legal system, religious practice, education, topography, migration, origins of surnames, etc.

Hey, D. (1996) *The Oxford companion to local and family history*, Oxford University Press
Over 2000 entries summarizing social, urban, agricultural, legal, family and ecclesiastical history.

Holton, G. S. and Winch, J. (2003) *Discover your Scottish ancestry: internet and traditional resources*, Edinburgh University Press

O'Neill, R. K. (2002) *Irish libraries, archives, museums and geneaological centres: a visitor's guide*, Ulster Historical Foundation

Genealogical services directory (2001) Genealogical Services Directory
Family and local history handbook.

Raymond, S. A. (2006) *Family history on the web*, Federation of Family History Societies

Ryan, J. G. (1997) *Irish records: sources for family history*, Ancestors

Timothy Owston's Pages **http://freespace.virgin.net/owston.tj/index.htm**
How to research your family history. Excellent suite of links.

Waddell, D. (2005) *Who do you think you are?* BBC
Popular introduction to tracing your family tree, emphasizing the human and emotional side of the activity.

Wagner, A. (1983) *English genealogy*, 3rd edn, Phillimore
The origins of English families from documentary sources.

www.bbc.co.uk/history/familyhistory
An excellent beginner's guide.

General databases

British Origins **www.origins.net**
Access to records held by the Society of Genealogists, including Boyd's Marriage Index.

Cyndi's List **www.cyndislist.com**
Cyndi Howell's site has links to over 30,000 genealogical sites worldwide including immigration, religions, military and passenger lists. US bias.

Family History Online **www.familyhistoryonline.net**
The Federation of Family History Societies Pay-as-view database.

Find My Past **www.findmypast.com**
A 'pay-per-view' website.

Free bmd **www.bmd.org.uk**
Provides free access to Civil Registration indexes, transcribed records and some censuses

Genealogy Gateway **www.gengateway.com**
Over 40,000 listings

GENUKI (Genealogical Service of the UK and Ireland) **www.genuki.org.uk**
Over 10,000 pages of UK genealogical information.

National Archives **www.nationalarchives.gov.uk**
Access to a wide variety of records such as passenger lists and wills. Free printable leaflets available. A successor to the Public Record Office (PRO) and Historical Manuscripts Commission (HMC) websites. See also Bevan (2006) above.

Rootsweb **www.rootsweb.com**
> A large and longstanding free genealogy website and host to various discussion forums and message boards. US emphasis.

Scotland's People **www.scotlandspeople.gov.uk**
> Indexes and copies of civil registration records, parish registrers, censuses and wills.

Biographical sources

See chapters on BIOGRAPHIES and HERALDRY & COATS OF ARMS, but the following can be useful and may be in stock in the larger libraries:

Army List; *Navy List*; and *Air Force List* (Annual, except for war years)
> These list armed forces personnel.

Clergy List and *Crockford's Clerical Directory*
> For Anglican priests and clergy.

Gentlemen's Magazine (1731–1868)
> A good source for local worthies.

Foster, J. (ed.) (1888) *Alumni Oxonienses 1500–1714, 1715–1886*, Parker & Co., 4 vols

Venn, J. (ed.) (1922–54) *Alumni Cantabrigensis*, Cambridge University Press, 10 vols
> These two works list graduates of the two universities.

Burgess and electoral rolls, voters' lists

These annual publications list the people who were eligible to vote in local elections from 1848 onwards, and in local and national elections from 1879 onwards. Rarely are they indexed by name and the enquirer will need to know an address since names are arranged alphabetically within wards (and polling districts) until 1883, thereafter in house order within street (or part of street) within each ward and polling district. Wards and polling districts regularly change, making these sources difficult to use. Many libraries produce their own street indexes.

Gibson, J. S. W. (1990) *Electoral Registers since 1832, and Burgess Rolls*, 2nd edn, Federation of Family History Societies

Census data

The UK national census started in 1801, and has been taken every tenth year (except 1941). From 1841, the census gives details of every person living at a specific address. Since personal information is confidential for 100 years, the latest census available is that for 1901.

The information in census returns is arranged by area and street, and not by name, though local history groups and others may have compiled indexes for their own localities.

The census returns for 1841–1901 for England and Wales are kept at the Family Records Centre, Myddleton Place, Myddleton Street, London EC1R 1UW, though they are available on microfilm for purchase by local libraries and family history societies. The 1881 Census is available free on **www.familysearch. org**. The 1901 census is available via the internet at **www.census.pro.gov.uk** and **www.1901censusonline.com**.

Ancestry Library **www.ancestrylibrary.com**

A subscription services often provided free by libraries. Provides access to all censuses. **www.ancestry.co.uk** is a personal subscription service of the above.

Civil registration

Introduced in 1837, the details on the forms that were filled in when a birth, marriage or death was registered contain important legal information. These documents are of key importance for family history as they give precise dates, parentage and other related information. If the exact dates are known, the certificates can be obtained from the Family Records Centre in London, the local registry office in the district where registration took place (which are sometimes more accurate than the GRO ones); or by post from the GRO, PO Box 2, Southport, Merseyside PR8 2JD. Visit **www.gro.gov.uk** for more information. If exact dates are not known, indexes will need to be searched to find that information. Some libraries and record offices have these indexes on microform (the 'St Catherine's House indexes').

Ancestry Library **www.ancestrylibrary.com**

A subscription services often provided free by libraries. Provides access to civil registration indexes for births, marriages and deaths and for all censuses. **www.ancestry.co.uk** is a personal subscription service of the above.

Other websites giving the indexes to the GRO records for England and Wales include:

www.freebmd.org.uk
Has links to all the sites with online versions of local registrar's indexes.

www.findmypast.com

www.familyrelatives.com

www.1901censusonline.com

www.bmdindex.co.uk (a subscription service)

www.thegenealogist.co.uk

The equivalent indexes for Scotland, and for transcripts of the original records, are on **www.scotlandspeople.gov.uk**, which also includes parish records, censuses and wills.

For baptisms (not births), marriages and burials (not deaths) before 1837, consult the IGI (see below) or parish registers (see chapter on PARISH REGISTERS).

Colwell, S. (2002) *The Family Records Centre: a user's guide*, Public Record Office

Price, V. J. (1993) *Register Offices of Births, Deaths and Marriages in Great Britain and Northern Ireland*, 2nd edn, Brewin

For information on registering births, marriages and deaths today, contact your local Registrar of Births, Deaths and Marriages (listed in the phone book). Information is also available at **www.gro.gov.uk/gro/content**.

Deeds

Deeds relate to property transactions. Old deeds are generally located in local archive and county record offices.

Directories to resources

www.genuki.org.uk
Directory to UK and Irish genealogical services.

Federation of Family History Societies **www.ffhs.org.uk**
Database of contacts and news.

www.ancestry.co.uk
> For UK sources.

www.genealogy.com
> For US sources.

The National Archives (formerly Royal Commission on Historical
Manuscripts) **www.nationalarchives.gov.uk**
> Information on manuscripts and the National Register of Archives.

Familia **www.familia.org.uk**
> Directory of family history resources held in public libraries in the UK and
> Ireland.

There are many local family history societies, most of whom will have their own
websites and directories.

Directories (local)

Local directories were published, as telephone directories are now, which list
principal inhabitants, their occupations, and frequently their address. The nature
of these will vary from place to place. Kelly's is a well-known publisher of
directories. Refer enquirers to the local history libraries for more details. See also
LOCAL HISTORY

International Genealogical Index (IGI)

The IGI is an index on microfiche compiled by the Church of Jesus Christ of
Latter-Day Saints (Mormons), which covers baptisms and some marriages (but
not burials) up to about the 1880s. Many of the entries are taken from published
or microfilmed registers, and generally from Church of England parish registers.
Arranged by country, then by county, surname and Christian name. (Note that
surnames are arranged phonetically, so that names that sound the same but spelt
differently are arranged together.) Most local studies libraries have this index. It
is also available online at **www.familysearch.org**. See also PARISH REGISTERS.

Marriages

The Civil Registration records and parish records are the usual source used to find
marriages from 1837 (see above). For records before this date see PARISH REGISTERS.

Migration and shipping records

www.theshipslist.com
Passenger lists and shipping including South Africa and Australia.

www.ellisisland.org
Information on emigrants to North America.

www.movinghere.org.uk
Records and information covering 200 years of migration to England.

Monumental inscriptions and cemeteries

The information on gravestones can provide useful genealogical information, particularly of relatives. See PARISH REGISTERS for records of gravestones in churchyards. Many local history societies have compiled records and these may be in local history libraries. Refer the enquirer to local archive and local studies libraries. Municipal and other cemeteries and crematoria will keep their own indexes to graves, as do some churches.

Cemetery Transcription Library **www.internment.net**
Four million cemetery records from 9000 cemeteries worldwide.

Commonwealth War Graves Commission, *Soldiers who died in the War*, 80 vols
Supplements cover later conflicts. **www.cwgc.org.uk**
Gives grave details. The service number enables names to be traced at The National Archives.

Newspapers

Local newspapers are valuable for family history. They are rarely indexed though local family history societies and libraries have often compiled indexes to, for example, obituaries and personal names.

Gibson, J. S. W. (1987) *Local newspapers 1750–1920, England and Wales: a select location list*, Federation of Family History Societies

British Library (1975) *Catalogue of the Newspaper Library*, 8 vols, British Museum Publications; also available on the British Library website **www.bl.uk**

Newsplan **www.newsplan2000.org**
Newsplan is a joint project between libraries to co-ordinate their holdings of local newspapers. The website contains an index to holdings.

Occupations

Raymond, S. A. (1996) *Occupational sources for genealogists*, 2nd edn, Federation
   of Family History Societies

Waters, C. (1999) *A directory of old trades, titles and occupations*, Countryside Books

Wills

Before 1858 the proving of wills was an ecclesiastical responsibility. Wills proved
at the Prerogative Court of Canterbury are at the Family Records Centre. Most
wills proved in the Archbishopric of York are at the Borthwick Institute of
Historical Research in York.

From 1858 wills were proved at the appropriate District Probate Registry, or at
the Principal Probate Registry in London, which also received copies of all wills
proved locally. Annual indexes to post-1858 wills for England and Wales are
published. Copies of wills and letters of administration (used when no will was left)
from 1858 are held by the Probate Department, Principal Registry of the Family
Division, First Avenue House, 42–49 High Holborn, London WC1V 6NP.

Camp, A. J. (1974) *Wills and their whereabouts*, Society of Genealogists

Gibson, J. S. W. (1994) *Probate jurisdictions: where to look for wills*, 4th edn,
   Federation of Family History Societies

Gibson, J. S. W. (1974) *Wills and where to find them*, Federation of Family
   History Societies

Scotland's People **www.scotlandspeople.gov.uk**

Record searchers

There are people trained to search records who offer their services for a fee. A list
of local searchers may be maintained in your library. Record searchers may also be
found in the advertisement pages of journals such as *Ancestors*, *Local History
Magazine*, *Family Tree Magazine*, *Practical Family Tree Magazine* and *Genealogists'
Magazine*.

The Association of Genealogists and Record Agents (AGRA), details below,
maintains a list of accredited members.

Other sources

Local archive departments and registry offices are listed in telephone directories.

Achievements of Canterbury **www.achievements.co.uk**
79–82 Northgate, Canterbury, Kent CT1 1BA
Tel: 01227 462618; Fax: 01227 765617
Provides services for genealogists.

Association of Genealogists and Record Agents (AGRA)
29 Badger's Close, Horsham, West Sussex RH12 5RU
E-mail: agra@agra.org.uk

Church of Jesus Christ of Latter Day Saints, UK Distribution Centre, 399
Garrett's Green Lane, Birmingham B33 0UH
Tel: 0121 784 9555.
Provides CD-ROMs, microfiche and online databases for genealogical
information.

Family Records Centre
Myddleton Place, Myddleton Street, London EC1R 1UW
Tel: 020 8392 5300
www.familyrecords.gov.uk/frc.htm

Federation of Family History Societies
PO Box 2425, Coventry CV5 6YX
E-mail: info@ffhs.org.uk
www.ffhs.org.uk
The FFHS is the umbrella organization for over 220 family history
societies worldwide with 180,000 members. It publishes a wide range of
useful guides. Many libraries will subscribe to these.

General Register Office
Smedley Hydro, Trafalgar Road, Southport, Merseyside PR8 2HH
www.statistics.gov.uk/nsbase/registration/general_register.asp
Responsible for all the registers of births, marriages and deaths

Jewish Genealogical Society of Great Britain
PO Box 13288, London N3 3WD
www.jgsgb.org.uk

The National Archives
Kew, Richmond, Surrey TW9 4DU
Tel: 020 8876 3444; Fax: 020 8392 5286
www.nationalarchives.gov.uk

The National Archives were formed by the amalgamation of the Public Record Office and the Historical Manuscripts Commission.

Society of Genealogists

14 Charterhouse Buildings, Goswell Road, London EC1M 7BA

Tel: 020 7251 8799; Fax: 020 7250 1800

www.sog.org.uk

Finally, for those wishing to live for ever, there is Posterity Online (**www.posterity. com**), a subscription website where you can add your autobiography, and keep adding to it, for your descendants.

Tips and pitfalls

Refer interested people to local family history societies, both in their local area and in the area they are interested in. Here they will get informed assistance from like-minded enthusiasts and, sometimes, resources not available in libraries. Keep a list of local groups.

More than any other subject, staff need to get involved in the individual case in order to understand what help is needed. This brings the danger of getting *too* involved and doing research for the enquirer instead of them doing it themselves. Do keep objective.

Keep a supply of leaflets on the resources available for people to take away and consult at leisure. And keep the leaflets up to date; family history is a rapidly developing subject. A good way of keeping up to date is to trace your own family!

Make sure you understand how to work the various microfilm machines, printers and where the supplies of paper and replacement bulbs are kept.

FILMS & CINEMA

See also Actors & Actresses; Awards & Prizes; Television & Radio

Typical questions

*   Who directed the film *Planes, trains and automobiles*?
*   In which year was *Chariots of fire* released?

Considerations

There are one or two 'standard' references which will be of use here. And there are some magnificent resources on the internet.

Where to look
Printed sources

Halliwell, L. (ed.) *Halliwell's film, video and DVD guide*, HarperCollins.
Annual
This is the best guide available. Over 23,000 films are included, arranged by title. Information includes year of release, country of origin, running time, synopses, principal cast lists, and credits for writer, director, producer, music, etc.

Walker, J. (ed.) (2006) *Halliwell's who's who in the movies*, 4th rev. edn, HarperCollins

Gifford, D. (2001) *The British film catalogue*, 3rd edn, Fitzroy Dearborn
Volume 1 covers fiction film 1895–1994 and Volume 2 non-fiction film 1888–1994. A total of 28,158 films are covered.

British national film and video guide, British Library
Since 1977 this has listed all copyright films and videos cleared by the British Film Institute. Strong on non-commercial, educational films.

Goble, A. (1996) *The international film index*
Available on CD-ROM as *The complete index to world films*.

There is a useful guide to older world cinema, which goes into more descriptive detail than Halliwell's:

Wilhelm, E. (1999) *VideoHound's world cinema*, Visible Ink Press

Dyja, E. (ed.) *The BFI film and television handbook*, BFI. Annual
Contains a large amount of statistical data as well as listings for production companies, organizations, cinemas, film festivals and funding bodies.

Organizations

The British Film Institute
21 Stephen Street, London W1T 1LN
Tel: 020 7255 1444
www.bfi.org.uk

Journals

Screen International

> EMAP Business Communications Ltd
> Weekly
> **www.screendaily.com**
> The main journal for industry news. This also includes reviews. They also produce an annual *Film and video directory*, which is essential for those interested in the industry.

Sight and Sound Magazine

> British Film Institute
> Monthly
> **www.bfi.org.uk/sightandsound/**
> A useful source for current film reviews.

Electronic sources

If you do not have a printed source, the internet will come to your rescue. The excellent *Internet Movie Database* lists most films and includes more detailed information than Halliwell's guide. Simply type in the name of a film and hey presto! Cast lists, reviews, video availability, links. All your enquirer could want:

www.imdb.com.

If you are interested in censorship or need to know the content of a film, try the excellent British Board of Film Classification website: **www.bbfc.co.uk**.

For film reviews try the excellent Movie Review Query Engine **www.mrqe.com.**

Tips and pitfalls

For most enquiries, it is quicker to use the internet than search through printed guides.

FLAGS

Typical questions

- What does the flag of Angola look like?
- I have seen a flag that is sky blue with a yellow cross. Do you know which country this belongs to?

Considerations

Looking for the flag of a particular country should not pose many problems. It is more difficult to find a flag from a vague description. This is where the internet can be quite helpful.

Where to look
Printed sources

Most encyclopedias will include pictures of international flags. There are also specialist flag books, which will go into more detail about flags and give their histories. Try and make sure the book you use is current. New flags are appearing all the time.

Znamierowski, A. (1999) *World encyclopedia of flags*, Lorenz

Complete flags of the world (2002) Dorling Kindersley
Some of the older texts are still useful, even though some of the newer countries' flags will not be listed.

Barraclough, E. M. C. and Crompton, W. G. (1985) *Flags of the world*, Warne
This book covers all international flags and their histories. There are also sections on the flags of international organizations and on yachts and merchant ships.

Talocci, M. (1989) *Guide to flags of the world*, Sidgwick and Jackson
This is even more comprehensive and shows state arms and some county and provincial flags.

Electronic sources

Flags of the World **http://flagspot.net**
Contains every world flag with description and histories.

World Flags Database **www.flags.net**

Flag Detective **www.flags.av.org/flags**
A great site. If you know what a flag looks like but do not know which country it belongs to, you can search a database of different flag designs and colours. You can select the pattern of the flag and then add the colours and the site will tell you which country your flag belongs to.

FOOD & DRINK

See also Agriculture & Farming; Beers & Brewing; Catering & Cookery; Retailing & Consumer Spending; Wine

Typical questions
- Can you tell me a particular company's brands?
- What does this term on the menu mean?
- I'm doing a college project on chocolate; I need to know what is the most popular selling chocolate confectionery.
- How much does the average family spend on food?

Considerations

The food and drink industry is vast. There are so many questions that could be asked. You really need to clarify with the enquirer what it is they need. Food manufacturers, processors, suppliers, importers and exporters are all covered well in the directories listed below. If you do not have specialized trade directories such as the ones listed, some of the more general directories such as *Kompass*, *Kelly's* or *Key British enterprises* are excellent. See COMPANIES for details. For statistics and market research Mintel or Keynote reports are excellent; both cover a huge range of food products. These are both subscription services. For those not lucky enough to have such things, try some of the websites mentioned below.

Supermarkets are now such a force in the food industry that the two terms have become entwined. Students often have projects comparing two supermarkets or food retailers. The *Retail trade directory* will give you details, but do use other sources like those listed under COMPANIES.

You may get asked about food issues, e.g. biotechnology, food safety and hygiene, and the consumer. Again some of the websites listed may be good starting points. There is an excellent website covering just about everything on food law: **www.rdg.ac.uk/foodlaw**.

Where to look
Food terms

Labensky, S., Ingram, G. and Labensky, S. (2007) *Prentice Hall essentials dictionary of culinary arts*, Prentice Hall

Collin, S. (2000) *Menu readers' dictionary: a guide to international menu terms*, Peter Collin Publishing

Food law

Jukes. D. J. (1997) *Food legislation of the UK: a concise guide*, 4th edn, Butterworth Heinemann

Directories

Food trades directory of the UK and Europe, 2 vols, Hemming Information Services
Volume 1 contains details of over 12,000 companies and organizations in the UK and is arranged by type of activity. Also provides sections on trade organizations, research institutes, consultants, education establishments and major food groups. There are also listings of food suppliers – manufacturers, processors, importers, exporters, agricultural producers and brokers. In addition, there is a guide to UK manufacturers of plant equipment and machinery, hygiene services and packaging materials; and a list of continental agents located in the UK. Volume 2 covers details of over 6000 supplies of food products and ingredients in 30 countries of continental Europe. The directory also lists details of 950 leading European companies involved in the manufacture and supply of food industry equipment and services.

Also check:

Food Trades Directory of the UK & Europe Online, Hemming Information Services **www.foodtrades.co.uk**
This allows limited results to non-subscribers but those subscribing to the hard copy can subscribe to the website for one year for an extra £30.

Food manufacturer directory (2008) William Reed Business Media
A buyer's guide to the food manufacturing industry, includes the top 50 food and drink manufacturers, and the food and drink industry production chain.

The Grocer directory of manufacturers and suppliers, UK edition, William Reed Business Media
This provides information on over 8300 top food and non-food manufacturers, including turnover, market share and league tables.

The Grocer directory of manufacturers and suppliers, European online edition, William Reed Business Media

227

This has information on over 9000 food and drink manufacturers and suppliers across Europe.

Retail directory of Europe, Hemming Information Services
Aims to provide details on all significant companies involved in retailing in Europe, some of which are from the food industry. Entries provide addresses, telephone numbers and in some cases the names of individual executives and buyers.

World food marketing directory (2008) 2 vols, Euromonitor
Volume 1 profiles 1500 leading food companies worldwide. There are company profiles on the top 50 food multinationals. Volume 2 is a global directory of food operators.

For more specific food enquiries try:

Baker's online directory **www.bakery.co.uk**

Fish industry yearbook **www.fishindustryyearbook.eu**

Frozen and chilled foods yearbook (2007) Sherwin Publications

Frozen and chilled food web directory **www.frozenandchilledfoods.com/web-directory.html**

Who's who in the meat industry (2008) Meat Trades Journal

Journals

Frozen and Chilled Foods
Sherwin Publications
Tel: 01732 868288
Six issues per year

Grocer
William Reed Publishing
Tel: 01293 613400; Fax: 01293 610330
Weekly
Everything relating to the food industry.

Food and Drink International
Haychart
Tel: 01472 310305; Fax: 01472 310317

Monthly
Current issues relating to the food and drink industry.

Food & Beverage
Direct Publishing
Tel: 0870 7013536
Quarterly

Food & Drink News
The Planet Group (UK) Ltd
Tel: 01484 321000; Fax: 01484 321001
Monthly
Providing up-to-date news and views on all aspects of the food and drink industry.

Food Industry News
GFJ Publishing
Tel: 0797 6525628
24 issues per year
News and information on the food and drink industry.

Food Manufacturer
William Reed Publishing
Tel: 01293 613400; Fax: 01293 610330
Monthly

Statistics

Many of the food organizations and associations provide statistics; it is worth looking at their websites, many of which are given below.

PRODCOM annual industry reports, Office for National Statistics
Excellent source of manufacturer sales, imports and exports statistics. Available to download free of charge from:
www.statistics.gov.uk/onlineproducts/PRODCOM2006_annual.asp

National diet and nutrition survey, Office for National Statistics

2000 National Food Survey (2001) commissioned by the Department for Environment, Food and Rural Affairs, carried out by Social Survey Division, The Stationery Office

The latest annual NFS statistics and a range of other statistics can be found under the heading 'Research and analysis' at Department for Environment, Food and Rural Affairs **www.defra.gov.uk**. This is extensive in coverage and well worth a visit.

Family food (report on the expenditure & food survey), Annual
    Available to download freely from:
    http://statistics.defra.gov.uk/esg/publications/efs/default.asp

Structure of the UK food industry: the role played by SMEs, Food and Drink Federation
    www.fdf.org.uk

The voice of the industry (2007)
    Available free to download at
    www.fdf.org.uk/annual_review/FDF_Annual_Review_full.pdf

Food and Agriculture Organization of the United Nations **www.fao.org**
    This has FAOSTAT **www.faostat.fao.org**, which is an online and multilingual database covering international statistics on food and food production, food aid, agriculture and land use and population.

Also look at:

State of food and agriculture, FAO's annual report.

Market research

Mintel reports, Mintel International Group
    For more details visit **www.mintel.co.uk** or Tel: 020 7606 4533; Fax: 020 7606 5932. These reports provide in-depth research into many different food and drink products. Also available on CD-ROM.

Key Note reports, Key Note
    For free executive summaries of report titles listed under 'Food & Catering' and 'Drinks & Tobacco' visit **www.keynote.co.uk**. For details of obtaining full reports, contact Key Note (Tel: 020 8481 8750; Fax: 020 8783 0049).

A further interesting source is:

Millstone, E. and Lang, T. (2008) *The atlas of food: who eats what, where and why*, 2nd edn, Earthscan Atlas series
    This atlas maps every aspect of the food chain, from farming, production and retail to the food on our plates.

Websites

There are so many food organizations worldwide it is probably worth checking the chapter ASSOCIATIONS & ORGANIZATIONS for directories to use for contact details. Some of the more popular are listed below.

Food company and industry information

British Egg Information Service **www.britegg.co.uk**

Meatmatters.com **www.meatmatters.com**

Potato Council **www.potato.org.uk**

Canadean **www.canadean.com**
Good for drinks industry news.

Dairy Council **www.milk.co.uk**

Federation of Bakers **www.bakersfederation.org.uk**
All about bread and the bread-making industry, both UK and European. Some excellent fact sheets available to download for free.

Flour Advisory Bureau **www.fabflour.co.uk**

Food and Drink Federation **www.fdf.org.uk**
Excellent for links to organizations and companies.

Food from Britain **www.foodfrombritain.com**

Honey Association **www.honeyassociation.com**

Just-Drinks **www.just-drinks.com**
Good for drinks industry news.

Just-Food **www.just-food.com**
Good for food industry news.

Meat Info **www.meatinfo.co.uk**
Packed with information.

Mushroom Bureau **www.mushroom-uk.com**

Red Tractor **www.myredtractor.co.uk/site/rtc_season.php**
This has a 'What's in Season' section, which is very useful.

Salt Manufacturers Association **www.saltinfo.com**

Sea Fish Industry Authority **www.seafish.org**

United Kingdom Tea Council **www.tea.co.uk**
Provides an online directory of tea companies and services, statistics and news.

Other food matters

Beat – Eating Disorders Association **www.b-eat.co.uk**

British Nutrition Foundation **www.nutrition.org.uk**

Co-operative Society **www.co-op.co.uk**
Good for food ethical policy.

Eat well, be well **www.eatwell.gov.uk**
Covers health issues and diet.

Fiveaday **www.5aday.nhs.uk/WhatCounts/PortionSizes.aspx**
Provides a portion guide table for fruit and vegetables.

Food and Agriculture Organization of the United Nations **www.fao.org**
Packed with statistical information on agriculture, fisheries, forestry, nutrition, news, topical issues. Excellent and well worth a visit.

Food and Behaviour Research **www.fabresearch.org**

Food Commission **www.foodcomm.org.uk**

Food Fitness **www.foodfitness.org.uk**

Food Standards Agency **www.foodstandards.gov.uk**

Foodlink **www.foodlink.org.uk**
For food safety and hygiene.

Soil Association **www.soilassociation.org**

Sustain **www.sustainweb.org**
The alliance for better food and farming.

Vegetarian Society **www.vegsoc.org**

World Food Programme (United Nations) **www.wfp.org**

Tips and pitfalls

The food industry is littered with brand names, which should be kept in mind when checking for company details. Enquirers wanting to know more about particular food companies should check the internet for company sites. Many of the major food manufacturers and suppliers have excellent websites. If financial information is required Carol (Company Annual Reports On-Line) **www. carolworld.com** is well worth a visit.

GAMES RULES (INCLUDING SPORTS)

Typical questions

- What are the dimensions of a standard crown bowling green?
- Have you got the rules for pool?

Where to look
Printed sources

Encyclopedias may provide an overview of some sports rules. If you need more detail, try some of the following:

Rules of the game (1990) rev. edn, St Martins Press
    This 'essential' has the rules for over 150 sports. The coverage can be fairly limited, but it is certainly a good starting point.

For more in-depth coverage, try:

Pocock, T. (2003) *Official rules of sports and games*, 19th edn, Hamlyn
    This thousand-page work goes from Archery to Water Polo.

See also some of the official sports yearbooks, e.g. Lawn Tennis Association, Amateur Athletic Association.
    For card and board games, *The new complete Hoyle* (1991) Doubleday, is a good bet. This is the definitive source for the rules of all card and other indoor games.

Electronic sources

There is a great website covering card game rules at **www.pagat.com**.

Tips and pitfalls

The associations governing bodies of different sports all have websites nowadays. These sites can sometimes be useful for finding out rules.

GARDENS, GARDENING & FLOWERS

See also Natural History

Typical questions

- When are the gardens at Parham open?
- What's the best way to make compost?

- What is this flower?
- Where can I buy unusual plants?

Considerations

People often ask for details of famous or interesting gardens, about which there are several directories, or for help to identify plants or flowers. Don't forget the library's lending stock.

Where to look
General

Bagust, H. (1998) *The gardener's dictionary of horticultural terms*, Brockhampton

Hamilton, G. (1993) *The Gardener's World directory*, 2nd edn, BBC Books
   A compendium of gardening information.

Goode, P. and Lancaster, M. (eds) (2001) *The Oxford companion to gardens*, 2nd edn, Oxford University Press

Huxley. A. J. (ed.) (1991) *New Royal Horticultural Society dictionary of gardening*, Macmillan
   The four-volume 'bible'.

Ettlinger. S. (1990) *The complete illustrated guide to everything sold in garden centres (except the plants)*, Macmillan
   Mulches, nematodes, etc., etc.

Gardenweb **www.gardenweb.com**
   Discussion-based, but good for gardening advice, plant directory, and answers to questions.

Greenfingers **www.greenfingers.com**
   Gardens to visit, finding a gardener, tips, reports and general advice.

Owen, J. and Gavin, D. (2004) *Gardening through time*, BBC Books
   An illustrated guide to 200 years of garden design giving timelines and background.

Symes, M. (2006) *A glossary of garden history*, Shire Books

Taylor, P. (2006) *Oxford companion to the garden*, Oxford University Press

G GARDENS, GARDENING & FLOWERS

Plants and flowers

Bagust, K. (comp.) *Hutchinson dictionary of plant names: common and botanical*, Helicon

Brickell, C. (ed.) (1999) *New encyclopedia of plants and flowers*, 3rd edn, Dorling Kindersley

Brookes, J. and Beckett, K. A. (1987) *The gardener's index of plants and flowers*, Dorling Kindersley
Plant information in tabular form.

Flowerbase **www.flowerbase.com**
Enables you to look up any plant and its picture. Searches on part words.

Forey, P. (1997) *Wild flowers of the British Isles and Northern Europe*, Parkgate Books
Large-format illustrations.

Griffith, H. (1994) *Index of garden plants: the new Royal Horticultural Society dictionary*, Timber Press.

Marinelli, J. (2005) *Plants*, Dorling Kundersley
A visual reference guide to plants of the world.

Martin, W. K. (1965) *The new concise British flora*, M. Joseph
The classic illustrated guide to UK flora.

Preston, C. D., Pearman, D. A. and Dines, T. D. (2002) *New atlas of the British and Irish flora: an atlas of the vascular plants of Britain, Ireland, the Isle of Man and the Channel Islands*, Oxford University Press
Shows distribution of plant species with background information.

Reader's Digest (2001) *Field guide to trees and shrubs of Britain*, 2nd edn, Reader's Digest Associates

Reader's Digest (1999) *New encyclopaedia of garden plants and flowers*, 2nd edn, Reader's Digest Associates
Two large-format encyclopedias. Photographs rather than Keble Martin's watercolour paintings.

Royal Horticultural Society (2002) *New encyclopedia of herbs and their uses*, 2nd edn, Dorling Kindersley

Directories

Gardenworld **www.gardenworld.co.uk**
> Lists over 600 garden centres and horticultural sites, plus links to other related websites. Sections on wildlife, advice, societies and specialist information.

Gardens of England and Wales open for charity, National Gardens Scheme. Annual
> Gardens of quality and interest open to the public for charity; called 'the Yellow Book'.

Hudson's historic houses and gardens: castles and heritage sites, Hudsons. Annual
> Over 2000 properties.

Johansens historic houses, castles and gardens, Johansens. Annual

King, P., *The good garden guide*, Bloomsbury. Annual

National Trust handbook, National Trust. Annual
> Gives brief descriptions of over 200 gardens and landscaped parks owned by the National Trust and open to the public. Contact and access details.

Buying guides

Consumers Association, *Gardening Which?*, Which? Publications. Ten per annum

Royal Horticultural Society, *RHS plant finder*, Dorling Kindersley. Biannual
> A large listing of uncommon plants and the nurseries where they can be bought.

Organizations

Royal Botanic Gardens, Kew **www.kew.org.uk**

Royal Horticultural Society
> 80 Vincent Square, London SW1P 2PE
> **www.rhs.org.uk**

National Society of Allotment and Leisure Gardens **www.nsalg.org.uk**

The National Trust **www.nationaltrust.org.uk**
> More than 200 gardens and buildings of outstanding interest.

Museum of Garden History (to be renamed The Garden Museum)
> Lambeth Palace Road, London SE1 7LB

Tel: 020 7401 8865; Fax: 020 7401 8869
E-mail: info@museumgardenhistory.
www.museumgardenhistory.org

The Alpine Garden Society
AGS Centre, Avon Bank, Pershore, Worcestershire WR10 3JP
Tel: 01386 554790; Fax: 01386 554801
E-mail: ags@alpinegardensociety.org
www.alpinegardensociety.org

The Hardy Plant Society
Little Orchard, Great Comberton, Pershore, Worcestershire WR10 3DP
Tel: 01386 710317
www.hardy-plant.org.uk

The Woodland Trust
Autumn Park, Dysart Road, Grantham, Lincolnshire NG31 6LL
Freephone: 0800 026 9650
www.woodland-trust.org.uk
Established in 1972, the Trust has created or saved over 1000 woods, planted over three million trees, and is the largest charity devoted to woodland conservation.

For community gardens, contact the local authority.

Tips and pitfalls

Know which of your colleagues are garden enthusiasts, and use them. Don't be shy of suggesting that enquirers use lending libraries and bookshops; gardening is a popular activity well supplied with popular books.

GEOGRAPHY, GEOLOGY & EARTH SCIENCES

See also Atlases & Gazetteers; Countries; Environment & Green Issues; Maps; Names; Weather

Typical questions

- What's a 'drumlin'?
- Do I live in a floodplain?

- Where is Middlesex?
- What causes an earthquake?

Considerations

'Geography' is one of those words that has changed its meaning over time, and particularly from generation to generation. Do find out precisely what the enquirer wants. Is it geography in the old-fashioned sense of places and their physical setting, or is it social geography, or the physical environment, travel or geopolitics? Many of your enquirers will be school children and students doing projects. Geography is one of the most distributed subjects in the Dewey classification system. 'Environmental studies' is perhaps the new 'geography'.

With geography we are getting into prime textbook territory; don't ignore these, they are usually well indexed.

Where to look
General

Bryant, E. (2004) *Natural hazards*, 2nd edn, Cambridge University Press
    Covers floods, drought, fires, storms, earthquakes and volcanoes.

CIA world factbook **www.odci.gov/cia/publications/factbook/index.html**
    Has profiles of every country in the world.

Clark, A. N. (1990) *Dictionary of geography*, Penguin Books

The Houghton Mifflin dictionary of geography (1997) Houghton Mifflin
    A good standard dictionary of 'people and places'.

Lincoln, R. J. and Boxhill, G. A. (1990) *Cambridge illustrated dictionary of natural history*, Cambridge University Press

Mayhew, S. (1997) *Oxford dictionary of geography*, Oxford University Press

McGraw-Hill concise encyclopedia of earth sciences (2005) McGraw-Hill

Oxford Reference Online (**www.oxford.com**) has a section called 'Earth & Environmental Science'.

Newton, D. E. (2003) *Encylopaedia of water*, Greenwood Press

Pitzl, G. R. (2004) *Encyclopedia of human geography*, Greenwood

Porteous, A. (2000) *Dictionary of environmental science and technology*, 3rd edn, Wiley

Visible Earth **www.visibleearth.nasa.gov**
A searchable topic-based directory of satellite pictures and animations of the Earth.

Your Environment **www.environment-agency.go.uk/your_env**
Information on the environment. The 'What's in your backyard' feature allows the users to access local environmental data by postcode.

Journals

Geographical Magazine, Royal Geographical Society. Monthly

Geography: an international journal, The Geographical Association. Quarterly

National Geographic, National Geographic Society. Monthly

Earthquakes

Bolt, B. A. (1999) *Earthquakes*, 4th edn, W. H. Freeman

Gems and minerals

Crowe, J. (2006) *Jeweller's directory of gemstones*, A&C Black

Manutchehr-Denai, M. (2005) *Dictionary of gems and gemology*, Springer

Read, P. G. (1988) *Dictionary of gemology*, 2nd edn, Butterworths

Wallis, K. (2006) *Gemstones: understanding, identifying, buying*, Antique Collectors' Club

Webster, R. (1998) *Gemmologist's compendium*, 7th edn, NAG Press

Geology

Allaby, A. and Allaby, M. (1990) *The concise Oxford dictionary of earth sciences*, Oxford University Press

Busbey, A. B. (ed.) (1996) *Rocks and fossils: the illustrated guide to the earth*, HarperCollins

The Dynamic Earth **www.mnh.si.edu/earth**
A multimedia presentation of rocks, stones and minerals from the Smithsonian Institute.

Earth Science World: Gateway to Geosciences, American Geological Institute
www.earthscienceworld.org
A collection of free databases.

Gradstein, F. and others (2004) *A geology time scale*, Cambridge University
Press

Pinna, G. (1985) *The illustrated encyclopedia of fossils*, Facts on File

The British Geological Survey publishes geological maps of the UK. Note
the two versions, 'drift' (for surface features) and 'solid' (for deep structures):
www.bgs.ac.uk/catalogue/home.html.

Names

Getty Thesaurus of Geographic Place Names
http://shiva.pub.getty.edu/tgn_browser
This database covers some 1 million names and other information about
places, both modern and historical.

See also NAMES.

Oceans and water

Dasch, J. (ed.) (2003) *Water: science and issues*, Macmillan Reference, 4 vols

Newton, D. E. (2003) *Encyclopedia of water*, Greenwood Press

Svarney, T. E. (2000) *The handy ocean answer book*, Visible Ink

Volcanoes

Feature stories in newspapers and magazines are popular with students doing
projects. If you come across any, photocopy them and file.

Scarth, A. (1999) *Vulcan's firing: man against the volcano*, Yale University Press
Features 16 famous volcanoes.

Volcano Live **www.volcanolive.com**
4000 pages covering 1562 live volcanoes.

Volcanoes of the World **www.volcano.si.edu/gvp/world**
A site managed by the Smithsonian Institution.

Other sources

Geographical Association
160 Solly Street, Sheffield S1 4BF
Tel: 0114 296 0088; Fax: 0114 296 7176
E-mail: ga@geography.org.uk
www.geography.org.uk
Publications programme, including journals, conferences and educational services.

Department for Environment, Food and Rural Affairs (DEFRA)
www.defra.gov.uk

Environment Agency **www.environment-agency.gov.uk**

National Geographic **www.nationalgeographic.com**
People, photos and maps.

Tips and pitfalls

Many atlases feature geographical information in both tabular and illustrated detail.

GOVERNMENT

See also Acts & Regulations; Election Results; European Information; Members of Parliament; Politics & International Relations

Typical questions

- I need the address of the Home Office.
- Could you tell me the members of my local council?

Considerations

It is important to realize that queries regarding government can relate to international, central or local governments. It is good practice to have details and lists of your own local government to hand. These should be kept up to date. Questions on government departments and government practice can be varied. There are, however, a number of good directories listed below which, in the main, will answer most general queries. In addition, in these days of open government, all the government departments and groups have excellent websites. The *Weekly Information Bulletin* provides a round-up of the week's activities in

Parliament and is available on **www.parliament.uk**.

In addition, *Hansard* provides a record of what is said each day in the House of Commons and is available also on the website.

If you require European Parliament information, look at the sources and websites listed in the chapter EUROPEAN INFORMATION.

Where to look
Directories

For a general overview of the UK's system of government look no further than *UK 2005: the official yearbook of the United Kingdom of Great Britain and Northern Ireland*, The Stationery Office. This provides an update on the progress of devolution and the effect on the four parts of the UK.

Civil Service yearbook, The Stationery Office. Annual
> Provides details of Parliamentary officers, ministries and other public organizations and their officials. There is an online version available.

Local government

Municipal yearbook, Hemming Information Services.
> This is indispensable for queries relating to government. It provides an A–Z listing of all local authorities in the UK and covers every aspect of local government. It also provides chapters on UK central government, international and European local government. It is now only available online, through **www.localgov.co.uk**.

The directory of English regional government (2007) Carlton Publishing and
> Printing
> A new reference work, focusing on the emerging structure of England's regional government.

Devolved government

The directory of Scottish government (2008) Carlton Publishing & Printing

The directory of Welsh government (2008) Carlton Publishing & Printing

The directory of Northern Ireland government (2007/8) Carlton Publishing &
> Printing

The directory of London government (2007/8) Carlton Publishing & Printing

Local government companion (2003) The Stationery Office
: This provides detailed information on local government, including the political composition of councils and the names of senior officers.

Local government gateway **www.info4local.gov.uk**
: This provides a gateway for local authorities to access local government-related information that is published on the websites of central government departments and agencies.

There is also a useful portal at:

www.oultwood.com/localgov/countries/england.php
: This is an excellent site for both local and national government links to department and council sites. It has an alphabetical listing for ease of use and links to councillors' websites.

Central government

The Times guide to the House of Commons (2005) Times Books

The guide to the House of Lords (2008) Carlton Publishing & Printing

The directory of Westminster and Whitehall (2006) Carlton Publishing & Printing

See also the Dod's Vacher series:

Dod's Parliamentary companion, Vacher Dod. Annual

Dod's Scottish Parliament companion, Vacher Dod. Annual

Dod's civil service companion, Vacher Dod. Annual
: These all include biographical information, constituency profiles, details of electoral systems, polling results and contact information.

In addition you can use many of the sources mentioned in the chapter MEMBERS OF PARLIAMENT.

For details about Parliamentary archives for the House of Commons and the House of Lords contact the House of Lords Record Office (Tel: 020 7219 3074; Fax: 020 7219 2570 or **www.parliament.uk**).

International government

See *Europa world yearbook*, details given under EUROPEAN INFORMATION.

Government publications

UKOP (United Kingdom Official Publications) is a comprehensive catalogue of UK official publications. It combines The Stationery Office (TSO) catalogue with the *Catalogue of British Official Publications* (COBOP), to which government departments must submit copies of their non-TSO publications. Published by TSO and available online via subscription.

Websites

Below are listed the websites for a few government departments and bodies. The listing is certainly not comprehensive. For access to other departments, regional assemblies and other government bodies visit **www.direct.gov.uk.**

Direct.gov is the government portal providing access to a wide range of government information and service. It is aimed at the general public rather than the specialist.

Benefits **www.dwp.gov.uk**
British monarchy **www.royal.gov.uk**
Cabinet Office **www.cabinetoffice.gov.uk**
Child Support Agency **www.csa.gov.uk**
Department for Culture, Media and Sport **www.culture.gov.uk**
Department for Children, Schools and Families **www.dcsf.gov.uk**
Department for Environment, Food and Rural Affairs **www.defra.gov.uk**
Department for Transport **www.dft.gov.uk**
Department for Work and Pensions **www.dwp.gov.uk**
Department of Health **www.dh.gov.uk**
Department of Business, Enterprise and Regulatory Reform **www.berr.gov.uk**
Foreign and Commonwealth Office **www.fco.gov.uk**
Health and Safety Executive **www.hse.gov.uk**
Home Office **www.homeoffice.gov.uk**
Land Registry **www1.landregistry.gov.uk**
Ministry of Defence **www.mod.uk**
No. 10 Downing Street **www.number-10.gov.uk**
Public Record Office (PRO) **www.pro.gov.uk**
The Stationery Office **www.tso.co.uk**
Treasury **www.hm-treasury.gov.uk**
UK Houses of Parliament **www.parliament.uk**
UK Identity and Passport Service **www.ips.gov.uk**

Tips and pitfalls

Government departments are constantly changing their names and websites. Keep checking **www.direct.gov.uk** for the latest information.

GRANTS & FUNDING

See also Benefits; Charitable Organizations

Typical questions

- How do I get an educational grant?
- How do I find out about grants?
- Is there any regional funding available for single parents to do . . .?
- How do I apply for a scholarship?

Considerations

In the main, you will probably find that you are asked about sources of educational grants. However, there are other types of grants, including housing grants, disabled facilities grants, business grants, and grants and funding for projects, to name a few. It is worth knowing a few reliable sources for each and certainly the relevant local authority departments. The websites listed below cover a wide range of available grants and funding; however, this list is not comprehensive. Grants for education are well covered by the directories listed below. It would be good practice to have contact details for your local education authority to hand. Your local Citizens Advice Bureau may also be able to provide assistance and information.

Where to look
Directories

The following are excellent reference works for grant contact details:

Guide to the major trusts (2007–2008) Directory of Social Change

Directory of grant making trusts, Directory of Social Change
    Comprehensive reference book covers 2500 grant-making trusts.
    Also available on CD-ROM.

The grants register: a complete guide to postgraduate funding worldwide, Palgrave
    Macmillan. Annual
    This directory provides details of grants available for students at or above
    postgraduate level and for professional/advanced vocational training.

Scholarships and bursaries, ISCO. Annual
A guide to scholarship and bursary awards made by UK universities and colleges.

Heap, B. (2002) *University scholarships and awards*, Trotman
Gives details of scholarships, bursaries and departmental awards made by over 100 universities and other professional bodies and organizations to applicants, undergraduates and overseas students.

Springboard funding guide, Hobsons
Listing of awards and bursaries in the UK.

Try also:

Forrester, S. and Lloyd, D. (2002) *Arts funding guide*, 6th edn, Directory of Social Change
This covers the National Lottery, official sources in the UK and Europe, companies and trusts.

French, A. (2005) *Welsh funding guide*, Directory of Social Change

Eastwood, N. (2002) *Youth funding guide*, 2nd edn, Directory of Social Change

French, A. (2006/2007) *A guide to local trusts in London*, Directory of Social Change

Smyth, J. (2006/2007) *A guide to local trusts in the Midlands*, Directory of Social Change

Ryland, R. (2008) *A guide to local trusts north*, Directory of Social Change

Lynch, G. (2006/2007) *A guide to local trusts south*, Directory of Social Change

Traynor, T. (2006/2007) *A guide to Scottish trusts*, Directory of Social Change

Holly, K. *Directory of European grantmakers 2006–2007*, Chapel and York
This provides details of 1000 private trusts and foundations that fund charities, nonprofits and individuals.

Directory of American grantmakers 2008-2009, Chapel and York
This provides details of 700 American foundations offering grants to charities and individuals working outside the USA.

Holly, K. *Directory of Asia Pacific grantmakers 2007*, Chapel and York
This provides details of 900 independent grantmakers.

Harland, S. and Griffiths, D. (2006–2007) *Educational grants directory*, Directory of Social Change

French, A. (2006–2007) *A guide to grants for individuals in need*, 8th edn, Directory of Social Change

For company and corporate giving try:

Smyth. J. (2007) *Guide to UK company giving*, 6th edn, Directory of Social Change
Available as a CD-ROM.

International directory of corporate philanthropy, Europa Publications
A guide to the 1200 national and international corporations in 100 countries which make charitable donations internationally.

For sponsorship use:

Hollis sponsorship & donations yearbook, Hollis (annual) or the *UK sponsorship database* **www.uksponsorship.com.**

Websites

Allavida (Alliances for Voluntary Initiatives and Development)
www.allavida.org
This is an international non-profit organization.

Architectural Heritage Fund **www.ahfund.org.uk**
Helps with repairs to historic buildings in the UK.

Arts and Humanities Research Board **www.ahrb.ac.uk**
Funding for university museums, galleries and postgraduate research.

Arts Council **www.artscouncil.org.uk**

Arts Council of Northern Ireland **www.artscouncil-ni.org**

Arts Council of Wales **www.artswales.org.uk**

Association of Charitable Foundations **www.acf.org.uk**

Awards for All **www.awardsforall.org.uk**
Lottery grants scheme for local communities.

British Council **www.britcoun.org**

Charities Aid Foundation Grants Council **www.cafonline.org/grants/**

Childcare Grant **www.dcfs.gov.uk/studentsupport**
Includes the Childcare Grant and other financial help for student parents in higher education.

Community Fund **www.community-fund.org.uk**
The independent organization set up by Parliament in 1994 to distribute money raised by the National Lottery to charities and groups.

Department for Children, Schools and Families **www.dcsf.gov.uk**

Department of Culture, Media and Sport **www.culture.gov.uk**

Environment Awards Net **www.environmentawards.net**

European Foundation Centre **www.efc.be/**

Funders Online **www.fundersonline.org/index.asp**
Search Europe's online philanthropic community.

Funding Information **www.fundinginformation.org**

Heritage Lottery Fund **www.hlf.org.uk**

Higher Education and Research Opportunities in the UK **www.hero.ac.uk**

J4b **www.j4b.co.uk**
Helps businesses find out about grants and loans.

National Endowment for Science, Technology and the Arts (NESTA)
www.nesta.org.uk

Scholarship Search **www.scholarship-search.org.uk**

Scottish Arts Council **www.sac.org.uk**

Tips and pitfalls

Bear in mind that grants and funding may place certain requirements on the individual or group. As a library worker you can only present the information; it would be unwise to advise an enquirer on which grants to apply for.

HEALTH & HEALTHCARE

See also Dentists; Doctors; Medicines & Drugs; Opticians

Typical questions
- Can you give me the address of . . . hospital?
- Do you know an organization for . . .?
- What are the symptoms of . . .?

Considerations

Healthcare queries can be those about particular medical conditions, health issues or finding contact details of a hospital or healthcare institute or organization. As well as using the specialized sources, it is useful to use the *Directory of British associations*, CBD Research, for enquiries relating to organizations involved in health or medical conditions and issues. For enquiries relating to prescriptive drugs and medicines see MEDICINES & DRUGS.

Where to look
Dictionaries

There are some excellent medical dictionaries and encyclopedias available, which will probably answer in sufficient detail the lay person's medical queries, particularly *Black's medical dictionary*, edited by Dr Harvey Marcovitch, 41st edition, 2006, Scarecrow Press. This gives 5000 definitions and descriptions of medical terms with cross-referencing to further information.

Stedman's abbreviations, acronyms and symbols (2003) 3rd edn, Lippincott
    Williams & Wilkins
    75,000 abbreviations in the field of health and medicine.

Try also:

Lock, S., Last, J. and Dunea, G. (2001) *Oxford illustrated companion to medicine*,
    Oxford University Press
    This covers all the major medical and nursing subjects as well as the history
    of medicine and complementary therapies.

There are also a number of excellent family health encyclopedias available:

British Medical Association complete family health guide (2005) Dorling Kindersley
A medical encyclopaedia which features information on screening, drug treatments and surgery with symptom charts to aid in the interpretation of symptoms. There is also an explanation of medical genetics and what they mean for your health and 2000 medical websites on every disorder.

British Medical Association A–Z family medical encyclopedia (2004) Dorling Kindersley

Apple, M. (1999) *Hamlyn encyclopedia of family health*, Hamlyn
This offers diagnosis and treatments for more than 200 ailments using orthodox and complementary medicines.

Komoroff. A. L, *Harvard family health guide*, Cassell

Carroll, S. (2003) *The Which? guide to men's health*, Which?

Robinson, A. (2003) *The Which? guide to women's health*, Which?

Directories
For contact details for hospitals and trusts there are a number of directories but remember also to use telephone directories for listings under hospitals.

The Institute of Healthcare Management yearbook, Beechwood House Publishing Ltd. Annual
This provides a comprehensive reference to both the NHS and independent healthcare. It includes details of departments, agencies and management contacts.

Binley's Directory of NHS Management, Beechwood House Publishing
Published three times a year. It provides a comprehensive directory to the NHS, having 12 main sections. These include a hospitals index, primary care trust index, NHS organizations, NHS circulars, NHS press releases and much more.

Dale, P. (2001) *Guide to library and information sources in medicine and healthcare*, British Library
Details of 812 organizations.

For details of people and organizations in the medical profession look no further than the:

Medical directory, 2 vols, Informapharma
> Provides information on 120,000 medical practioners and 15,000 NHS and independent healthcare and independent establishments.

For details of organizations involved in complementary healthcare try:

British register for alternative practice (2002) Milestone Publishing
> Covers individual therapies, directory of practitioners and legislative background.

Directory of organisations in allied and complementary health care (2000) British Library

NHS directory of complementary and alternative practioners, NHS Trusts Association
> **www.complementaryalternatives.com**

There is now also a move towards global healthcare communication and information. The *International directory of ehealth and telemedicine*, The Stationery Office, offers contacts for a range of services offered through this new healthcare provision.

Journals

There are numerous journals on health, medicine and the healthcare industry, details of which can be found in *Willings press guide* (see JOURNALS & PERIODICALS). In addition, many medical/health journals are available online; details of websites can also be found in *Willings*.

Market research

Laing's Healthcare Market Review (2007–8), 20th edn, Laing and Buisson
As well as having market reviews of certain areas of healthcare, it provides a wide range of reports on healthcare concerns and issues.

Baggott, R. (2004) *Health and healthcare in Britain*, 3rd edn, Palgrave Macmillan.

Key Note reports, Key Note
> For free executive summaries of report titles listed under healthcare and medical visit **www.keynote.co.uk**. For details of obtaining full reports, contact Key Note (Tel: 020 8481 8750; Fax: 020 8783 0049).

For further guidance try:

Madge, B. (2001) *How to find information – health care*, British Library

Madge, B. (2001) *How to find information – complementary and alternative health care*, British Library

Ryder, J. (ed.) (2002) *Directory of health library and information services in the UK and the Republic of Ireland 2002–3*, 11th edn, Facet Publishing

Statistics

Key data on health, Eurostat
   This covers the countries of the EU, looking at population, mortality, lifestyles, health status and healthcare.

Health statistics in the UK (2006) Office for National Statistics
   This covers a wide range of healthcare issues and systems, including mortality and determinants of health, health education and healthcare. There is some European comparison.

On the state of public health: the annual report of the Chief Medical Officer, Department of Health
   Excellent publication, available free to download at **www.dh.gov.uk**. Select 'Chief Medical Officer'.

Health Survey for England, Department of Health
   This is a cumulative work that looks at the health of different groups of people each year. Available at **www.dh.gov.uk**. Select 'Publications' then 'Surveys'.

O'Donovan. D. (2008) *The atlas of health*, Earthscan Atlas Services
   This provides a profile of global health. Excellent for understanding trends in health and disease and looks at health services and policy.

Organizations

Department of Health
   Richmond House, 79 Whitehall, London SW1A 2NS
   Tel: 020 7210 4850
   www.dh.gov.uk

Parlimentary and Health Service Ombudsman
www.ombudsman.org.uk
The Health Service Ombudsman considers complaints about any aspect of NHS provision if these are not dealt with adequately by the body concerned. Also looks at complaints against private health providers if the treatment was funded by the NHS.

Carers

Ramsey, R. et al. (2001) *Mental illness: a handbook for carers*, Jessica Kingsley Publishers
The 13 chapters of Part 1 cover specific illnesses, while the 18 of Part 2 cover mental health services. Resources are listed in a useful appendix.

Health and travel

You can check the Foreign and Commonwealth Office travel health advice website before you take your holiday at **www.fco.gov.uk/en/travelling-and-living-overseas**. Select travel advice by country.

Websites

You may find the following publication useful to consult if you intend to use the internet for health or medical information:

Wilkinson. S., *Medicine and health on the internet: your essential guide to online resources*, Internet handbooks, The Stationery Office

Don't forget that you can also use the health portal of one of the major search engines such as:

Yahoo! **http://uk.dir.yahoo.com/Health**

BBC Online (Health and Fitness) **www.bbc.co.uk/health**

British Medical Journal **www.bmj.com**

Children's Growth Calculator **www.healthatoz.com**

Department of Health **www.dh.gov.uk**

Health AtoZ **www.healthatoz.com**
A comprehensive, well-integrated health and medical resource developed by healthcare professionals.

Health Information **www.patient.co.uk**

Healthy Schools **www.healthyschools.gov.uk**

INTUTE **www.intute.ac.uk**
This is a database of 31,000 resources covering the health and medical industry. Select 'Health & Life Sciences'.

Lancet **www.thelancet.com**

Medline Plus **http://medlineplus.gov**

Medical Research Council **www.mrc.ac.uk**

Medicines and Healthcare products Regulatory Agency **www.mhra.gov.uk**

NetDoctor **www.netdoctor.co.uk**
The UK's independent health website.

NHS Direct **www.nhsdirect.nhs.uk**

Royal Society of Medicine **www.rsm.ac.uk**

Surgery Door **www.surgerydoor.co.uk**

World Cancer Research Fund **www.wcrf-uk.org**
Provides online lesson plans for teachers and families (4–11-year-olds).

World Health Organization **www.who.int/en**
Excellent for publications on research, statistics and international medicine.

HERALDRY & COATS OF ARMS

See also Family History & Genealogy

Typical questions

- Can you tell me what my family's coat of arms is?
- This diagram of a shield is in black and white. What are the colours?
- What's the translation of this motto?
- Whats's a 'quartering'? And what's 'sable'?

Considerations

With heraldry we come to one of those areas of impenetrable jargon and esoteric knowledge where the gulf between the specialist and the layperson is immense and barely bridgeable. Heraldry has its own arcane form of knowledge best left to the College of Heralds and others of that ilk. The encyclopedias and guides below will help, but, as in other areas of reference work, all the librarian can hope to do is point the enquirer in the correct direction and perhaps unscramble some of the jargon – such as 'or', 'argent', 'supporters' and 'couchant'. The librarian can also counter the rather naive belief that because someone in the past had a coat of arms, then someone of the same name today can use it: a belief encouraged by some of the companies that advertise genealogies and coats of arms. A knowledge of the differences between peerages, baronetages and knightages, and between Debrett's and Burke's, would be useful to learn too.

The term 'heraldry' applies to the system of personal and family graphics that were portrayed on shields, which evolved in Europe in the 12th century to meet the military and civil purposes of identification. Strict rules apply to the use of coats of arms.

Enquiries will often come from genealogists and family historians, who are referred to the classic sources such as Burke's, Debrett's and Cockrayne. People expect the larger libraries to stock these.

Where to look
General

Brooke-Little, J. P (1975) *An heraldic alphabet*, 2nd edn, Macdonald and James

Brooke-Little, J. P. (1978) *Boutell's heraldry*, 2nd edn, F. Warne

Fox-Davies, A. C. (1985) *A complete guide to heraldry*, rev. edn, Bloomsbury Press

Friar, S. and Ferguson, J. (1999) *Basic heraldry*, A&C Black

Friar, S. (2004) *The Sutton companion to heraldry*, Sutton

Friar, S. (1987) *A new dictionary of heraldry*, A&C Black

Wood, A. (1996) *Heraldic art and design*, Shaw and Sons

Woodcock, T. and Robinson. J. H. (1988) *The Oxford guide to heraldry*, Oxford University Press

Zieber, E. (1895, 1909) *Orders and decorations in America*, Bailey, Bank and Biddle

Armories

These are lists of surnames against which the heraldic devices used by that family are illustrated.

Burke, J. B. (1884) *The general armory of England, Scotland, Ireland and Wales*, Harrison

Cockayne, G. E. (1910–1959) *The complete peerage of England, Scotland, Ireland, Great Britain and the United Kingdom extant*, extinct or dormant, 2nd edn, St Catherine Press.
First published between 1887 and 1898, this 13-volume second edition was reprinted by Sutton Publishing in 2000 in six volumes. *The complete peerage* gives a full historical and genealogical account of all peerages created in England, Scotland and Ireland between the Norman Conquest and the early twentieth century. The main text includes details of every peer's birth, parents, honours, offices, marriage, death and burial, while the footnotes deal with people's wills, incomes, royal charters, rent rolls, illegitimate children, romances, treasons, public achievements, works of art and literature.

Cockayne, G. E. (1983 reprint) *The complete baronetage*, Alan Sutton

Debrett's peerage and baronetage, Debrett's Peerage Ltd. Biannual

Fox-Davies, A. C. (1970) *Armorial families*, David & Charles

Mosley, C. (ed.) (1999) *Burke's peerage and baronetage*, 106th edn, 2 vols, Fitzroy Dearborn
Gives bearings and genealogy.

Burke's landed gentry: the Kingdom in Scotland, 19th edn

Burke's landed gentry: England and Wales, 18th edn

Burke's peerage and gentry online database **www.burkes-peerage.net**
A subscription website covering over 1 million names from the titled and landed families of the UK, Ireland and USA.

Pyne, L. (1972) *New extinct peerage 1884–1971*, Heraldry Today

Mottoes

Elvin, C. N. (1971) *A hand-book of mottoes*, revised by R. Pinches, Heraldry Today

Pine, L.G. (1983) *A dictionary of mottoes*, Routledge

National heraldry

Briggs, G. (1973) *National heraldry of the world*, Dent

Ordinaries

These are books that illustrate heraldic devices, either graphically or using verbal descriptions, giving the families who used them.

Fairbairn, J. (1968) *Fairbairn's book of crests of the families of Great Britain*, Genealogical Publishing Co.
Illustrations.

Papworth, J. and Morant, A.W. (1874, 1977) *Papworth's ordinary of British armorials*, Tabard Publications
Arms are listed A–Z under heraldic terms.

Paul, J. B. (1969) *An ordinary of arms contained in the public register of all arms and bearings in Scotland 1672–1901*, William Green & Sons

Other sources

Burke's Peerage and Baronetage
Millennium Court, Stokesley Business Park, Stokesley, N Yorkshire T59 5JZ
Tel: 01642 714484; Fax: 01642 713517
E-mail: admin@burkes-landed-gentry.com
www.burkes-peerage.net

The College of Arms
Queen Victoria Street, London EC4V 4BT
Tel: 020 7248 2762; Fax: 020 7248 6448
www.college-of-arms.gov.uk
The repository of the registered grants and confirmations of arms in the British Commonwealth. Has FAQs.

Court of the Lord Lyon
New Register House, Edinburgh EH1 3YT
Tel: 0131 556 7255; Fax: 0131 557 2148

Genealogical Office
2 Kildare Street, Dublin 2

Tips and pitfalls

This is a technical area unfamiliar to most library staff; refer enquirers to books or websites on the subject.

HISTORIC HOUSES & CASTLES

See also Museums & Galleries

Typical questions

- What are the opening hours and entrance charges for Lyme Park Estate?
- I would like to find out about the history of East Riddlesden Hall.

Considerations

The first step is to try and find out what the enquirer actually wants! Do they want opening hours, charges, facilities, history or architecture of a specific house or castle?

Where to look
Printed sources

Tyack, D. and Brindle, S. (1994) *Blue guide to the country houses of England*, A&C Black
This gives a county-by-county guide to nearly 400 country houses regularly open to the public. Descriptions include details about the architecture and the history of the properties and their families.

Hudson's historic houses and gardens 2008 (2007) Norman Hudson and Co.
This concentrates more on the commercial aspect of houses and castles, covering opening hours, admission charges, contact details, facilities, accessibility, etc.

Reynard, K. W. (2003) *Directory of museums, galleries and buildings of historic interest in the United Kingdom*, 3rd edn, Europa

There will also be texts that go into much more detail about certain historic houses or castles. Check your library's catalogue for details.

Electronic sources

Some smaller libraries may not have access to the publications mentioned above.

They will be able to find current information on the internet though. Many of the owners of the country houses and castles now have websites.

English Heritage lists all their properties and give details such as opening hours, entry fees, descriptions, facilities, directions and even lists of events:

English Heritage
    23 Savile Row, London W1X 1AB
    www.english-heritage.org.uk

The National Trust provide a similar, excellent website:

The National Trust
    PO Box 39, Bromley, Kent BR1 3XL
    Tel: 0870 458 4000
    www.nationaltrust.org.uk

British Castles, Stately Homes and Houses **www.castles.org/britain**
    This is a list of links to the websites of most British castles, stately homes and houses.

Tips and pitfalls

As with many tourist attractions, the enquirer should always phone before visiting a place, to check that it is open when they intend to visit. Don't forget to suggest this to them!

HISTORY

> **See also** Archaeology; Dates, Calendars & Anniversaries; Local History

Considerations

Enquiries on historical topics tend to be fairly straightforward; the terminology is known and most people have a reasonable knowledge of history, although one must be aware of differing cultural backgrounds and attitudes. Thus be careful in using words such as 'English' and 'British', 'American' and 'North American', 'Arab' and 'Muslim'.

Note the distinction between 'archaeology' and 'history'. Each subject is treated separately in this 3rd edition of KIAFIF. Archaeology is the scientific study of artefacts whereas history is primarily the study of events through written records. The boundary is not always clear, but the distinction is useful.

HISTORY **H**

Where to look
Printed sources

There are so many excellent histories that it would be pointless to itemize them here. Cambridge and Oxford University Presses publish classic multi-volume series such as the *Cambridge Ancient History, Cambridge Medieval History, Cambridge Modern History*, and the Oxford histories of Britain, Africa, Asia, etc. Single volume series such as the *Blackwell Companion*s to *British history, History, European history, American history* and *World history* are also excellent. Many of these are on the reference shelves of the larger libraries.

Buisseret, D. (ed.) (2007) *Oxford companion to world exploration*, Oxford University Press

Butt, J. J. (2006) *The Greenwood dictionary of world history*, Greenwood Press

Castleden, R. (2005) *Events that changed the world*, Time Warner
Narrative accounts of 263 events from ancient times to the 2004 Tsunami.

Dictionary of world history (2006) 2nd edn, Oxford University Press

Hornblower, S. and Spawforth, A. (eds) (2003) *Oxford classical dictionary*, 3rd edn, Oxford University Press

Marsden, H. (2005) *Chambers dictionary of world history*, ChambersHarrap

Cambridge concise histories, e.g. France, Greece, Hungary, India, Italy.

Oxford Reference Online (**www.oxfordreference.com**) has a section 'History & Prehistory'.

British history

Arnold-Baker, C. (1996) *The companion to British history*, Longcross Press
A 1400-page 'treasure trove' of facts.

Cook, C. and Stevenson, J. (2003) *The Routledge companion to world history since 1914*, Routledge

Gardiner, J. and Wenborn, N. (eds) (1995) *The History Today companion to British history*, Collins and Brown
4500 entries on events, people and movements.

Hey, D. (2002) *How our ancestors lived: a history of life a hundred years ago*, Public Record Office

Kenyon, J. P. (ed.) (1994) *A dictionary of British history*, 2nd edn, Secker & Warburg
3000 entries.

The History Today who's who in British history (2000) Collins and Brown
4000 biographical entries.

The Oxford classical dictionary (1996) 3rd edn, Oxford University Press.
CD-ROM available.

Philip's world history encyclopedia (2000) G. Philip
An illustrated global history with 6500 entries.

The Victoria history of the counties of England, Boydell & Brewer, for the Institute of Historical Research
The standard history of the counties of England. Publishing in progress: visit **www.victoriacountyhistory.ac.uk** for more information.

Victorian Research Web **http://victorianresearch.org**
Free website giving information about the Victorian era.

Haigh, C. (1990) *Cambridge historical encyclopedia of Great Britain and Ireland*, Cambridge University Press

Journals

Historical Abstracts (1955–) ABC-Clio. 3 p.a.
An abstracting journal giving details of articles and books on a wide range of historical subjects. Excludes North America. Also available on CD-ROM and on a subscription website.

America: History and Life (1964–) ABC-Clio. 3 p.a.
An abstracting journal giving details of articles and books on US and Canadian history from 1800 journals. Over half a million references. Also available on CD-ROM and on a subscription website **www.abc-clio.com/products**.

Annual register (1759 to date)

Mitchell, B. R. (1962) *Abstract of British historical statistics*, Cambridge University Press. *Second abstract*, 1971.

Electronic sources

The National Archives **www.nationalarchives.gov.uk**
>   National archives information, catalogue to resources and printable leaflets.

Oral History Society **www.ohs.org.uk**

BBC History **www.bbc.co.uk/history**

Britannia **www.britannia.com**
>   Comprehensive coverage of British history from a US provider.

British History Online **www.british-history.ac.uk**
>   A free website published by the Institute of Historical Research. A digital library containing some of the core printed and secondary sources for the medieval and modern history of the British Isles. Search options are places, subjects, periods, sources, maps and 'text search'.

English History **http://englishhistory.net**

History On-Line **www.history.ac.uk**
>   Over 30,000 records on books, journals, articles, historians, theses and seminars; service provided by the Institute of Historical Research.

History Channel **www.thehistorychannel.com**

The Institute of Historical Research (IHR) website (**www.history.ac.uk**) includes 'Reviews in History', an online journal with reviews of the latest books, news of conferences and free guides to history practice.

Other sources

The Historical Association
>   59a Kennington Park Road, London SE11 4JH
>   Tel: 020 7735 3901
>   **www.history.org.uk**
>   The Historical Association is the leading UK society for the study of history. Publishes journals and has local branches from Aberdeen to Plymouth.

National Monuments Record
>   Kemble Drive, Swindon SN2 2GZ
>   Tel: 01793 414600
>   **www.english-heritage.org.uk**

The public archive of English Heritage. Holds more than 10 million photographs and provides information on the architecture and archaeology of England.

The Royal Commission on Historical Manuscripts
www.nationalarchives.gov.uk
Set up to meet the demand for a systematic investigation of manuscript sources. Combined with the Public Record Office in 2002 to form The National Archives. Maintains the National Register of Archives, a collection of some 40,000 lists and catalogues. These lists may be consulted in the public search rooms. The indexes for these lists may be consulted on The National Archives website. Offers advice on manuscript matters.

Royal Historical Society
c/o University College London, Gower Street, London WC1E 6BT
Tel/Fax: 020 7387 7532
E-mail: royalhistsoc@ucl.ac.uk
http://ihrinfo.ac.uk/rhs
Founded to promote the study of history by means of papers and proceedings.

Institute of Historical Research, Senate House, Malet Street, London WC1E 7HU
Tel: 020 786 28740; Fax: 020 786 28811
E-mail: ihr@sas.ac.uk
www.ihrinfo.ac.uk
The IHR has been the University of London's centre for advanced study in history since 1921. It provides a wide range of services for scholars worldwide.

There are many local and regional historical societies.

Tips and pitfalls

Do check *which* country's history is required! Beware the loose definition of the word 'archaeology'. People often confuse 'pre-history' (the story of events before the invention of writing) with 'archaeology' (the science of locating, excavating, preserving and interpreting material artefacts).

HOMEWORK

See also Research & Study

Typical questions

- Are there any websites to help with my child's homework?
- Can you help me with my homework, miss?
- How much homework should my child have?

Considerations

This is normally the sort of enquiry where concerned parents want to help their child with a homework project or give extra tuition for a particular subject. However, depending on what part of the library you work in it can also be the sort of question you get from children themselves. These should be taken seriously and the information given should be appropriate for the age of the child, with as much help as necessary for the child to get started. This is, after all, where good information skills start and a positive experience is essential for a return visit. Homework questions can be answered using just about everything in your library and a little lateral thinking can produce good results. We are great advocates of using the printed word to answer homework enquiries as so many children these days believe all they need is the internet. However, having said that there are some absolutely wonderful websites available to use which we can highly recommend. Basically, choose appropriately and try to use a selection of good printed sources and selected websites.

Where to look
Homework guidelines

Homework Guidelines **www.direct.gov.uk/en/Parents**
    Select 'Schools', 'Learning & Development', 'Extra-Curricular activities'.

For homework standards:

Homework Standards **www.standards.dcsf.gov.uk/homework**

Encyclopedias

Oxford Reference Online **www.oxfordreference.com**
    This is now available in almost all public libraries in England as a result of an agreement between OUP and the Museums, Libraries and Archives

Council. It is absolutely fantastic, with hundreds of sources, dictionaries, illustrations, maps etc.

Encyclopeadia Britannica Online Library edition **www.library.eb.com**
Junior ages 5–11
Student ages 12–18

Websites

BBC Schools **www.bbc.co.uk/schools**
Learning resources for home and school.

Channel 4 Learning **www.channel4learning.net**
Online education resources, games and activities for primary and secondary schools.

Connexions direct – Homework **www.connexions-direct.com**
Select 'Learning' then 'Help with Study'.

HomeWork Elephant **www.homeworkelephant.co.uk**
5000 selected internet resources to help with homework.

How Stuff Works **www.howstuffworks.com**
Absolutely fascinating.

Michael Multilingual Inventory of Cultural Heritage in Europe
www.michael-culture.org.uk
Access to digital collections from UK museums, libraries and archives. Search by subject, place, time, people or type of material. Excellent.

National Geographic **http://kids.nationalgeographic.com**

Topmarks **www.topmarks.co.uk**
Allows searching for sites by subject and/or age group.

Woodlands Homework Help for Primary Kids
www.woodlands-junior.kent.sch.uk/Homework

Tips and pitfalls

Many of the sections in this book will offer sources and websites which can be used for specific homework subjects. After years of market research, I can confidently say that many websites offer sections on resources for teachers and parents, it is just a case of looking carefully and thinking laterally. When you do find good ones it is worth bookmarking them, especially if you frequently find yourself answering homework project questions. Don't skimp on answering homework questions. These people are your future users and you are playing a part in their information skill development. Point them to good-quality information so they do well and this will only encourage them to use those sources again and to look at using others for further information.

HOTELS & GUESTHOUSES

Typical questions
- I want a list of hotels in St Tropez.
- Are there any cheap bed-and-breakfast places in St Ives?

Considerations
The short-break travel market is ever expanding and more and more people are deciding to 'tailor' their own short breaks. Most large libraries will have a decent directory of hotels and bed-and-breakfasts in the UK. The problems start arising when people are looking for hotels abroad.

Where to look
Printed sources
There are many hotel guides covering the UK and Ireland. For instance:

RAC inspected hotels, Great Britain and Ireland, BBC Worldwide Publishing

If the customer is looking for hotels abroad, some of the foreign guidebooks recommend hotels and lodgings. Make sure the guide you are looking at is current, though.

Electronic sources
If you are short of hotel guides, you can always try the internet. This is in many ways better than looking at a guidebook and is much more up to date. Many smaller hotels, which may not get into guidebooks, can afford to set up websites. Another advantage is that you may be able to book instantly, and searching for hotels abroad could not be easier.

The best way to find hotels is simply to use a good search engine and type, for example, 'hotels St Ives'. Alternatively, look for the town or city's local tourist information centre. They usually have websites with lists of recommended accommodation.

Tips and pitfalls

Most tourist information centres have directories of UK hotels and many provide a bed-booking service throughout the UK. Refer your enquirer to them if you are having problems.

HOUSING & BUYING A HOUSE

See also Architecture & Planning; Social Welfare

Considerations

There are many books available on buying or selling property; your library will probably have a selection in its lending department. Providing these are up to date, they will probably answer many of the queries you are likely to get. There are some detailed information sources given below. Information about properties for sale in the UK can be obtained from estate agents and local newspapers. If you require lists of estate agents, the Yellow Pages or **www.yell.com** will provide contact details. Most estate agents have websites for buying and selling houses and properties. These usually include property details and both internal and external pictures. Statistical information, such as comparing house prices by region, can be found in a number of sources. Many of the building societies have good information on their web pages. Your local authority is probably the best source of information for local land searches. For queries about land ownership contact the Land Registry. Information about housing matters such as homelessness, student accommodation and the state of housing can be found either from government official statistics or through organizations. Some of the best are listed below.

Where to look
Buying or selling a house

Here is just a small selection of the type of books available on moving house. Make sure that you are using up-to-date editions; if not, make sure the user is aware that changes may have occurred in the interim.

Which? Buy, sell and move house (2007) The Consumers Association

Abbey, R. and Richards, M. (2007) *A practical approach to conveyancing*, 9th edn, Oxford University Press

The Council of Mortgage Lenders **www.cml.org.uk**
    An excellent website, which includes some useful publications. Among

these are: *The guide to home buying and selling in England and Wales*, *Mortgage complaints*, *Buy-to-let* and *Debt following mortgage possessions*. The website also provides information on housing finance, the housing and mortgage markets and housing policy in the UK. These include statistics. It provides data on house prices both in the UK and in Europe. Well worth a visit.

Moneyextra Homepages **www.homepages.co.uk**
Covers everything to do with moving house.

Home Information Pack **www.homeinformationpacks.gov.uk**
Everything you needed to know about home information packs

Royal Institution for Chartered Surveyors (RICS) has an excellent range of guides available to download. They include selling your home, buying a home, letting a property to name just a few. Available at **www.rics.org/usefulguides.**

Renting and letting

Wilde, P. and Butt, P. (2002) *Which? Renting and letting*, Consumers Association
History of houses

Barratt, N. (2001) *Tracing the history of your house: a guide to sources*, Public Record Office

Rights

Randall, G. *Housing rights guide*, Shelter
An annual guide to legislation and practice.

Statistics
House prices

Halifax Bank of Scotland house price index
www.hbosplc.com/economy/HousingResearch.asp

HM Land Registry **www.landreg.gov.uk/houseprices**

Mypropertyspy **www.mypropertyspy.co.uk**
Enter a postcode or town to find UK house prices.

To find out how much your house could be worth try the house price calculator **www.nationwide.co.uk/hpi/calculator.asp.**

General

For general housing statistics and housing policy look no further than the Communities and Local Government **www.communities.gov.uk**.

This is excellent and provides a list of housing statistics which includes *Housing statistics annual, Housing statistics quarterly, Local housing statistics, Homelessness statistics* and *Sales of council house statistics*. There is also a survey section which includes 'Survey of English homes', 'English house condition survey' and *Housing surveys bulletin*.

Housing issues

For housing issues and housing policy there are a number of excellent organizations:

Chartered Institute of Housing
> Octavia House, Westwood Business Park, Westwood Way, Coventry CV4 8JP
> Tel: 024 7685 1700
> **www.cih.org**
> This has an excellent site for information and links.

Housing Ombudsman Service
> 81 Aldwych, London WC2B 4HN
> Tel: 020 7421 3800
> **www.ihos.org.uk**

Joseph Rowntree Foundation
> The Homestead, 40 Water End, York YO30 6WP
> Tel: 01904 629241
> **www.jrf.org.uk**

National Housing Federation
> Lion Court, 25 Procter Street, London WC1V 6NY
> Tel: 020 7067 1010
> **www.housing.org.uk**
> Excellent for research and policy publications.

Shelter
> 88 Old Street, London EC1V 9HU
> Tel: 0845 458 4590; Fax: 020 7505 2030
> Shelterline: 24 hour helpline 0808 800 4444

www.shelter.org.uk
Excellent for downloadable guides, briefings and toolkits.

For Wales try **www.sheltercymru.org.uk**

Websites

Empty Homes Agency **www.emptyhomes.com**

Homecheck **www.homecheck.org.uk**

Homeless International **www.homeless-international.org**

Homeless Link **www.homeless.org.uk**

Homeless Pages **www.homelesspages.org.uk**

Land Registry **www.landreg.gov.uk**

Land Registers of Northern Ireland **www.lrni.gov.uk**

Leasehold Advisory Service **www.lease-advice.org**

National Association of Estate Agents **www.naea.co.uk**
Use 'Find an Agent' facility for specific postcode area.

INFORMATION TECHNOLOGY

Typical questions

- What is the difference between RAM and ROM?
- Can you recommend any internet sites on art?
- I'm buying a new PC. Have you any recent guides?
- Can you explain what 'Web 2.0' is?

Considerations

Information technology is constantly an area of great interest. As you can see from the typical questions above, this can be a wide-ranging subject. And of course the whole area of IT is constantly changing, so it is important that you try and keep up with what is going on. Texts that are relevant one year may be obsolete the next. If you are going to keep right up to date with what is going on you should consider subscribing to a relevant journal or magazine.

Where to look

It is essential that you have a good, up-to-date dictionary of IT and computing terms. Peter Collin publish a useful set including:

Black, A. and C. (2008) *Dictionary of computing and the internet*, 4th edn, A&C Black

There are thousands of books available on computers, computing and IT. One of the most important publishers is Microsoft, which has a UK website at: **www.microsoft.com/uk/mspress**.

Magazines

What PC is a good guide for potential PC buyers. There are many other similar titles on the market. Try a few to see which suits your enquirers the best.

There are also several magazines that deal with the more technical aspects of PCs and software. Check Willings press guide for a complete listing.

Internet

There are a number of publications available which cover the internet and which recommend websites. One of the most useful is:

Buckley, P. and Clark, D. (2007) *The Rough Guide to the Internet*, 13th rev. edn, Rough Guide Publishing

Written in plain English, it covers everything from getting online for the first time to newsfeeds, internet telephony and advanced tips and tricks guaranteed to turn casual surfers into net gurus. This fully revised guide covers all the latest sites and crazes, including Skype, blogging, MySpace and other social networks and online video.

Poulter, A. (2005) *The library and information professional's internet companion*, Facet Publishing

This book will help information professionals to fully understand new internet technologies and applications in a workplace context, and acts as a springboard to further sources of information.

An excellent publication for keeping up to date with new internet websites and internet technology is:

Tips and Advice Internet

Indicator Advisors & Publishers

Calgarth House, 39–41 Bank Street, Ashford, Kent TN23 1BA

Tel: 01233 653500; Fax: 01233 647100

www.indicator.co.uk/internet

Fortnightly

There is a great website with free information about all aspects of the internet at **www.philb.com**.

Tips and pitfalls

Nobody working in libraries could have failed to notice the impact that IT is having nowadays. Nearly all libraries now provide internet access and other facilities such as word-processing. Staff now need a basic knowledge of IT in order to be able to answer simple enquiries. Taking the European Computer Driving Licence should make more staff computer literate and give them confidence to answer enquiries. However, they cannot learn everything, so having some print-based resources available is a great help. Make sure you keep these resources current, though, as the IT world is changing constantly.

INSURANCE

Typical questions

- Can you give me the address of . . . insurance company?
- Can you give me the address of . . . assurance company?
- Have you got insurance claims statistics?

Considerations

First, let's clarify what the terms assurance and insurance mean.

Assurance: in Britain this is the term used for insurance policies relating to death, about something that will definitely happen. **Insurance** is the agreement that, in return for regular payments, a company will pay for loss, damage, injury or death. A common dilemma is to know the difference between insurance and assurance.

For enquirers wanting information on insurance companies the directories below will provide company details. If a user has a complaint against an insurance company then refer them to the Financial Ombudsman Service.

Where to look
Directories

Post Online **www.insurance-directories.com**
> Able to search by product, service or company.

UK insurance directory: a guide to hundreds of insurance websites in the UK
> **www.ukinsurancedirectory.com**

Insurance pocket book, NTC Publications
> Provides profiles of insurance groups, and key facts and figures of industry trends.

ABI yearbook, Ten Alps Publishing
> The yearbook of the Association of British Insurers.

The Association of Friendly Societies yearbook, Association of Friendly Societies
> A listing of companies and their products in the sector of the UK insurance market.

Kluwer's insurance buyer's guide, Kluwer Publishing Ltd

Kluwer's insurance register, Croner

This directory provides details of UK insurance companies. There is a useful 'Who owns whom' list.

Tolley's insurance handbook, Lexis Nexis Tolley

An invaluable one-stop shop of information published annually. The new edition takes into account the changes to the law resulting from the Financial Services and Markets Act 2000.

Tolley's life and allied insurance handbook, Tolley and Chartered Insurance Institute

CIR Services Guide, Perspective Publishing **www.cirguide.com**

Includes products and services for the professional insurance, risk and business continuity buyer.

Run off and restructuring 2008: yearbook and directory of run off service providers, BD Communications

A directory of insurance and reinsurance services.

Journals

There are numerous journals for the insurance industry, details of which can be found in *Willings press guide* (see JOURNALS & PERIODICALS).

Market research

The Association of British Insurers has an excellent website for free downloadable research publications and statistics: **www.abi.org.uk**.

Key Note reports, Key Note.

For free executive summaries of report titles listed under financial services (insurance companies and UK insurance market) visit **www.keynote. co.uk**. For details of obtaining full reports, contact Key Note (Tel: 020 8481 8750; Fax: 020 8783 0049).

Statistics

UK insurance key facts, Association of British Insurers **www.abi.org.uk**

International insurance statistics

www.international insurance.org/ international/toc

Insurance statistics by country and ratings by country and company.

International insurance factbook 2007/2008, Insurance Information Institute

■ INSURANCE

Organizations

For complaints contact:

Financial Ombudsman Service
> South Quay Plaza, 183 Marsh Wall, London E14 9SR
> Tel: 020 7964 0500
> Consumer Helpline 0845 080 1800
> **www.financial-ombudsman.org.uk**
> Deals with complaints about health and loan protection, household and buildings, motor, private medical and travel insurance as well as life assurance.

For tracing lost insurance policy accounts, advice on what to do is available at Association of British Insurers **www.abi.org.uk** or use the Unclaimed Assets Register **www.uar.co.uk**, which is an excellent search service that helps you find your lost assets.

Websites

The Acturial Profession **www.actuaries.org.uk**

A. M. Best **www.ambest.com**
> Insurance company directory and worldwide ratings service.

Association of British Insurers **www.abi.org.uk**
> Provides lots of links.

Association of Consulting Actuaries **www.aca.org.uk**
> Provides advice to individuals, institutions, the government and corporate bodies on pensions, life and general insurance and other financial issues.

Association of Insurance and Risk Managers (Airmic) **www.airmic.com**

British Insurance Brokers' Association (BIBA) **www.biba.org.uk**
> An independent insurance body, representing both the consumer and the professional insurance broker.

Chartered Insurance Institute **www.cii.co.uk**
> The professional and educational body for insurance and financial services. The UK pages list regulators, professional organizations and reference sources.

Chartered Institute of Loss Adjusters (CILA) **www.cila.co.uk**
> The authority of insurance claims issues.

276

Insurance Industry Internet Network **www.iiin.com**
> International websites directory for companies, agents and brokers, corporate counsels and other insurance resources. Lists over 1000 insurance companies.

Insurance Institute of London **www.iilondon.co.uk**

Insurance Times **www.insurancetimes.co.uk**

International Underwriting Association of London **www.iua.co.uk**
> For international organizations and websites use:

Insurance Information Institute **www.iii.org/international/resources**
> This is excellent for world links.

Worldwide Insurance Links **www.insurance-links.com**

INTERVIEWS

Typical questions

- I'm trying to find out about a company/organization that I am going to have an interview with.

Considerations

First, ask the user when their interview is and how much time they have to do their research. Frequently, users are on their lunch-hour, hoping to quickly 'grab' some information like they grab a sandwich. In such cases there are probably two important things to establish: (a) if the company (or organization) is registered or unincorporated – if it's part of a group and you're struggling for information, the parent company may provide some leads; (b) the main business activity of the company/organization – the user may tell you this but always check so you have it clear in your own mind. With these facts established you can proceed to a more thorough investigation. There is a wealth of company information available but even if your library doesn't have many business sources there are numerous websites to refer to. If the user has left enough time you can advise them to telephone the company for their annual report or check out some of the websites listed below.

As well as providing company information, you can suggest the user considers looking at the industry as a whole to have an understanding of the wider picture. This doesn't have to be in any major detail but could include the company's competitors, potential customers, product sales and ranking, who buys the product/service and maybe even a few notes on the industry's future. Now, that should impress a would-be employer!

Where to look
Directories

Please refer to the directories listed under COMPANIES.

Market intelligence

Please refer to the market research reports listed under MARKET RESEARCH.

Newscuttings

Subscription-based news articles databases such as Infotrac are great for full-text news. However, by their very nature they tend to cater for the bigger companies and organizations. Check which services your library subscribes to and get familiar with its contents and searching facility.

Local company news

This is probably something that your library has to tackle itself. It could be in the form of simply keeping newscuttings from local publications, arranged alphabetically by company.

Guides

There are numerous books dealing with help on job interviews – check your library catalogue. Try also:

Lees, J. and Deluca, M. (2008) *Job interviews: top answers to tough questions*, McGraw-Hill

Popovich, I. (2003) *Teach yourself winning at job interviews*, Teach Yourself Books

There are hundreds of websites offering tips and help with interviews, some are better than others. It is probably best to be selective and bookmark your selection. Here are two of the best:

Job applications, letters and interviews: **www.direct.gov.uk**. Select 'Employment' then 'Jobseekers'.

Prospects: the UK's official graduate careers website **www.prospects.ac.uk**
Select 'Jobs & Work' for a whole section on interviews.

Websites

Carol (Company Annual Reports OnLine) **www.carolworld.com**
Not only the UK but for the rest of Europe as well as the USA and Asia.

Companies – Business Profiles **www.bized.ac.uk**
Select 'Company Information' then 'Business Profiles'.

Companies House **www.companieshouse.gov.uk**

Tips and pitfalls

Avoid comment on the merits or problems of individual companies and organizations. You simply don't know if it's a good job or a good place to work. It is also an area where a little lateral thinking yields results. If you are getting nowhere with the company or organization name, don't be afraid to approach the search via the industry or product route. Many of the sections in this book will be useful for all sorts of interviews such as jobs at schools, universities etc. Look at the resources at the appropriate section.

INVENTIONS, PATENTS & TRADE MARKS

See also Copyright & Legal Deposit

Typical questions

- Who invented television?
- When was the first motor car invented?
- How do I patent something?
- How do I register a trade mark?
- Can I check a trade name?

Considerations

When, where, and by whom things were invented are popular sources of enquiry. They often form part of student projects and pub quizzes. More seriously, many people invent things and want to know how to protect their invention, that is, take out a patent. In fact it is often quite difficult to establish who invented things, especially before patents were established. Much depends on how precise people are, or want to be.

A trade mark is a unique symbol, sign or logo used by a business to identify its product or service. The 1994 Trade Marks Act clarifies what constitutes a trade mark in law and it would be sensible to refer serious enquirers to this. There is also a definition on the UK Intellectual Property Office website.

Where to look
General

UK Intellectual Property Office (UK-IPO) **www.ipo.gov.uk**

The British Library **www.bl.uk/bipc/protect.html**
  Provides links to many other databases as well as giving information for inventors. (BIPC = Business & Intellectual Property Centre.)

Inventions

Most encyclopedias have information on the more high-profile inventions. Check the library shelves at Dewey 608 and 609.

About.Com, **http://inventors.about.com/education/inventors**

Invent Now, **www.invent.org**

The Lemelson Center for the Study of Invention and Innovation, **www.si.edu/lemelson**

Arrangement by broad topics

Acton, J., Adams, T. and Packen, M. (2006) *Origins of everyday things*, Pan Macmillan

Giscard d'Estaing, V.-A. (1991) *The book of inventions and discoveries*, Macdonald

Brown, G. I. (1996) *The Guinness history of inventions*, Guinness Publications

Homer, T. (2006) *Book of Origins*, Portait Press
  22 subject categories with index.

Petrovski, P. (1993) *The evolution of useful things*, Knopf

Reader's Digest (1998) *The origin of everyday things*, Reader's Digest

Robertson, P. (1994) *The new Shell book of firsts*, Headline
Includes an index by place.

Arrangement alphabetically by invention

Baker, R. (1976) *New and improved: inventors and inventions that have changed the world*, The British Library
Gives patent numbers, mostly British, for 363 inventions.

Brown, T. (1994) *Historical first patents: the first United States patents for many everyday things*, Scarecrow Press

Tibballs, G. (1994) *The Guinness book of inventions: the 20th century from aerosol to zip*, Guinness Publications

Berens, M. (1992) *How it all began: the stories behind those famous names*, Smith Settle
An illustrated guide to Airfix, Ambrosia, Anchor and other famous brands.

Webb, P. and Suggitt, M. (2001) *Gadgets and necessities: an encyclopedia of household innovations*, ABC-Clio

Zoom Inventors and Inventions, **www.enchantedlearning.com/inventors**
Alphabetical index of historical inventions, plus a timeline and thematic and geographical arrangements of inventions.

Arrangement chronologically by invention

Desmond, K. (1987) *The Harwin book of inventions, discoveries from pre-history to the present day*, Constable
Lacks detail but a good index by specific topic leads to the inventor and date.

Oxford illustrated encyclopedia of invention and technology (1992) Oxford University Press
Large format. A–Z by subject and name.

Van Dulken, S. (2000) *Inventing the 20th century: 100 inventions that shaped the world*, British Library
Page-length accounts of many familiar products from the biro and velcro to the ring-pull and the Dyson.

▋ INVENTIONS, PATENTS & TRADE MARKS

How things work

eHow.com **www.ehow.com**

How Everyday Things are Made
  http://manufacturing.stanford.edu/hetm.html
  Describes, and shows in short videos, how things are made and how
  technical processes work.

How Stuff Works **www.howstuffworks.com**
  Thousands of illustrated articles classified into themes.

How Products are Made: an illustrated guide to product manufacturing, Gale
  Research. Biennial.

The Cutting Edge: an encyclopedia of advanced technologies (2000) Oxford
  University Press

Made How **www.madehow.com**
  Includes biographies.

Firsts

Harrison, I. (2003) *The book of firsts*, Cassell

Richardson, M. (1997) *The Penguin book of firsts*, Penguin

Patents

Adams, S. R. (2006) *Information sources in patents*, 2nd edn, K. G. Saur

Elias, S. and Stim, R. (2004) *Patent, copyright and trademarks*, Nolo
  Has US emphasis.

European Patent Office **www.epo.org**
  European patents searchable by keyword. Gratis.

Hunt, D., Nguyen, L. and Rodgers, M. (2007) *Patent searching: tools and
  techniques*, Wiley

Patents Information Network **www.bl.uk/collections/patents/html**
  Includes a list of patent offices in other countries.

The UK Intellectual Property Office (formerly Patent Office)
  www.patent.gov.uk

Gives information about how to apply for a patent.

US Patent and Trademark Depository Library **www.uspto.gov/go/ptdl**

Van Dulken, S. (1999) *British patents of invention, 1617–1977: a guide for researchers*, The British Library

Van Dulken, S. (ed.) (1998) *Introduction to patent information*, 3rd edn, The British Library

Sharpe, C. C. (1999) *Patent, trademark and copyright searching on the internet*, McFarland

Wherry, T. L. (2002) *The librarian's guide to intellectual property in the digital age: copyright, patents, and trademarks*, American Library Association

Other sources for patent information

The British Library

Patents Information, The British Library, 96 Euston Road, London NW1 2DB

Tel: 020 7412 7919; Fax: 020 7412 7480

E-mail: patents-information@bl.uk

www.bl.uk/collections/patents.html

The British Library holds 44 million patent specifications from 38 countries. It also offers general information on patents.

The UK Intellectual Property Office

Concept House, Cardiff Road, Newport, South Wales NP9 1RH

Tel: 0845 9500 505

E-mail: patent-enquiries@patents.gov.uk

www.patent.gov.uk

The UK Intellectual Property Office (formerly the Patent Office) is a government department and is responsible for intellectual property (copyright, designs, patents and trade marks). Brochures may be obtained free of charge. Supplies of brochures about patents are supplied to larger libraries.

Trade marks

There is a definition of 'trade mark' on the UK Intellectual Property Office website **www.patent. gov.uk**.

Trade Marks Act 1994

This clarifies what constitutes a trade mark in law and it would be sensible to refer serious enquirers to this.

Michaels, A. (2001) *A practical guide to trade marks*, 3rd edn, Sweet & Maxwell

Registering a trade mark

For information about registering a trade mark contact the:

UK Intellectual Property Office, Concept House, Cardiff Road, Newport, Gwent NP9 1RH

Tel: 0845 9500 505 (Central Enquiry Unit)

www.patent.gov.uk

The UK Intellectual Property (formerly the Patent Office) also has an excellent site for understanding trade marks. Under 'Search our records' the user can search for brief trade mark information.

Trade mark information

For general information about trade marks contact:

Institute of Trade Mark Attorneys

4th Floor, Canterbury House, 2–6 Sydenham Road, Croydon CR0 9XE

Tel: 020 8686 2052

www.itma.org.uk

This is an excellent site for those who need to understand what is meant by trade marks. It also links to world patent offices.

Trade mark name searches

For information about trade mark name searches, contact:

Waterlow Signature

Tel: 020 7490 0049; Fax: 020 7549 8677

www.waterlow.com/wishome.htm

This is a subscription online information service for trade mark searching. It includes UK and European trade marks. Trade mark reports contain images and text on over 800,000 UK trade marks and 45,000 European Union trade marks.

Trademark World, Informa Publishing Group. 10 issues per year

Tel: 020 7017 5000

Views and reports on law relating to trade marks

Tips and pitfalls

With inventions and 'firsts', different sources often contradict each other. Check more than one source if possible. Distinguish between brand names and the process or object, thus Xerox is the name of a company and also the copyrighted name of a process; photocopying is a generalized name for the process.

Registering patents and trade marks is a technical process and enquirers seriously proposing to do so should consider seeking the services of a professional patents agent.

ISBNs & ISSNs

See also Publishing

Typical questions

* I'm publishing a book. How do I get an ISBN?
* Do I need to include ISBNs when I list books in a bibliography?

Considerations

ISBN stands for International Standard Book Number. Each ISBN is a unique number and one is allocated to every book title published. It is not part of copyright and books can be published without one. They are used by booksellers and librarians to avoid confusion over titles, joint authors and different editions. They are particularly useful since they are used in the electronic transmission of data (e.g. tele-ordering), shop stock control systems, and computer issue systems in libraries. The ISBN, which appears as a barcode printed on the back covers of books, is used by most shops. Since 2007 ISBNs have formed part of the full EAN number, the European Article Number.

ISSN stands for International Standard Serial Number. Like ISBNs, the ISSN is allocated to the individual titles of serial publications, journals and magazines.

Neither number is part of the essential bibliographical record of a book for the purposes of compiling bibliographies and reading lists; indeed, the same book title may have more than one ISBN if there are paperback and hardback versions, or a book has different publishers in different countries. But ISBNs are important for ordering purposes.

Since January 2007, all ISBNs consist of a 13-digit number, replacing the 10-digit number used previously. Old books do not have ISBNs.

▮ ISBNS & ISSNS

Where to look
General
Writers' and artists' yearbook, A&C Black. Annual

The writers' handbook, Macmillan. Annual

Both these guides have information on ISBNs and ISSNs.

International Standard Book Numbers (ISBNs)
For information about how to acquire ISBNs contact:
ISBN Agency
>   3rd Floor, Midas House, 62 Goldsworth Road, Woking, Surrey GU12 6LQ
>   Tel: 0870 777 8712; Fax: 0870 777 8714
>   E-mail: isbn@nielsenbookdata.co.uk
>   The agency (currently Nielsen Books) produce a printed guide.

www.iso.org for the standard
www.isbn-international.org

International Standard Serial Numbers (ISSNs)
ISSN UK Centre
>   The British Library, Boston Spa, Wetherby, West Yorkshire LS23 7BQ
>   Tel: 01937 546959; Fax: 01937 546979
>   E-mail: issn-uk@bl.uk
>   The ISSN Centre allocates International Standard Serial Numbers.

There are International Standard numbers for other formats, for example: ISBD(PM) International Standard Bibliographical Description for Printed Music.

Tips and pitfalls
Take care when transcribing ISBNs. The 13 digits include a check digit, which will validate the number. The number will not transmit if incorrect.

The same book title may have different ISBNs if it has different formats, publishers or editions.

JOBS

See also Careers & Qualifications; Employment – Law; Employment – Rights & Statistics

Typical questions

- I need a list of recruitment agencies?
- Can you tell me where to look for . . . jobs?

Considerations

There are numerous places where jobs are advertised. For instance, there are a number of specialized newspapers on the market that are devoted to advertising jobs in specific regions; see *Willings press guide* for title details. In addition, many of the trade and professional journals have a job section as do the national and local newspapers. Finally, there is the internet. There are hundreds of job sites, some better than others: it is probably useful to look at and bookmark a few which you feel would be beneficial to your library users. You may be asked about employment agencies, which can usually be found listed in the Yellow Pages. For research into job titles and social grades a useful book is *Occupation grouping: a job dictionary* (2006) 6th edn, Market Research Society.

Where to look
General

Executive grapevine: the UK directory of executive recruitment (2008) International edition, Executive Grapevine

Executive grapevine: UK directory of talent management (2007) Executive Grapevine

Britain's top employers (2008) Corporate Research Foundation
www.britainstopemployers.com

Major employers of Europe 2004 – the job finder's directory, 4th edn, Graham & Whiteside
Available at **www.biz-lib.com/info/80487.pdf**.

Apprenticeships

ApprenticeMaster Alliance
6 Blackstock Mews, London N4 2BT

Tel: 020 7359 8391
www.apprentice.org.uk
Links school leavers and graduates with experts for long-term apprenticeships.

Apprenticeships (Learning and Skills Council)
www.apprenticeships.org.uk

Volunteeering

Pybus, V. (2006) *Directory of international voluntary work,* 10th edn, Crimson Publishing

Virgin guide to volunteering, Virgin Books

Ausenda. F. (2007) *Green volunteers: the world guide to voluntary work in nature conservation,* Crimson Publishing

Ausenda. F. and McCloskey. E. (eds) (2008) *World volunteers: the world guide to humanitarian and development volunteering,* Crimson Publishing

Ford, L. (2007) *The 'Guardian' guide to volunteering,* Guardian Newspaper Ltd

Working abroad

For an excellent guide to considerations and further information consult:

Griffith, S. (2007) *Work your way around the world,* 13th edn, Crimson Publishing

Try also:

Boothby, D. (2002) *Directory of jobs and careers abroad,* 11th edn, Vacation Work

Griffith, S. (2008) *Summer jobs worldwide,* Crimson Publishing

Hobbs, G. (2006) *Directory of jobs and careers abroad,* Crimson Publishing

Overseas Job Centre **www.overseasjobcentre.co.uk**
Excellent for contacts for work, articles, links and publications.

Newspapers

Listed below are the days on which newspapers publish job advertisements.

Daily Telegraph

Thursday – General appointments

Saturday – Senior appointments

Financial Times

Monday – Accountancy (junior)

Wednesday – IT, Senior, Banking, Finance and General

Thursday – Accountancy (senior)

Guardian

Monday – Conservation, Environment, Housing, Media, Public appointments

Tuesday – Education, International

Wednesday – General appointments

Thursday – Commercial, Computing, Graduate, Technical

Friday – Housing, Public appointments

Saturday – General appointments

Independent

Monday – Computing

Tuesday – Accountancy, Financial, Marketing, Media and sales

Wednesday – City jobs

Thursday – General, Education, Public appointments

Friday – Legal

Times

Monday – Education

Tuesday – General management and legal

Wednesday – La crème de la crème, Accountancy, Finance, Media, Sales

Thursday – General, Executive supplement

Journals

Opportunities – Public Sector Recruitment and Career Development Weekly

www.opportunities.co.uk

J JOBS

Websites

Accountancy, banking, computing, education, healthcare and secretarial and
more: **www.reed.co.uk**.

Agency Central (recruitment agencies and job sites directory)
www.agencycentral.co.uk

Connexions Direct **www.connexions-direct.com**
Excellent for information and advice for young people on careers and job-
seeking.

European Job Mobility Portal **www.europa.eu.int/eures**

Get – Graduate Jobs **www.get.hobsons.co.uk/index.jsp**

Graduate jobs **www. prospects.ac.uk**

Jobcentre Plus **www.jobcentreplus.gov.uk**
The executive agency of the Department for Work and Pensions; provides
an excellent website, offering a search facility to find your local job centre;
it also includes information for employers and has links to related useful
sites.

Jobseekers **www.jobseekers.direct.gov.uk**

Jobtrack **www.jobtrack.co.uk**

Tips and pitfalls

This really is an area where you could find yourself offering too much to the
enquirer. It is best to have a few trusty resources which you feel offer good
coverage. There isn't one particular source of information that could be used for
all: jobs just aren't like that. In reality, most enquirers will want the latest job
adverts, which will mean looking at newspapers or journals. If your region does
a specific job advertisement publication, it would be sensible to subscribe to it.
It will certainly be well used.

JOURNALS & PERIODICALS

See also Articles in Journals; Media & the Press;
Newspapers & Magazines; Publishing

Typical questions

- Have you got the *Farmers Weekly*?
- Where can I get a journal you don't have?
- What periodicals are published on model making?

Considerations

A great amount of information, news and comment appears in journals, so it is little wonder that libraries get many questions about them. No library can have them all and many enquiries are about getting issues the library does not have. For this type of enquiry you will need to be aware of your library's procedures for obtaining them, or for referring people to other libraries that do stock them.

There is no clear demarcation between journals, periodicals, magazines and other categories such as serials, newsletters and proceedings. Generally we are referring here to publications produced commercially at regular intervals such as weekly, monthly or quarterly.

Where to look
Lists of journals and periodicals

Benn's media, Miller Freeman Information Services, 3 vols. Annual
  Gives full publication details of periodicals by subject.

BRAD (British Rate and Data) Emap Communications. Monthly

British Library, *Current serials received*. Annual
  Also available online at **www.bl.uk/serials**
  Over 40,000 serial titles currently received by the British Library.

Journal Info **http://jinfo.lulo.lu.se**
  Free service giving details of some 18,000 journals featured in 30 major databases. Approach is by browsing in broad subject areas.

Nobori, N. (ed.) (1998) *Books and periodicals online: a directory of online publications*, Library Technology Alliance

The serials directory: an international reference book, EBSCO. Annual
  Over 150,000 entries.

*Ulrich's international periodicals directory (incorporating irregular serials and
  annuals)*, Bowker.
  Online version **www.bowkerlink.com**.
  Gives details of major periodicals, directories and yearbooks published
  worldwide by subject.

Willings press guide, Hollis, 2 vols. Annual
  A–Z within countries. Gives prices, addresses and brief content
  descriptions to over 50,000 periodicals, magazines and broadcast media.
  Includes advertising rates.

Writers' and artists' yearbook, A&C Black. Annual
  Lists popular British and Irish journals and magazines.

Abbreviations

Cryptic abbreviations to journal titles are a problem encountered from time to time.
A recent resource is:

Alkire, L. G. and Westerman-Alkine, C. (eds) (2007) *Periodical title
  abbreviations*, Thomson Gale
  This lists some 230,000 periodicals by title and abbreviations. Covers
  periodical title abbreviations, database abbreviations and selected
  monograph abbreviations. Emphasis on US titles.

Indexes to articles

  See ARTICLES IN JOURNALS

For older journals

British union catalogue of periodicals (1955–58) 4 vols, Butterworths
  A record of periodicals of the world, from the 17th century to the present
  day. Despite the date, the work is still useful for identifying established and
  older titles and locations.

British Library Catalogue **http://blpc.bl.uk**
  Use the advanced mode to access periodicals.

There are a number of co-operative journal databases, but these are generally available only on subscription, e.g. LAMDA, the journal collections of ten academic libraries.

Electronic sources

The publication of journals in electronic formats (either alongside print versions, or just as e-journals) and the existence of services providing CD-ROMs and website access to a range of indexes or even the full text makes this is a confusing and volatile area. Subscription services such as Ebsco (**www.ebsco.com**) and Ingenta (**www.ingentaconnect.com**) offer massive listings of titles and often full text retrieval of articles to subscribers. See chapter on ARTICLES IN JOURNALS for further details.

Google Scholar (**http://scholar.google.com/scholar/librarylinks.html**) provides texts, abstract and listing of periodical articles. Many publishers archive their journals electronically and offer access by subscription. An example is **www. emeraldinsight.com** for the journals published by Emerald. Your library, or a nearby academic library, may offer some of these services. Do check. Use a search engine such as Google to find information on individual titles.

Tips and pitfalls

Beware journals that have changed their titles, have amalgamated with others, have titles identical with others, or have simply ceased. Check for any lists, catalogues and OPACs (online public access catalogues) that other local libraries have; referral is often necessary with journals.

KINGS & QUEENS, RULERS & HEADS OF STATE

Typical questions
- When was Victoria queen of England?
- Does Belgium have a king?

Where to look
Printed sources

Cannon, J. and Griffiths, R. (2000) *Oxford illustrated history of the British monarchy*, 2nd rev edn, Oxford University Press
> This covers the history of the period from c.400 to the present day and lists all the monarchs.

For rulers worldwide, Guinness have produced the useful:

Carpenter, C. (1978) *Guinness book of kings, rulers and statesmen throughout the world, from 300 BC to the present day*, Guinness Publications

A more recent addition is:

Arnold, J. (2002) *The royal houses of Europe*, Patricia Arnold
> Separate volume for Great Britain. Consists mainly of genealogical tables.

There are also many biographies available on both the current royal family and kings and queens of the past. Check your shelves for availability. Encyclopedias are generally good on royalty and heads of state.

Electronic sources

There is a useful website listing all heads of state and rulers from around the world, both past and present:

www.info-regenten.de/regent/regent-e

You could also try:

www.rulers.org
www.worldstatesmen.org
www.cia.gov/cia/publications/factbook/

For the history of the UK monarchy, try the official site:

www.royal.gov.uk

LANGUAGES & TRANSLATING

See also Alphabets & Scripts; Dictionaries

Typical questions

- How can I get this article translated?
- What language do they speak in India?
- When do I use 'which' and when 'that'?

Considerations

We include grammar here, but many dictionaries contain information about grammar and other language-related topics (see chapter on DICTIONARIES). Pronunciation matters are also covered under Dictionaries.

Where to look

General

Campbell, G. (2000) *Compendium of the world's languages*, 2nd edn, 2 vols, Routledge
Over 300 A–Z entries on languages and dialects. A concise edition was published in 1998.

Crystal, D. (2003) *The Cambridge encyclopedia of the English language*, 2nd edn, Cambridge University Press.

Crystal, D. (2003) *The Cambridge encyclopedia of language*, 2nd edn, Cambridge University Press
Large format, illustrated, and relatively non-technical.

Dalby, A. (1998) *Dictionary of languages: the definitive guide to more than 400 languages*, Bloomsbury
Feature article on every language.

Katzner, K. (2002) *The languages of the world*, 3rd edn, Routledge
Gives examples of printed text and brief background.

Longman dictionary of English language and culture (2005) 3rd edn, Longman/Pearson Educational
A wider focus than just language.

Mugglestone, L. (2006) *The Oxford history of English*, Oxford University Press

L LANGUAGES & TRANSLATING

Grammar

Huddleston, R. and Pullum, G. K. (2002) *The Cambridge grammar of the English language*, Cambridge University Press

Jarvie, G. (2007) *Bloomsbury grammar guide*, 2nd edn, A&C Black

Linguistics

Crystal, D. (2008) A *dictionary of linguistics and phonetics*, 6th edn, Blackwell

Fawley, W. J. (ed.) (2003) *International encyclopedia of linguistics*, 2nd edn, Oxford University Press, 4 vols

Matthews, P. H. (2007) *The Oxford concise dictionary of linguistics*, 2nd edn, Oxford University Press

Institute of Linguists
Saxon House, 48 Southwark Street, London SE1 1UN
Tel: 020 7940 3100; Fax: 020 7940 3101
E-mail: info@iol.org.uk
www.iol.org.uk

Translating

AltaVista's *Babel Fish* allows you to type in up to 150 words, or even a website address, and claims to translate it into eight languages: **http://babelfish.yahoo.com/**

See Yellow Pages and Thomson directories for local translators and translating services.

Many libraries and information units compile lists of local translators. Check to see if any local lists are produced.

Local colleges and universities may have staff knowledgeable in different languages.

Institute of Translation and Interpreting
Exchange House, 494 Midsummer Boulevard, Central Milton Keynes MK9 2EA
Tel: 01908 255905; Fax 01908 255700
E-mail: info@iti.org.uk
www.iti.org.uk
Includes a directory of members.

Association of Language Excellence Centres
  PO Box 178, Manchester M60 1LL
  Tel: 0161 228 1366

Language Matters (UK) Ltd **www.languagemattersuk.com**
  Provides language training, translation and interpreting services.

Tips and pitfalls

For short translations, try colleagues, and even your regular users – but make sure you can trust them!

LAW

> **See also** Acts & Regulations; Companies – Law; Licences & Licensing; Police & Security; Rights

Typical questions

- What is the law on . . .?
- What does 2AER stand for?
- What's the most I can get for this offence?
- What's a 'tort'?

Considerations

A request for information on a legal topic is a request we fear. Apart from the complexity of law as a subject, there is always the fear of 'What if I get the answer wrong and give incorrect information?' We are right to fear this, though as long as we are not knowingly providing incorrect information, the worst 'they' can get us for is probably incompetence. In addition, most staff will be covered by their employer's indemnity policy. But we still have to be careful. Always preface your answer to a legal enquiry by saying it is only your understanding of the situation and quote the full source of your information. Always advise the enquirer to seek legal advice from a qualified lawyer. And never, even lightheartedly, voice a judgement. You may know you are ignorant, but some people believe librarians know everything!

The good news is that most legal enquiries do not require knowledge of the law, just knowledge of your library. Most enquiries, particularly those from students and smartly dressed strangers – lawyers – will be for specific books and named court cases. Precise details are probably known and the main difficulty may be helping the enquirer to interpret cryptic references and navigate confusing indexes. Request some training if you are not confident to cope with these.

Requests for 'the law on' a particular subject can be troublesome, especially if the enquirer seems unfamiliar with printed material. In such cases, and often these result from a summons, solicitor's letter, dispute, or accident, it is hard not to get drawn into the detail of the enquiry. Sad and hard-luck cases are legion: 'I can't afford a solicitor and the CAB won't help. You are my final hope!' At times one has to be tough-minded, even brutal.

Another point that surprises librarians is how often solicitors, barristers and other law professionals use the public library even though most have access to other libraries. The main reason is cost. The cost of law books, combined with frequent new editions, is phenomenal. Even solicitors can't afford them! This presents library managers with a dilemma and sometimes results in resource-sharing agreements.

Many law resources are available in electronic form. Law publishers such as Butterworths (e.g. *All England direct*) and Sweet & Maxwell offer many of their voluminous texts on databases, often combining many such resources. Details can be found on the publishers' websites.

Other points:

- Check *whose* law ('jurisdiction') is wanted: English, Scottish, European?
- Be aware of the *types* of books needed: practitioner, textbooks or non-technical books such as the *Which?* guides. Practitioner books are usually known by names such as Kemp & Kemp (on damages), Chitty (on contract), Emmett (on title), Tristram & Coote (on probate), Hill & Redmond (on landlord and tenant).
- Unusual words ('tort'), or even common words used in unusual ways ('minor'), can confuse. Do use law dictionaries.
- The dates of sources are critical since law can change rapidly.

Where to look
General

Oxford Reference Online **www.oxfordreference.com**
   This popular subscription site has a section on law.

Pester, D. (2003) *Finding legal information: a guide to print and electronic sources*, Chandos Publishing

Intute **www.intute.ac.uk/law**
   This is a huge gateway to internet resources giving access to information on

UK and international law. It is well organized and comprehensive (case law, organizations, societies, reference materials, journals) but beware the mix of free and subscription sites.

Legal Hub **www.legalhub.co.uk**

An online subscription resource for barristers and solicitors by the publishers Sweet & Maxwell. Includes access to The BarList, The Expert Witness Directory and In-House Lawyer Directory.

Venables **www.venables.co.uk**

This is a particularly useful gateway to legal resources relevant to the UK. Carries a huge number of resources for the public, lawyers, companies and students.

Crone, P. and Conaghan, J. (eds) (2008) *The New Oxford companion to the law*, Oxford University Press

Ward, R. and Wragg, A. (2005) *Walker & Walker's English legal system*, 9th edn, Oxford University Press
A standard textbook.

Practical guides

Community Legal Service
Tel: 0845 345 4345
www.clsdirect.org.uk
The website provides a directory of solicitors and legal advisers within a geographic area. Provides advice on your rights and whether you are entitled to legal aid. Numerous free downloadable leaflets on such key areas as employment, welfare benefits and debt.

Consumers Association (2000) *150 letters that get results*, Which? Books
Sample letters on legal problems.

Halsbury's laws of England, Butterworths
Continuous revision with looseleaf updating services, annual volumes and revised subject volumes. This brown multivolumed subject encyclopedia is the best-known standard source of English law and a good first source to consult. Note that the index references are to numbered paragraphs, not pages! Don't confuse *Halsbury's laws* with *Halsbury's statutes*, which is an encyclopedia of Acts of Parliament, and thus more specific than the *Laws*. Not the easiest work to use, but does give the background.

LAW

JustAsk **www.justask.org.uk**
> JustAsk is the website of the government's Community Legal Service. It is aimed at the general public and carries, among other material, 'How to find a solicitor', 'What are my rights on . . .?' and 'Can I get legal aid?', with free online leaflets. Tel: 0845 608 1122.

Lorton, R. (2001) *A–Z of neighbourhood law*, The Stationery Office

Martin, J. and Gibbins, M. (2003) *The complete A-Z law handbook*, 3rd edn, HodderHeadline

Richards, K. (1998) *401 legal problems solved*, Which? Books
> A question-and-answer handbook with directory section.

Shepperton, T. (2001) *Legal advice handbook*, Law Pack

See also:

Encyclopaedia of forms and precedents (continuously updated), Butterworths
> A multivolume collection of over 10,000 forms and precedents covering all aspects of non-contentious law. Popular with people doing their own legal work. Also available as a subscription website and on CD-ROM.

Current law yearbook, Sweet & Maxwell
> Gives recent changes in the law.

The Law Society publishes leaflets on a wide variety of common types of legal services free of charge. Many libraries get these for the public to have.

Dictionaries

Curzon, L. B. and Richards, P. (2007) *Dictionary of law*, 7th edn, Longman

Martin, E. A. and Law, J. (eds) (2006) *Dictionary of law*, 6th edn, Oxford University Press
> A popular one-volume dictionary

Rutherford, L. and Bone, S. (eds) (2005) *Osborn's concise law dictionary*, 10th edn, Sweet & Maxwell

Saunders, J. B. (ed.) (1998) *Words and phrases legally defined*, LexisNexis/Butterworth
> A heavyweight work used by law students and lawyers. In three volumes, with supplements.

Stewart, W. J. (2006) *Collins dictionary of law*, 3rd edn, Collins

Stroud's judicial dictionary of words and phrases (2006) 7th edn, Sweet & Maxwell
A comprehensive multivolume dictionary popular with practitioners. Also available on CD-ROM.

Abbreviations

Many problems relate to the cryptic citation of law reports. Legal reference sources usually provide a key to these abbreviations. *Osborn's concise law dictionary* and the first volume of *Halsbury's laws* (both noted above) have a key to abbreviations. For the more elusive try:

Raistrick, D. (2008) *Index to legal citations and abbreviations*, 3rd edn, Sweet & Maxwell

Directories

Boczek, B. A. (2005) *International law: a dictionary*, Scarecrow Press

Law Society's directory of solicitors and barristers, Law Society ('The Law List').
Annual
This is a directory of law firms in England and Wales with access by name of solicitor, firm and subject. It has information on choosing and using a lawyer. It is based on the records of the Law Society.
www.solicitors-online.com is the online version.

The Bar Directory **www.legalhub.co.uk**
A searchable online directory giving chambers and practising barristers in the UK; part of the Legal Hub (noted above).

Varsity directory of investigators and process servers, Shaw & Sons. Subtitle:
Featuring investigators, process servers, certified bailiffs, security consultants and many other services throughout Great Britain and Ireland. Annual

Francis, A. (2006) *Varsity directory of legal services*, 11th edn, Wychwood

Legal aid

Legal Aid Board (1998) *Legal aid handbook*, Sweet & Maxwell
Aimed at the specialist lawyer.

LAW

Courts

Anthony & Berryman's magistrates court guide, Butterworth. Annual
> A very accessible guide to offences tried in the magistrates courts, and procedures. Good rule-of-thumb guide to sentencing such as 'I've been done for speeding, what happens next?'

Family court practice, Family Law. Annual
> Also known as 'The Red Book', this is the standard guide to practice and procedure in family courts.

Shaw's directory of courts in the United Kingdom, Shaw & Sons. Annual

Stone's Justices' manual, Butterworths. Annual
> Stone's, commonly known as 'The Blue Book' (it has light blue covers), is a three-volume compendium of English law. It is compiled for lay magistrates and can be found in most reference libraries.

The Civil Court practice, Butterworths. Annual with supplements
> Known as 'The Green Book', this sets out civil procedure rules, protocol and practice, and a court guide. Also available on CD-ROM and a subscription website.

The White Book service, Sweet & Maxwell. Annual
> Covers court procedure. Similar to 'The Green Book' above.

Court Service **www.courtservice.gov.uk**
> The Court Service is an agency of the Lord Chancellor's Department which is responsible for the running of the Court Service. It gives details about the courts and a large amount of other information such as wills and probate, being called as a witness, etc. It's a bit cumbersome, but worth getting to know.

Law reports

Law reports are a special class of literature with their own structure, style of citation, rationale and publishing patterns. Law reports are the detailed record of court cases which feature important points of law. Such reports record the facts, issues, decisions and, more importantly, the legal principles on which the judgment was made. These reports influence subsequent decisions and are, therefore, often cited and requested. Generally such cases appear in the High Courts or Courts of Appeal.

Note that most of the high profile cases featured in the press have no 'report' in the sense used here since they do not involve matters of legal interpretation. For further details of other cases, try newspaper indexes, a search engine, or apply to the court concerned.

Two rival weekly publications which carry details of the judgments and a report of the arguments of council are:

All England law reports, Butterworths. Weekly with annual cumulations

Weekly law reports, Incorporated Council of Law Reporting for England
www.lawreports.co.uk

See also:

Times law reports, Butterworths. Fortnightly with cumulations
Cases cover every branch of law and a wide range of jurisdictions.

The law reports, Incorporated Council of Law Reporting for England. Annual
These are the 'official' reports of cases and are checked by the judges. They are the series preferred in the courts. Over the years there have been several series; currently there are four: Appeal Cases (AC), Chancery Division (Ch), Queen's Bench (QB) and Family Division (Fam.). These cover only English law.

The digest, Butterworths. Updated replacement volumes
Formerly known as *The English and Empire digest*, this multivolume encyclopedia gives a subject approach to law reports. It is particularly useful for legal jurisdictions beyond England (but not beyond the Commonwealth) and for older cases.

There are many other series of law reports. Examples are the *European human rights reports*, *Industrial cases reports* and *VAT tribunal reports*. Only the larger or specialist law libraries are likely to have these.

There is quite a lot of free case law on the internet, though it can be difficult to locate without specialist knowledge. One of the best sites is **www.lawreports.uk**, provided by the ICLR. The site provides *Daily law reports*, cases that will eventually appear in *Weekly law reports*.

Case citators

To find out if, and where, a court case is reported, the following may help:

Current law case citator (1972 to date) Sweet & Maxwell. Revised, cumulated
volumes produced annually

The digest, noted above, has separate volumes indexing the cases the publication features. *All England reports* lists all the cases it features in its consolidated tables and indexes.

Law reports indexes index not only the law reports themselves but also cases published in the *AER*, *Criminal appeal reports*, *Lloyds law reports*, *Local government reports*, *Road traffic reports* and *Tax cases*.

Halsbury's laws of England also has detailed indexes to cases cited in each of its volumes, though the subject area needs to be known first.

Subject sources

As indicated above, many branches of law have their own, regularly updated, specialist reference sources. Most of the standard 'named' works include details of current legislation and regulations, as well as relevant court cases. Particularly popular are *Wilkinson's road traffic offences* (2002) and *Archbold: common pleading, evidence, and practice* (2004). Both are Sweet & Maxwell publications.

Other jurisdictions (systems of law)

Examples of books on non-English law are:

Hussain, J. (1999) *Islamic law and society: an introduction*, Federation Press

Manson-Smith, D. (2004) *The legal system of Scotland*, 3rd edn, The Stationery Office

Murdoch, H. (2004) *A dictionary of Irish law*, 4th edn, Tottel

United Nations (2000) *International Court of Justice: questions and answers*, United Nations

Other sources

Citizen's Advice Bureaux **www.adviceguide.org.uk**
   Provide advice on a wide range of legal problems for the general public. The CAB have local offices and leaflets that can be downloaded from their website.

The Law Society
   113 Chancery Lane, London WC2A 1PL
   Tel: 020 7242 1222

E-mail: info.services@lawsociety.org.uk
www.lawsociety.org.uk
The professional body for solicitors in England and Wales. Provides services and support for solicitors, sets standards, and works to improve access to the law.

The Bar Council
3 Bedford Row, London WC1R 4DB
Tel: 020 7242 0082
www.barcouncil.org.uk
The Bar Council is the governing body of the Bar – the professional body for barristers (those who represent people in the courts). The site provides information for barristers and the public, including details of how to complain about a barrister.

Family Law Consortium
Tel: 020 7420 5000

Tips and pitfalls

Be aware of local specialist law collections, for example in magistrates and Crown courts, but note that access may be restricted. Sometimes special arrangements can be negotiated for library staff to gain access on an enquirer's behalf, or specific cases can be supplied as photocopies.

Get to know how law books are arranged in the library; there are many different versions of most classifications. Books on the law of specific subjects may be shelved with other books on the same subject, for example, child law in a social welfare section rather than with other law books. Take time to familiarize yourself with the arrangement of *Halsbury's laws* and popular websites such as JustAsk.

Be prepared, when referring someone to a solicitor, for the response, 'But I *am* a solicitor!' Or for the joker who asks for the case 'Jarndyce v. Jarndyce' (in the novel *Bleak House* by Charles Dickens).

LIBRARIES & INFORMATION SERVICES

See also Archives

L LIBRARIES & INFORMATION SERVICES

Typical questions

- What is the address and telephone number of my local public library?
- Can I see the library catalogue on the internet?
- Are there any libraries that specialize in philately?
- Can anyone use the British Library?

Considerations

Most questions about libraries tend to centre around addresses and opening hours, and whether or not they have a certain book or periodical in stock.

Where to look

General

Dictionary of information and library management (2006) 2nd edn, A&C Black

Drake, M. A. (ed.) (2003) *Encyclopedia of Library and Information Science*, 2nd edn, Dekker, 4 vols

Feather, J. and Sturges, P. (eds) (2003) *International encyclopedia of information and library science*, 2nd edn, Routledge

Prytherch, R. (2005) *Harrod's librarians' glossary and reference book*, 10th edn, Ashgate
Over 10,200 terms in information management, library science, publishing and archives.

Reitz, J. M. (2004) *Dictionary for library and information science*, Libraries Unlimited
Has a US emphasis.

Pedley, P. (2006) *Essential law for information professionals*, 2nd edn, Facet Publishing.

Hoare, P. (ed.) (2006) *Cambridge history of libraries in Britain and Ireland*, Cambridge University Press, 3 vols

Directories

Reynard, K. W. (ed.) (2004) *Aslib Directory of Information Sources in the United Kingdom*, 13th edn, Europa
10,741 sources listed.

World guide to libraries (2002) 17th edn, K. G. Saur
43,000 entries. Available on CD-ROM as *World guide to libraries plus 2002/2003*, 7th edn, 2002, with 56,000 libraries listed.

Libraries and information services in the United Kingdom and the Republic of Ireland, Facet Publishing. Annual
Lists some 3000 library and information services (public, school and academic), as well as selected government, national and special libraries. There are also useful lists of departments of librarianship and information science and of key library agencies. Note that many individual libraries are not listed since sometimes only the library authority will be included. Contact the authority website or local telephone directories for further details.

Walker, I. (ed.) (2004) *The libraries directory: a guide to the libraries and archives of the United Kingdom and Ireland*, 49th edn, James Clarke & Co.
Also available on CD-ROM.

Directory of university libraries in Europe (2004) 2nd edn, Europa

Dale, P. and Wilson, P. (eds) (2002) *Guide to libraries and information services in government departments and other organisations*, 34th edn, British Library
Around 600 entries.

Dale, P. (2000) *Guide to libraries and information sources in medicine and health care*, 3rd edn, British Library
812 library and information services listed.

Ryder, J. (ed.) (2001) *Directory of health library and information services in the United Kingdom and the Republic of Ireland 2002–3*, Facet Publishing

McKenzie, E. (ed.) (2003) *Guide to libraries in key UK companies*, British Library

McBurney, V. and Wilson, P. (2004) *Guide to libraries in London*, 2nd edn, British Library
About 700 entries.

What's in London Libraries **www.londonlibraries.org.uk**

Dunshire, G. and Robertson, P. (eds) (2004) *Scottish library and information resources*, 16th edn, CILIP in Scotland

O'Neill, R. K. (2002) *Irish Libraries, archives, museums and genealogical centres: a visitor's guide*, Ulster Historical Foundation

Schweizer, M. (ed.) (2005) *World guide to library, archive and information science associations*, 2nd edn, K. G. Saur

Ker, N. and Perkin, M. (2004) *A directory of the parochial libraries of the Church of England and the Church in Wales*, 2nd edn, Bibliographical Society

For library and careers news, the journal of the library and information profession in the UK is *Library + Information Update*, published by CILIP.

Individual libraries

Most UK library authorities will have their own websites showing locations and opening hours of libraries. Some may even give access to their catalogues. For public libraries try the local authority's website and there should be links from there. Or there is a list on the following website:

http://dspace.dial.pipex.com/town/square/ac940/weblibs.html

Library catalogues

The internet is the ideal platform for accessing library catalogues. Many libraries now have their catalogues on the world wide web. These include:

The British Library online catalogue and website **www.bl.uk**
> This gives free access to the catalogues of the British Library collections, including the main collections in London as well as the collections held at the Document Supply Centre at Boston Spa in Yorkshire (which supplies interlibrary loans):

For library university and college catalogues on the internet **www.hero.ac.uk/ uk/reference_and_subject_resources/institutions_facilities/online_ library_catalogues_3792.cfm**

For other library catalogues on the internet
www.hero.ac.uk/uk/reference_and_subject_resources/resources/opacs_in _britain_and_ireland_3795.cfm

For national libraries worldwide **www.library.uq.edu.au/natlibs**

Try also COPAC **http://copac.ac.uk**
> A merged online catalogue of major university and national libraries in the UK and Ireland. Allows user to search individual catalogues, or all in combination.

European Library Portal **www.europeanlibrary.org**
> Gives access to the combined resources of the 43 national libraries of Europe, including books, magazines, journals, etc., both digital and non-digital.

E-libraries

Several websites provide the texts of books electronically, often supplied from a variety of sources. Some are subscription sites, but larger libraries may be subscribers.

Google Book Search **http://books.google.com**
> Free. Full text of out-of-print books from five major research libraries.

Project Gutenberg **www.gutenberg.org**
> Free, c.25,000 texts.

World Cat **www.worldcat.org**
> A network of library catalogue content and services. Subscription site.

World eBook Library **http://worldlibrary.net**
> 400,000 titles. Subscription site.

World Public Library **http://worldlibrary.net**
> 6000,000 titles. Subscription site.

Organizations

For further information about libraries and information work in the UK and Northern Ireland contact:

CILIP (Chartered Institute of Library and Information Professionals)
> 7 Ridgmount Street, London WC1E 7AE
> Tel: 020 7255 0500; Fax: 020 7255 0501; Text phone: 020 7255 0505
> E-mail: info@cilip.org.uk
> **www.cilip.org.uk**
> CILIP was formed in April 2002 by the merger of the Institute of Information Scientists and The Library Association.

Association of Independent Libraries **www.independentlibraries.co.uk**
> AIL is an association of independently funded libraries, mostly historical in nature, that continue to function. Includes cathedral libraries, stately

houses, mechanics's institutes, subscription, proprietary and society libraries.

Tips and pitfalls

Always suggest that the user phones the library concerned before visiting as opening hours can change and collections can be relocated.

Warn potential visitors to check if they are allowed to use another library before visiting. Sometimes you will be asked to write a letter of recommendation.

LICENCES & LICENSING

See also Copyright & Legal Deposit; Inventions, Patents & Trade Marks

Typical questions

- Can pensioners get a free TV licence?
- What are the rules about holding a raffle?
- Is it true a society can't charge admission if it holds a public meeting?
- Do I need a licence to perform a play? Or to fish in a canal?

Considerations

Licences are needed for a wide variety of activities; for the places where activities are held; and to do some jobs. Often people do things without realizing they need a licence. This need usually has the force of law so we have to be careful in giving information.

Ministers of religion, airline pilots, child minders and residential homes all need to be 'licensed'. Other people need to be 'certificated' or have professional qualifications to practise – doctors, solicitors, librarians.

Excluded here are all the licences needed to import and export certain goods, licence products, etc. See books on commercial law or contact the local Chambers of Commerce.

Where to look

The standard printed source is:

Paterson's licensing acts, Butterworths. Annual
    The latest edition has sections on: Public Entertainment, Health and Safety; Liquor Licensing; Night Cafés; Betting; Gaming; and Lotteries.

Each section features a commentary, the text of relevant statutes and statutory instruments, forms, and additional information. Users may find Paterson a touch 'heavy'; and watch out when using the index – numbers refer to parts and paragraphs, not pages – but it is the standard and authoritative source.

Local authorities

Want to provide karaoke, music and dancing? Want to hold a street collection or run a raffle? Then your local authority is the body responsible. Contact them for advice on all aspects of public entertainment, alcoholic and late night refreshment houses, small lotteries, etc.

Lottery and fund raising

Lotteries need the permission of your local authority or the Gaming Board for Great Britain (Berkshire House, 168–173 High Holborn, London WC1V 7AA). The Charity Commission issue advice in their publication CC20 – *Charities and fund-raising*. This can be viewed on their website (**www.charitycommission. gov.uk**). Their helpline is: Tel: 0870 333 0123.

Professional practice

To check if someone is licensed, authorized or qualified to do a job, contact their employer and/or their professional organization, e.g. British Medical Council for doctors, the Law Society for solicitors, Institute of Chartered Accountants for accountants (see ASSOCIATIONS & ORGANIZATIONS). Given reasonable notice, the people concerned should be able to produce their certification (if it is not already on their office wall or on an identity badge).

Performances

Check with the manager of the venue or the local authority's theatres or leisure department. For plays and music, more that just a licence is needed (see MUSIC; PLAYS).

Television

Current licence information is available at **www.tv-l.co.uk**; Tel:0845 602 33 34. Licences are no longer available from post offices, but can be obtained from local payment centres.

Cars

Cars need to be registered and drivers need to be licensed. The local post office, motoring organizations and the Driving and Vehicle Licensing Agency will advise on current regulations. The latter have information on their website **www.dvla.gov.uk** and on two freephones. For driving licence enquiries telephone 0870 240 0009; for vehicle registration enquiries telephone 0870 240 0010.

Fishing

Rivers, canals and reservoirs are all owned by someone. And this includes the fish in them! Many owners lease fishing rights to angling clubs. Your local angling shop will have details and may even be authorized to issue licenses. Check Yellow Pages for their addresses.

Millichamp, R. I. (1987) *Anglers' law*, A&C Black

LITERATURE

See also Books & Bibliographies; Poems & Poetry; Plays; Quotations & Speeches; Writers & Writing

Typical questions

- What books did Anne Brontë write?
- I'd like to know more about the Shakespeare authorship controversy.
- What is a trope?
- Who wrote *The Good Companions*?
- What Indian classics are available in English?
- Who else writes like . . .?

Considerations

There are numerous reference books on literature. As always, seek clarification: misunderstandings, misconceptions and, importantly, mis-spellings, can all result in wasted time. 'Literature' is usually taken to mean novels, plays and poetry that have received critical acclaim and whose popularity has lasted, but, technically, all written work is 'literature'.

We exclude here the works of, and works about, individual authors. Library staff should be aware of the status of different editions of individual novels. Thus 'critical' editions will feature the best original texts, supported by comprehensive introductions, clear explanatory notes, chronologies and bibliographies, and edited by leading scholars. The Oxford Standard Authors series, reprinted in paperback as Oxford World's Classics, is an example. Dent's Everyman editions are also good for serious readers. Popular are the 'Notes' series such as the Methuen, Brodies, and Collins study aids. These are geared for school examination levels and do not feature the text of the novel itself. Popular paperback versions of novels, although perfectly adequate for general reading, lack such critical status At the other end of the scholarly spectrum are 'variorum' editions, which include variant texts and facsimiles of manuscripts.

Some classic authors have their own publisher's editions. An example is the Arden Shakespeare, which is the standard critical edition to Shakespeare's plays, a volume for each one. The Loeb Classics, red for Latin authors, green for the Greek ones, is the standard series for the classical authors, with the text in both the original language and in an English translation.

Where to look
General

Entries on literary topics and authors can be found in a wide variety of resources, including general encyclopedias. Advise readers to check the indexes of books as well as the main A–Z sequences. The widely available subscription service, *Oxford Reference Online* (**www.oxfordreference.com**), has a selection of reference texts on literature from Oxford University Press. The *Literature Resource Centre* (**http://gale.cengage.com**) provides a similar resource combining reference works from Gale, Scribner, Twayne and other publishers.

Bibliographies

New Cambridge bibliography of English literature, edited by G. W. Watson and I. R. Willison (1969–1977) Cambridge University Press, 5 vols
This was the 2nd edn of the *Cambridge bibliography of English literature* (1940, Supplement 1957). It is being replaced by:

Cambridge bibliography of English literature, 3rd edn, Cambridge University Press, to be in 5 vols
The first volume of this edition to be published is Volume 4, 1800–1900, edited by J. Shattock (1999).

Bibliography of American literature (1955–1991) Yale University Press

Annual bibliography of English language and literature (1922–) Modern Humanities Research Association.

Comprehensive source for recent work in literary studies. Includes periodical articles as well as books. Good for keeping abreast of recent criticism. Online and CD-ROM versions available.

See also the British Library and Library of Congress Library catalogues – details in the chapter LIBRARIES & INFORMATION SERVICES.

Selected lists: recommended reading

Bradbury, M. (2001) *The modern British novel 1878–2001*, 2nd edn, Penguin Books
Discursive text but with extensive listing of authors and titles.

Farrow, N. et al. (1990) *An English library: a bookman's guide*, 6th edn, Gower/Book Trust
An annotated guide to the best books. Earlier editions were by M. Seymour-Smith.

Raphael, F. and McLeish, K. (1981) *The list of books: a recommended library of over 3,000 works*, Mitchell Beazley
Wider subject coverage but less annotation than Farrow above.

Rogers, J. (ed.) (2001) *Good fiction guide*, Oxford University Press
34 subject essays and 1000 writers in A–Z order.

Seymour-Smith, M. (1998) *The 100 most influential books ever written: the history of thought from ancient times to today*, Citadel Press

Biography *see* chapter on WRITERS & WRITING

Children's literature

Lansberg, M. (1988) *The world of children's books*, Simon & Schuster
Includes over 400 recommended titles.

This, and others, are updated by the annual *100 best books*, published by Booktrust.

Warren, V. and Yardley, M. (2007) *Who next . . . ? A Guide to children's authors*, 3rd edn, Loughborough University

Encyclopedias

Benet, W. R. (1998) *The reader's encyclopedia*, 4th edn, edited by B. Murphey, A&C Black

A one-volume encyclopedia on world literature. Some 10,000 biographies of poets, playwrights, novelists and essayists, plot summaries, sketches of principal characters, myths, legends and folklore, biographies of artists, musicians and historical personages, as well as recipients of major literary awards.

Cody, G. H. and Sprinchorn, E. (eds) *The Columbia encyclopedia of modern drama*, Columbia University Press, 2 vols

Drabble, M. (ed.) (2000) *Oxford companion to English literature: a thousand years of English literature*, 6th edn, Oxford University Press
Just one of the many Oxford companions; other examples are the *Oxford companion to French literature*, the *Oxford companion to American literature* and *Oxford companion to German literature*.

Encyclopedia of American literature (1999) Gale

McGraw-Hill encyclopedia of world drama (1983) 2nd edn, McGraw-Hill

Kruegar, C. L. and others (2003) *Encyclopedia of British writers*, Facts on File
Two volumes covering 19th and 20th-century writers and literary movements.

The literary encyclopedia **www.litencyc.com**
Subscription service. Over 48,000 articles and 21,000 works listed.

Stapleton, M. (1983) *The Cambridge guide to English literature*, Cambridge University Press
An A–Z encyclopedia.

Guides, handbooks and companions

The Cambridge and Oxford University Presses publish a large number of excellent companions and handbooks to individual literatures. Only a few can be noted here. The Cambridge companions also publish several in-depth studies to individual authors, e.g. Christopher Marlowe.

Forster, J. W. (2006) *The Cambridge companion to the Irish novel*, Cambridge University Press

Head, D. (2006) *Guide to literature in English*, 3rd edn, Cambridge University Press

Hicken, M. (2004) *Adult sequels*, 3rd edn, CILIP Career Development Group
Identifies novels which are connected, using the same characters, etc. Authors are listed alongside book titles and publication dates (rather than dates), which is useful for guiding readers wanting to read related books in order.

Huse, R. and Huse, J. (eds) (2005) *Who else writes like . . .?: a reader's guide to fiction authors*, 5th edn, Loughborough University

Ousby, I. (ed.) (1993) *Cambridge guide to literature in English*, Cambridge University Press

Reference guide to world literature 3rd edn (2003), St James Press, 2 vols

Widdowson, P. (2004) *The Palgrave guide to English literature and its contexts, 1500-2000*, Palgrave

Three websites which have guides to literature are:

Novelist **www.ebsco.com/novelist**
A subscription site which lists over 155,000 fiction titles with discussion guides.

Fiction Connection **www.fictionconnection.com**
Subscription site with synopsis and reviews.

Nonfiction Connection: **www.nonfictionconnection.com**

For translated fiction see **www.translatedfiction.org.uk**
A website set up by the charity Booktrust.

Guides to content

Many enquirers, usually quiz and crossword enthusiasts, want to know details of characters or places in a particular novel. Two, rather dated, but still useful, sources are:

Magill, F. (ed.) (1949, 1952, 1960) *Masterpieces of world literature in digest form*, 3 vols, Harper

Haydn, H. and Fuller, E. (1949) *Thesaurus of book digests*, Arco

Histories and chronologies

New Cambridge history of English literature, 15 vols, Cambridge University Press

Each volume covers a different period and is revised periodically, replacing the volumes in the older *Cambridge history of English literature*.

Trent, W. P. (2007) *The Cambridge history of American literature*, Cambridge University Press

Kelleher, M. and O'Leary, P. (eds) (2006) *Cambridge history of Irish literature*, 2nd edn, Cambridge University Press

There are Cambridge histories for the literatures of many other countries, e.g. Spanish and American literature.

Conrad, P. (2003) *Cassell's history of English literature*, 2nd edn, Cassell

Cox, M. (ed.) (2002) *The Oxford chronology of English literature*, Oxford University Press
A year-by-year digest of 15,000 significant and representative works of literature published in English since 1475. Cox (2004) also edited a *Concise Oxford chronology of English literature*, OUP.

Oxford English literary history, Oxford University Press, 13 vols. In progress.
A revised series of individually authored volumes replacing the previous *Oxford history of English literature*.

Literary characters

Chambers dictionary of literary characters (2004) 2nd edn, Chambers Harrap

Locations and regional novels

Eagle, D. et al. (eds) (1985) *The Oxford illustrated literary guide to Great Britain and Ireland*, Oxford University Press

Ousby, I. (1990) *Blue guide: literary Britain and Ireland*, 2nd edn, A&C Black

Snell, K. D. M. (2003) *Bibliography of regional fiction in Britain and Ireland, 1800–2000*, Ashgate

Reviews

Times Literary Supplement. Weekly

London Review of Books. Monthly

Most broadsheet newspapers (particularly the Sunday papers) and periodicals review books.

Science fiction, fantasy, crime and horror

D'Ammassa, D. (2006) *Encyclopedia of fantasy and horror fiction*, Facts on File

James, E. and Mendlesohn, F. (2003) *The Oxford companion to science fiction*, Oxford University Press

Ousby. I. (1997) *The crime and mystery book: a reader's companion*, Thames & Hudson

Priestman, M. (ed.) (2003) *The Cambridge companion to crime fiction*, Cambridge University Press

Science fiction and fantasy research database
http://lib-oldweb.tamu.edu/ cishing/sffrd
Indexes articles, books and other material

Stapleford, B. (2005) *The A–Z of science fiction literature*, Scarecrow Press

Stapleford, B. (2005) *Historical dictionary of fantasy literature*, Scarecrow Press

Theory

Gale publish a number of study guides to literary topics, e.g. magic realism (1999).

Cuddon, J. A. (1999) *The Penguin dictionary of literary terms and literary theory*, 4th edn, Penguin

Ferber, M. (2001) *A dictionary of literary symbols*, Cambridge University Press

Hawthorne, J. (1998) *A glossary of contemporary literary theory*, Arnold

Martin, R. and Ray, S. M. (eds) (2003) *The Bedford glossary of critical and literary terms*, 2nd edn, Palgrave

Wolfreys, J. (2003) *Critical keywords in literary and cultural theory*, Palgrave

Electronic sources

Bibliomania **www.bibliomania.com**
Hundreds of searchable full-text works of classic and popular fiction, short stories, drama, poetry, research and religious texts. Includes *Brewer's dictionary of phrase and fable*, *Webster's dictionary*, *Roget's thesaurus* and *Biographical dictionary of English literature*. Includes literary criticism. A huge resource.

A similar project is Bartleby **www.bartleby.com**

BUBL Language and Literature **http://bubl.ac.link/lan.html**
A catalogue of selected internet resources.

Register of UK Societies **www.uksocieties.com**
Directory of over 500 British-based literary and historical societies.

Literary resources **www.andromeda.rutgers.edu/-jlynch/Lit**

IPL Online Literary Criticism Collection **www.ipl.org/ref/litcrit**

Online texts
The Online Books Page **http://onlinebooks.library.upenn.edu**

Project Gutenberg **http://promo.net/pg/list.html**

Internet Classics **http://classics.mit.edu**

Other sources
In addition to web-based literature resources, there are a number of reprint and microfiche services available, such as ProQuest's 'The Nineteenth Century' collection of over 13,000 texts available on microfiche. The online catalogue is free at **http://c19.proquest.co.uk.**

The Alliance of Literary Societies (ALS) **www.sndc.demon.co.uk**
Author societies exist for some 200 authors, of which the Trollope Society, Dickens Society and Brontë Society are three of the largest. Most have meetings, publish newsletters and/or journals, hold conferences and have chat lines. The ALS is an umbrella society, though most individual societies can be accessed using a search engine.

Tips and pitfalls
A distinction needs to be made between 'English Literature', and 'Literature in English'. The latter has a wider coverage since it covers literature in English from around the world, such as South Africa, the Commonwealth and other countries.

LOCAL HISTORY

See also Archives; Family History & Genealogy; History; Parish Registers

L LOCAL HISTORY

Typical questions
- I want to research my locality. Where do I start?
- What's a tithe award?
- Who lived in my house before me?

Considerations
Local history is the subject of a large number of enquiries. Typically they require a knowledge of what is available in the nearest local studies library, the local history sections of larger libraries, and local archives and record offices. Do know where these are, but before referring enquirers to them, ascertain that referral is necessary, and warn enquirers that seeking local history information can be a lengthy process.

While a number of general principles apply, for which some of the handbooks listed below may be useful, each locality is different, each has a different history, and therefore each has material unique to itself. What may be the case in one place may not apply in another.

Unlike most of the other chapters in this book, many of the sources needed will be old and out-of-print books dating from the nineteenth century and earlier; old newspapers, too. On the other hand, a great deal of information on all localities, not in print form, is available on the internet, provided by local newspapers and local community associations.

Where to look
General sources

Campbell-Kease, J. (1989) *A companion to local history research*, A&C Black
320 pages of reference for the local historian.

Carter, P. and Thompson, K. (2005) *Sources for local historians*, Phillimore
Handbook based on the resources of The National Archives.

Dymond, D. *Researching and writing history: a practical guide for local historians*, British Association of Local History.

The family and local history handbook (2008) 11th edn, Robert Blatchford Publishing

Friar, S. (2002) *Sutton companion to local history*, Sutton Publishing
Over 2000 entries on local history, archaeology, architecture and landscape.

Hey, D. (2000) *How our ancestors lived: a history of life a hundred years ago*, Public Record Office

Hey, D. (ed.) (2008) *The Oxford companion to local and family history*, 2nd edn, Oxford University Press
Over 2000 entries.

The Local Historian (quarterly) **www.balh.co.uk**
Journal of the British Association for Local History. Articles and book reviews.

Local History Magazine. Six issues per year
Useful advertisements and news items.

Local History Online **www.local-history.co.uk**
Includes news, bookshop and links to some 300 related websites

Martin, C. T. (1976) *The record interpreter*, 2nd edn, Phillimore
Provides a glossary of abbreviations and archaic terms, together with Latin forms of British names

Richardson, J. (2003) *The local historian's encyclopedia*, 3rd edn, Historical Publications
Gives meanings of terms as well as detailing legislation.

Riden, P. (1998) *Local history: a handbook for beginners*, 2nd edn, Merton Priory Press

Ryan, J. G. (1997) *Irish records: sources for family and local history*, Ancestry

Sinclair, C. (1994) *Tracing Scottish local history: a guide to local history research in the Scottish Record Office*, Scottish Record Office

Stephens, W. B. (1973) *Sources for English local history*, Manchester University Press
Although out of date in many details, Stephens is still an excellent guide on how to study local history.

Stuart, D. (2001) *Latin for local and family historians*, Phillimore

Winterbotham, D. and Crosby, A. *The local studies library: a handbook for local historians*, British Association for Local History

Specialist sources

Local history enquiries often entail consulting the rich (and confusing) variety of local printed and non-book material. Consult or refer enquirers to your nearest local history library or archives office.

Biographies

For prominent people, see the chapter BIOGRAPHIES. The indexes to *The Times* newspapers (online version: *Times Digital Archive*) and the *Oxford dictionary of national biography* (ODNB) contain obituaries and biographical information on deceased people to quite local levels. Features and obituaries in local newspapers are an important source of information. Some libraries index them.

Electoral rolls

The annual lists of people entitled to vote can be a useful source of information. See section 'Burgess and electoral rolls, voters' lists' in the chapter FAMILY HISTORY & GENEALOGY.

Local newspapers

These are invaluable for local history, but rarely are they indexed. Researchers need to spend a long time searching unless they can find dates from other sources. Many are on microfilm. Check your local studies library for details of what is available. (*The Times* and other national papers may be available and may contain news of local events. *The Times* is on microfilm and on subscription website back to 1785, and is indexed.)

Newsplan, the British Library project to microfilm all UK local newspapers, has compiled a directory of newspaper holdings to areas of the UK. For details of volumes see **www.bl.uk/collections/nplan.html**.

Maps

Maps are a particularly important source of local history. See chapter on 'MAPS', but more importantly refer enquirers to the local studies library of the locality itself.

Smith, D. (1988) *Maps and plans for the local historian and collector: a guide to types of maps of the British Isles produced before 1914 valuable to local and other historians and mostly available to collectors*, Batsford

Tithes: maps, apportionments and the 1836 Act: a guide for the local historian, British Association for Local History

Oral history

Recordings of people talking about topics in a locality are collected by local history societies and local libraries.

Oral History Society **www.ohs.org.uk**

Photographs

Most local studies libraries have collections of local photographs. See also:

Francis Frith Collection **www.francisfrith.com**
> Over 100,000 photographs of British towns and villages taken between 1870 and 1900. Available to view (free) and purchase.

Geograph British Isles **www.geograph.org.uk**
> A database which aims to have geographically representative photographs and information for every kilometre square of Great Britain and Ireland. Over 800,000 images to date.

Images of England **www.imagesofengland.org.uk**
> This is a large database of some 300,000 images maintained by English Heritage.

Regional histories

Victoria County Histories. The hundred or so volumes that make up the histories of the counties of England in the 'VCH' are the standard starting point for local research. Published by the Institute of Historical Research, the contents of the volumes can be seen on British History Online: **www.british-history.ac.uk**. The detail can be quite technical (compilers worked at the parish level), publishing has taken place over a long period of time, and a few counties have not been completely covered, but most large libraries have volumes for the local counties.

Other modern and older histories should be consulted. Check library catalogues for these, and see also:

Currie, C. R. J. and Lewis, C. P. (eds) (1994) *English county histories: a guide*, Alan Sutton.
> Bibliographic essays of each county.

The villages of Britain series published by Countryside Books, is an A–Z of villages by county, compiled by the Federation of Women's Institutes. They give page-length characterizations of the many villages not normally featured in guide books.

West, J. (1997) *Village records*, 3rd edn, Phillimore

Telephone directories

Old copies of these may be kept in your local studies library. They are useful for finding address of people in the recent past.

Trade directories

From the late 18th century until today, directories form a valuable source of local information. The amount of information varies from directory to directory, but most contain a general account of the district, details of local government, a list of streets and their residents, an alphabetical list of residents, and a classified trades section. The Post Office directories appearing from the 1880s are particularly useful. After World War 2 the Barrett directories, then the Thomson directories, continued the tradition. Check with your local studies library for details of what is available. See:

Shaw, G. and Tipper, A. (1989) *British directories: a bibliography and guide to directories published in England and Wales (1850–1950) and Scotland (1773–1950)*, Leicester University Press

Shaw, G. (ed.) *Directing the past: directories and the local historian*, British Association of local history

Waters, C. (1999) *A directory of old trades, titles and occupations*, Countryside Books

Other printed sources

Other printed sources include: local journals and magazines, newscuttings, illustrations and photographs, census enumerators' returns, local authority documents, parish and nonconformist registers (see PARISH REGISTERS), monumental inscriptions, pamphlets and leaflets.

Series such as the *Camden Society, Harleian Society, List & Index Society, The Thoresby Society* and the *Surtees Society* reprint documentary material. These are often asked for by scholars. An index to these is:

Mullins, E. L. C. (1958, 1983) *Texts and calendars: an analytic guide to serial publications*, Royal Historical Society, 2 vols
A listing of, and index to, historical serial publications of official bodies, national societies, and major local history societies.

Electronic sources

Most places have a large variety of local websites. Just type in the place name on a search engine. The BBC and local newspapers host many local web pages.

Up My Street **www.upmystreet.com**
Contemporary information by postcode.

The National Archives: **www.nationalarchives.gov.uk**
> The government site for state records formed by the amalgamation of the Public Record Office and the Historical Manuscripts Commission. Useful archives information and printable leaflets.

Borthwick Institute **www.york.ac.uk/inst/bihr**
> A centre for the north of England.

Local record searchers

A number of people offer their services to search records for a charge. Their knowledge of the location of local resources, experience of using these resources, and understanding of local history make it convenient to use their services, especially for people living away from the area. Local history libraries often have a list of local searchers, and staff know the strengths and special interests of individuals. Further record searchers may be found in the advertisement pages of journals such as *Local History Magazine, Family Tree Magazine, Genealogists Magazine* and local or regional magazines such as *The Dalesman.*

Association of Genealogists and Researchers in Archives (AGRA)
> 29 Badgers Close, Horsham, West Sussex RH12 5RU
> **www.agra.org.uk**
> AGRA provides training courses in record searching and gives accreditation to successful candidates.

British Association for Local History (BALH)
> PO Box 1576, Salisbury, Wiltshire SP2 8SY
> Fax: 01722 413242
> E-mail:info@balh.co.uk
> **www.balh.co.uk**
> BALH organize forums, visits, publication, awards, and publish *The Local Historian* (Q): articles and reviews, and *Local History News*, which includes reports of local groups, news on topical issues, and news about museums, libraries and education.

Other sources

Local history groups have knowledgeable members. It may be appropriate to refer enquirers to one of these. For details of local history groups see *The family and local history handbook*, 19th edn (2006) published by Blatchford, or contact the British

L LOCAL HISTORY

Association of Local History (mail@balh.co.uk), which has nearly 600 local history groups as members.

Local history libraries or departments and local archives and record offices have a variety of special collections, catalogues and indexes. Refer enquirers to them.

Tips and pitfalls

Many of the resources useful for local history are fragile and restrictions may be made about their use. Warn enquirers that many will also be on microfilm and microfiche.

MANUFACTURING

Typical questions

- What is the UK's manufacturing output?
- What is the state of manufacturing in xxx?

Considerations

When enquirers are asking about manufacturing make sure they understand what it is. *Kompass*, *Dun & Bradstreet's key British enterprises* and *Kelly's* all provide lists of manufacturers for all types of products. You will find details of these directories in COMPANIES. In addition, look at specific subject headings for specific sources.

Where to look

Directories

As well as the above try:

Kelly's OnLine **www.kellysearch.com**
> This covers the manufacturing industry. The enquirer can search by company name, product/services, and by country.

Statistics

Manufacturing worldwide: industry analysis statistics (1999) Gale Group
> This provides data on 500 manufactured products and commodities. It also gives details of 4000-plus companies in 119 countries.

PRODCOM annual and quarterly industry reports
> An excellent source of manufacturer sales figures, available to download from **www.statistics.gov.uk/OnlineProducts/default.asp**.

Economic and labour market trends, Producer prices indices: the economy, Manufacturing productivity, Index of manufacturing
> These are available to download at **www.statistics.gov.uk**. Then select 'Economy'.

Websites

Confederation of British Industry **www.cbi.org.uk**
> Offers numerous publications to download free. Lots of links and information on the CBI's Manufacturing Council.

BEAMA **www.beama.org.uk**
> Excellent for publications, downloads, statistics and lots more.

EEF: The Manufacturers Organisation **www.eef.org.uk**
> The voice of the engineering and manufacturing in the UK. Excellent for publications.

Heavy Industry News **www.heavyindustry.com**

Institute for Manufacturing
> Mill Lane, Cambridge CB2 1RX
> **www.ifm.eng.cam.ac.uk**
> Excellent site, including *Cambridge Manufacturing Review*, available to download freely. It is worldwide in coverage.

Manufacturing Chemist **www.manufacturingchemist.com**

MAPS

> **See also** Atlases & Gazetteers; Geography, Geology & Earth Sciences

Typical questions
- I want an Ordnance Survey map of the Yorkshire Dales.
- Have you any old maps of Bulgaria?
- Do you have a Victorian map of Plymouth?

Considerations

It is not necessary to list all the different types of maps and atlases available. Most encyclopedias contain basic maps, and as for Ordnance Survey maps, simply go and check to see what you have on the shelves. Problems are more likely to be encountered in smaller branch libraries where stock may be limited, though even here the OS Landranger maps and street atlases for their local areas should be available.

Where to look
Old maps

Most local studies departments of libraries stock old maps of their areas. Check your local studies department to see what is available.

Road maps and street atlases

Books of road and route maps are widely available, often called road atlases. At the larger scales these become street atlases. Geographia, the Ordnance Survey and the Automobile Association all publish excellent editions.

Useful address

Ordnance Survey, Romsey Road, Southampton SO16 4GU
Tel: 08456 05 05 05; Fax: 023 8079 2615
www.ordnancesurvey.co.uk

Electronic sources

You can download maps at some of the following sites:
www.mappy.com
www.old-maps.co.uk
www.multimap.co.uk
http://maps.google.co.uk

There is an excellent collection of country and historical maps at the following:

www.lib.utexas.edu/maps/index.html

Tips and pitfalls

Beware of copyright on maps, especially OS ones. As a simple rule, you are allowed to take four A4 copies of a single extract from an OS map, and these must be for private use only. OS will send you a notice if you ask them.

Local tourist offices often have free maps of the area to give away.

MARKET RESEARCH

See also European Information; Statistics

Typical questions

- I'm doing some market research on. . .
- What is the potential future trend for. . .?
- How do children spend their pocket money?

Considerations

Market research is either primary or secondary, or put another way, field or desk.

Field research is actually going out and collecting the raw data, and desk research is using printed sources of data already available. For people interested in doing field research for themselves, look no further than *Business information factsheets* for one-page easy guides. Those carrying out desk research for either a business plan or an academic project can use reports prepared by specialist market research companies or some of the vast range of statistics available. However, for those with limited access to printed sources there are lots of excellent websites to use. There is an extensive list given here, which should offer a range of free reports and surveys.

Where to look
Directories

For market research companies use:

International directory of market research organizations, a joint venture between
The Market Research Society and Norton Sterling Associates, IMRI Ltd
www.IMRIresearch.com
The website is useful for market research links.

Research buyer's guide UK and Ireland 2008. Available to search online at
www.rbg.org.uk

Books

Adams, K. and Brace.I. (2006) *An introduction to market & social research: planning & using research tools and techniques*, Kogan Page

Birn, R. (ed.) (2002) *International handbook of market research techniques*, 2nd edn, Kogan Page

Brace, I. (2004) *Questionnaire design: how to plan, structure and write survey material for effective market research*, Kogan Page

Hague. P., Hague. N. and Morgan. C. (2004) *Market research in practice: a guide to the basics*, Kogan Page

Hamersveld, M. and Bont. C. de (2007) *Market research handbook*, 5th edn, ESOMAR Publications

Global market research 2007, 19th annual industry study, ESOMAR

Market intelligence

Mintel reports, Mintel International Group

These market reports provide in-depth research. They look at market factors, market segmentation, the consumer and the future. Also available on CD-ROM. For details visit **www.mintel.co.uk** or Tel: 020 7606 4533; Fax: 020 7606 5932.

Key Note reports, Key Note

For free executive summaries of report titles visit **www.keynote.co.uk**. For details of obtaining full reports, contact Key Note (Tel: 020 8481 8750; Fax: 020 8783 0049).

Other fee-based market research companies include:

Datamonitor
Tel: 020 7675 7000
www.datamonitor.com

Euromonitor
Tel: 020 7251 8024
www.euromonitor.com

Frost and Sullivan
Tel: 020 7730 3438
www.frost.com

Websites

Cabinet Office (People's Panel) **www.cabinet-office.gov.uk**

ESOMAR **www.esomar.org**
World organization dealing with research.

Government National Statistics **www.statistics.gov.uk**

Key Note **www.keynote.co.uk**
For free executive summaries.

Major Market Profile **www.majormarketprofiles.com**
For free summaries of international market reports.

Market Research Portal **www.marketresearchworld.net**
> An excellent site offering online resources, explanations, articles, news and more. Well worth a visit.

Market Research Society
> 15 Northburgh Street, London EC1V 0JR
> Tel: 020 7490 4911
> **www.mrs.org.uk**
> Excellent website for publications, market research and links. Includes *A newcomers' guide to market and social research* to freely download, and the MRS code of conduct and guidelines.

Mori **www.mori.co.uk**
> Excellent site for reports.

Mystery Shoppers **www.mysteryshop.org**

Research Buyers Guide **www.rbg.org.uk**
> A directory of market research providers and support services.

Research Council UK **www.rcuk.ac.uk**

Research Index **www.researchindex.co.uk/data/home.htm**

Tips and pitfalls

Market research sometimes requires persistence and patience. Sometimes you can find things quickly, other times the subject area may need more time. It is important that your enquirer appreciates this. You may need to use more than one report or set of statistics to build up a picture and it is sometimes hard to get this across to enquirers. However, if you can produce something fairly quickly that provides some basic information that the user can be working on, such as *Annual abstract of statistics*, you can then feed other sources through to build up a good picture. By which time the user has settled down into 'doing research' and not hoping for a quick answer.

MEDALS & DECORATIONS

See also Antiques; Coins & Stamps; Etiquette & Forms of Address; Uniforms

Typical questions

- I found this medal when sorting through some junk. What is it?
- Have you a list of winners of the Victoria Cross?
- What are these medals worth?

Considerations

Distinguish between enquiries that have a family connection, such as where a medal was awarded to an ancestor, and those about militaria and memorabilia. They need different treatment.

Among the current generation, knowledge of campaign and war medals is generally poor, and answering questions on the subject perhaps distasteful. However, the librarian must bear in mind that decorations were worn with pride and often represented great courage and sacrifice. One must be aware of the attitudes and context of the time when the medals and decorations were awarded, and for what they were awarded.

Medals and other commemorative objects extend into other areas of public service, and beyond, into the field of 'collectables'.

Where to look

General

Buckland, C. *The medal yearbook*, Pen and Sword
  Guide for medal collectors, giving prices and availability.

Clarke, J. D. (2001) *Gallantry medals and decorations of the world*, Pen and Sword
  270 decorations for 43 countries. Includes ribbons.

Holmes, R. (ed.) (2001) *The Oxford companion to military history*, Leo Cooper

The London Gazette, HMSO. Weekly
  The official government publication where awards are announced and citations given. These details will get reported in national and relevant local newspapers.

Biographical sources

Honoured by the Queen: recipients of honours (1995) Belgrave Press
   Lists some 200,000 people honoured 1952–94.

Commemoratives and non-service

Eimer, C. (1989) *An introduction to commemorative medals*, Seaby

Setchfield, F. R. (1986) *The official badge collector's guide*, Longman
   Hobby badges rather than medals. The 'official' designation is surely
   'tongue-in-cheek'!

Gordon, L. L. (1979) *British battles and medals*, 5th edn, Spink
   Covers 18th to 20th centuries.

Arlsby, C. (1989) *Allied combat medals of World War II. Volume 1: the British, the
   Commonwealth and Western European nations*, P Stephens Ltd

Description and identification

Abbott, P. E. and Tamblin, T. A. (1971) *British gallantry awards*, Guinness
   Superlatives

Churchill, C. and Westlike, R. (1986) *British army collar badges, 1881 to the
   present: an illustrated reference guide for collectors*, Arms & Armour Press

Davis, B. L. (1988) *British army cloth insignia, 1940 to the present: an illustrated
   reference guide for collectors*, 2nd edn, Arms and Armour Publications

Dorling, H. T. (1983) *Ribbons and medals*, 20th edn, Osprey

Gaylor, J. (1996) *Military badge collecting*, Leo Cooper

Hieronymussen, P. (1975) *Orders, medals and decorations of Britain and Europe*,
   2nd edn, Blandford Press

Joslin, E. C. et al. (1988) *British battles and medals: a full list from 1588*, Spink

Kipling, A. L. and King, H. I. (1978) *Head-dress badges of the British army*, 2nd
   edn, P. Muller

Mericka, V. (1976) *Book of orders and decorations*, Hamlyn
   Gives background.

Ripley, H. (1976) *Buttons of the British army 1855–1970: an illustrated reference guide for collectors*, Arms and Armour Press
Updated price guides issued from time to time.

Shortt, J. G. (1988) *Special forces insignia, British and Commonwelth units: an illustrated reference guide for collectors*, Sterling Press

Wilkinson, F. (1992) *Badges of the British army, 1820 to the present: an illustrated guide for collectors*, Arms and Armour Press

Etiquette

Tinson, A. R. (1999) *'Medals will be worn.' Wearing medals past and present, 1844–1999*, Token Publishing

Prices and valuations

Arden, Y. (1976) *Military medals and decorations: a price guide for collectors*, David & Charles

Litherland, A. R. and Simpkin, B. T. (1990) *Spink's standard catalogue of British and associated orders, decorations and medals, with valuations*, Spink

Victoria Cross

Arthur, M. (2004) *Symbols of courage: a complete history of the Victoria Cross*, Sidgwick & Jackson

Harvey, D. (2001) *Monuments to courage*, 2 vols, distributed by Pat M. da Costa, 124 Oatlands Drive, Weybridge Drive, Surrey KT13 9HL
Fully illustrated guide to each of the 1350 VCs.

The register of the Victoria Cross (1988) 2nd edn, Beshara Press
Gives brief details and photographs of recipients.

Other sources

Pen and Sword **www.pen-and-sword.co.uk**
Specialist publisher website; includes Leo Cooper books.

Orders and Medals Research Society
PO Box 248, Snettisham, Kings Lynn PE31 7TA
www.omrs.org.uk

Spink and Son Medal Service
   69 Southampton Row, London WC1B 4ET
   E-mail: info@spinkandson.com
   www.spink-online.com
   Commercial dealer.

Tips and pitfalls

The usual librarianly caveat about giving advice and opinion applies, particularly to the enquiries: 'What's this worth?' and 'What's this?'

MEDIA & THE PRESS

See also Books & Bibliographies; Journals & Periodicals; Newspapers & Magazines; Publishing; Television & Radio

Typical questions

• Can you advise me in which papers to place an advert?
• I want to publicize my new book. Which sources are best?

Considerations

The term 'media' covers a large variety of publications, printed, broadcast and electronic, so do check the *see also* headings above. Advertising and public relations also relate to the subject. This is a volatile commercial topic and there is a danger – a certainty almost – that much information is out of date as soon as it is printed. Do check websites.

Note also that 'media' can refer to the various formats in which data can be stored, such as film, video, sound recording and computer discs. See Schopflin, K. (ed.) (2008) *A handbook for media librarians*, Facet Publishing.

Where to look
General

Crone, T. M. (2002) *Law and the media*, 4th edn, Focal Press

Barendt, E. and Hitchen, L. (2000) *Media law: cases and materials*, Longman

Balnaves, M. et al. (2001) *The global media atlas*, British Film Institute
   Over 50 colour maps with commentary showing the global diffusion of old and new media – print, phones, film, internet, etc.

Hansen, B. (1997) *The dictionary of multimedia terms and acronyms*, Fitzroy
  Dearborn

Media UK **www.mediauk.com**
  Independent media directory for the UK. Covers radio stations, TV
  channels, newspapers and magazines.

Orlebar, J. (2003) *The practical media dictionary*, Arnold

Smith, C. and Crewdson, S. (eds) *Media issues*, Independence Publishing
  Vol. 142 in the *Issues* series reprinting significant articles from the press.

Directories

Bell, E. and Alden, C., *Media directory*, Media Guardian. Annual
  Contacts and feature articles

*Benn's media: the guide to newspapers, periodicals, television, radio and on-line
  media*, CMP Information. Annual.
  4-volume listing of media that accepts advertising (v.1: UK; v.2: Europe;
  v.3: North America; v.4: World).

BRAD (British Rate and Data): monthly guide to advertising media, Emap
  Information
  A media information database containing over 13,500 entries for
  advertising media from magazines and newspapers to radio stations and
  websites. Gives rates.

Gale directory of publications and broadcast media, Thomson Gale. Annual

Hollis media guide, Hollis.Publishing. 2 p.a.
  Contact details and profiles on 10,000 UK media titles: newspapers,
  magazines, TV, radio and online.

Hollis UK, press & public relations annual, Hollis Publishing
  Over 20,000 contacts in government, official bodies and PR consultancies.
  Also available as a subscription website.

Hollis UK public relations annual, Hollis Publishing
  Information on in-house contacts at 10,000 commercial and public
  organisations, plus public and government relations consultancies and key
  media contacts at major newspapers, TV and radio.

Peak, S. *The Guardian media guide*, Guardian Books. Annual
  Over 10,000 media contacts.

Watson, J. and Hill, A. (2003) *Directory of media and communication studies*, 6th edn, Hodder/Headline

Willings press guide, Waymaker Ltd, 3 vols. Annual
Available as a subscription website at **www.willingspress.com**. Includes advertising rates.

Other sources

Media Wise **www.mediawise.org.uk**
Considers and advises on complaints against the press.

National Media Museum (formerly National Museum of Photography, Film and Television)
Bradford BD1 1NQ
Tel: 01274 202030; Fax: 01274 723155
www.nationalmediamuseum.org.uk

National Union of Journalists **www.nuj.org.uk**

Ofcom (Office of Communications) **www.ofcom.org.uk**

MEDICINES & DRUGS

See also Health & Healthcare

Typical questions

- What are the side effects if I take xxx?
- I want to learn more about the medicine that my doctor has prescribed me.
- What does 'street drugs' mean?

Considerations

Many people like to check the drugs they have been given to see what is in them and what effects they may have. It is common practice nowadays to include information leaflets with prescribed drugs. But the enquirer may want an independent point of view.

Where to look
General sources

There are several useful reference books that cover this topic. Try and make sure you have something similar to:

Henry, J. (ed.) (2007) *BMA new guide to medicines and drugs: medicines*, Dorling Kindersley Publishers
This is a home reference guide to 2500 medicines.

For much more in-depth information the BNF is essential:

British national formulary, British Medical Association and Royal Pharmaceutical Society of Great Britain
Provides current information about the use of medicines.

British national formulary for children, British Medical Association and Royal Pharmaceutical Society of Great Britain **http://bnf.org/bnf**
Information on the safe and effective use of medicines to treat childhood disorders covering newborns to adolescents.

British pharmacopoeia 2008, TSO. Annual
www.pharmacopoeia.co.uk
The official UK standard for medicines.

European pharmacopoeia, 2 vols, Council of Europe – European directorate for the quality of medicines

Websites

It is probably best to bookmark a few reputable UK websites from trusted sources. Many sites are US in origin and carry a note of caution for UK users. The following should cover most if not all enquiries:

Electronic Medicines Compendium **http://emc.medicines.org.uk**
Allows you to search by brand name, generic name, company's name or a specific word of phrase. Provides summaries of product characteristics and patient information leaflets. Well worth a visit.

Health Supplements Information Service **www.hsis.org**
Information on vitamins, minerals and food supplements. A–Z factsheets.

Medicine Chest **www.medicine-chest.co.uk**
A directory of medicines and food supplements available over the counter.

Medicines and Healthcare Products Regulatory Agency
www.mhra.gov.uk/index.htm
An executive agency of the Department of Health, to safeguard the health of the public by ensuring medicines and medical devices work.

National Pharmaceutical Association **www.npa.co.uk**

NHS Direct **www.nhsdirect.nhs.uk**
Click on 'Health encyclopedia'. Then 'Medicines'.

Patient UK **www.patient.co.uk/dils.asp**
803 leaflets on specific medicines and drugs, with alphabetical arrangement.

Royal Pharmaceutical Society **www.rpsgb.org**

UK Medicines Information **www.ukmi.nhs.uk**

Illegal drugs

For queries on illegal or street drugs check your library shelves to see what you have on the subject or try the following:

Emmett, D. and Nice. G. (2005) *Understanding street drugs: a handbook of substance misuse for parents, teachers and other professionals*, Jessica Kingsley Publishers

Forsyth, A. J. M. (2000) *Psychoactive drugs: the street pharmacopoeia*, The Stationery Office

Websites

There are some excellent sites which may be worth bookmarking.

Childline **www.childline.org.uk**
Click on 'More Info', then 'Damaging Yourself', then 'Drugs'.

Drug Information database **www.uksport.gov.uk**

Drugs **http://drugs.homeoffice.gov.uk**
Excellent. Well worth a visit.

Drugscope **www.drugscope.org.uk**
Excellent. Well worth a visit.

Live Well **www.nhs.uk/LiveWell/Drugs**
Advice and articles.

Know the Score **www.knowthescore.info**
Information and advice on drugs in Scotland.

Release (for legal information) **www.release.org.uk**
   Advise on drug use and associated legal matters.

Street Drugs Names **www.drugrehab.co.uk/street-drug-names.htm**

Tips and pitfalls

Remember not to advise the enquirer about specific medicines. Guide them only in the direction of the relevant books or publications. Try to make sure these are up to date. If a user wants advice, refer them to their doctor or chemist. For organizations that deal with drug addiction check the directories listed in ASSOCIATIONS & ORGANIZATIONS and use your local telephone directories. It is worth knowing some local organizations and keeping their details up to date. This can be an emotive enquiry area either from drug addiction or through serious illness; the secret is to be patient, offer reliable sources of information and show consideration. This is an area where it is essential to make the enquirer feel at ease.

MEMBERS OF PARLIAMENT

See also Election Results; Government

Typical questions
- Who is my local MP?
- Can you give me the address of my local MP?
- What is the name of the Education Secretary?
- Who is my MEP?

Where to look
Directories

Dod's parliamentary companion 2006, Vacher Dod Publishing
   This provides an alphabetical listing of all MPs, giving for each their age, education, marital status and details of their parliamentary career. It includes contact details both in the constituency the MP represents and at the House of Commons. In addition it lists alphabetically all the constituencies in the UK in order to locate the MP for that area. Also gives an alphabetical listing of the members of the House of Lords.

Vacher's Parliamentary profiles, Vacher Dod Publishing
   Detailed profiles of all UK MPs.

M MEMBERS OF PARLIAMENT

Contacting an MP

MPs deal with enquiries and concerns from their constituents. If the enquirer does not know the constituency in which they live, the internet service Constituency Locator is a must:

www.locata.co.uk/commons

Enquirers can write to their MP's office at:

House of Commons
London SW1A 0AA

For ex- or deceased MPs try:

Stenton, M. and Lees, S. (eds) (1981) *Who's who of British Members of Parliament 1832–1979*, 4 vols, Harvester Press

In addition you could try *Who was who* or *Who's who*.

Other sources

Rush, M. (2001) *Role of the Members of Parliament since 1868*, Oxford University Press

Register of Members' Interests
www.publications.parliament.uk/pa/cm/cmregmem.htm

The code of conduct together with the guide to the rules relating to the conduct of members **www.publications.parliament.uk/pa/cm/cmpocrules.htm**

Jacobs, F., Corbett, R. and Shackleton, M. (2007) *The European Parliament*, John Harper Publishing

Websites

Europarl **www.europarl.org.uk**
Another excellent site for everything to do with the European Parliament including MEPs.

Political Links **www.politicallinks.co.uk**
Published by Vacher Dod Publishing. This is an excellent site. You won't need anything else to answer questions on parliament and politicians.

Another useful site is:

FaxYourMP.com **www.faxyourmp.com**
> By inputting your postcode this site lets you know the name of your MP, councillor, MEP, MSP or Northern Ireland, Welsh or London Assembly member.

MONEY

See also Coins & Stamps; Prices

Typical questions

- What is the euro exchange rate against the dollar?
- What currency is used in Poland?
- What was £1 worth 20 years ago?

Where to look
Directories

If you are looking for details on monetary units and denominations for any country in the world look no further than the website of

Economist **www.economist.com**
> Click on 'Markets & Data' for currencies of the world, converter and exchange rates.

For information on the euro, look no further than:

Euro Information: the Official Treasury Euro Resources **www.euro.gov.uk**
> This is an excellent, informative site. It provides pictures of the notes and coins. It also has lots of publications which can be downloaded.

For information on the history of money try:

Davies, G. (2005) *A history of money from ancient times to the present day,* Julian Hodge Bank Ltd

Statistics

For notes and coins in circulation use *Annual Abstract of Statistics*, ONS.

Financial Times. Daily
> World currencies listed on Monday.

Investors Chronicle. Weekly

Exchange rates can be found in the Statistics section.

Old Money: Current Value

www.projects.ex.ac.uk/RDavies/arian/current/howmuch.html
An excellent and fascinating website. Even if you haven't got an enquiry it is well worth a visit. Packed with information and links.

Purchasing power of British Pound **www.measuringworth.com**
Excellent, just type in amount, original year and desired year.

Banknotes of different countries (in the past and now)

www.geocities.com/prysjan/in_91.html

The state of the nation's savings 2007/2008, available free to download at:

www.abi.org.uk/Bookshop/default.asp

To search for your lost money use the Unclaimed Assets Register **www.uar.co.uk**. This is a search service that helps you find your lost assets and re-establish contact with financial institutions.

Journals

The Economist

The Economist Newspaper
Tel: 020 7839 2968
www.economist.com
Weekly
Gives currency and exchange rates.

Moneyfacts

Moneyfacts Group
Tel: 0845 1689689
www.moneyfacts.co.uk
Monthly
A guide to the UK savings and mortgage rates.

Money Management

FT Magazine
Monthly
www.ftadviser.com

Websites

Currency Converter **www.iccfx.com**

Current Exchange Rates **www.oanda.com**
Allows you to convert from any currency to any currency.

MUSEUMS & GALLERIES

See also Art & Design, The Arts; Tourism & Travel

Typical questions

- What are the opening hours and charges of Tate Modern?
- Which exhibitions are on at the Lowry Centre in Salford at the moment?

Considerations

Most main libraries should have a directory of museums, showing opening hours, charges, etc. For up-to-date information regarding current exhibitions, though, the internet is ideal.

Where to look
Printed sources

Museums of the world (2002) 9th edn, K. G. Saur
A brief description of 42,000 museums in 200 countries.

Museums yearbook, Museums Association. Annual
Contains a directory of museums, listing museums alphabetically by town. Information includes admission charges, opening hours and facilities. There is also a listing of members of the Museums Association and a directory of related organizations, e.g. suppliers.

Redington, C. (2002) *A guide to the small museums of Britain*, I. B. Tauris

Reynard, K. W. (2003) *Directory of museums, galleries and buildings of historic interest in the United Kingdom*, 3rd edn, Europa
3255 entries.

Collections in museums, galleries and historic houses, Tomorrow's Guides Ltd. Annual
Details of over 1600 museums, art galleries and historic houses in the UK. Online version at **www.mghh.co.uk**.

Electronic sources

There is a huge listing of UK museums by area at:

www.24hourmuseum.org.uk
You can also search this site for specific collections.

For world museums try:

http://Vlmp.museophile.com/world.html#museums

For news, contacts and links from the Museums Association, try their website:

www.museumsassociation.org

Tips and pitfalls

If your enquirer is looking for details of a particular museum and its current exhibitions, simply use a search engine on the internet and type in the name of the museum.

MUSIC

Typical questions

- How much are these records worth?
- How can I buy an old record?
- When was Bill Haley's 'Rock around the clock' a hit?
- How many number ones did Elvis Presley have?
- What's the story behind *Die Fledermaus*?

Considerations

The literature of music is huge. The subject is huge. Most general enquiries about composers and music history can be answered from the many, many general dictionaries and encyclopedias.

Occasionally, a knowledge of music notation is required. Know which members of staff have this knowledge. It is also useful to know the musical tastes of staff. Downloading performances via the internet is not considered here, nor indeed the supply of different musical media, print, audio or video, for loan or in-house listening or viewing.

Where to look
General

The new Grove dictionary of music and musicians (2001) 2nd edn, Grove Music
This is the standard 'biggie' 29-volume classic resource. There is an online version **www.grovemusic.com** of the texts of the *New Grove dictionary of music and musicians*, the *New Grove dictionary of opera*, and the *New Grove dictionary of jazz*. This is a subscription service available in many libraries.

Chambers dictionary of music (2006) Chambers

Griffiths, P. (2006) *A concise history of Western music*, Cambridge University Press

Latham, A. (ed.) (2002) *The Oxford companion to music*, Oxford University Press

Latham, A. (ed.) (2004) *The Oxford dictionary of musical terms*, Oxford University Press

Harrap's illustrated dictionary of music and musicians (1990) Harrap

Jacobs, A. (1996) *Dictionary of music*, 6th edn, Penguin

Kennedy, M. (2006) *Oxford dictionary of music*, 5th edn, Oxford University Press

Kennedy, M. (1994) *Oxford guide to music*, 2nd edn, Oxford University Press

Music Search **www.musicsearch.com**
A search engine for music.

Musicians' & songwriters' yearbook, A&C Black

Nettle, B. and others (2003) *Garland encyclopedia of world music*, Routledge
A 10-volume heavyweight.

New Oxford history of music (1974) 11 vols, Oxford University Press

Randel, D. M. (ed.) (2003) *The Harvard dictionary of music*, Harvard University Press

Sadie, S. (ed.) (1985) *The Cambridge music guide*, Cambridge University Press
Chapter-length essays with detailed index.

Baker's biographical dictionary of musicians (2001) 9th edn, Gale
A six-volume heavyweight containing over 41,000 addresses.

International music directory 2004/2005, K G Saur
> A two-volume successor to the *European music directory*. Covers orchestras, choirs, theatres, concert management and promotion agencies, educational institutions, libraries, research, etc.

Contemporary musicians

Cummings, D. M. (ed.) *International who's who in music and musician's directory*, vol. 1: *Classical and light classical fields*, International Biographical Centre. Bi-annual

Gregory, A. (2003) *International who's who in popular music*, 5th edn, Europa

Festivals

Adams, R. (1986) *A book of British music festivals*, R. Royce

Instruments

Examples are:

Coelho, V. A. (ed.) (2003) *Cambridge companion to the guitar*, Cambridge University Press

Palmieri, R. and M. W. (2003) *Piano: an encyclopedia*, 2nd edn, Routledge

Price guides

Hamlyn, N. (1997) *The Penguin price guide for records and CD collectors*, Penguin
> Over 14,000 valuations.

Pelletier, P. (ed.) (1991) *The essential British price guide to collecting 45/78 rpm singles 1950–1960*, Record Information Services

Record Collector (2000) *Rare record collector*, Record Collector
> Over 100,000 entries.

Publishing

Music publishers international ISMN directory (2000) 3rd edn, K G Saur

Recordings

Penguin guide to compact discs (1999) Penguin

Classical good CD guide, Gramophone Publications. Annual

Songs and lyrics

Amin, K. and Cochrane, J. (1986) *The great British songbook*, Faber

Lax, R. and Smith, F. (1989) *The great song thesaurus*, 2nd edn, Oxford University Press

Lyrics **www.lyrics.com**
Words to pop songs.

Kennedy, P. (ed.) (1975) *Folksongs of Britain and Ireland*, Oak Publications
A classic heavyweight collection of folksongs.

Reed, W. L. and Bristow, M. J. (eds) (1985) *National anthems of the world*, 6th edn, Blandford Press

Popular American songs (2001) 10 vols, Gale

The rock song index: essential information on the 7,500 most important songs of rock and roll (1997) Schirner Reference

Song File **www.songfile.com**
Lyrics to pop music.

Themes

Barlour, H. and Morgenstern, S. (eds) (1970) *A dictionary of musical themes*, Benn
Classical music; requires knowledge of music notation.

Barlour, H. and Morgenstern, S. (eds) (1956) *A dictionary of vocal themes*, Benn

Gelfand, S. (1994) *Television theme recordings: an illustrated discography 1951–1994*, Popular Culture Ink.
Gives details of the original music.

Titles

Room, A. (ed.) (2000) *A dictionary of music titles: the origin of the names and titles of 3,500 musical compositions*, McFarland

Types of music
Blues

Russell, T. (1998) *The Blues*, Gale

MUSIC

Blues **www.bluesworld.com**

Classical

Griffiths, P. (ed.) (2005) *Penguin companion to classical music*, Penguin

Henley, D. (2006) *Classic FM: the friendly guide to music*, Hodder Arnold
A popular guide for the novice. Includes a listing of music used in films.

International music directory (2004/2005) K G Saur
Over 35,000 entries with emphasis on classical music

International who's who in music and musician's directory (2002) 17th edn, Melrose
Covers classical and light classical music.

Head, L. (ed.) *British and international music yearbook*, Rheingold. Annual
A two-volume directory of the classical music industry.

Staines, J. (ed.) (2005) *The Rough Guide to classical music*, Rough Guides

Classicalmusic **www.classicalmusic.co.uk**
Articles, news, guides and concert listings.

Classic FM Magazine (Monthly) Haymarket **www.classicfm.co.uk**
Includes details of up-coming concerts and events.

The Gramophone (Monthly) Haymarket **www.gramophone.co.uk**
Published since 1923 for the classical record industry.

Country

Kingsbury, P. (ed.) (2005) *The encyclopedia of country music*, 2nd edn, Oxford
University Press

Stambler, I. and Landon, G. (2000) *Country music – the encyclopedia*, Griffin

Jazz

Kernfeld, B. (ed.) (2001) *The new Grove dictionary of jazz*, 3 vols, 2nd edn,
Grove Music

Kirchner, B. (ed.) (2000) *Oxford companion to jazz*, 2nd edn, Oxford University
Press

New Grove dictionary of jazz (1992) 2nd edn
www.grovemusic.com

Shipton, A. (2001) *A new history of jazz*, Continuum

Jazz Online **www.jazzonln.com**

Jazze.com **www.jazze.com**

Jazz Corner **www.jazzcorner.com**

Light

Ganzel, K. (ed.) (2001) *Encyclopedia of musical theatre*, 2nd edn, Gale

Opera

Bogden, M. (2007) *The Rough Guide to opera*, Rough Guides

Forman, D. (1994) *The good opera guide*, Phoenix

Harewood, Earl of, and Peattie, A. (eds) (1997) *The new Kobbé's opera book*, 11th edn, Putnam

Henley, D. and Lihoreau, T. (2005) *Classic ephemera*, Boosey & Hawkes
Classical music facts, stories and trivia.

International dictionary of opera (1993) 2 vols, St James Press

New Grove dictionary of opera (1992) Oxford University Press, 4 vols

Operadata: **www.operadata.co.uk**
Listings and background.

See also **www.opera.co.uk**

Popular music

Clarke, D. (ed.) (1989) *The Penguin encyclopedia of popular music*, Viking

Grammond, P. (1991) *The Oxford companion to popular music*, Oxford University Press

Hardy, P. and Laing, D. (1990) *The Faber companion to 20th century popular music*, Faber

Jeffries, S. (2003) *Encyclopedia of world pop music, 1980–2001*, Greenwood Press

Larkin, C. (ed.) (1997) *The Virgin encyclopedia of popular music*, Virgin

Larkin, C. (ed.) *Guinness encyclopedia of popular music*, Guiness World Records, 6 vols

Larkin, C. (ed.) (1998) *Encyclopedia of popular music*, Palgrave Macmillan, 8 vols

The encyclopedia of popular music, 3rd edn, Macmillan
Eight-volume compendium of biographies, genre articles and information on musicals, record companies, song index (50,000 titles), fanzines and bibliographies.

Larkin, C. (1998) *The Virgin encyclopedia of dance music*, Virgin

International who's who in music, Vol. 2: pop music (2000) 3rd edn, Melrose

Clickmusic **www.clickmusic.co.uk**
Gives details of bands, gigs and groups.

Ultimate Band List **www.ubl.com**
Huge database of groups and singles.

VirginMega **www.virginmega.com**
One of many useful retailer sites with large listings.

Pop charts

Roberts, D. et al. (2000) *British hit singles*, 14th edn, Guinness Publications

Bronson, F. (1997) *The Billboard book of number one hits*, 4th edn, Billboard Publications

Gambaccini, P. (ed.) (1992) *Top 40 charts*, Guinness Publications

Rice, T. (ed.) (1986) *Guinness British hit albums*, Guinness Publications

Warwick, N., Kutner, J. and Brown, T. (2004) *The complete British charts: singles and albums*, 3rd edn, Omnibus Press

Whitburn, J. (2000) *The Billboard book of USA top 40 hits*, 7th edn, Billboard Publications

The complete book of the British charts (2004) 3rd edn, Omnibus Press

Rock

The Rough Guide to rock (1999) 2nd edn, Rough Guides

Stambler, I. (1980) *The encyclopedia of pop, rock and soul*, Macmillan

Tips and pitfalls

Get to know the taste in music of your fellow staff. Help for librarians dealing with music can be obtained from the International Association of Music Librarians (IAML) **www.iaml-uk.org**.

MYTHS & MYTHOLOGY

See also Fairy Tales & Nursery Rhymes

Typical questions

- Who was the Roman god of love?
- I want to know more about the Norse god Odin.

Considerations

This subject area is relatively straightforward and should not cause too many problems. The more obscure mythologies are the most difficult to find information about.

Where to look
Printed sources

There are many sources to turn to here. There are the basic encyclopedias which cover the more common myths, and more specialized ones concentrating solely on the subject. An excellent text is:

Coulter, C. R. and Turner, P. (2000) *Encyclopedia of ancient deities*, Fitzroy
    Dearborn

You can also try some of the other standard references if you do not have the above:

Willis, R. (2000) *Dictionary of world myth*, Duncan Baird

Cotterell, A. (2008) *Encyclopedia of mythology*, Anness

Leeming, D. (2005) *Oxford companion to world mythology*, Oxford University
    Press.

Most enquiries will be about the more common mythologies, such as Greek, Roman, etc. and most libraries should have individual texts on these mythologies.

Electronic sources

There is an excellent resource at:

Encyclopedia Mythica **www.pantheon.org**
    This should be the only site you will need!

NAMES

See also Pseudonyms

Typical questions
- Have you got a book about the meanings of Christian names?
- I am trying to find out where the name Skipton originates from.

Considerations
You can generally split this area into three subjects: the meaning of place names, the meaning of surnames, and the meaning of first names. Enquirers may be researching a place, doing their family tree, or choosing a name for their baby.

Where to look
Printed sources
There are no general encyclopedias that will cover these subjects. You will need to look at more specialist dictionaries.

People's names
For first names there are several useful texts available:

Cresswell, J. (1990) *Bloomsbury dictionary of first names*, Bloomsbury

Dunkling, L. and Gosling, W. (1983) *Everyman's dictionary of first names*, Everyman Reference.

*Hanks, P. and Hodges, F. (1990) *A dictionary of first names*, Oxford University Press

For surnames, two of the best books available are:

*Hanks, P. and Hodges, F. (1988) *A dictionary of surnames*, Oxford University Press

Reaney, P. H. (1991) *A dictionary of English surnames*, 3rd edn by R. M. Wilson, Routledge

*These titles have been partially incorporated into Hanks, P. et al. (2002) *The Oxford names companion*, Oxford University Press.

There are also many books available about names around the world and their meanings. For example there are books on Welsh, Scottish, Irish, Muslim, Jewish and African names.

Place names

Try the following titles for British place names:

Mills, A. D. (2003) *A dictionary of British place-names*, 2nd edn, Oxford University Press

Room, A. (1988) *Dictionary of place-names in the British Isles*, Bloomsbury

For world place names, the following is a good bet. It covers over 1000 of the world's more familiar place names:

Room, A. (1987) *Place-names of the world*, Angus and Robertson

Electronic sources

An excellent site for first names is:

Behind the Name: the etymology and history of first names
www.behindthename.com

For last names try:

www.last-names.net

NATIONALITY & IMMIGRATION

See also Law

Typical questions

- How do I get a passport?
- On what grounds can an overseas national qualify to be British?
- Is 'English' a nationality?

Considerations

This subject is one to treat carefully. While, rightly, library staff must be wary of getting too involved in personal cases, enquiries may just be for student projects. There may also be language difficulties, and not just foreign languages. The differences within English can be a problem: thus describing someone as an 'immigrant', or an 'alien', or even 'English' rather than 'British', can cause unintended offence.

Be ready with other sources of referral such as local Social Services departments, Citizens Advice Bureaux, law centres, Home Office, and local solicitors' phone numbers. Many solicitors and agencies specialize in nationality matters.

Where to look
General

Firth, L. (ed.) (2007) *Citizenship and national identity*, Independence Publishers
Vol. 131 in the *Issues* series of booklets reprinting recent articles from the press.

Moving Here **www.movinghere.org.uk**
Historical website documenting 200 years of migration to England.

Shah, P. A. (2000) *Refugees, race, and the legal concept of asylum in Britain*, Cavendish Press

Practical advice

Chatwin, M. (ed.) (1999) *Immigration, nationality and refugee law handbook: a user's guide*, Joint Council for the Welfare of Immigrants

Halsbury's laws of England, Vol. 18, Part 2, Butterworths
Look under 'Foreign Relations – Law – Nationality'.

Home Office, Immigration and Nationality Directorate
www.ind.homeoffice.gov.uk
Useful current information. Includes asylum seeking.

Jones, R. (1994) *How to emigrate: your complete guide to a successful future overseas*, How To Books

Macdonald, I. A. and Blake, N. J. (1995) *Immigration law and practice in the United Kingdom*, 4th edn, Butterworths.
900-page legal textbook.

Migration and social security handbook (2007) 4th edn, CPAG

Parliament *Immigration and Asylum Act 1999*, The Stationery Office

Phelan, M. (2001) *Immigration law handbook*, 2nd edn, Blackstone Press

Radar: refugee resources in the UK 2003, Refugee Council
A CD-ROM directory for organizations providing services for refugees and asylum seekers.

Refugee Council Information service (annual) *An information survival kit for public and voluntary sector employees working with refugees and asylum seekers* Looseleaf format available on annual subscription.

Seddon, D. (2002) *Migration and social security handbook*, 3rd edn, CPAG

Citizenship

Citizenship Foundation **www.citizenshipfoundation.org.uk**

Home Office (2007) *Life in the United Kingdom*, 2nd edn, The Stationary Office
Official handbook for the *Life in the UK* citizenship test.

Passports and visas

The UK Passport Service, an agency of the Home Office, provides a website to assist new applicants and existing passport holders who are British nationals:

www.ukpa.gov.uk
Tel: 0870 521 0410

The Foreign and Commonwealth Office provides a website giving information about visas and obtaining a UK passport while overseas:

www.fco.gov.uk

Race and multiculturalism

Cashmore, E. (2004) *Encyclopedia or race and ethnic studies*, Routledge

Commission for Racial Equality **www.cre.gov.uk**

Institute of Race Relations **www.irr.org.uk**

Kenrick, D. (2007) *Historical dictionary of the gypsies (Romanies)*, 2nd edn, Scarecrow Press

Other sources

Office of the Immigration Services Commissioner (OISC)
6th Floor, Fleetbank House, 2–6 Salisbury Square, London EC4Y 8JX

Tel: 020 7211 1500; Fax: 020 7211 1553
www.oisc.org.uk

Immigration Advisory Service
Tel: 020 7378 9191
24-hour service for people who have been refused asylum or have immigration problems.

Immigration Law Practitioners' Association
Lindsey House, 40–42 Charterhouse Street, London EC1M 6JN
Tel: 020 7251 8383; Fax: 020 7251 8384
E-mail: info@ilpa.org.uk
www.ilpa.org.uk (includes a directory of practitioners).

Refugee Council
3 Bondway, London SW8 1SJ
Tel: 020 7820 3000; Fax: 020 7582 9929
E-mail: info@refugeecouncil.org.uk
www.refugeecouncil.org.uk

Tips and pitfalls

Check *which* nationality is of concern before rowing up the wrong creek! Terminology is vital here: immigration vs emigration; refugee vs asylum.

NATURAL HISTORY

See also Animals, Pets & Vets; Birds; Gardens, Gardening & Flowers; Environment & Green Issues

Typical questions

- What's the difference between an ash tree and a willow?
- Have you a picture of Tyranosaurus Rex?
- Is there a local naturalist club?

Considerations

The term 'natural history' covers a vast number of subjects, from dinosaurs to evolution, and queries range from the need to identify specimens to their environmental context. There is a need for good quality illustrated books, such as the pocket-sized ones published by Collins and the larger ones published by

Dorling Kindersley. General encyclopedias and search engines will be the main resources. Do clarify the aim of the enquiry and the level of expertise of the enquirer.

Where to look
General

Allaby, N. (ed.) *The Oxford dictionary of natural history*, Oxford University Press

Collins complete guide to British wildlife (1997) Collins

Oxford Reference Online **www.oxfordreference.com**
   This popular subscription service has a selection of reference books on natural history.

Biology

Cambridge dictionary of human biology and evolution (2004) Cambridge
   University Press
   13,000 terms, specimens, sites and names.

Botany: plants and trees

Allaby, M. (2006) *A dictionary of plant science*, Oxford University Press

Johnson, O. and Moore, D. (2004) *Collins tree guide: Britain and Europe*,
   HarperCollins

Sterry, P. (2007) *Collins complete guide to British trees*, Collins

Woodland Trust
   Autumn Park, Dysart Road, Grantham, Lincolnshire NG31 6LL
   Purchases threatened woodland and protects it for future generations; creates new native woods and encourages public understanding and enjoyment of the country's woodland heritage; lobbys Government to give threatened woodland better protection.

Dinosaurs

Fastovsky, D. E. and Weishampel, D. B. (2004) *The evolution and extinction of
   dinosaurs*, 2nd edn, Cambridge University Press
   A popular standard text.

Ecology

Allaby, M. (ed.) (2005) *A dictionary of ecology*, 3rd edn, Oxford University Press

Evolution and genetics

Reeve, E. C. R. (2001) *Encyclopedia of genetics*, Fitzroy Dearborn

Ragel, M. (ed.) (2002) *Encyclopedia of evolution*, Oxford University Press

Insects

New encyclopedia of insects and their allies (2002) Oxford University Press

Capinera, J. L. (ed.) (2004) *Encyclopedia of entomology*, Kluwer Academic

Resh, V. H. and Cardé, R. (2002) *Encyclopedia of insects*, Academic Press

Reptiles

New encyclopedia of reptiles and amphibians (2002) Oxford University Press

NEWSPAPERS & MAGAZINES

See also Journals & Periodicals; Media & The Press

Typical questions

* Have you got last week's *Times*?
* Where can I get a copy of a Polish paper?
* What newspapers cover Tamworth, and where can I get them?
* Where can I get an issue of a paper from when my father was born?

Considerations

Newspapers are one of the most important of information resources and getting hold of newspapers a frequent requirement. Sometimes what is wanted is the account of an event in the past; sometimes the enquirer has been given a particular reference. Few libraries keep newspapers for more than a few weeks unless they are local. In the latter case the local studies library is the place to refer people to. Few newspaper offices keep their own papers for long and tend to refer people to the local library. Advising people how they can get hold of papers the library does not have is a common task. Many subscription websites are available, both for individual titles, and jointly. Check what your library has.

Where to look

Directories

Willings press guide, Waymaker Ltd. 3 vols. Annual
Newspaper and magazine listings.
Available online at **www.willingspress.com**

See also *Benn's media* and *BRAD* in the chapter on MEDIA & THE PRESS.

The Paperboy **www.thepaperboy.com**
Lists newspapers from around the world.

General

Keeble, R. (2001) *The newspapers handbook*, 3rd edn, Routledge

Locations

Finding back numbers of newspapers is a common need and hard to resolve. The British Library has the largest collection:

www.bl.uk/collections/newspaper/newscat.html

Local newspaper offices will hold backfiles of their own papers, but will probably refer enquirers to the local public library!

Indexes

The lack of indexes to newspapers is one of the most common problems. Two UK newspapers that do have printed indexes are:

The Times (1785 to date) Primary Source Microfilm (Gale)

The Guardian (1986 to date) UMI/IPI
Both are available in hard copy and on microfilm.

See also:

Clover Information Index (quarterly with annual cumulations), Clover Publications
Also available on CD-ROM and online (**www.cloverweb.co.uk**). Indexes a wide range of newspapers.

Infotrack **http://infotrac.galegroup.com**
Full text articles from selected national daily and Sunday newspapers as well as popular journals.

Electronic sources

There are several subscription CD-ROM and web-based services that provide the text of newspapers. For example Proquest provides CD-ROM and web versions of many UK national papers and the Gale Group has digitized *The Times* from 1785 to 1985.

Most newspaper publishers now provide their papers on their websites, but usually only for a short time and only for a selection of the text.

Express **www.express.co.uk**

Guardian **www.guardian.co.uk**

Daily Telegraph **www.telegraph.co.uk**

Mirror **www.mirror.co.uk**

Times/Sun **www.thetimes.co.uk**

Times Digital Archive 1785–1985 **www.galeuk.com/times**
This subscription site has every page as published, including advertisements and illustrations.

Sunday Times **www.Sunday-times.co.uk**

Financial Times **www.ft.com**

Independent **www.independent.co.uk**

Star **www.megastar.co.uk**

Overseas newspaper websites

See AJR Newslink for newspapers in the UK and around the world:

http://ajr-newslink-org/news.html

Other sources

A number of commercial services provide presentation copies of old papers. One is:

W H Smith Historic Newspapers
PO Box 3, Newton Stewart, Wigtownshire DG8 6TQ
Tel: 01988 402222

The British Library Newsplan project has sponsored a number of projects to microfilm local papers. Contact your local studies library or the Newsplan website **www.newsplan.co.uk**.

Tips and pitfalls

Some newspapers have more than one edition so that even if someone has the correct date and page number, the item may not be in the issue the library has. These editions may relate to different times of the day – morning, afternoon and evening editions – or to different parts of a region.

OPTICIANS

Typical questions
- Can you give me the telephone number of . . . optician?
- How do I find out if . . . optician is registered?

Where to look
Directories

For an alphabetical list of opticians use the *Opticians' register*, General Optical Council:

www.optical.org

Try also:

Optical yearbook, Reed Business Information. Annual

or

Find an optician **www.nhs.uk/England/Opticians**

Journals

Optician
Reed Business Information
Tel: 020 8652 8250
Weekly

Websites

Association of Contact Lens Manufacturers **www.aclm.org.uk**
Excellent links to other eyecare sites.

Eyecare Information Service **www.eyecare-information-service.org.uk**

General Optical Council
41 Harley Street, London W1G 8DJ
Tel: 020 7580 3898
www.optical.org
The statutory body that regulates the optical professions.

 OPTICIANS

Complaints

For complaints against an optician refer to the General Optical Council: www.optical.org.

PARISH REGISTERS

See also Family History & Genealogy; Local History

Typical questions

- How can I find details of my grandfather's birth?
- Where can I find the marriage registers for a particular church, chapel or synagogue?

Considerations

The 1538 Act of Elizabeth I decreed that every church should maintain a register listing baptisms, marriages and burials in the parish. Parish registers in the UK officially started in 1538, but in many places not until 1598 or later. They show baptism (*not* birth), marriage, and burial (*not* death) records. The amount of detail varied considerably until the introduction of printed registers for marriages in 1754, and for baptisms and burials in 1813. 'Parish registers' here are those of the Church of England, the established church in the UK. All baptisms, marriages and burials had to be registered with the local parish church until 1837. Thereafter parish registers were still maintained for those people who chose to marry in church, baptize their children, or be buried in the parish churchyard.

Where to look

General

Present-day registers are generally kept at the relevant parish church, but most older ones will have been deposited in local record offices.

Some registers have been printed by regional societies such as the Yorkshire Parish Register Society. Check with your local record office or local history library to see if this is the case in your area, since, if so, the task of tracing entries is considerably eased. The existence of indexes is also important. In many cases the registers may have been transcribed and/or microfilmed.

BMD Registers **www.bmdregisters.co.uk**

Includes Nonconformist registers for England and Wales.

UKBMD **www.ukbmd.org.uk**

This site has links to all the sites with online versions of local registrars' indexes (which are sometimes more accurate than the ones at the General Record Office).

Humphrey-Smith, C. R. (2003) *The Phillimore atlas and index of parish registers*, 3rd edn, Phillimore.
Coloured county maps showing the boundaries of individual parishes.

National index of parish registers: a guide to Anglican, Roman Catholic and Non-Conformist registers with information on bishop's transcripts, modern copies and marriage licences (1968–) Society of Genealogists. In progress
This multi-volume index is a useful location source. Available on the internet at **www.sog.org.uk**.

Scotland's People **www.scotlandspeople.gov.uk**
Includes indexes and records of parish registers.

Society of Genealogists (1987) *A catalogue of parish register copies in the Society of Genealogists' collection*, 8th edn, Society of Genealogists

Society of Genealogists (1974) *A catalogue of parish register copies other than in the Society of Genealogists' collection*, 2nd edn, Society of Genealogists

Webb, C. C. (1987) *A guide to parish records in the Borthwick Institute of Historical Research*, Borthwick Institute

Many local and regional and national societies have published parish records. Examples are the Canterbury and York Society and the Catholic Record Society.

Bishops' transcripts

From 1598 copies of registers had to be sent annually to the Diocesan Registry. Sometimes these include information not in the parish registers. Many parish registers are incomplete with parts missing; compliance with requirements was sometimes lax and survival over the centuries fitful. A number have been lost. This has proved the value of having the bishops' transcript copies, though the transcriptions were often poorly done.

Gibson, J. S. W. (1997) *Bishops' transcripts and marriage licences, bonds and allegations: a guide to their location and indexes*, 4th edn, Federation of Family History Societies.

Marriage bonds and allegations

These were required when people married by licence rather than banns. The licence would have been kept by the couple who were to marry, but the allegation, a statement made by the intending bride and groom, and the bond, assurances by bondsmen (usually friends or relatives), were kept at the Diocesan Registry. Those for the Diocese of York for the years 1660 to 1950 are at the Borthwick Institute. Some lists have been published. See the Gibson book above.

Boyd's marriage index

This index sometimes gets asked for. It contains entries for marriages in many parts of the UK from 1538 to 1837. The original is at the Society of Genealogists, but a limited number of copies were made and may be available locally. Available online at the British Origins section of **www.origins.net**. See also Massey, R. W. (1987) *A list of parishes in Boyd's marriage index*, 6th edn, Society of Genealogists. This early index sometimes contains records not found elsewhere.

Non-parochial registers

For the registers created by Nonconformist denominations, Roman Catholic, Jewish and other faiths, consult local archives departments or record offices; the guides published by the Federation of Family History Societies; or the offices of the denomination or faith in question. Many registers of Nonconformist and non-Christian communities are now at the Family Records Centre.

The International Genealogical Index (IGI)

In their quest to retrospectively baptize the past generations of Christians, the Church of Latter-Day Saints ('Mormons') have microfilmed and digitized a large percentage of existing parish records (and other genealogical records). Most large libraries have the IGI, usually on microfiche, and this is a convenient first check for personal details. Genealogists are advised to check back with the original records since the IGI information is limited.

Other sources

The Parish Register Society was founded in 1896 to print the parish registers of England and Wales. It was dissolved in 1934, its work being continued by the Society of Genealogists.

Society of Genealogists

14 Charterhouse Buildings, Goswell Road, London EC1M 7BA
Tel: 020 7250 8799; Fax: 020 7250 1800
E-mail: library@sog.org.uk
www.sog.org.uk

Tips and pitfalls

Genealogy, and the esoterica of parish registers, are areas of enquiry to be referred to specialist local historians, record searchers and archivists. The general librarian's role is mainly to clarify the enquiry so that useful information about sources can be given and relevant referrals made.

PHILOSOPHY & PSYCHOLOGY

Typical questions

- What is a hedonist?
- What is a psychopath?
- Have you got any IQ tests?
- Have you got anything on the determinism versus freewill debate?

Considerations

Philosophy and psychology are often lumped together in the popular mind, but academically they are quite distinct disciplines. 'What is the key to happiness?' might be a popular 'philosophy of life' question, while the title of Dale Carnegie's 1953 book *How to win friends and influence people* might stand for the populist view of psychology. Academically speaking, philosophy is concerned with the nature of knowledge and with what we can, or cannot, know, while psychology is more about behaviour. As with all subjects, the librarian needs to be a psychologist (to observe the enquirer's behaviour – verbal and non-verbal) and a philosopher (to structure a meaningful response)!

Where to look
General

Bothamley, J. (1993) *Dictionary of theories*, Gale Research

Bullock, A. and Trombley, S. (eds) (1999) *The new Fontana dictionary of modern thought*, 3rd edn, HarperCollins

Gregory, R. L. (ed.) (2004) *The Oxford companion to the mind*, 2nd edn, Oxford University Press

Oxford Reference Online **www.oxfordreference.com**
    Has a section covering reference sources on religion and philosophy.

Philosophy

Audi, R. (1999) *The Cambridge dictionary of philosophy*, 2nd edn, Cambridge University Press

Blackburn, S. (1994) *The Oxford dictionary of philosophy*, Oxford University Press

Bunnin, N. and Tsui-James, E. P. (eds) (2003) *The Blackwell companion to philosophy*, 2nd edn, Blackwell

Craig, E. (ed.) *The shorter Routledge encyclopedia of philosophy*, Routledge

Routledge also have an online encylopedia of philosophy: **www.rep.routledge.com**

Honderich, T. (ed.) (2005) *The Oxford companion to philosophy*, 2nd edn, Oxford University Press

Encyclopedia of philosophy (Stanford University Press) **http://plato.stanford.edu**

Internet encyclopedia of philosophy **www.utm.edu**

Psychology

Campbell, R. J. (2004) *Campbell's psychiatric dictionary*, 8th edn, Oxford University Press

Colman, A. M. (2006) *The Oxford dictionary of psychology*, 2nd edn, Oxford University Press

Corsini, R. J. (2002) *Encyclopedia of psychology*, 3rd edn, Wiley

PsychNet-Uk **www.psychnet-uk.com**
Free website of some 350 pages and over 9000 links to websites suitable for both academics and the general public.

Reber, A. S. and E. S. (2001) *The Penguin dictionary of psychology*, 3rd edn, Penguin

Smith, E. E. and others (2003) *Hilgard and Atkinson's introduction to psychology*, 14th edn, Wadsworth/Thomson
A popular standard textbook.

Sutherland, N. S. (1995) *Macmillan dictionary of psychology*, 2nd edn, Macmillan

Winstanley, J. (ed.) (2006) *Key concepts in psychology*, Palgrave Macmillan

Psychology topics

Personality tests
> **www.bbc.co.uk/science/humanbody/mind/index_surveys.shtml**
> 21 short personality tests.

PsychINFO and Psyc ARTICLES www.apa.org/psycinfo
> Two subscription databases published by the American Psychological Assoc-
> iation. The former indexes behavioural, psychological and mental health
> resources, the latter is a full-text database of leading journals in the field.

Tips and pitfalls

Beware the pitfall of confusing psychology (an academic discipline), psychiatry
(the treatment of mental disorders) and psycho-analysis (a once fashionable
theory of mental functioning).

Note that personality and IQ tests are often asked for, but as they are subject
to stringent copyright and licensing requirements, they are not generally available
to the public.

PHOTOGRAPHS & PHOTOGRAPHY; ILLUSTRATIONS

Typical questions

- Where can I locate a picture of women workers in shawls?
- Can you give me advice on looking after old photographs?
- Can I use an old photograph in a book I'm writing?
- How can I best take pictures indoors?
- I have an old camera I want to repair.

Considerations

The internet has made available millions of images. Many art galleries, for
example, now make their collections digitally available, and many commercial
suppliers use the internet as a shop window.

Copyright queries can be troublesome. Bear in mind that the ownership of a
picture or photograph is not the same thing as having the right to give permission
to copy; that is usually the right of the photographer or whoever commissioned

them. Art galleries and museums usually charge a fee to use an image of one of their pictures in addition to the cost of reproduction; and they may also collect royalties on behalf of the photographer. Warn enquirers to be particularly careful if they plan to publish. Copyright usually lasts for 70 years from the photographer or illustrator's death.

Camera technology has developed rapidly with the advent of digital photography. Cameras that use film have all but disappeared from shops; black and white film is hard to find. Refer enquiries on how to use cameras to local camera shops or the manufacturers (who may provide assistance on their websites).

Where to look
General
Jeffrey, I. (1997) *The photography book*, Phaidon
> Strong on artistic aspects.

Lenman, R. (ed.) (2005) *Oxford companion to the photograph*, OUP

Buying guides
Which Camera **www.whichcamera.co.uk**

Camera Review **www.camerareview.com**

Collections of images
Printed sources

There are many books featuring photographs; general collections such as:

Ultimate visual dictionary (1997), Dorling Kindersley
> Some 6000 colour photographs and illustrations on a wide range of themes.

Or collections of the work of particular photographers or genres.

Internet search services
Most general search engines have options for pictures. Examples are:

Alta Vista **www.altavista.com/image/default**
> 112,723 images in 3188 categories.

Google Image Search **http://images.google.com**
> A search engine which gathers together some 425 million images culled from Google's webpages.

Lycos Images **www.lycos.com/picturethis**
> A database of 80,000 freely available images plus access to over 18 million on the web.

Yahoo! **http://images.search.yahoo.com**

Multi-search engines (services that cover several search engines – though rarely all the same!) include:

Ez2 Find **ww.ez2find.com**
Fagan Finder **www.faganfinder.com/img/**
Fazzle **www.fazzle.com**
Picsearch **www.picsearch.com**
Stopstock **www.1stopstock.com**

There are also a number of specialist search services such as:

Ditto.com **http://ditto.com/**
Image Surfer **http://isurf.interpx.com**

For audio and video, try Whoopie! **www.whoopie.com.**

Specialist collections of images on the internet

Many specialist websites have collections of images. Typically, web-based collections allow small images to be accessed free, but a fee is payable for downloading full images, etc. Examples are:

Art Photo Gallery **www.artphotogallery.org**
> A 'gallery' of the work of famous photographers with commentary.

Corbis **www.corbis.com**
> A large online picture library of some 2 million images.

Education Image Gallery **http://edina.ac.uk/eig**
> An online resource of 50,000 curriculum-specific images available on subscription.

Freefoto **www.freefoto.com**
> A large database of images, free for non-commercial use.

Free Images **www.freeimages.co.uk**

Getty Images **http://creative.gettyimages.com**
> A provider of imagery, film and digital services.

Mirror Pix **www.mirrorpix.com**
Pictures from the Mirror Group newspapers' photo archive.

Photos To Go **www.photostogo.com**
Over 200,000 images.

Picture Collection Online (PCO) **http://digital.nypl.org/mmpco/index.cfm**
A collection of 30,000 digitized images from books, magazines and
newspapers as well as original photographs, prints and postcards, mostly
created before 1923. Administered by the New York Public Library.

Time Inc. Photo Collection **www.thepicturecollection.com**
Images from a company famous for its photo journalism.

United Press International Photos database **www.upi.com/photos/index.cfm**
Large press photo archive.

Among the many art galleries that have databases of their collection are:

National Gallery **www.nationalgallery.org.uk**

New York Metropolitan Museum of Art **www.metmuseum.org/collection**

National Portrait Gallery **www.npg.org.uk**

Tate Gallery **www.tate.org.uk**

Picture agencies

The British Association of Picture Libraries and Agencies has a directory of picture
libraries in the UK: **www.bapla.org.uk**

Evans, H. and M. (2001) *Picture researcher's handbook*, 7th edn, Pira
International, Routledge
International guide to picture sources and how to use them.

Technical aspects

Ang, T. (2006) *Digital photographer's handbook*, 3rd edn, Dorling Kindersley

Cope, P. (2002) *The digital photographer's A–Z*, Thames & Hudson

Freeman, J. (2007) *Collins digital SLR Handbook*, Collins

Harman, D. (2007) *The digital photography handbook*, Quercus

Hedgecoe, J. (1997) *The new photographer's handbook: the definitive reference manual of photographic techniques, procedures and equipment*, 2nd edn, Ebury Press

Kelby, S. and Kloskowski, S. (2008) *The Photoshop book for digital photography*, New Pinders

Tomosy, T. (1997) *Camera maintenance and repair: a comprehensive, fully illustrated guide*, Amherst Media
Tomosy has compiled several specialist repair guides.

Stroebel, L. D. and Zakia, R. D. (eds) (1993) *Focal encyclopedia of photography*, 3rd edn, Focal Press
Covers technical aspects.

Zakia, R. and Stroebel, L. (1993) *The Focal encyclopedia of photography*, 3rd edn, Focal Press

Betterphoto **www.betterphoto.com**

Other sources

For images of places in the UK, see the chapter LOCAL HISTORY.

British Journal of Photography **www.bjphoto.co.uk**
An online magazine, which includes an archive of articles, visits to galleries, information on careers and equipment suppliers.

National Media Museum (formerly National Museum of Photography, Film and Television), Bradford BD1 1NQ
Tel: 01274 202030; Fax: 01274 723155
www.nationalmediamuseum.org.uk

The Royal Photographic Society (RPS)
The Octagon, Milson Street, Bath BA1 1DN
Tel: 01225 462841; Fax: 01225 448688
www.rps.org
The leading society for the advancement of photography. Has some 10,000 members in 59 countries. Gives details of latest news and exhibitions with a good range of links to other websites.

Tips and pitfalls

Local photographic societies are a useful source of information, advice and expertise. Likewise local art galleries and museums. Get to know the details of specialist camera shops in the locality. Local studies departments of libraries often hold photographic collections for their area.

PLAYS

See also Literature; Television & Radio; Theatre & Acting

Typical questions

- Who wrote *An inspector calls*?
- Is *An inspector calls* being performed anywhere in this area?
- Where can I get multiple copies of a play so we can have a group reading?
- What plays can you suggest for seven characters?

Considerations

On the question of getting a 'play set', i.e. enough copies of a play so that every character can have a copy, check your library's facility to borrow sets from a regional centre. Most regional library systems have play collections. They may also have a catalogue of what is available.

In order to perform a play in public, permission must be obtained if the play is in copyright. Even if the play is long out of copyright, the actual text being used may be in copyright. Also bear in mind that public performances may need to be licensed. If performance is contemplated, suggest the enquirer contacts a local dramatic society for advice.

Where to look

General

Matlaw, M. (1972) *Modern world drama: an encyclopedia*, Secker & Warburg
    80 countries, 688 playrights, 1058 plays and drama terms.

Krasne, D. (ed.) (2005) *A companion to twentieth century American [US] drama*,
    Blackwell

Patterson, M. (2005) *The Oxford book of plays*, Oxford University Press
    Around 1000 of the most significant plays of world literature.

PLAYS

Bibliographical information

British national bibliography and the *British Library catalogue* are useful in identifying published plays. See Books & Bibliographies.

Biographical Information

McGraw-Hill encyclopedia of world drama (1972) 4 vols, McGraw-Hill

Contemporary dramatists (1998), Gale

Performance

Jones, C. (2005) *Make your voice heard: an actor's voice*, 2nd edn, Back Stage Books

Indexes and play selection

Connor, B. M. (1993) *Ottemiller's index to plays in collections: an author and title index to plays appearing in collections published between 1900 and 1986*, 7th rev. edn, Scarecrow Press

The guide to selecting plays for performance, Samuel French Ltd. Annual
The standard guide (annotated) to plays. French's make available plays for amateur performances in the UK. Includes information about rights and copyright.

Play index (1949–), H. W. Wilson.
A multi-volume work listing plays written in, or translated into, English. Also available as a subscription website: **www.hwwilson.com/Databases/playindex_e.htm.**

Shipley, J. T. (1956) *Guide to great plays*, Public Affairs Press (USA)
Gives outlines and performance histories.

Shank, T. J. (ed.) (1963) *A digest of 500 plays; plot outlines and production notes*, Collier-Macmillan

Other sources

Amateur Theatre Network **www.amdram.co.uk**

National Drama Festivals Association
Hon. Sec. Tony Broscomb, Bramleys, Main Street, Shudy Camp, Cambridgeshire CB1 6RA
Tel: 01799 584920; Fax: 01799 584921

Performing Right Society (PRS) (now incorporated into the MCPS-PRS Alliance)

29–33 Berners Street, London W1T 3AB

Tel: 020 7580 5544; Fax: 020 7306 4050

www.mcps-prs-alliance.co.uk

Samuel French Ltd

52 Fitzroy Street, London W1P 6JR

Tel: 020 7387 9373; Fax: 020 7387 2161

E-mail: theatre@Samuelfrench-London.co.uk

www.samuelfrench-london.co.uk

French's Theatre Bookshop stock acting editions. French's is also the licensing agent for performances of the plays by many authors.

Local drama groups and societies are useful in all sorts of ways.

Tips and pitfalls

Your local or regional library bureaux may have their own catalogue of play sets. If so, it would be clever to advise a potential borrower to select from what *is* available rather than what is not.

Note the distinction between the prose version of a play and an acting edition.

POEMS & POETRY

See also Literature; Publishing; Quotations & Speeches; Writers & Writing

Typical questions

- Have you the poem 'There's a yellow one-eyed god to the north of Khatmandu'?
- I'm trying to remember a poem I learnt at school, but I've forgotten its title. Can you help?
- Have you a poem suitable for a leaving 'do'?

Considerations

Where the author is known, finding a particular poem is relatively straightforward. The library may have a volume of the poet's works, or a selection of some of them. If that fails, try the many anthologies and collections of poetry that are published.

Most of them will have indexes of poets, first lines and sometimes subjects.

Poems are generally listed in indexes by title and by first lines. Where neither of these is known (or misremembered – the poem in the first question above is, in fact, 'There's a one-eyed yellow idol to the north of Khatmandu'), then the librarian has to use dictionaries of quotations or try the approach by subject.

Where to look
Anthologies

Palgrave, F. T. (1994) *Palgrave's golden treasury of the best songs and lyrical poems in the English language*, 6th edn, updated by Press, J., Oxford University Press
Palgrave's *Treasury* is perhaps the best known of all poetry anthologies.

Ricks, C. (1999) *The Oxford book of English verse*, Oxford University Press
Contains 850 favourite poems.

The English poetry full-text database (1995) Chadwyck-Healey
A CD-ROM database of some 16,500 poems by 1250 poets.

Poets Corner **www.poets-corner.org**
A massive database of out-of-copyright poems with author, title and subject indexes, plus other poetry-related information.

Biographical sources

Bold, A. (1985) *Longman dictionary of poets: the lives and works of 1,000 poets in the English language*, Longman
Brief outlines.

International who's who in poetry and poets' encyclopedia, Melrose Press. Bi-annual

Indexes to titles and first lines

Granger, E. (2005) *The Columbia Granger's index to poetry in collected and selected works*, Columbia University Press
Granger's index is one the most famous of all reference books. Fiche and CD-ROM versions are available. Also available online on subscription: **www.columbiagrangers.org** containing over 300,000 poem citations and 100,000 full-text poems.

Other sources

The Poetry Society
> 22 Betterton Street, London WC2H 9BX
> Tel: 020 7420 4818; Fax: 020 7240 4818
> E-mail: info@poetrysoc.com
> **www.poetrysoc.com**
> The Poetry Society publishes *Poetry News* and *Poetry Review* and offer many other membership benefits. They also answer information enquiries.

Poetry Library **www.poetrylibrary.org.uk/poetry/index.html**
> Has a 'Lost Quotations' message board.

Tips and pitfalls

Some poems are regulars, always being asked for. It is worth keeping a handy index of details to save staff time in the future, and it may be worth having copies of the most popular poems themselves to hand out or photocopy, to save time.

Many queries can be resolved using a good search engine such as **google.com** to find sources.

Half-remembered poems can result in endless searches and may occasionally force you to say, 'I give up!' However, recourse to fellow staff can sometimes bring answers!

POLICE & SECURITY

Typical questions

- How do I get into the Police Force?
- I want the number of a private detective.
- Do you have any information on Basque terrorist groups?

Considerations

This is quite a large area to tackle. Luckily there are some useful websites around to make your job easier. For crime statistics, *see* STATISTICS.

Where to look
Police

The Police and constabulary almanac lists all the UK's police forces, fire brigades, ambulance services and civil defence/emergency planning.

Unfortunately, there is no UK Police website anymore. Most regional police forces have their own websites, so check with a good search engine.

Police Information is a one-stop shop and information centre for police, security and criminal justice sector workers who are engaged in law enforcement in the UK. The site contains information on how to join the police, police jobs, police news, police pay and police law:

www.police-information.co.uk

For information on joining the police see **www.policecouldyou.co.uk**.

Security

The Security Service (MI5) is responsible for protecting the UK against threats to national security. This website provides information about the Security Service, the threats it counters, links to sources of security advice and details of careers with the Service:

www.mi5.gov.uk

For private detectives try:

Varsity directory of investigators and process servers, Shaw and Sons Ltd. Annual

Terrorism

Atkins, S. E. (2004) *Encyclopedia of modern worldwide extremists and extremist groups*, Greenwood Press

Chaliand, B. and Blin, A. (2007) *History of terrorism: from antiquity to Al Qaeda*, University of California
This authoritative work covers the history of terrorism up to the present day.

Combs, C.C. (ed.) *Encyclopedia of terrorism* (2007) 2nd rev. edn, Facts on File
Thoroughly updated and expanded by terrorism experts, the *Encyclopedia of terrorism* provides students, researchers, journalists and policymakers with a complete survey of what seems to be an intractable problem. More than 350 entries.

There are some useful government terrorist sites, loaded with information. Try:

www.homeoffice.gov.uk/security/terrorism-and-the-law
www.homeoffice.gov.uk/security

The Centre for the Study of Terrorism and Political Violence (CSTPV), based at St Andrews University, has an excellent website, with up-to-date newsfeeds in their online library. Most of the articles in the library are free to access:

www.st-andrews.ac.uk/~cstpv/resources/elibraryintro.php

For a list of terrorism and counter terrorism organizations:

www.psr.keele.ac.uk/sseal/terror.htm

POLITICS & INTERNATIONAL RELATIONS

See also Biographies; Countries; Election Results; Government; History; Members of Parliament; United Nations

Typical questions
- What, exactly, is a Marxist?
- Have you got copies of the election manifestos?

Where to look
General

Dale, I. (2001) *Directory of political websites*, Politico Publishing
    3500 websites listed.

Guide to US elections (2005) 5th edn, C Q Press, 2 vols

Intute **www.intute.ac.uk**
    Intute (formerly Sosig – Social Science Information Gateway) is a free online service giving access to the best websites in the social sciences, including a large quantity of political information.

Jones, B. (2004) *Dictionary of British politics*, Manchester University Press

Miller, D. (ed.) (1987) *The Blackwell encyclopaedia of political thought*, Blackwell Reference

Oxford Reference Online **www.oxfordreference.com**
    There is a category for Politics and Social Sciences in this popular subscription website.

Ramsden, J. (2002) *Oxford companion to twentieth century British politics*, Oxford University Press

Robertson, D. (2002) *A dictionary of modern politics*, 3rd edn, Europa

Scruton, R. (2007) *The Palgrave Macmillan dictionary of political thought*, 3rd edn, Palgrave Macmillan

ukpolitics@ **www.ukpolitics.org.uk**
Free guide to British politics including details of parliamentary constituencies, local councils and historical background.

International relations

Calvert, P. (ed.) (2004) *Border and territorial disputes of the world*, 4th edn, John Harper Publications
Summaries and details on 93 ongoing disputes.

Council on Foreign Relations **www.cfr.org**

Day, A. J. et al. (2002) *A political and economic dictionary of Eastern Europe*, Europa
Includes biographies and addresses.

East, R. et al. (2007) *A political and economic dictionary of Eastern Europe*, 2nd edn, Routledge

Evans, G. (1998) *The Penguin dictionary of international relations*, Penguin

Griffiths, M. (ed.) *Encyclopedia of international relations and global politics*, Routledge

Weigall, D. (2002) *International relations: a concise companion*, Arnold
Over 1500 entries relating to the 19th and 20th centuries.

Biographies

Baylen, J. and Grossman, N. (1979–88) *Biographical dictionary of modern British radicals*, Harvester Press, 3 vols

Dictionary of Labour biography (1972–2004), Palgrave Macmillan, 12 vols

Economist (1991) *Dictionary of political biography*, Economist Books
Brief biographies. 'The essential guide to who really counts in the world of international politics.'

Hutchinson encyclopedia of modern political biography (1999) Hutchinson

Robbins, K. (ed.) (1990) *The Blackwell dictionary of British political life in the twentieth century*, Blackwell Reference

World statesmen **www.worldstatesmen.org**

Compilations

Cook, C. and Stevenson, J. (eds) (1980) *British historical facts 1688–1760*, Palgrave Macmillan

Cook, C. and Stevenson, J. (eds) (1988) *British historical facts 1760–1830*, Palgrave Macmillan

Cook, C. and Stevenson, J. (eds) (1975) *British historical facts 1830–1900*, Palgrave Macmillan

Butler, D. (2001) *Twentieth century British political facts, 1900–2000*, Palgrave Macmillan

Cook, C. and Paxton, J. (1981) *European political facts, 1789–1848*, Macmillan

Cook, C. and Paxton, J. (1978) *European political facts, 1848–1918*, Macmillan

Cook, C. and Paxton, J. (1992) *European political facts, 1918–1990*, Macmillan

Corbett, R. et al. (2000) *The European parliament*, 4th edn
A standard reference source.

Gilliard, K. and Kennedy, F. (eds) (Annual) *Irish political studies data yearbook*, Frank Cass

Diplomacy

A dictionary of diplomacy (2003) 2nd edn, Palgrave Macmillan
Covers legal terms, political events, international organizations and major figures of 500 years of diplomacy.

Foreign and Commonwealth Office, *The diplomatic service book*, The Stationery Office. Annual
Lists senior staff and departments in the Foreign and Commonwealth Office; details of British embassies and missions abroad and biographical details of staff.

Treaties and alliances of the world (2007) 8th edn, John Harper Publishing

Events and yearbooks

Newspapers are a prime source for political events (see MEDIA & THE PRESS, NEWSPAPERS & MAGAZINES). Particularly useful are the weeklies *New Society*, *New Statesman*, *Newsweek* and *Time* magazine.

Almanac of American politics, National Journal (Washington DC). Annual

Annual register of world events: a review of the year (1758–) Keesings Worldwide
Good for national and international events.

Britain: an official handbook, The Stationery Office. Annual

Drost, H. (1995) *What's what and who's who in Europe*, Cassell
Information on people, places, organizations, events and terms.

Europa yearbook, Europa Publications
Gives statistics and information for each country.

International Institute for Strategic Studies, *Strategic survey*, Routledge. Annual
An annual series of essays on the political problems of the world and its regions.

International yearbook and statesman's who's who, Nijhoff. Annual
Standard reference directory to international organisations, states of the world and some 6000 leaders and statesmen.

Political handbook of the world, CQ Press (Washington). Annual

Statesman's yearbook: the politics, cultures and economies of the world, Palgrave Macmillan. Annual
Available online on subscription, **www.statesmansyearbook.com**.

Whitaker's almanack, A&C Black. Annual
Contains a great deal of information on world conditions and events during the year. Lists embassies and consulates in the UK, and UK embassies overseas.

Yearbook of world affairs, Institute of World Affairs. Annual

Parties and movements

Barberis, P. et al. (2000) *Encyclopedia of British and Irish political organizations: parties, groups and movements of the twentieth century*, Pinter

Blevins, D. (2006) *American political parties in the 21st century*, McFarland

Craig, W. F. S. (ed.) (1988) *British general election manifestos 1959–1987*, 3rd edn, Dartmouth Publications

Day, A. J. (ed.) (2000) *Directory of European Union political parties*, J. Harper Publishing

Hewitt, C. and Cheetham, T. (2000) *Encyclopedia of modern separatist movements*, ABC-Clio

Luther, K. R. (2004) *Political parties of the world*, John Harper Publishing

Marxist Internet Archive **www.marxist.org**
Free website on Marxist literature, history and contemporary socialist movements and political parties. Over 35,000 documents and writings of over 300 authors.

Mercer, P. (1994) *Directory of British political organizations*, Longman

Party election manifestos **www.psr.keele.ac.uk/area/uk/man.htm**

Revolutionary and dissident movements: an international guide (1991) 3rd edn, Longman

Szajkowski, B. (2005) *Political parties of the world*, 6th edn, John Harper Publishing
A reference directory to some 2550 political parties and 230 national political systems.

Szajkowski, B. (ed.) 2004 *Revolutionary and dissident movements of the world*, 4th edn, John Harper Publishing

Other sources

Most political parties have their own websites, e.g.

Conservatives **www.conservatives.com**
Labour **www.labour.org.uk**
Liberal Democrats **www.libdems.org.uk**

Scottish National Party **www.snp.org**

For a complete list of political parties' websites try:

http://bubl.ac.uk/uk/parties.htm

Fabian Society
>   11 Dartmouth Street, London SW1H 9BN
>   Tel: 020 7227 4900; Fax: 020 7976 7153
>   E-mail: info@fabian-society.org.uk
>   **www.fabian-society.org.uk**

POPULATION

Typical questions
* What is the population of . . .?
* What percentage of the UK population is married?
* Can you provide a breakdown of the ethnic population for . . .?

Considerations

There can be a whole range of queries regarding population; there are, after all, several different levels to consider – world, continent, country, regional and district. In addition, groups of people with certain characteristics are also small populations. Therefore questions about ethnic groups, number of married people that live in a certain area, numbers of people employed in various sectors, are all questions about populations. Your library will probably keep local population and characteristic statistics based on Census details. It may be that your local council, based on their own data, produces an economic profile that includes local population data. Population statistics are widely available in many publications; a list of the most authorative is given below. For quick reference you can use *Whitaker's*.

There are also numerous websites providing population statistics; some of the best are listed below.

Where to look
UK statistical publications

The Stationery Office provides a number of excellent publications which all include population data:

Annual abstract of statistics, Palgrave Macmillan
A comprehensive collection of statistics covering the UK, including population.

Population trends, Palgrave Macmillan
This provides the latest quarterly information on births, marriages, divorces, migration (internal and international), population estimates and projections.

Social trends, Palgrave Macmillan
A compendium of social statistics from a wide range of government departments and other organizations, presenting a broad picture of the British. Includes population data.

Monthly digest of statistics, Palgrave Macmillan
There is a chapter on population and vital statistics.

Regional trends, Palgrave Macmillan
A compendium publication with the most comprehensive official statistics about regions of the UK. It has a section on population and households.

Census

The 2001 Census data is now available on the National Statistics Neighbourhood Statistics website **www.statistics.gov.uk/neighbourhood**, which is excellent. It also collates local statistics from local authorities and public bodies.

International statistics

Demographic yearbook, United Nations
This is an international source of statistics on 200 countries. It includes data on distribution and trends in population.

Compendium of human settlements statistics 2001, United Nations
Although slightly dated this is an excellent source of information on settlement and housing conditions for 243 countries or areas and 315 cities.

Population and vital statistics report, United Nations

Europa world year book, 2 vols, Routledge/Europa
A statistical survey is given for 250+ countrries. This includes population statistics by country, regions and principal towns.

P POPULATION

Eurostat yearbook: Europe in figures, European Commission Eurostat

Provides comparative population data between countries, looking at age and gender for past, present and future. Available free to download as a pdf document from **http://bookshop.europa.eu**.

Monthly bulletin of statistics, United Nations Statistics Division

Provides monthly population statistics for over 200 countries and territories of the world.

Eurostat regional yearbook, European Commission Eurostat

Provides data on EU population. Available free to download as a pdf document from **http://bookshop.europa.eu**.

State of world population 2007, UNFPA Publishing

Available to download from **www.unfpa.org/swp**. Excellent report and fantastic website. Well worth a visit.

Statistical yearbook, United Nations

This provides population statistics on over 200 countries or areas of the world for which data was available. It is also available on CD-ROM. For more details take a look at **www.un.org**.

Trends in Europe and North America 2001, United Nations Economic Commission for Europe

Includes population size, mortality rates and life expectancy statistics.

Encyclopaedia of population, Gale Group

Websites

Government Official Statistics **www.statistics.gov.uk**

NationMaster **www.nationmaster.com**

Excellent site for country-specific information. Enables the user to rank and compare countries. Well worth a visit.

United Nations Population Information Network (POPIN) **www.un.org/popin**

Especially useful for population projections.

United Nations **www.un.org**

Produces a huge number of publications on population.

PRICES

See also Employment – Rights & Statistics; Money

Typical questions
- What is the latest figure for the Retail Price Index?
- What are the latest Consumer Price Indices?
- I would like a breakdown of the purchasing power of the pound since 1990.

Where to look
Statistics

Consumer Price Indices, The Stationery Office. Monthly
> A monthly publication which provides all you need to know about the cost of living from monthly changes to historical indexes. It provides a full picture of inflation and consumer prices in the UK. Available to download free on **www.statistics.gov.uk**.

Annual abstract of statistics, The Stationery Office
> This has an excellent chapter on prices. It covers the Producer Price Index, Retail Price Index, Tax and Price Index and the purchasing power of the pound. Available to download free at **www.statistics.gov.uk**.

Economic and labour market review, The Stationery Office. Monthly
> Has a regular feature on prices.

Monthly Digest of Statistics, The Stationery Office
> Provides a section on prices and wages.

International prices

Main Economic Indicators, Organization for Economic Co-operation and Development (OECD). Monthly
> Provides economic indicators for the 30 OECD members and six non-member countries.

Share prices

London Stock Exchange **www.londonstockexchange.com**
> Use to find share prices for companies and data on world indices. Also has a 'prices and news' page. Select from the home page.

Journals

Investors Chronicle
FT Business
Tel: 0844 8480106
Weekly
Provides a section called 'Statistics', which includes UK and international economic indicators.

Financial Times
Financial Times
Tel: 020 7873 3000; Fax: 020 7873 3922
Daily
Look in 'Companies and Markets' section.

PRISONS & PROBATION

See also Crime & Criminals, Law; Police & Security

Typical questions

- How many prisoners are there in the UK?
- What does probation mean?
- From what age can you be sent to prison?

Considerations

Many of the enquiries in this area focus on prison statistics for projects or on contact details for UK prisons. A very good starting point is the excellent **www.direct.gov.uk**. Select 'Crime, Justice and the Law', then 'Prison and Probation'. There are sections on *Visiting family members in prison, Community sentencing* and lots more. The websites given below also offer some of the best information available from reputable sources.

Where to look
General and legislation

For details of prisons in the UK use:

Prisons handbook (2008) Prisons.org.uk Ltd
Annual guide to prisons in England and Wales.

For legislation on prisons and probation use the excellent website:

www.opsi.gov.u
> Select 'UK Legislation', then 'Acts', and use the keyword search facility to find a specific piece of legislation.

Statistics

Use **www.statistics.gov.uk/onlineproducts/default.asp** for *The prison population in England and Wales*, or **www.homeoffice.gov.uk/rds**, which is excellent for statistical publications relating to crime including *Crime in England & Wales* and *British crime survey.*

Websites

There are some very good websites covering all the aspects of prisons and probation.

Action for Prisoners' Families **www.prisonersfamilies.org.uk**
> The national voice of organizations supporting families of prisoners. Excellent, especially for publications to help families.

H M Inspectorate of Prisons **http://inspectorates.justice.gov.uk/hmprisons**
> For reports.

H M Prison Service **www.hmprisonservice.gov.uk**
> Excellent. Packed with information. Includes *Prison population figures* and *Prison services performance ratings.*

National Probation Service **www.probation.homeoffice.gov.uk**

Prisons.org.uk **www.prisons.org.uk**
> Independent website dedicated to the penal system of England and Wales.

Prisons and Probation Ombudsman for England and Wales **www.ppo.gov.uk**

Prisoners Abroad **www.prisonersabroad.org.uk**
> Includes prisoners abroad statistics.

Prison Reform Trust **www.prisonreformtrust.org.uk**

Scottish Government prison statistics
> **www.scotland.gov.uk/Topics/Statistics/15730/3320**
> Select 'Prisons'.

Scottish Prison Service **www.sps.gov.uk**

Social Exclusion Task Force
www.cabinetoffice.gov.uk/social-exclusion-task-force.aspx

PROOFREADING & EDITING

See also Publishing; Writers & Writing

Typical questions

- Have you a list of the marks used to proofread a text?
- What does 'stet' mean on this typescript?
- How do I get my book proofread?

Considerations

The general points of preparing texts for publication are covered in the chapter WRITERS & WRITING; this chapter is about the specific task of checking texts destined for publication or presentation. Writers may be asked to check their own scripts, or deal with those proofread by someone else. Standard conventions apply, although each publisher has their own preferences. Suggest to the enquirer to check with the publisher to see if they have a preferred style.

Where to look

Most books on writing will contain a section of proofreading marks. These include *The writers' and artists' yearbook, The writer's handbook*, and *Whitaker's almanack*.

There are many specialist books for editors and proofreaders:

Butcher, J., Drake, C. and Leach, M. (2006) *Butcher's copy-editing: the Cambridge handbook for editors, copy-editors and proofreaders*, 4th edn, Cambridge University Press
The classic handbook.

The Chicago manual of style (1993), 14th edn, University of Chicago Press

The Economist style guide (2001) Economist Books

Mackenzie, J. (2005) *The editor's companion*, Oxford University Press

The Oxford dictionary for writers and editors (2000) Oxford University Press

Ritter, R. M. (2003) *The Oxford style manual*, Oxford University Press

The British Standard is: BS 5261–2: 1976 (1995) *Specification for typographic requirements, marks for copy preparation and proof corrections, proofing procedure*, British Standards Institution

Other sources

Society of Editors and Proofreaders (SfEP)
Erico House, 93–99 Upper Richmond Road, Putney, London SW15 2TG
www.sfep.org.uk

Society of Authors
84 Drayton Gardens, London SW10 9SB
www.societyofauthors.org

Local writers' circles and writing groups will have knowledgeable members who may give advice and help.

Tips and pitfalls

The important thing in proofreading a text is that the printer understands what corrections to make. Better to write out in full what you want rather than use symbols you don't understand.

PROVERBS

See also Quotations & Speeches

Typical questions

- Where does the phrase 'Handsome is as handsome does' come from?
- What's the meaning of 'To pay through the nose'?

Considerations

There are many books of proverbs about. Most good reference libraries should have one or two decent dictionaries of proverbs.

Where to look

Here are some examples of texts available:

Stevenson, B. (1987) *Macmillan book of proverbs, maxims and famous phrases*, Macmillan

Simpson, J. (2004) *Oxford dictionary of proverbs*, Oxford University Press

Tips and pitfalls

Make sure that the phrase is actually a proverb, and not a famous quotation. If you are not sure, it may be worth checking a dictionary of quotations too.

PSEUDONYMS

See also Biographies; Literature; Names

Typical questions

- What's the real name of Elton John?
- Which other names does P. D. James write under?

Considerations

Many famous people use pseudonyms – false names – without us knowing. Often that is how they wish it to be. The need to find out the 'real' name is generally that of the quiz and puzzle addict, or to settle a bet! Cataloguers and bibliographers may want to know too.

Where to look
Dictionaries and indexes

Atkinson, F. (1982) *Dictionary of literary pseudonyms: a selection of popular modern writers in English*, 3rd edn, Clive Bingley
Some 4000 authors listed under both their real names, giving the pseudonym they used, and under the pseudonym, giving their real name.

Carty, T. J. (1995) *A dictionary of literary pseudonyms in the English language*, Mansell

Halkett, S. and Laing, J. (1926–62) *Dictionary of anonymous and pseudonymous English literature*, Oliver and Boyd
The nine-volume standard.

Houghton, W. E. (1966–88) *Wellesley index to Victorian periodicals 1824–1900: tables of contents and identification of contributors*, 4 vols, University of Toronto Press
Nineteenth-century journalism/literature.

Room, A. (2004) *Dictionary of pseudonyms: 11,000 assumed names and their origins*, 4th edn, McFarland

Sharp, H. S. (1975) *Handbook of pseudonyms and personal nicknames*, 2 vols, Scarecrow Press

Library catalogues

The catalogues of national and university libraries are particularly good for identifying pseudonyms. See LIBRARIES & INFORMATION SERVICES.

See also dictionaries and encyclopaedias in the subject area concerned.

Electronic sources

http://en.wikipedia.org/wiki/List_of_pseudonyms

For literary pseudonyms try

www.trussel.com/books/pseudo.htm

PUBLISHING

See also Books & Bibliographies; Copyright & Legal Deposit; ISBNs & ISSNs; Proofreading & Editing; Media & the Press

Typical questions

- Can you give me a list of publishers of children's books?
- How do I get in touch with publishers about a book I've written?
- Who is the publisher of XXX journal?

Where to look
Book publishers

Directory of UK and Irish book publishers, Joint publication by The Booksellers Association and Nielsen BookData
Also available online at **www.booksellers.org.uk**.

Directory of publishing: United Kingdom and the Republic of Ireland, Continuum
and the Publishers Association
Provides information on 950 publishers.

Journal publishers

Willings press guide, 3 vols, Cison UK Ltd
Excellent three-volume publication providing details of thousands of
newspapers, magazines, periodicals and broadcasting in the UK (Vol. 1),
Western Europe (Vol. 2), and the rest of the world (Vol. 3). Lists over 75,000
contacts. Also available online at **www.willingspress.com**.

BRAD: the monthly guide to advertising media, Emap Communications
BRAD is a classified directory of media in the UK and the Republic of
Ireland that carries advertising. It is divided into eight market sectors
including national newspapers, regional newspapers, consumer press and
the business press. Each sector has a classification index.

Benn's media, 4 vols, Hollis Publishing
This covers the UK, Europe, North America and the rest of the World. It
has 28,000 named contacts from 208 countries.

Statistics

UK book industry statistics yearbook (2007) Publishers Association

Getting published

Writers' & artists' yearbook, A&C Black
An excellent source of information for all budding authors, whether it's
writing books, poetry or newspaper articles. Try also the *Children's writers'
and artists' yearbook*.

The Publishers Association website provides sections on getting published and
careers in publishing:

www.publishers.org.uk

Websites

Booksellers Association of the UK and Ireland **www.booksellers.org.uk**

British Newspapers and News Online **www.wrx.zen.co.uk**

Includes all the British newspapers publishing online news and information.

Independent Publishers Guild **www.ipg.uk.com**

Music Publishers Association (MPA) **www.mpaonline.org.uk**

Newspaper Society **www.newspapersoc.org**
Excellent, includes Find a Publisher, publisher websites and Facts and Figures.

Periodical Publishers Association **www.ppa.co.uk**

Publishers Association **www.publishers.org.uk**
Excellent for publishing issues, market information and statistics.

Publishers Licensing Society **www.pls.org.uk**

Publishing News **www.publishingnews.co.uk**

Publishing Scotland **www.publishingscotland.org**

Society of Young Publishers **www.thesyp.org.uk**

Welsh Books Council **www.wbc.org.uk**

QUOTATIONS & SPEECHES

See also Literature; Poems & Poetry; Proverbs

Typical questions

- Who said 'Let them eat cake'?
- Can you suggest some humorous quotes I can use for a talk I am giving?
- What's the correct wording of 'All that glitters is not gold'?

Considerations

Finding the source of quotations is a frequent task for library staff. There are numerous compilations of quotations. It is a subject beloved of crossword and quiz compilers. Writers and after-dinner speakers are also regular enquirers. Bear in mind that there is sometimes genuine uncertainty about the first recorded use of a 'quote' and it is worth checking more than one source if there is time.

Collections of quotations are arranged in many ways, by subject, by first word, and by the person quoted. Although most books have indexes for the approach not chosen in the main sequence, it is useful to know which books in your stock are best for which purpose. There are numerous books on quotations; often you will have to look through all of them on the library shelves in search of the elusive quote. This is one of those categories of enquiries, especially for the phone enquirer doing a crossword, where one has to put a time limit on how long to spend searching. Perhaps a check in three sources is enough for the quiz addict.

There are also books of quotations on particular subjects. These are generally located with other books on that subject, for example, medical quotes, biblical quotes.

Where to look
Quotations

Andrews, R., Biggs, M. and Seidel, M. (1996) *The Columbia world of quotations*, Columbia University Press
65,000 quotations from 5000 authors with 6500 subject categories. The 1996 print edition of *The Columbia world of quotations* is available online at **www.bartleby.com/66**

Bartleby **www.bartleby.com/100**
A website based on the 1919 edition of Bartlett's *Familiar quotations*. It has some 11,000 quotations.

Bartlett, J. (1993) *Familiar quotations*, 16th edn, Little, Brown and Co.

Cohen, J. M. and Cohen, M. J. (1998) *The new dictionary of quotations*, Penguin

Farkas, A. (2002) *The Oxford dictionary of catchphrases*, Oxford University Press

Jeffares, A. N. and Gray, M. (1995) *Dictionary of quotations*, HarperCollins

Kemp, P. (2002) *The Oxford dictionary of literary quotations*, 2nd edn, Oxford University Press

Knowles, E. (2000) *The Oxford dictionary of quotations*, 5th edn, Oxford University Press
20,000 quotes from 2500 people.

Knowles, E. (2002) *The Oxford dictionary of modern quotations*, 2nd edn, Oxford University Press

Quoted **www.geocities.com/~spanoudi/quote.html**
About 25,000 entries.

Rees, N. (2006) *Brewer's famous quotations*, Weidenfeld & Nicolson
5000 quotations and the stories behind them.

Sherrin, N. (ed.) (2000) *The Oxford dictionary of humorous quotations*, Oxford University Press
A personal selection of 5000 quotations.

Shapiro, F. R. (2006) *The Yale book of quotations*, Yale University Press
An oustanding work in the genre of quotation books.

Speeches

Burnet, A. (ed.) (2006) *Chambers book of speeches*, Chambers
Full texts of over 250 famous speeches by over 200 people.

Fadiman, C. and Bernand, A. (2000) *Bartlett's book of anecdotes*, 2nd edn, Little, Brown and Co.

The Quotations Page **www.thequotationspage.com**
A quote-of-the-day for those wanting quotes to use.

Tips and pitfalls

A check round colleagues is often useful. Bear in mind that the Bible, Milton and Shakespeare between them account for a large percentage of quotes. Which of your colleagues has had a classical, humanist or liberal education?

RAILWAYS

See also Timetables & Journey Planning

Typical questions

- Have you got maps of where old railway lines used to go?
- Who owns all the various railway services?
- Can I go by train to Gainsborough?
- How many passengers use the trains every day?

Considerations

There is a huge interest in railways, both from the historical perspective (cultural and local history) and the modern concern for improving public transport services and reducing carbon emissions. Not forgetting the train spotters and model makers!

Where to look

General

Butcher, A. C. (ed.), *Railways restored*, Ian Allen. Annual
    Overall picture plus technical details.

A comprehensive guide to Britain's railways, 9th edn, Emap. Annual
    Guide and directory to the routes, operating companies and infrastructure of today's rail network.

Glover, J. (2005) *'Modern Railways' dictionary of railway industry terms*, Ian Allan

Holland, J. (2007) *Amazing and extraordinary railway facts*, David & Charles

Jackson, A. A. (2006) *The railway dictionary: worldwide railway facts and terminology*, 4th edn, Sutton Publishing

The modern railway: directory, review, opinion, reference, Ian Allen. Annual
    Standard reference source for the railway industry.

Thomas, D. St. J. et al. (1960–) *A regional history of the railways of Great Britain*, David & Charles
    The standard 14-volume series covering the UK.

Ottley, G. (1983) *A bibliography of British railway history*, 2nd edn, HMSO; Supplement (1988), HMSO

Railway directory, DVV Media UK. Annual
> Worldwide coverage of companies, personnel, statistics, suppliers and maps. Available also as subscription website.

Journals and magazines

Modern Railways Ian Allen. Monthly
> Fairly technical.

The Railway Magazine, IPC. Monthly

Today's Railways, Platform 5 Publishing. Monthly

Maps and atlases

Baker, S. K. (2007) *Rail atlas of Great Britain and Ireland*, 11th edn, Midland Counties Publications.
> Every operating line, whether passenger, private, freight or narrow gauge.

Ball, M. G. (1996) *European railway atlas*, Ian Allen, 3 vols

Wignall, C. J. (1985) *Complete British railways maps and gazetteer from 1825 to 1985*, OPC Railprint

Timetables

Bradshaw's April 1910 railway guide (1968 reprint) David & Charles
> Bradshaw's railway timetables were published from 1840. This reprint shows the full extent of the UK rail network at its height.

European rail timetable, Thomas Cook. Monthly
> Covers 40 countries including the UK, but does not give full details of purely local services.

National Rail Enquiries **www.nationalrail.co.uk/planmyjourney**

UK rail timetable, The Stationery Office. Biannual
> Complete coverage for the UK.

Tips and pitfalls

There is a huge 'sub-culture' of carriage stock books, rail company liveries, engine numbers and best viewing points beloved of rail enthusiasts. See the railway magazines for details of these.

RECORDS (ACHIEVEMENT)

Typical questions

- What is the longest suspension bridge in the world?
- Who was the tallest ever living human being?
- What is the fastest animal on four legs in the world?

Where to look
Printed sources

There is one obvious place to look for facts like these:

Guinness book of records, Guinness Publications. Annual
> The format of the book seems to change year by year, but you should be able to find answers in here. It is indexed and this should make your job easier, as the format can be difficult to navigate.

Another useful publication is;

Ash, R. (2008) *The top ten of everything*, Dorling Kindersley
> This annual includes records, facts and trivia. For example, it will give you Britain's best-selling comics, the world's longest running musical, and the top ten soft drinks. It has a wealth of information and facts. Try and have a look at the book and you will be amazed at its contents.

Electronic sources

Guinness have a useful website in addition to the printed version of their book of records:

www.guinnessworldrecords.com

RELIGION

See also Myths & Mythology; Parish Registers; Saints

Typical questions

- Have you got the 'authorized' Bible?
- When is the festival of Diwali?

R RELIGION

Considerations

Religion, like sex and politics, can be a dangerous subject! Be very careful not to pass a personal opinion. While most enquirers are likely to be open and straightforward, there are some who will be neither.

Each religion, denomination and sect has its own literature, reference books and local organizations. Religion quickly shades into cultural issues; indeed, the distinction between religion and culture is not accepted in many faiths, so beware of making distinctions where none exists.

Where to look
General

Adherents.com **http://adherents.com**
Free website giving references to published membership/adherent statistics and congregation statistics for over 4200 religious churches, denominations, religious bodies, faith groups, tribes, cultures, movements, ultimate concerns, etc. US focus.

American religious data archive (ARDA) **www.thearda.com**

Brown, A. (ed.) (1998) *Festivals in world religions*, Longman

Encyclopedia of world religion (2006) 2nd edn, Facts on File

Firth, L. (ed.) (2008) *Religious beliefs*, Independence publishers
Vol. 148 in the Issues series, which features recent articles from the press.

Hinnells, J. R. (ed.) (2003) *A new handbook of living religions*, 3rd edn, Blackwell
One of the best in a large number of alternatives.

Oxford Reference Online **www.oxfordreference.com**
Has a section Religion & Philosophy with texts from major reference books.

Weller, P. (ed.) (2001) *Religions in the UK: a multi-faith directory*, 3rd edn, The Multi-Faith Centre, University of Derby
A guide to the nine main world religions in the UK, listing 3500 local, regional and national organizations. Over 600 pages.

MacGregor, G. (1990) *The Everyman directory of religion and philosophy*, Dent

SHAP calendar of religious festivals (2001) Shap Working Party

The world's religions: a Lion handbook (1994) 2nd edn, Lion Publishing
Basic, colourful, factual.

Sacred books

The Bible, the Koran, the Torah, and other writings that form the basis of Christianity, Islam, Judaism, etc., are to be found in many different versions. Details of them will be found in the general sources above. In addition to the different versions (which will appeal to different branches of followers), there may be commentaries, dictionaries and concordances to these on the library shelves.

Buddhism

Buswell, R. E. (2004) *Encyclopedia of Buddhism*, Macmillan, 2 vols

Encyclopedia of Buddhism (2008) Facts on File

Keown, D. and Prebish, C. S. (2007) *Encyclopedia of Buddhism*, Routledge

Christianity
General

Cross, F. L. and Livingstone, E. A. (1997) *The Oxford dictionary of the Christian Church*, 3rd edn, Oxford University Press.

Friar, S. (2003) *The Sutton companion to churches*, 2nd edn, Sutton Publishing

Humphrey, S. (1991) *Churches and chapels: Northern England*, Blue Guides

Humphrey, S. (1991) *Churches and chapels: Southern England*, Blue Guides

Livingstone, E. A. (ed.) (2006) *The concise dictionary of the Christian Church*, 2nd edn, Oxford University Press

Melton, J. G. (ed.) (2005) *Encyclopedia of Protestanism*, Facts on File

Taylor, R. (2003) *How to read a church: a guide to images, symbols and meanings in churches and cathedrals*, Rider

Venning, T. (2005) *Compendium of British office holders*, Palgrave Macmillan
Includes holders of religious office in the British Isles since the fifth century.

World Christian encyclopedia (2000) 2nd edn, Oxford University Press
Covers contemporary Christianity.

World Council of Churches
PO Box 2100, 150 Route de Ferney, 1211 Geneva 2, Switzerland
www.wcc-coe.org

The Bible

The Bible is the sacred book of Christianity. The 'Authorized' or 'King James' version of 1611 version was 'authorized to be read in Churches' by King James I and is a standard text of the Bible. Although only infrequently used in churches now, it is often referred to and requested. The Roman Catholic Church uses a different version of the Bible which goes back to the Duay-Rheims Bible of 1609. There are now many different translations and versions of the Bible. Larger libraries may have the Greek New Testament.

The Bible, New Revised Standard version, Cambridge University Press

Harvey, A. G. (2004) *A companion to the New Testament: the new revised standard version*, Cambridge University Press
A detailed commentary on the popular modern edition.

Metzger, B. M. and Coogan, M. D. (eds) (1993) *Oxford companion to the Bible*, Oxford University Press

Be aware of how parts of the Bible are cited. Generally citations consist of three elements: name of 'book' or part of the Bible, followed by the chapter number, followed by the verse number or numbers. This arrangement dates from the Vulgate version of the year 405 and is enshrined in the Authorized version. Thus 'Proverbs 3: 6–11' would refer to verses six to eleven of the third chapter of the Book of Proverbs. OT and NT refer to the Old Testament and New Testament respectively.

The Anglican Church

Includes the Church of England, the Church in Wales, the Scottish Episcopal Church and the Church of Ireland.

Anglican Online **http://anglicanonline.org**
A large database of information, resources and links.

Church of England yearbook, Church House Publishing. Annual

Directory of parishes and organisations of the Established Church.

Crockford's clerical directory: a directory of the clergy of the Church of England, the Church in Wales, the Scottish Episcopal Church, the Church of Ireland, Church House Publishing. Annual
The standard list of Anglican clergy and churches.

Methodism

Methodist Recorder Weekly newspaper

Yrigoyen, C. and Warrick, S. E. (eds) (2005) *Historical dictionary of Methodism*, 2nd edn, Scarecrow Press

The Religious Society of Friends in Britain (Quakers)

Friends House, 173 Euston Road, London NW1 2BJ
The website **www.quaker.org.uk** lists local groups, news and events.

The Roman Catholic Church

Catholic directory of England and Wales, Gabriel Communications Ltd. Annual

The Catholic Herald Weekly newspaper

Encyclopedia of Roman Catholicism, Facts on File

Glazier, M. and Hellwig, M. K. (eds) (2004) *The modern Catholic encyclopedia*, Liturgical Press

Martin, C. (2007) *A glimpse of heaven: Catholic churches of England and Wales*, English Heritage
A guide to 100 catholic churches.

New Advent Catholic encyclopedia **www.newadvent.org**
Online version of the 15 vol. *Catholic encyclopedia*, edited by C. G. Herberman and others (1907–1914).

Hinduism

Cush, D., Robinson, C. and York, M. (2007) *Encyclopedia of Hinduism*, Routledge

Encyclopedia of Hinduism (2007) Facts on File

Rinehart, R. (ed.) (2004) *Contemporary Hinduism: ritual, culture, and practice*, ABC-Clio

Islam

Coughlin, K. M. (ed.) (2006) *Muslim culture today: a reference guide*, Greenwood Press

Crescent International Weekly newspaper

Encyclopedia of Islam (2007) Facts on File

Exposito, J. L. (ed.) (2003) *The Oxford dictionary of Islam*, Oxford University Press

Exposito, J. L. and others (2004) *The Islamic world past and present*, Oxford University Press, 3 vols

Martin, R. C. et al. (ed.) (2004) *Encylopedia of Islam and the Muslim World*, Macmillan

Muslim Heritage **www.muslimheritage.com**

Rippin, A. (ed.) (2006) *The Blackwell companion to the Qur'an*, Blackwell

Judaism

Abrahamson, G. (ed.) (2005) *Encyclopedia of Modern Jewish culture*, Routledge, 2 vols

Encyclopedica Judaica **www.encyclopediajudaica.com**

Jewish Chronicle Weekly newspaper

Jewish encyclopedia **www.jewishencyclopedia.com**
Based on the 1901–06 print version. Free.

Encyclopedia of Judaism (2000–3) Brill, 4 vols

Other religions, groups and organizations

British Humanist Association **www.humanism.org.uk**

Clarke, P. (ed.) (2006) *Encyclopedia of new religious movements*, Routledge

Ekklesia **www.ekklesia.co.uk**
A think-tank that promotes theological issues in public life.

Encyclopedia of new religions: new religious movements, sects and alternative
  spiritualities (2004), 2nd edn, Lion Publishing

Religious Tolerance **www.religioustolerance.org.uk**
  A foundation for human rights and tolerance.

Tips and pitfalls

Most religions and denominations have websites and yearbooks. Local telephone
directories have good coverage of places of worship.

This is not a subject that library staff should get too involved with unless they,
or a colleague, feel confident of their knowledge, and can dispense it without bias.
In religion, like politics, an enquiry for information can quickly develop into an
argument. Even when the librarian is sure the enquirer is wrong there are times
when it is wise to be quiet. Be aware, also, that most religions have their
fundamentalist–orthodox and modernist–liberal communities. Don't get caught
in the middle!

General encyclopedias are usually very good on religions and religious topics.

RESEARCH & STUDY

See also Books & Bibliographies; Homework; Writers &
Writing

Typical questions

- What research has been published on . . .?
- I've been told to look at a particular thesis. Can you get it for me?
- What's special about writing a dissertation?

Considerations

The word 'research' is one of those words used so loosely that one has to interrogate
further to identify what level of research is intended. Originally the province of
postgraduate students and scholars, the word is now used by school children and
quiz buffs. There is also a need to be careful over the terms 'dissertation' and 'thesis'.
Although both words are used loosely for the reports of research, more specifically,
a (UK) 'thesis' is the written work done for a doctorate, which is a 'dissertation'
in the USA. A 'dissertation' in the UK generally refers to work done for a
Bachelor's or Master's degree. However, since schoolchildren use both words for
their 'research', care needs to be taken over what, exactly, the enquirer wants.

In a school, college, university or industrial library, staff should be familiar with the needs of their users; specialist resources in those libraries are not featured here. Such specialist needs, particularly if tied to a curriculum or subject field, usually have their own printed literature guides, internet portals, and subscription services. Probably, even, there are specially prepared instructional guides. For queries in public libraries reference to the other chapters in this guide may be sufficient, but the library might have some guides to research sources and many people will ask for guidance.

Indexes and abstracts to, for example, theses and dissertations, may be stocked and can provide information about what, if anything, has been already researched on a subject. Since they are, usually, unpublished, the many thousands of theses and dissertations that have been written represent a huge pool of knowledge not indexed by the standard indexes and bibliographies which relate to published work. Be warned, though, that advice may be needed from library colleagues who deal with interlibrary lending on any restrictions that may apply in obtaining or using this category of literature. A formal declaration may be needed and use will, almost certainly, be restricted to within the library.

Many of the indexes that were formerly purchased in print form are now available on subscription websites.

Finally, beware of getting drawn into doing peoples' research for them. It is a slippery slope from assisting someone to use materials to using them for them!

Where to look
General

Allison, B. (1997) *The student's guide to preparing dissertations and theses*, 2nd edn, Routledge

Blaxter, L., Hughes, C. and Tight, M. (2006) *How to research*, 3rd edn, Open University Press

Hock, R. (2007) *The extreme searcher's internet handbook: a guide for the serious searcher*, 2nd edn, Cyber Age Books.
See **www.extremesearcher.com** for links to websites covered.

Rumsey, S. (2004) *How to find information: a guide for searchers*, Open University Press

Turabian, K. L. (1996) *A manual for writers of term papers, theses and dissertations*, 6th edn, University of Chicago Press

Theses and dissertations

ASLIB (1950/1–) *Index to theses accepted for higher degrees in the universities of Great Britain and Ireland*
Abstracts arranged in broad subject areas, with author index.

British Standards Institution (1990) *Presentation of theses and dissertations*, 2nd edn, BSI

The Brits index: an index to the British theses collection (1971–1987) held at the British Library Document Supply Centre and London University (1989) 3 vols, British Theses Service

Comprehensive dissertation index, 1861–1972 (1973) 73 vols, Xerox University Microfilm
Over 417,000 dissertations.

Dissertation abstracts international (1938–) University Microfilms International. Monthly, cumulated
Lists US doctoral dissertations available on microfilm or as xeroxed reproduction. Includes European theses from 1969. Arranged by broad subject with keyword and title indexes.

ETD [Electronic Theses and Dissertations] Digital Library **www.theses.org**
Links to websites which list theses and dissertations.

University Microfilms International (now Proquest) **www.proquest.com**
Subscription website to over 1.4 million dissertations.

Website portals and e-libraries

British Library Direct **http://direct.bl.uk**
Provides access to 20,000 journals and their texts, which can be purchased using credit cards.

Gale Virtual Reference Library **www.cengage.com**
A database of encyclopedias and specialized reference sources for multidisciplinary research.

Google Scholar **http://scholar.google.co.uk/imtl/en/scholar**
Provides access to peer-reviewed papers, theses, books, abstracts and articles.

Intute **www.intute.ac.uk** (formerly SOSIG)

> Intute is a free online service providing access to the best web resources for education and research. The service is managed by a network of UK universities and other partners. Subject specialists select and evaluate the websites and write objective descriptions of the resources. The database contains some 125,000 records.

Ovid Search Solver **www.ovid.com/site/help/documentaion/searchsolver.jsp**

> A single search access to a wide range of resources including journals, databases, portals and OPACS.

Oxford Scholarship Online

> **www.oxfordscholarship.com/oso/public/index.html**
> Gives full text of over 750 humanities and social science titles published by Oxford University Press. Subscription applies to the full texts but there is free access to view abstracts and keywords.

Other sources

Scholarly Societies Project **www.scholarly-societies.org**

> Gives details of over 4000 societies worldwide with links to 3815 websites.

Tips and pitfalls

Students doing projects often come in droves, often for the same topic. Tell colleagues what seems to be the latest topic, else you will find all the useful resources 'missing'! Pool knowledge and information on useful materials. Many topics keep popping up and librarians often compile 'project files', or subscribe to the Independence Press *Issues* series. Keep in touch with teachers if you can and ask them to forewarn you before the hordes descend.

Be careful not to get too involved in someone else's research.

RETAILING & CONSUMER SPENDING

See also Consumer Information; Food & Drink

Typical questions

- Have you got a list of supermarkets?
- Have you got a list of factory outlets?
- I've got to do a project on the retail industry.
- How much do people spend on . . .?

Considerations

There is both the retailer and the consumer to consider when looking at the retail industry. Is the enquirer interested in consumer patterns or are they themselves the consumer? What type of retail outlet is the user interested in? The retail industry covers a wide range of outlets, including supermarkets, department stores, mail order/home shopping, chemists, factory and discount stores, and market traders.

When more in-depth comment on the retail industry is required, market research reports are an excellent source of statistics and analysis.

Users may also want to complain about goods they have bought. It is best to refer to the Trading Standards Institute, National Consumer Council or the Office of Fair Trading. For more details of the above and consumer law see chapter on CONSUMER INFORMATION.

Where to look
Directories

World retail directory and sourcebook, Euromonitor
> This provides information on leading retailers in over 52 countries and global trends in retailing.

Retail directory of the UK, Hemming Information Services
> This directory provides details of the most significant retailing companies both in the UK and the Republic of Ireland. In addition to company details it also provides, if available, the names of individual buyers and managers.

Retail directory of Europe, Hemming Information Services

World's top retailers, Hemming Information Services
> Information on 25,000 stores from 90 countries.

Retail and shopping centre directory, William Reed Directories
> This provides alphabetical listings of shopping centres in the UK and the Republic of Ireland, multiple retailers and commercial property agents, owners and developers. Includes details of 13,800 companies. There is also an online version free with the directory.

Market yearbook, World's Fair
> This publication provides market details (type of market, market days, charges and contacts) arranged geographically.

Refer also to the directories mentioned under COMPANIES.

Journals

There are numerous journals that cover retail and retailers, details of which can be found in *Willings press guide* (see JOURNALS & PERIODICALS).

European Retail Analyst
> Research and Markets
> Tel: 00 353 1 481 1716
> **www.researchandmarkets.com**
> Monthly
> Market intelligence on retail sector in Europe.

Statistics

Consumer trends, The Stationery Office. Quarterly
> This provides data on household expenditure. Available to download from **www.statistics.gov.uk**.

Economic & labour market review, The Stationery Office. Monthly
> Includes the Retail Price Index and GDP.

Monthly digest of statistics, The Stationery Office
> Includes national accounts, retailing statistics and both the Retail Price Index and the Consumer Price Index.

World retail data and statistics, Euromonitor
> This directory provides retailing statistics from 52 countries in addition to socio-economic trends and consumer expenditure patterns.

Market research

Mintel retail reports, Mintel International Group
> This provides in-depth research into the retail industry. It looks at market factors, market segmentation, the consumer and the future. Also available on CD-ROM. For details visit **www.mintel.co.uk** (Tel: 020 7606 4533; Fax: 020 7606 5932). Mintel website allows free access to press releases on new reports; these provide a synopsis of the report.

Key Note reports, Key Note
> For free executive summaries of report titles listed under retailing visit **www.keynote.co.uk**. For details of obtaining full reports, contact Key Note (Tel: 020 8481 8750; Fax: 020 8783 0049).

The Competition Commission is a useful place to look for information on the retail industry. It has documents and press releases on mergers, markets and the regulation of the major regulated industries **www.competition-commission.org.uk**.

Websites

British Chambers of Commerce **www.britishchambers.org.uk**

British Retail Consortium **www.brc.org.uk**
> Excellent for retail policies and issues, surveys and statistics. It has loads of publications available to download.

RIGHTS

See also Consumer Information; Employment – Rights & Statistics; Equal Opportunities; Law; Social Welfare

Typical questions

- I'm in dispute with a neighbour. What are my rights?
- What rights do children have?
- What have you got on the Human Rights Act?

Considerations

'Rights' is a topic of great concern. They present a problem for the librarian as the subject did not exist in its modern form when the Dewey classification was established. The 323s (political rights) is one place to find books on rights, another is in law, and a third is in ethics (179). 'Rights' as an abstract concept (ethics) needs to be distinguished from the 'rights' of a particular group (politics), animals included. Legal rights is another category. An element of preliminary interrogation is often needed to get the librarian on the right wavelength. Be aware, also, that this is an area of both legal necessity and passionate concern.

For the rights of a particualar subject, e.g. employment, look under that subject.

Where to look
General

Allen, R. (2000) *Employment law and the Human Rights Act 1998*, Blackstone Press

▪R RIGHTS

Arat, Z. F. K. (2006) *Human rights worldwide: a reference handbook*, ABC-Clio

Brownlie, I. (1992) *Basic documents on human rights*, 3rd edn, Clarenden Press
International and regional agreements.

Citizens Advice Bureau (2008) *Citizen's advice guide to your rights: the ultimate
survival guide to life in Britain today*, CAB

Cooper, I. (1983) *Which? way to complain*, Consumer Association

Directgov **www.direct.gov.uk**
A government website providing a wide range of practical information on
social issues. Numerous downloadable leaflets.

Fenwick, H. (2007) *Civil liberties and human rights*, 4th edn, Routledge
A 1604-page compendium.

Foreign and Commonwealth Office and Department for International
Development, *Human rights*, The Stationery Office. Annual
A useful annual survey.

Guild, E. and Lesieur, G. (1999) *The European Court of Justice on the European
Convention on Human Rights: who said what, when?* Kluwer Law
International

Halsbury's laws of England, Butterworths
This multivolume legal encyclopedias may be useful here.

Humana, C. (1992) *World human rights guide*, 3rd edn, Oxford University Press
Tabled guide to countries of the world.

Leckie, D. and Pickersgill, D. (1999) *The 1998 Human Rights Act explained*,
The Stationery Office.
A brief introduction.

Parliament, *Human Rights Act 1998*, HMSO

Robertson, D. (2004) *A dictionary of human rights*, 2nd edn, Europa

United Nations human rights yearbook, UN. Annual

Wadham, J. and Crossma, G. (eds) (2000) *Your rights: the Liberty guide to human
rights*, 7th edn, Pluto Press
Includes selected texts and directory information. UK law.

Wadham, T. and Mountfield H. (1999) *Blackstone's guide to the Human Rights Act 1998*, Blackstone Press

Wiseman, S. (2001) *How to complain effectively*, Law Pack Publishing

Organizations

National Association of Citizens' Advice Bureaux **www.nacab.org.uk**
CABs provide information on civil rights among many other social topics. See telephone directories for local offices.

National Information Forum
Post Point 905, BT Burne House, Bell Street, London NW1 5BZ
Tel: 020 7402 6681; Fax: 020 7402 1259
E-mail: info@nif.org.uk
http://nif.org.uk
Campaigns for access to information as a basic civil right

Animals *see* chapter on ANIMALS, PETS & VETS for information on animal rights.

Children

Alston, P. et al. (eds) (1992) *Children, rights and the law*, Oxford University Press

Data protection

Carey, P. (2000) *Data protection in the UK*, Blackstone Press

Carey, P. (2004) *Data protection handbook*, Law Society

Information Commissioner's Office (Previously Data Protection Commission)
Wycliff House, Water Lane, Wilmslow SK9 5AF
Tel: 01625 545740
www.ico.gov.uk
The UK's independent authority to promote access to official information and to protect personal information. This office issues numerous information leaflets.

Leigh-Pollitt, P. and Mullock, J. (2001) *Data Protection Act explained*, The Stationery Office (Point of Law series)

Parliament, *Data Protection Act 1998*, HMSO
  Covers information on electronic and manual records.

Disabled

Equality and Human Rights Commission (previously Disability Rights
  Commission) **www.equalityhumanrights.com**

Elderly

O'Dempsey, D. et al. (2006) *Age discrimination handbook*, Legal Action Group

Freedom of information

The Campaign for Freedom of Information **www.cfoi.org.uk**

Carey, P. and Turle, M. (eds) (2006) *Freedom of information handbook*, Law Society

Brook, H. and Hislop, I. (2006) *Your right to know: a citizen's guide to the
  Freedom of Information Act*, 2nd edn, Pluto Press

Local Government Association Constitution Unit (2001) *Freedom of
  information: practical guide for local authorities*

Macdonald, J. and Jones, C. (eds) (2003) *The law of freedom of information*,
  Oxford University Press

Ministry of Justice (previously Department of Constitutional Affairs)
  www.justice.gov.uk
  Many links to freedom of information bodies.

Parliament, *Freedom of Information Act 2000*, HMSO

Wadham, J. et al. (2001) *Blackstone's guide to the Freedom of Information Act
  2000*, Blackstone Press
  Provides text of act, commentary, and chapters on open government and
  freedom of information in other countries.

Organizations

The AIRE (Advice on Individual Rights in Europe)
  17 Red Lion Square, London WC1R 4QH
  Tel: 020 7831 3850
  www.airecentre.org

The Freedom Association
PO Box 2820, Bridgnorth, Shropshire WV16 6YR
Tel: 01746 861267
www.tfa.net

Health
Mind (2001) *Legal rights and mental health: the Mind manual*, 14th edn, Mind

Homes
Child Poverty Action Group (1998) *Rights guide for home owners*, 12th edn, CPAG

Minorities
Equality and Human Rights Commission (previously Commission for Racial
Equality)
Elliot House, 10–12 Allington Street, London SW1E 5EH
Tel: 020 7828 7022
www.equalityhumanrights.com

Lesbian and gay men and bisexual equality issues **www.stonewall.org.uk**

Liberty (National Council for Civil Liberties)
21 Tabard Street, London SE1 4LA
Tel: 020 7403 3888
www.liberty-human-rights.org.uk
An independent human rights organization.

Minority Rights International
379 Brixton Road, London SW9 7DE
Tel: 020 7978 9498
www.minorityrights.org

Prisoners
Amnesty International
1 Easton Street, London WC1X 0DW
www.amnesty.org
Worldwide campaigning movement with particular concern for prisoners
of conscience.

Tips and pitfalls

As with all legal enquiries, let the texts speak for themselves. And if you don't understand them, admit it. Refer enquirers to the CAB or to a legal aid scheme if appropriate.

SAINTS

See also Religion

Typical questions
- Who is the patron saint of librarians?
- I want to know more about St Ia.

Considerations

General encyclopedias cover the more common saints but try and make sure you have a specific dictionary or encyclopedia, too.

Where to look
Printed sources

Farmer, D. H. (2004) *The Oxford dictionary of saints*, Oxford University Press
  This dictionary contains concise accounts of the lives, cults and artistic associations of around 1250 saints from Great Britain and Europe. Make sure you have a copy!

Watkins, B. (2002) *The book of saints*, 7th edn, ARC Books
  Biographical dictionary of 10,000 saints.

Electronic sources

Catholic Online: Saints and Angels **www.catholic.org/saints**
  An excellent resource. Most saints are covered. Lives, patronages and feast days are all shown.

SIGNS & SYMBOLS

See also Alphabets & Scripts

Typical questions
- What's the sign for a low bridge?
- What does the symbol on this packaging mean?
- What does '?' in chess notation stand for?

Considerations

Signs and symbols are used almost everywhere, on labels giving washing instructions, on the machines that do the washing, on keyboards and on documents. And this is before looking at the symbolism used in art and in cultural history. Information about many symbols, in art or on road traffic signs, for example, will be covered in books on the subject or in general encyclopedias in the case of cultural symbols such as the cross or swastika. A number of specialist works do exist which display symbols whose meaning may be unknown. Obviously, arrangement is problematical!

Where to look
Printed sources

Foley, J. (1993) *The Guinness encyclopedia of signs and symbols*, Guinness Publications
    Modern symbols such as trade marks.

Liungman, G. (1995) *Dictionary of symbols*, W. W. Norton
    Strong on classical symbols.

Shepherd, R. and Shepherd, R. (2002) *1000 symbols: what shapes mean in art and myths*, Thames & Hudson

For domestic symbols, such as washing temperatures and cleaning symbols, books on household work are useful, such as:

Phillips, B. (1989) *The Daily Mail book of household hints and tips*, Dorling Kindersley

Electronic sources

Symbols **www.symbols.com**
    4500 Western signs in 54 groups from 'ideograms carved in mammoth teeth by Cro Magnon man, to hobo signs and subway graffiti'. Interactive facility whereby you can describe the symbol you want.

Alternatively try **www.symbols.net**

SOCIAL WELFARE

See also Benefits; Charitable Organizations; Childcare; Death, Funerals & Bereavement; Health & Healthcare; Nationality & Immigration; Rights; Volunteering

Typical questions

- What are the rules about when people can go into care?
- How can a disabled person get help?

Considerations

A distinction needs to be drawn between those enquirers who are seeking help, and students doing projects.

Librarians on information desks frequently encounter people who are in genuine need or in distress. Some guidelines and useful addresses which can be produced quickly are needed, such as the local Salvation Army (and how to get there). Sometimes the police may have to be contacted – have their local number to hand. Such encounters can be upsetting, but help given tactfully can be rewarding.

Where to look
General

Bramner, A. (2004) *Social work law*, 2nd edn, Longmans

Child Poverty Action Group (2008) *Social security legislation*, 9th edition, CPAG, 4 vols

Child Poverty Action Group (2007) *Migration and social security handbook*, 4th edn, CPAG

Davies, M. (ed.) (1997) *The Blackwell companion for social work*, Blackwell

Ennals, S. *Social security and state benefits: a practical guide*, 6th edn, Tottel

Guide to the social services: social policy and legislation explained, Waterlow. Annual
Includes directory information.

Jacobs, M. (ed.) (1998) *The care guide: a handbook for the caring professions and other agencies*, Cassell

Kinrade, D. and Wark, P. (2007) *Where to find information*, National Information Forum and CILIP
A guide to information sources on disability, health and money, young people, homelessness and consumer information against a 'right to know' background.

Llewellyn, A., *Society Guardian NHS and social services directory*, Guardian Books and Sage Publications. Annual

Lowe, R. (2004) *The welfare state in Britain since 1945*, 3rd edn, Palgrave Macmillan

Social services year book, Longman. Annual
Over 50,000 contact details for all social services related organizations in the UK. Covers voluntary, charitable and private organizations. Also available on CD-ROM.

Thomas, H. and Pierson, J. (1995) *Dictionary of social work*, Collins Educational

Tonge, K. (2002) *Social security and state benefits: a practical guide*, Tolley

Vernon, S. (ed.) (1998) *Social work and the law*, Butterworths

For government documents try **www.direct.gov.uk**.

Community care

Mandelstam, M. (1998) *An A–Z of community care law*, Jessica Kingsley Publishers

National Carers Association
20–25 Glasshouse Yard, London EC1A 4JS
Tel: 020 7490 888; Fax: 020 7490 8824
www.carersuk.org.uk

Disability

Blue Badge Scheme (Parking concessions for disabled and blind people) Tel: 020 7944 6800

Darnborough, A. and Kinrade, D. (1998) *Directory for disabled people*, 7th edn, Prentice Hall

Dial UK Tel:01302 310123
> Network of disability information and advice services run by people with direct experience of disability.

Disability Net **www.disability.net.uk**
> The information centre for individuals with disabilities. Good links to UK government and non-government agencies. Includes job agencies.

Disabled Living Foundation
> 380 Harrow Road, London W9 2VU
> Helpline: 0845 130 9177
> **www.dlf.org.uk**
> UK national charity working for disabled people.

Paterson, J., *Disability rights handbook*, Disability Alliance. Annual
> A guide to benefits and services for all disabled people, their families, carers and advisers.

RNID for Deaf and Hard of Hearing People **www.rnid.org.uk**

Royal National Institute of the Blind **www.rnib.org.uk**

Elderly

Age Concern England
> Room C696, Astral House, 1268 London Road, London SW16 4ER
> Tel: 020 8765 7200 or 020 8679 8000; Fax 020 8765 7211
> **www.ageconcern.org.uk**
> Advice and information relating to the welfare of older people. Provides free factsheets and a welfare rights advice line. Age Concern Information Line: 0800 00 99 66; Freephone 0808 800 6565
> **www.ace.org.uk**

Agelink Tel: 0500 600090
> Guidance for older people on contacting and using services.

Ashton, G. R. (2008) *Elderly people and the law*, 2nd edn, Tottel

Careline Alarm System (telephone alarm from home): contact the local authority.

Carers' Association Tel: 020 7490 8818

Carers' National Line Tel: 08457 573369

Contact The Elderly
   15 Henrietta Street, London WC2E 8QH
   Tel: 020 7240 0630; Freephone 0800 716543
   www.contact-the-elderly.org
   A voluntary organization for supporting the elderly.

Darnborough, A. and Kinrade, D. (1992) *Directory for older people*, 2nd edn, Woodhead Faulkner

Elder Abuse Tel: 0845 606 0606
   Action on Elder Abuse (national helpline) Tel: 0808 808 8141

Help the Aged
   St James's Walk, Clerkenwell Green, London EC1R 0BE.
   Tel: 020 7253 3303
   www.helptheaged.org.uk

Seniorline – Freephone: England, Scotland and Wales: 0800 00 99 66; Northern Ireland: 0808 800 7575
   Advice and information service for older people.

National Association of Widows/Widowers Advisory Trust
   54-57 Albion Street, Digbeth, Birmingham B5 5TH
   Tel: 0121 643 8348

Pre-Retirement Association
   9 Chesham Road, Guildford, GU1 3LS
   Tel: 01483 301170; Fax: 01483 300981

Shukla, R. B. and Brooks, D. (1996) *A guide to the care of the elderly*, HMSO

Family and parents (see also CHILDCARE)

Hershman, D. and McFarlane, A. (2001) *Children Act handbook 2001*, Family Law
   Contains amended and annotated texts and the 1989 Children Act and other relevant documents.

Contact A Family **www.cafamily.org.uk**
   For families who care for children with disabilities and special needs.

Child Line UK **www.childline.org.uk**

Tel: 0800 1111

A 24-hour helpline for children and young people in trouble or danger.

National Council for One Parent Families (Gingerbread)
225 Kentish Road, London NW5 2LX
Tel: 020 7428 5400; Fax: 020 7482 4851; Helpline: 0800 018 5026
E-mail: info@oneparentfamilies.org.uk
www.oneparentfamilies.org.uk;

NSPCC Child Protection Helpline
Freephone: 0808 800 5000
24-hour helpline for children for children and young people, or anyone concerned about a child or young person at risk of abuse.

Parentline Plus
Freephone: 0808 800 2222
Helpline for support and information for parents or anyone in a parenting role.

Housing

Care homes for older people: national minimum standards (2001) The Stationery Office

Shelterline
Freephone: 0808 800 444
24-hour housing advice offering independent information and advice in confidence to anyone with a housing problem.

Missing people

Message Home Helpline
Freephone: 0800 700 700
24-hour helpline for people who have left home or run away; enables callers to send messages to their families or carers.

National Missing Persons Helpline
Tel: 0500 700 700 (free)
24-hour helpline providing advice, practical help and support for anyone missing relatives or immediate family members.

Rogers, C. D. (1986) *Tracing missing persons: an introduction to agencies, methods and sources in England and Wales*, Manchester University Press

Red Cross International Tracing and Message Service
Tel: 020 7235 5454
www.redcross.org.uk

Salvation Army
www1.salvationarmy.org.uk
See telephone directories for your local branch.

Marriage and relationships

Feltham, C. and Dryden, W. (2004) *Dictionary of counselling*, 2nd edn, Whurr

Lesbian and Gay Switchboard
Tel: 020 7837 7324
24-hour helpline offering support and information for lesbians and gay men.

RELATE (Previously Marriage Guidance Council)
Herbert Grey College, Little Church Street, Rugby, Warwickshire CV21 3AP
Tel: 01788 573241
www.relate.org.uk
Check telephone directories for local centres. Advice and counselling on personal relationship issues.

Pensions

Pension Service, *Pensioners' guide: making the most of government help and advice*. Annual
Free booklet available from local offices of the Department for Work and Pensions. Or contact the Pension Service (Tel: 0845 606505; **www.dwp.gov.uk**). See chapter on BENEFITS.

Suicide

The Samaritans **www.samaritans.org.uk**
Tel: 08457 909090
Gives reports and information. Provides a 24-hour confidential and emotional support helpline for anyone in crisis.

Volunteering *see* **chapter on** VOLUNTEERING

Other sources

Refer people to the local authority information offices, the local offices of the Department of Work and Pensions (previously Social Services) or the Citizens Advice Bureau.

National Association of Citizens Advice Bureaux **www.citizensadvice.org.uk**
Tel: 0870 128 8080 or 020 7833 2181 or phone book for local CAB office.

National Information Forum
Post Point 905, BT Burne House, PP205, Bell Street, London NW1 5BZ
Tel: 020 7402 6681; Fax:020 7402 1259
E-mail: info@nif.org.uk
www.nif.org.uk
Campaigns to improve access to information for the disadvantaged.

Telephone Helplines Association (2006) *Telephone helpline directory*, THA
3rd/4th Floor, 9 Marshalsea Road, Borough, London SE1 1EF
E-mail: info@helplines.org.uk
www.helplines.org.uk
The THA provide information about non-profit UK helplines and provide quality standards.

Tips and pitfalls

Stay objective. Check local telephone directories, e.g. Yellow Pages under 'Counselling and Advice' and 'Charitable Organizations'. The preliminary pages also give useful relevant information. Have the address of the local Citizens Advice Bureau (**www.citizensadvice.org.uk**) at hand.

SPORTS

See also Games Rules

Typical questions

* Who won the FA Cup in 1953?
* Who was in the team that played in the World Cup final for England in 1966?
* Who won the men's championship at Wimbledon in 1982?
* Where do Durham play their home cricket matches?

S SPORTS

Considerations

The range of queries you may receive about sports is vast. There are so many different kinds of sports, and so many different types of questions that could be asked in this popular subject area. Enquirers may be looking for sports' histories, winners of competitions, rules, teams, records, even colours of shirts.

Where to look
Printed sources

There is not space in this book to cover every individual sport. The general sports encyclopedias only are covered. You can also find basic information in a general encyclopedia.

Cuddon, J. A. (1980) *The Macmillan dictionary of sports and games*, Macmillan
　　Has around 6000 entries for sports, events, awards and teams.

Arlott, J. (ed.) (1977) *The Oxford companion to sports and games*, Oxford University Press
　　Describes around 200 sports and games with historical notes.

There are also many yearbooks for specific sports. These can be of great use when looking up previous seasons' results, records, teams, etc. Some examples are:

Sky Sports football yearbook

Wisden cricketers' almanack

Olympics

A key book in this field is:

Greenberg, S. (2003) *Whitaker's Olympic almanack 2004*, A&C Black
　　This little gem contains coverage of every summer and winter Olympics, with descriptions of venues, sports, competitors and records.

The same author also wrote:

Greenberg, S. (1991) *Guinness Olympic factbook*, Guinness

Past Olympic results are available at **www.databaseolympics.com**

The official Olympic website is **www.olympic.org**.

Electronic sources

There are thousands of good sports websites. Again, each individual sport will have its own good websites. As a starting point, try some of the following:

http://sports.yahoo.com
http://directory.google.com/Top/Sports
http://en.wikipedia.org/wiki/Sport

For up-to-date sports news and scores try:

www.bbc.co.uk/sport
www.sportinglife.com

Tips and pitfalls

Check your library shelves to see what reference books you have on sport. Try and familiarize yourself with them and their contents. This will make life much easier when dealing with enquiries. Also, get to know the sporting interests of your colleagues. You could be amazed at the knowledge they possess.

STATISTICS

See also European Information; Market Research; Population

Typical questions

- Have you got any statistics for pet ownership?
- How do I locate statistics on health?

Considerations

Statistics can be either official – from government – or unofficial, e.g. from trade associations, companies, independent market research companies and banks. Vast amounts of statistics are produced and it is difficult to know about them all. Undoubtedly, the best way to find out about government-produced statistics is to use the excellent government statistics website **www.statistics.gov.uk**. This allows you to search by keyword or specific title. Many of the titles can be downloaded freely or the site gives you purchase details. Unofficial statistics are produced by such a wide variety of organizations that it would be impossible to provide a list here. However, the *World directory of non-official statistical sources* (2007) Euromonitor may help. This is an excellent tool to locate reports, statistics and surveys produced by companies, banks and trade associations. In addition, a lot of the suggestions in the Market Research and European Information chapters are useful for tracking down statistics.

Where to look
Background
Everitt, B. S. (2006) *The Cambridge dictionary of statistics*, 3rd edn, Cambridge University Press

International

World statistics pocketbook, 2 vols, United Nations
Provides international statistics on 215 countries, covering basic economic, social and environmental data. The data is drawn from 20 international statistical sources. Also look at the United Nations Statistical Division website **www.un.org/Depts/unsd/**.

Statistical abstract of the United States, US Census Bureau **www.census.gov**
Also provides other US statistics.

National

Annual abstract of statistics, Office for National Statistics
A comprehensive collection of statistics covering the UK. Contains data on population, manufacturing, social services, finance, education, transport and defence.

Social trends, Office for National Statistics
A compendium of social statistics from a wide range of government departments and other organizations presenting a broad picture of the British. Contains data on population, households and families, education, employment, income and wealth, expenditure, health, social protection, crime and justice, housing, environment, transport and leisure. Data are in the form of tables, charts and interpretative commentary. In addition some editions contain special reports on specific topics.

Monthly Digest of Statistics, Office for National Statistics
Compendia of the latest social and economic statistics. Contains data on the population, employment, social services, production and output, transport, national income and expenditure, law enforcement, agriculture, food,

drink, tobacco, energy, chemicals, metals, engineering and vehicles, textiles, construction, retailing, external trade, overseas and home finance, prices and wages, leisure and weather.

Regional

Regional trends, Office for National Statistics
A compendium publication with the most comprehensive official statistics about regions of the UK. Contains profiles of each of the 11 standard regions, data on the regions across the European Union, and social or economic topic areas which allow comparisons to be made. Also includes data for the sub-regions and key statistics for the local authority districts.

Financial

Economic and Labour Market Review, Office for National Statistics
A monthly publication, by the Office for National Statistics in collaboration with the statistics divisions of government departments and the Bank of England, which brings together all the main economic indicators.

Financial Statistics, Office for National Statistics
A monthly publication which contains data on public sector finance, central government revenue and expenditure, money supply and credit, banks and building societies, interest and exchange rates, financial accounts, companies and capital issues, balance sheets and balance of payments.

Historical

Mitchell, B. R. (1988) *British historical statistics*, Cambridge University Press
This provides statistics of the UK since 1700.

Mitchell, B. R. (2007) *International historical statistics 1750–2005*, 3 vols
Palgrave Macmillan (Africa, Asia & Oceania, Americas, Europe)

Websites

Government Official Statistics **www.statistics.gov.uk**

World Trade Organization **www.wto.org**
Includes the International Trade Statistics, which are free to download.

Tips and pitfalls

Despite popular belief, statistics are not available for every situation, topic or issue that hits the headlines. It may be necessary to approach some enquiries from a wider perspective or various different angles but the one thing to remember is you cannot provide statistics that simply don't exist. Finding statistics does require a creative mind, in the sense that a bit of lateral thinking is often rewarded. Market research reports and surveys are great sources of statistics as are reports from associations and organizations. It is not out of the question either to ask for a few statistics over the telephone from relevant groups. Furthermore, don't be afraid to suggest, especially to students, that they could collect their own data specific to their project.

Another useful way of finding statistics is to check for relevant associations. Many now put their research publications on the internet. For details of associations and web addresses use the *Directory of British associations*, or one of the other directories listed in ASSOCIATIONS & ORGANIZATIONS.

TAX

See also Benefits

Typical questions

- Where can I find the contact for my local tax office?
- What is inheritance tax?
- I need some help with my council tax, who do I talk to?

Considerations

Tax information is for the tax specialist. There are a number of general publications which can clarify basic enquiries. If these are not sufficient for the query you are dealing with refer the enquirer to a local tax consultant or one of the contacts below. Some of the most commonly asked questions are about forms of tax, such as income tax, VAT, corporation tax, inheritance tax, capital gains tax and council tax. There is an excellent section on government revenue in *UK Yearbook*, The Stationery Office. It explains the collection of taxes and taxation policy and defines the main forms of taxes, dividing them into taxes on income, taxes on capital, and taxes on expenditure. It also mentions local government revenue.

Where to look
Directories

Any of the following are good for tax rates and facts. It is essential that you are using the current edition:

Homer, A. and Burrows, R., *Tolley's tax guide 2007–8*, Butterworth

Vass, J., *Daily mail tax guide 2007/2008,* Profile Books Ltd

Levene, T., *The tax handbook 2008/9: a complete guide to the UK tax system,* Which?

For more analysis and developments try:

International Tax Review
Euromoney Institutional Investor
Tel: 020 7779 8999
www.internationaltaxreview.com
Ten issues per year

T TAX

BDO Stoy Hayward's orange tax guide, Lexis Nexis
> This contains up-to-date legislation relating to National Insurance contributions, stamp duty and VAT.

BDO Stoy Hayward's guide yellow tax guide, Lexis Nexis
> This contains up-to-date legislation relating to income tax, statutes, corporation tax and capital gains tax.

Walton. K. and Dolton, A. (2007) *Tolley's tax cases*, Lexis Nexis Butterworths

Council tax

Queries regarding council tax are best dealt with by the council tax department of your local authority. You will find the telephone number in your local telephone book or use **www.yell.com** or **www.upmystreet.com** to locate. There is a significant amount of information on the internet which may answer some enquiries. Go to the Local Government Finance Index **www.local.communities.gov.uk/finance/stats/ctax.htm**.

For Northern Ireland, where rates are still paid, queries will be dealt with by the Land and Property Services: an executive agency with the Department of Finance and Personal for Northern Ireland: contact details and offices are given in the local telephone book under the Government of Northern Ireland.

To find local tax offices use:

www.hmrc.gov.uk/local

Statistics

Inland Revenue tax receipts, Inland Revenue Analytical Services Division, Office for National Statistics

Websites

Digita Tax Centre **www.digita.com/taxcentral**

Revenue and Customs **www.hmrc.gov.uk/stats**

Road Tax Calculator **www.parkers.co.uk/cars/road-tax**

National Insurance Contributions **www.hmrc.gov.uk/nic**

Tax Advice **www.taxaid.org.uk**

Tax Associations **www.taxsites.com**
    American but useful for international tax associations.

Tax Calculator **www.digita.com**

Tax Payers' Alliance **www.taxpayersalliance.com**

Tax Zone **www.accountingweb.co.uk/tax/index.html**

Treasury **www.hm-treasury.gov.uk**

TELEPHONE DIRECTORIES

See also Addresses & Postcodes

Typical questions

- Can you give me the phone number of the Royal Albert Hall?
- What is the code for Birmingham?
- Which area does this code relate to?

Considerations

First, the codes for all UK areas and international telephone codes can be found at the front of all telephone books. So even if you only have your local telephone book you can answer dialling code queries. Telephone books are marvellous publications providing you have certain pieces of information. If your library is lucky enough to have a full set of UK phone books then you will need to refer to the Phone Book Index to find the number of the volume you need for the town or city requested.

The White Pages and the Yellow Pages do not always share the same volume number. The Yellow Pages in many cases cover a number of towns or cities; using the *National planner*, you can look up the town and be referred to the correct volume. The White Pages are divided into two sections: the first section is an alphabetical list of businesses and organizations, the second section is an alphabetical list of individuals. The Yellow Pages are a classified directory that businesses and others pay to be included in. This is something to bear in mind. It is arranged alphabetically by subject. There is an index at the back that suggests other terms to use if you are having trouble finding what you are looking for.

Where to look
UK telephone directories

For a known business or service or name use the relevant White Pages. To find contacts for a particular industry, service or public service use the Yellow Pages.

Dialling codes can be found in all White Pages or BT's *Phone book companion*. This is available to purchase from BT (Tel: 0800 833 400) and contains all the UK codes listed numerically by code and alphabetically by name. It also includes an international code list and decoder.

For help locating the right telephone book use: *National planner*, Marketing Services Group.

The following are also helpful:

Telephone helpline directory, Telephone Helplines Association
> This directory contains details of 1000 national, regional and local telephone helplines throughout the UK.

Directory enquiries

Many organizations can provide their own enquiry services. The best place to get a full listing of the services including costs is to look at **www.magsys.co.uk/telecom/dialdirq.htm**.

International directories

For availability contact BT's International Directories Unit, Tel: 0800 731 8114.

Websites

Ofcom (Office of Communications) **www.ofcom.org.uk**
> Excellent website, packed with information.

Telephone Directories of the World **www.infobel.com/teldir**
> An excellent site, with 400 links to Yellow Pages, White Pages, business directories, e-mail addresses and fax listings from over 170 countries all around the world.

Yellow Pages **www.yell.co.uk**

White Pages **www.thephonebook.bt.com**

Tips and pitfalls

Don't be surprised not to find some businesses in the Yellow Pages; remember it costs to be included. Also, the majority of trade directories will provide telephone numbers, so don't assume that if you haven't found a business in the phone book it doesn't exist. Using international telephone directories either in hard copy or via the internet can be frustrating because of the language barrier. Looking up terms in a language dictionary is one way to muddle through or you could try one of the translation services via the internet which allows you to type in phrases as well as single words. Try AltaVista's Babel Fish (see LANGUAGES & TRANSLATING).

TELEVISION & RADIO

See also Actors & Actresses; Media & the Press

Typical questions

- What was the cast of 'Fawlty Towers'?
- What is the frequency of Classic FM?
- Have you got details of CB Radio?
- What's 'Freeview'?

Considerations

Programme information, past, present and future, is a regular subject of enquiry, but such is the all-pervasive nature of television and its offshoots such as video, that TV-related enquiries are bound to increase. Wider still is 'media', a more general term for public communication, with a large range of social and technical aspects (see chapter on MEDIA & THE PRESS). We concentrate on directory information here.

Where to look
Radio

Fleming, C. (2002) *The radio handbook*, 2nd edn, Routledge

Media UK **www.mediauk.com**
  Lists 603 radio stations, gives background on the history of radio, and has articles on topics such as digital radio.

Radio Academy **www.radioacademy.org**
  Covers all things to do with radio and has a list of all UK stations.

BBC **www.bbc.co.uk/radio**
Information on radio stations and a comprehensive listings service.

Television

Baskin, E. (1996) *Serials on British television 1950–1994*, Scolar Press

Evans, J. (2006) *The Penguin TV companion*, 3rd edn, Penguin
A large A–Z compendium of programmes and personalities. Includes cast lists and the addresses of television companies.

Holland, P. (2000) *The television handbook*, 2nd edn, Routledge
Covers aspects of television in general.

Media UK **www.mediauk.com**
Full coverage of television facts. Lists 329 TV channels.

Newcomb, H. (ed.) (2000) *Encyclopedia of televsion*, 2nd edn, Fitzroy Dearborn, 4 vols
Available as a free website: **www.museum.tv/archives/etv/index.html**.

Channels

Most television channels have their own website, e.g.:

BBC **www.bbc.co.uk**
A massive website with numerous features and regional sections.

ITV **www.itv.co.uk**

Listings

Printed lists of forthcoming programmes are to be found in newspapers, *Radio Times*, *TV Choice* and *TV Times*. Website listings include:

www.radiotimes.beeb.com

www.teletext.co.uk – a lot faster than from the television itself!

Mightyv **www.mightyv.com**
Information on what's available on a wide range of TV channels.

Other sources

National Media Museum (formerly National Museum of Photography, Film
    and Television)
Bradford, BD1 1NQ
Tel: 01274 202030; Fax: 01274 723155
www.nationalmediamuseum.org.uk

THEATRE & ACTING

See also Actors & Actresses; Plays

Typical questions

* What theatres are there in Leeds?
* Which plays are on in the local theatre?
* How do I get to be an actor?

Where to look

For enquiries concerning local venues and events there will be local publicity and
contacts, such as the events pages in the local press, reception desks and telephone
enquiry lines at the venue concerned, and various local websites. There are
probably numerous free leaflets in local libraries as well! First check which
locality is required.

Printed sources

Banham, M. (ed.) (1995) *The Cambridge guide to theatre*, 3rd edn, Cambridge
    University Press
    A major reference source of over 3500 entries.

Billington, M. (1982) *The Guinness book of theatre facts and feats*, Guinness
    Superlatives

Bordman, G. (2004) *The Oxford companion to American theatre*, Oxford
    University Press

Cambridge history of British theatre (2003) 3 vols, Cambridge University Press

Chambers, C. (ed.) (2002) *The Continuum companion to twentieth century theatre*,
    Continuum
    A mixture of brief entries and essays.

Harrison, M. (1993) *Theatre*, Carcanet
A dictionary of words used in the theatre world.

Hartnoll, P. and Found, P. (1992) *Oxford companion to the theatre*, 2nd edn, Oxford University Press

Taylor, J. R. (1993) *The new Penguin dictionary of the theatre*, 3rd edn, Penguin

The Stage, The Stage. Weekly

Biography

Griffith, T. R. and Woddis, C. (1991) *Bloomsbury theatre guide*, 2nd edn, Bloomsbury

Directories

British performing arts yearbook, Rhinegold Publishing. Annual
A comprehensive directory of UK performing arts.

Williams, R., *The original British theatre directory*, Richmond House.

Artistes and agents, Richard House Publications. Annual

Aloud.com **www.aloud.com**
Directories, events and reviews.

Events

Most weekend newspapers give theatre listings. See also:

Time Out
A magazine, which gives reviews and listings for the London theatres.

Sunday Times Culture Section

News and reviews **www.whatsonstage.com**

UK Theatre Web **www.uktw.co.uk**

Acting and production

Chapman, A. (2007) *The actor's handbook 2007–2008*, Casting Call Pro
The actors handbook is the definitive guide for aspiring and rising actors, offering advice on all areas of vocational acting, from training to self-promotion, finding work to career development.

Cassin-Scott, J. (1979) *Costumes and settings for historical plays*, 4 vols, Batsford

Morrison, H. (2003) *Acting skills*, 3rd rev. edn, A&C Black

Buchman, H. (1989) *Stage makeup*, Watson Guptill

Tardivel, M. (2007) *Artistes and agents 2007*, Richmond House Publications

Other sources

Performing Right Society Ltd (now incorporated into MCPS-PRS Alliance)
> 29–33 Berners Street, London W1P 4AA
> Tel: 020 7580 5444; Fax: 020 7306 4054
> **www.mcps-prs-alliance.co.uk**
> The PRS administers rights, royalties, permissions and licensing on behalf of playwrights.

The Society for Theatre Research
> The Theatre Museum, Tavistock Street, London WC2E 7PA
> **www.str.org.uk**

The Theatre, Musicals and Actors Web is at **www.tmaw.co.uk/homepage.html**.

The various national arts councils also provide advice and (some) support for the dramatic arts.

TIMETABLES & JOURNEY PLANNING

Typical questions

- I want to know the times of trains from Leeds to Blackpool.
- Do you keep local bus timetables?

Considerations

The main types of timetables people will ask for are for trains, long distance coaches, and local buses. Most main libraries should keep copies of the British Rail and National Express timetables. Some keep local bus timetables too. However, these may not be available at smaller branches. Do not worry, though. This is where the internet can prove very useful, with every imaginable type of timetable on there somewhere.

For European travel, the Thomas Cook European timetables are available in some libraries, but are not, as yet, online.

If your customers do not have Sat Nav they can use one of the many useful journey planners online.

Where to look

UK rail timetable, The Stationery Office, 2 p.a.

National Express coach timetable, National Express, 2 p.a.

Thomas Cook European rail timetable, Thomas Cook, 2 p.a.

Thomas Cook rail map of Europe (2007) 16th edn, Thomas Cook

Websites

For European rail timetables try the excellent **www.seat61.com/Europe.htm**.

or **www.raileurope.com/us/index.htm**
www.europeanrail.com/timetables.asp.

National Rail Timetables **http://ojp.nationalrail.co.uk/en/pj/jp**

National Express **www.nationalexpress.com/**

Eurolines (European Coach Travel) **www.eurolines.com/**

For local bus timetables, the following site is excellent. It covers all travel by rail, air, coach, bus, ferry, metro and tram within the UK (including the Channel Islands, Isle of Man and Northern Ireland) and between the UK and Ireland, plus all rail, ferry and coach travel between the UK and mainland Europe. This is *the* definitive index to timetables, fares, ticket types, passenger facilities and lots more: **www.traveline.info**.

Also, Transportdirect is the only website that offers information for door-to-door travel for both public transport and car journeys around Britain. They also have an excellent place locator. Simply type in a place or postcode and a map appears showing all local bus stops and train stations: **http://transportdirect.info**.

For road journeys, try the following sites:

www.theaa.com/travelwatch/planner_main.jsp
www.rac.co.uk/web/routeplanner/

For European journeys try:

www.viamichelin.co.uk

TOURISM & TRAVEL

See also Aircraft & Airlines; Museums & Galleries; Timetables & Journey Planning; Transport

Typical questions
- Have you any books on Cape Town?
- Where do I get a passport from?
- I'm doing a tourism course. What useful sources do you have?

Considerations
This is a popular subject with students who are usually requiring tourism or leisure spending statistics. For this you will require statistical publications and/or market research reports, both of which can be expensive. If your library does not subscribe to such things then you could make use of the various sites on the internet. Some general publications also contain travel and tourism statistics, such as *Annual abstract of statistics*, *Social trends* and *Regional trends*. Strategic responsibility for tourism in England lies with the regional development agencies. A list of these can be found at **www.visitbritain.org** as well as a list of the regional tourist boards.

For travel advice and tips for British travellers on staying safe look at **www.fco.gov.uk/en/travelling-and-living-overseas**

For information on passports use the Identity and Passport Service **www.ips.gov.uk/passport/index.asp**.

Where to look
Directories
Travel trade gazette directory, CMP Information **www.ttglive.com/ttgdirectory**
Online alphabetical search facility to find company information on a wide range of travel categories, e.g. accommodation, car hire and tour operators.

Books
Youell, R. (2003) *Complete A–Z travel and leisure handbook*, 2nd edn, Hodder

Jenkins, T. (ed.) (2002) *Ethical tourism*, Hodder

Journals

There are numerous journals for the leisure industry, details of which can be found in *Willings press guide* (see JOURNALS & PERIODICALS).

Market intelligence

IRN research reports **www.irn-research.com**

Free to download executive summaries of research reports concerning the travel and tourism industry.

Mintel leisure reports, Mintel International Group

A fee-based service that provides in-depth research into the leisure and recreation industry. Looks at market factors, market segmentation, the consumer and the future. Also available on CD-ROM. For details visit **www.mintel.co.uk** or call Tel: 020 7606 4533; Fax: 020 7606 5932.

Key Note reports, Key Note

For free executive summaries of report titles listed under travel and tourism visit **www.keynote.co.uk**. For details of obtaining full reports, contact Key Note (Tel: 020 8481 8750; Fax: 020 87830049).

Statistics
Travel

Travel trends, Annual

Available to download at **www.statistics.gov.uk**.
Select 'Travel and Tourism' from the main page.

National travel survey

Available to download at **www.dft.gov.uk**.
Select 'Transport Statistics', 'Statistics' then 'Personal Travel'.

Tourism

Visit Britain **www.visitbritain.org**

Visit Britain is the national tourism agency which promotes Britain internationally. It provides a wealth of information for statistics and market research. Excellent. Well worth a visit.

World Tourism Organisation **www.unwto.org**

> Produces numerous statistical publications including *Yearbook of tourism statistics* (2007) 2 vols; *Compendium of tourism statistics* (2007); *Tourism market trends for Africa, Asia, and the Middle East* (2006); and *UNWTO world tourism barometer*.

Organizations and websites

There are hundreds of organizations dealing with the huge range of tourism and travel activities available. There is a very good selection of contacts in *Key organizations*, Carel Press. In addition, using one of the search engines such as **google.com** will also give good results. Don't forget your local Tourist Informaton Office.

Association of British Travel Agents **www.abta.com**

Association of Leading Visitor Attractions **www.alva.org.uk**

> Useful for visitor statistics for major UK attractions.

Britainonview **www.britainonview.com**

> The online image library of VisitBritain. Fantastic.

Department of Culture, Media and Sport **www.culture.gov.uk**

enjoyEngland **www.enjoyEngland.com**

> Official website for breaks and days out in England.

Freedom Days **www.freedom-days.co.uk**

> Day trips for all the family.

Holidaycare **www.holidaycare.org.uk**

> Holiday and travel information service for disabled and older people.

Information Britain **www.information-britain.co.uk**

Northern Ireland Tourist Board **www.nitb.com**

Travel GBI **www.travelgbi.com**

> Covers travel, holiday and tourism for the UK and Ireland.

UK inbound **www.ukinbound.org**

> Use for tour operators and suppliers within the industry dealing with oversea visitors.

Via Michelin **www.viamichelin.com**
> Includes maps, driving instructions, tourism information

VisitLondon **www.visitlondon.com**

VisitScotland **www.visitscotland.org**

VisitWales **www.visitwales.com**

World Travel Guide **www.worldtravelguide.net**
> Excellent guide to countries, cities, airports, beaches and much more. Includes a world clock and weather guides.

TRADE UNIONS

Typical questions
- Have you got the contact number for the local branch of my trade union?
- Can you tell me what . . . trade union has said about . . . issue?

Considerations
For enquiries that require trade union local branch contact details the local telephone directory should be sufficient. Most trade unions in the UK now have websites which will provide further information. Otherwise, the resources listed below all provide excellent information.

Where to look
Directories
Trade unions of the world, John Harper Publishing
> The main trade unions are given for each country listed; in addition, some historical background information is provided.

Websites
European Trade Union Confederation **www.etuc.org**

International Confederation of Free Trade Unions **www.icftu.org**
> Excellent site, which is packed with information including links to global unions.

TUC **www.tuc.org.uk**
> Excellent site for research publications and provides links to individual British unions.

TRANSPORT

See also Aircraft & Airlines; Railways; Timetables & Journey Planning

Typical questions

- Have you got the address of the local bus company?
- Have you statistics for rail usage in the UK and Europe?
- Can you tell me where the cycle lanes in the UK are?

Considerations

There is no end to the enquiries you could be asked regarding transport. Some are specific to timetables, contact details and how to get from A to B. In the main, most of these can be answered directly by the local bus or train companies. You can find contact details in your local telephone book or try **www.yell.com**. Or you could use some of the suggestions in the chapter TIMETABLES & JOURNEY PLANNING. Other enquiries may relate to statistics and the state of the transport industry, or come from those interested in policy and campaigns. Fortunately, the transport industry has some good sources of information which should offer answers or at least point you in the right direction.

Where to look
Directories

If you need information on the world's railway industry look no further than:

Railway directory, Railway gazette publication with DVV Media UK
This provides an alphabetical listing of the world's railways, maps, and manufacturers and suppliers of rail equipment.

For bus and coach information then use:

The little red book, Ian Allan Publishing
Provides detailed information on bus and coach operators throughout Britain.

Statistics

Annual bulletin of transport statistics for Europe and North America, United Nations Economic Commission for Europe

Available to download at **www.unece.org/trans/main/wp6/transstatpub.html**. Covers general transport statistics as well as rail, road, inland waterways and maritime.

Transport trends, Department for Transport (DFT)

Transport Statistics **www.dft.gov.uk**
Provides a wealth of transport statistical information including *Transport statistics GB* and *Transport trends*. Excellent.

Transport yearbook, Transport Statistics Users Group (TSUG) and the Stationery Office

Organizations and websites

Air Transport Users' Council
CAA House, 45–59 Kingsway, London WC2B 6TE
Tel: 020 7240 6061
www.auc.org.uk

Campaign for better transport **www.bettertransport.org.uk**

Chartered Institute of Logistics and Transport **www.ciltuk.org.uk**

Confederation of Passenger Transport UK **www.cpt-uk.org**

Cycleweb.co.uk **www.cycleweb.co.uk**
Good for links and cyclemaps directory.

Department for Transport **www.dft.gov.uk**

Office of the Rail Regulator
1 Kemble Street, London WC2B 4AN
Tel: 020 7282 2000
www.rail-reg.gov.uk
Excellent, provides statistics, industry structure, publications and much more.

Maritime.com **www.maritimenews.com**
Useful for finding world ports.

National Federation of Bus Users **www.nfbu.org**
Provides downloadable access to Bus Users UK annual report.

National Rail **www.nationalrail.co.uk/passenger_services**
   Provides lots of additional information for the public, train enthusiasts, teachers and children.

Passenger Focus **www.passengerfocus.org.uk**
   For rail passengers.

Sustrans **www.sustrans.org.uk**
   Sustainable transport charity. Excellent for information and links.

UKSuperweb.co.uk **www.uksuperweb.co.uk/public-transport.html**
   Excellent for links to everything to do with transport, journeys, operators and much more throughout the UK. Well worth a visit.

THE UNEXPLAINED

See also Myths & Mythology; Religion

Typical questions

- Have you any books on interpreting dreams?
- Where are the most haunted places in the UK?
- Where can I find something on the Bermuda Triangle?
- How can I work out my horoscope?

Considerations

The 'unexplained' covers a wide range of subjects from angels to zombies! Only a few of these subjects can be touched on here. Broadly speaking, the subjects fall outside the boundaries of orthodox science and one of the first considerations the librarian has is to find out whether the enquirer is a 'sceptic' or a 'believer', that is to say, is the enquirer investigating the subject, or are they serious about the subject? The sources used may vary accordingly. For better or for worse, there is a great popular interest in these subjects and there is a need to be well supplied with sources and information about them.

Where to look
General

Bord, J. and Bord, C. (1996) *Dictionary of earth mysteries*, Thorsons

Carall, R. T. (2003) *The skeptic's dictionary: a collection of strange beliefs, amusing deceptions, and dangerous delusions*, Wiley
Available online, free, at **http://skepdic.com**.

Guiley, R. E. (1992) *Harper's encyclopedia of mystical and paranormal experience*, HarperCollins

Picknett, L. (1990) *The encyclopedia of the paranormal: a complete guide to the unexplained*, Macmillan

Randles, J. (1996) *The paranormal source book; the comprehensive guide to strange phenomena worldwide*, Piatkus

Rickard, B. and Michell, J. (2000) *Unexplained phenomena: a Rough Guide special*, Rough Guides

Steiger, B. and Steiger, S. H. (2003) *The Gale encyclopedia of the unusual and unexplained*, Gale, 3 vols

Williams. W. F. (ed.) (2000) *Encyclopedia of pseudoscience*, Fitzroy Dearborn
2000 A–Z entries relating to superstitions, alternative medicine, frauds, hoaxes, mistaken therories, etc.

Wilson, C. (1987) *The encyclopedia of unsolved mysteries*, Harrap

Astrology

Parker, J. and D. (2001) *Parker's astrology: the definitive guide to using astrology in every aspect of your life*, 2nd edn, Dorling Kindersley

Goodman, L. (1968) *Linda Goodman sun signs*, Pan
The classic bestseller.

Fenton, S. (1998) *How to read your star signs*, Thorsons

Astrology.com **www.astrology.com**

Astrology Gateway **www.astrologygateway.homestead.com**

Dreams

The alleged 'meaning' of dreams can be addressed in a number of books compiled specifically for the purpose. The enquiries relating to such popular beliefs like astrology need to be distinguished from orthodox scientific enquiries about the physiology and psychology of sleep and consciousness. In terms of the Dewey classification, between the 135s and the 150s.

Numerous popular books are published on the subject, for example:

Miller. G. H. (1995) *Ten thousand dreams interpreted, or what's in a dream*, Ernest Benn

Pelton, R. W. (1983) *The complete book of dream interpretation*, Arco Publishing

Raphael, E. (1996) *The complete book of dreams*, Foulsham

Most general books on psychology and sleep contain information, as do encyclopedias. Try:

Gregory, R. L. (ed.) (1998) *The Oxford companion to the mind*, Oxford University Press

Dictionary of dream symbols **www.petrix.com/dreams**

Prophecy

Nostradamus, *The prophecies*. Many editions, e.g. *The prophecies of Nostradamus* (1989) Spearman

The complete book of fortune (1988) Chatto and Windus
Includes numerology, tea-leaves, palmistry, omens, graphology, etc.

Ghosts

Spencer, J. and Spencer, A. (2000) *Ghost hunter's guide to Britain*, Collins
A popular and reasonably factual geographical guide to alleged sightings of ghosts.

Spencer, J. and Spencer, A. (1996) *The encyclopedia of ghosts and spirits*, Headline

The Ghost Club
PO Box 160, St Leonards-on-Sea TN38 8WA
www.ghostclub.org.uk

Tarot and runes

Garen, N. (1989) *Tarot made easy*, Simon & Schuster

Blum, R. (2000) *Book of runes*, Connections

UFOs

Blevins, D. (2003) *UFO directory international: 1,000+ organizations and publications in 40+ countries*, McFarland

Randles, J. and Warrington, P. (1985) *Science and the UFOs*, Blackwell

UNIFORMS

See also Armed Forces; Costume & Fashion; Medals & Decorations

Typical questions

- Have you got a picture of the uniform of the Horse Guards?
- Which regiments wear the busby?

Considerations

There is a large literature related to the uniforms of the armed forces, much of it aimed at the specialist markets of the modeller, military historian and collector. Check which use is required, since the first will probably want coloured plates, the second well-documented prose, and the third current price guides. Be aware, also, of the distinction between badges and insignia, which are part of uniform, and medals and decorations, which may or may not be.

Where to look
Printed sources

Carman, W. Y. (1977) *A dictionary of military uniforms*, Batsford
A–Z by feature.

Newark, T. (1999) *Brassey's book of uniforms*, Brassey's

Illustrated sources

Barnes, R. M. (1972) *Military uniforms of Britain and the Empire*, Seeley
Line drawings.

Carman, Y. (1985) *Uniforms of the British army*, Webb and Bower

Knotel, H. and Sieg, H. (1980) *Uniforms of the world: a compendium of army, navy, and air force uniforms, 1700–1937*, Arms and Armour Press
Line drawings, historical background.

Lason, C. C. P. (1996) *A history of the uniforms of the British army*, 5 vols, Kay & Ward

There a number of publishers' series featuring a particular country, period, type of force or even particular regiments with coloured illustrations. These include:

Arms and uniforms series, Ward Lock

Osprey Elite series, Osprey Publications

Uniforms Illustrated series, Arms and Armour Press

Badges and insignia

Churchill, C. and Westlake, R. (1986) *British army collar badges, 1881 to the present: an illustrated reference guide for collectors*, 2nd edn, Arms and Armour Press

Davis, B. L. (1988) *British army cloth insignia, 1940 to the present: an illustrated reference guide for collectors*, 2nd edn, Arms and Armour Press

Short, J. G. (1988) *Special forces insignia, British and Commonwealth units: an illustrated reference guide for collectors*, Arms and Armour Press

All the above have price guides.

Hobart, M. C. (2000) *Badges and uniforms of the Royal Air Force*, Leo Cooper

Kipling, A. L. and King, H. I. (1978) *Head-dress badges of the British army*, 2nd edn, F. Muller Ltd
A two-volume definitive work.

Other sources

Imperial War Museum
Lambeth Road, London SE1 6HZ
Tel: 020 7416 5320
www.iwm.org.uk

UNITED NATIONS

See also Politics & International Relations

Typical questions

• Have you got the Universal Declaration of Human Rights?
• What's the Charter of the UN?
• Who are the members of the Security Council?

Considerations

General information on the UN is fairly easy to find: encyclopedias and books on international relations have material. Harder to locate, or obtain, are detailed accounts of the proceedings and texts of resolutions of the UN as only the larger libraries stock this material and the UN itself is very slow at publishing. The best sources are newspaper accounts and information on the UN's own website, which is extensive and helpful.

Where to look
Printed sources

Gareis, S. B. and Varwick, J. (2005) *The United Nations: an introduction*,
Palgrave Macmillan
This provides a systematic introduction to the main areas of activity of the
United Nations today and to its organization and evolution as well as an
evaluation of its likely role and prospects for reform in the 21st century.

Luard, E. (1994) *The United Nations: how it works and what it does*, 2nd edn,
Macmillan

Rengger, N. (ed.) (1995) *Treaties and alliances of the world*, 6th edn, Catermill
Has the texts of many of the international treaties and agreements that
feature the UN.

United Nations Yearbook. Annual

United Nations statistical yearbook, UNESCO/The Stationery Office. Annual
A comprehensive collection of statistics on all subjects, comparing most
countries of the world.

United Nations (2004) *Basic facts about the United Nations*, United Nations

Osmanczyk, E. J. *Encyclopedia of the United Nations and international agreements*
(2002) 23rd rev. edn, Taylor & Francis

Try news databases such as the indexes to *The Times* or newspaper websites (see
NEWSPAPERS & MAGAZINES) for recent events such as voting details in the Security
Council.

Electronic sources

United Nations **www.un.org**
A large site giving a wide range of information and text.

Other sources

United Nations Association of the UK **www.una-uk.org**
The United Nations Association of Great Britain and Northern Ireland
(UNA-UK) is the UK's leading independent policy authority on the UN
and a UK-wide grassroots membership organization.

Statesman's yearbook, *Whitaker's almanack* and many other current affairs sources have information about the UN.

The United Nations is a serious publisher of statistics, along with enormous amounts of English-language material. Some material can be ordered through The Stationery Office outlets. There are also a number of linked organizations, e.g. UNESCO, WHO (World Health Organization).

UTILITIES

See also Energy

Typical questions

- Have you got the contact details for . . . electricity supplier?
- How do I complain about my gas supplier?
- How do I find out about water meters?

Where to look
Water

The main directory to use is:

Who's who in the water industry, Faversham House Group

But try also:

Web4Water **www.web4water.co.uk**
    This includes an online directory and excellent links to everything to do with water and the water industry. Well worth a visit.

Clarke, R. and King, J. (2004) *The atlas of water: mapping the world's most critical resource*, Earthscan Atlas Series

Websites for electricity, gas and water

Association of Electricity Producers **www.aepuk.com**

Corgi **www.trustcorgi.com**
    The national watchdog for gas safety in the UK.

Drinking Water Inspectorate **www.dwi.gov.uk**

Department for Business, Enterprise and Regulatory Reform
    www.og.berr.gov.uk

Excellent for statistics, policy documents and reports on oil and gas.

Department for Environment Food & Rural Affairs
www.defra.gov.uk/environment/water.index.htm

Electricity Guide **www.electricity-guide.org.uk**
Provides information on the industry and the companies operating within it. Excellent.

Energywatch **www.energywatch.org.uk**
The gas and electricity watchdog that handles consumers' complaints against gas and electricity companies. Helpline 08459 06 07 08.

Gas Guide **www.gas-guide.org.uk**
Provides information on the industry and the companies operating within it. Excellent.

OFGEM (Office of Gas and Electricity Markets) **www.ofgem.gov.uk**

OFWAT (Office of the Water Services) **www.ofwat.gov.uk**
Useful for water companies' contact details and how to complain.

National Grid **www.nationalgrid.com/uk/electricity**

National Grid **www.nationalgrid.com/uk/gas**

Rigzone.com www.rigzone.com
The gateway to the oil and gas industry.

Water Aid UK site **www.wateraid.org.uk**
Excellent. Well worth a visit.

Water Guide **www.water-guide.org.uk**
Provides information about the UK water industry and the companies operating within it. Excellent.

Water UK **www.water.org.uk**
Provides a huge amount of information covering all aspects of the water industry.

VOLUNTEERING

See also Charitable Organizations; Jobs

Typical questions

- After college I would like to do voluntary work. Have you any addresses?
- I'm planning for my retirement and wonder if my skills would be useful.
- Where can I get volunteers for an environmental project?

Considerations

Questions on volunteering are among the more pleasing of enquiries to handle. This is a growing area now that there are more retired people and more people are concerned with helping the environment and helping other people.

Where to look
Organizations

British Trust for Conservation Volunteers
   Tel: 01795 583 850
   www.btcv.org.uk

International Voluntary Service
   7 Upper Bow, Edinburgh EH1 2NJ
   Tel: 0131 226 6722

National Association of Volunteer Bureaux
   New Oxford House, 16 Waterloo Street, Birmingham B2 5UC
   Tel: 0121 633 4555 (England); 029 2039 0477 (Wales)
   Places volunteers in a number of different projects across the country.

National Centre for Volunteering
   Regents Wharf, 8 All Saints Street, London N1 9RL
   Tel: 020 7520 8900
   www.volunteering.org.uk

National Council for Voluntary Organisations (NCVO)
   Regent's Wharf, 8 All Saints Street, London N1 9RL
   Tel: 020 7713 6161

National Women's Register (formerly National Housewives Register)
   Unit 3A, Vulcan House, Vulcan Road North, Norwich NR6 6AQ

Tel: 0845 4500 287 or 01603 406767; Fax: 01603 407003
E-mail: office@mwr.org
www.nwr.org;
Informal meetings and discussions.

Pybus, V. (ed.) (1997) *The international directory of voluntary work*, 6th edn
Vacation Work

REACH
Tel: 020 7928 1452
Arranges voluntary places for experienced managers or professionals.

Relatives Association
Tel: 020 7916 6055

Retired and Senior Volunteer Programme (RSVP)
Tel: 020 7278 6601 (England); 029 2039 0477 (Wales)

The voluntary agencies directory, NCVO Publications. Annual
Guide to over 2000 charities and voluntary organizations, with contact details.

WEATHER

Typical questions

- What will the weather be like in Madeira next week?
- What is the average summer temperature in Boston, USA?
- What was the weather like on 23 September 2000 in Lytham St Annes?
- Have you any information about tornadoes? I want to know how they are formed.

Considerations

There is much to consider here. Enquirers may want forecasts for holidays, or want to check previous weather for insurance purposes. They may be doing school projects on the weather. The possibilities are endless. However, with a few select resources, you should be able to manage most enquiries.

Where to look

General

Harding, M. (2001) *Weather to travel: the traveller's guide to the world's weather*, 3rd edn, Tomorrow's Guides Ltd
Weather profiles and what to wear for 205 countries.

Meteorological Office (1991) *Meteorological glossary*, 6th edn, HMSO
The definitive glossary.

Pearce, E. A. and Smith, C. G. (2000) *World weather guide*, 4th rev. edn, Helicon

Watts, A. (1994) *The weather handbook*, Waterline
A good general introduction to our weather systems.

Whitaker, R. (ed.) (1996) *Weather: the ultimate guide to the elements*, HarperCollins
A comprehensive and accessible guide to meteorology.

Longshore, D. (1998) *Encyclopedia of hurricanes, typhoons and cyclones*, Fitzroy Dearborn

The Met Office

The Met Office provide a wealth of information about weather.

Met Office
>FitzRoy Road, Exeter, Devon EX1 3PB
>Tel: 0870 900 0100; Fax: 0870 900 5050
>**www.metoffice.gov.uk**

Current forecasts are available from:

www.metoffice.gov.uk/weather/uk/uk_forecast_weather.html

Severe weather warnings from:

www.metoffice.gov.uk/weather/uk/uk_forecast_warnings.html

Links to other sites giving related warnings and advice are at:

www.metoffice.gov.uk/about/website/links.html

The National Meteorological Library and Archive is based at the Met Office. This is open to the public and exists to provide information for anyone with an interest in the weather and climate and includes a comprehensive collection of published literature on meteorology and related science and original weather records. The Library and the Archive for England and Wales are based in Exeter, with an Archive for Scotland in Edinburgh and weather records for Northern Ireland being held in Belfast. A searchable online catalogue is available, which will enable you to see what is available on a particular topic. There are also fact sheets to introduce topics on weather and meteorology, and subject guides, which give an idea of the literature on certain topics for those pursuing their interest for the first time. Staff are happy to assist with enquiries via telephone or e-mail during stated opening hours.

More information on the Library and Archive, including the catalogue, may be found at **www.metoffice.gov.uk/corporate/library/index.html**, with the fact sheets at **www.metoffice.gov.uk/corporate/library/factsheets.html**.

Electronic sources

There are some great weather sites around on the internet. Here are a selection:

Weather gateway **www.weather.co.uk**
BBC Weather **www.bbc.co.uk/weather**
The Met Office **www.metoffice.gov.uk**
Yahoo World Weather **http://weather.yahoo.com**

There is a useful site for flood warnings:

www.environment-agency.gov.uk/subjects/flood/floodwarning

Tips and pitfalls

Many libraries keep weather figures from their local weather stations. Check to see whether yours does or not. These figures are very popular for people putting in insurance claims for storm damage, etc. If you do not keep these then check local newspapers or contact your local weather observation station.

WEIGHTS & MEASURES

Typical questions

- What's 60 degrees Fahrenheit in centigrade?
- How much does a pint of water weigh?
- When do children's shoe sizes change to adult ones? Are they the same in the USA?

Considerations

Simple conversions from, say, imperial measures into metric, can be found in most desk diaries, even pocket diaries. Staff should check what is in theirs! More complex conversions, such as those used in engineering, may well be beyond the librarian's comprehension, but possibly within that of the engineer who asks!

Where to look

Whitaker's almanack, A&C Black. Annual
    Has conversion tables.

Diagram Group (1997) *Collins gem ready reference*, HarperCollins
    Over 130 quick conversion tables.

Economist (1998) *The Economist desk companion: how to measure, convert, calculate and define practically anything*, 3rd edn, The Economist
    272 pages and index.

Zwillinger, D. (ed.) (1996) *CRC standard mathematical tables and formulae*, 30th edn, CRC Press

Bolton, B. (2001) *Newnes instrumentation and measurement and measurement pocket book*, 3rd edn, Newnes
    Technical data.

Tips and pitfalls

Different countries use different sizes for clothes. The UK and USA still use some imperial (non-metric) measures, the USA more so, but not always the same ones! An example is paper sizes.

WINE

See also Food & Drink

Typical questions

- Where can I find recommendations for wines to buy?
- How many units in the average glass of wine?
- How much wine is consumed each year in the UK?

Considerations

Many food and drink directories have information on wine merchants, suppliers etc. However, there are some fantastic guides on the market and it is worth having at least one in your reference collection.

Where to look

To find out what a unit is visit **www.units.nhs.uk**, which explains and has a unit calculator.

Printed sources

For the history of wine try:

Gabler. J. (ed.) *Wine into words*, Bacchus Press
   A history and bibliography of wine books in the English language. For those with a serious interest in wine literature.

Hurley, J. (2005) *A matter of taste: the history of wine drinking in Britain*, Tempus Publishing

A dictionary of wine, Fitzroy Dearborn

Guides

There are numerous 'choosing wine' reference books available. Check your library shelves to see what you have available or try:

Parker, R. (2002) *Parker's wine buyer's guide*, 2 vols, 6th edn, Dorling Kindersley
A comprehensive round-up of the world's wine output, scores given to all wines tasted. The essential reference work for those seeking guidance in buying or drinking fine wines.

Robinson, J. (ed.) (2006) *Oxford companion to wine*, 3rd edition, Oxford University Press.
The world's most respected wine book having won every major wine book award on both sides of the Atlantic. This has 4000 entries covering every aspect of wine. It is fully illustrated with maps, diagrams and photgraphs. This should answer most questions from wine regions to the politics of wine.

World's best wines (2008) William Reed Business Media
Buyers' guide to wine and where to find it. Reviews of the UK's leading wine retailers and information on the world's top wine regions.

Also try:

Arkell, J. (2006) *Wine*, Collins
Practical guide to wine.

Bettane, M. and Desseauve, T. (2006) *World's greatest wines*, Stewart, Tabori & Chang

Broadbent, M. (2003) *Vintage wine*, Little Brown

Broadbent, M. (2000) *Winetasting*, Mitchell Beazley
The classic wine-tasting reference book.

Clarke, O. (2007) *Pocket wine book*, Little Brown

Johnson, H. (2007) *Pocket wine book*, Mitchell Beazley

Robinson, J. (ed.) (2001) *Concise wine companion*, Oxford University Press

Stevenson, T. (2002) *Christie's encyclopedia of champagne and sparkling wine*, Absolute Press
The definitive book on fizz.

Stevenson, T. (ed.) (2008) *The wine report 2008*, Dorling Kindersley
Gives vintage guides, recommended wines and in-depth information on all the world's wine regions.

Williamson, P. and Moore. D. (2008) *Wine behind the label*, 6th edn, Williamson and Moore
Covers 18,000 wines and 3000 producers.

Market research

Key Note reports, Key Note
For free executive summaries of report titles listed under drinks and tobacco visit **www.keynote.co.uk**. For details of obtaining full reports, contact Key Note (Tel: 020 8481 8750; Fax: 020 8783 0049).

Mintel market reports, Mintel International Group
Provides in-depth research the alcoholic drinks industry. Looks at market factors, market segmentation, the consumer and the future. For details visit **www.mintel.com** or Tel: 0207 606 4533.

Websites

All About Wine **www.allaboutwine.com**

Decanter **www.decanter.com**
An online wine magazine. Full of news, with a wine finder and recommendations. Useful section on learning about wine.

The interactive Taste Trainer Program **www.freewinecourse.com**
A fun interactive wine tasting course to do in your own time.

Uncork **www.uncork.biz**

Wine Education Service **www.wine-education-service.co.uk**
For information on wine courses, wine tastings and holidays.

Wine of the Week **www.wineoftheweek.com**
A web-zine for wine and food lovers.

Wine on the Web (WOW) **www.wineontheweb.co.uk**
The talking wine magazine.

Wine-pages **wine-pages.com**
Packed with information, news, wine region guides, tastings, links. Useful for the glossary of wine words.

Wine-Searcher.com **www.wine-searcher.com**

The resource for locating and pricing wines. Useful for the Wine Spectator's Top 100 wines.

Wine & Spirit www.wine-spirit.com
Information and news about the wine industry.

Wine & Spirit Education Trust www.wset.co.uk

WRITERS & WRITING

See also Biographies; Books and Bibliographies; Copyright & Legal Deposit; ISBNs and ISSNs; Literature; Proofreading & Editing; Publishing

Typical questions

- How do I write a dissertation?
- I've written a book. How do I get it published?

Considerations

It is natural that people interested in writing should ask a librarian. Many people, though, have a naive view of how easy it is to get published. Don't feed these expectations!

Where to look
General

Author.co.uk www.author.co.uk
A website supported by the Arts Council of England, which provides contacts, reviews, news, discussion groups and other web-based services.

The Author: Journal of the Society of Authors. **Monthly**
As well as feature articles this journal includes adverts for courses, prizes and agents. Good for 'official' news such as legislation and legal matters.

Bolt, D. (2000) *New authors handbook*, 2nd edn, P. Owen

Germano, W. (2001) *Getting it published: a guide for scholars and anyone else serious about serious books*, Chicago University Press

Hoffman, A. (2003) *Research for writers*, 7th edn, A&C Black
Includes many directory sections.

Kane, T. S. (1994) *The new Oxford guide to writing*, Oxford University Press

Legat, M. (1998) *An author's guide to publishing*, 3rd edn, Hale

International authors and writers who's who, Melrose Press. Bi-annual
A comprehensive directory to living authors worldwide.

Ritter, R. (2000) *The Oxford dictionary for writers and editors*, Oxford University Press
One of many handy works which lists words and abbreviations writers need to check for meaning and spelling.

Singleton, J. (ed.) (1999) *The creative writing handbook*, 2nd edn, Palgrave Macmillan
Sources, techniques and outlets.

Turner, B. (ed.) *The writer's handbook*, Macmillan. Annual
Both this and *The writers' and artists' yearbook* contain pretty well everything the aspiring writer needs, from information on how to present work, agents and publishers, to advice on copyright, rights and contracts, and much else in the literary and media marketplaces.

Writers' and artists' yearbook, A&C Black. Annual
Sub-title: 'A directory for writers, artists, playwrights, writers for film, radio and television, designers, illustrators and photographers'.

Writers' News. Monthly
A magazine giving advice on techniques and contacts published by Writers' News Ltd. Has a helpline.

Directories

Hayden, D. (2003) *Directory of writers' circles*, Diane Hayden (39 Lincoln Way, Harlington, Beds LU5 6NG)
Details of over 1200 writers' groups in the UK and Eire: Writers' Circles **www.writers-circles.com.**

Light, J. *Light's list: worldwide list of titles, addresses and a brief note of interests of over 1500 independent press magazines publishing poetry, short stories, articles, artwork market information, in English*, Photon Press. Annual

The writer's directory, St James Press. Annual
Biographical, bibliographic and contact information on 17,500 living authors from English-speaking countries.

Text preparation and style manuals

(see also PROOFREADING & EDITING)

The Chicago manual of style (2004) 15th edn, Chicago University Press
The essential guide for writers, editors and publishers.

Butcher, J., Drake, C. and Leach, M. (2006) *Butcher's copy-editing: the Cambridge handbook for editors, copy-editors and proofreaders*, 4th edn, Cambridge University Press
The classic handbook.

Modern Humanities Research Association (1996) *Notes for authors, editors and writers*, 5th edn, Maney Publishing
Details on copy preparation, proof correction, etc. More basic than Butcher.

BS 5261–1: 2000 *Copy preparation and proof correction*
Covers document layout, arrangement of headings and footnotes, choice of typography, etc.

Ritter, R. M. (2003) *The Oxford style manual*, Oxford University Press
Includes *Hart's rules for compositors and typesetters*.

Strunk, W. and White, E. B. (2000) *The elements of style*, 4th edn, Allyn & Bacon

Reports, etc.

There are numerous popular, low-priced guides to writing 'papers'. Examples are:

Berry, R. (1999) *The research project: how to write it*, 4th edn, Routledge

Oliver, P. (1996) *Teach yourself writing essays and reports*, Hodder & Stoughton

Turabian, K. L. (2001) *A manual for writers of term papers, theses, and dissertations*, 6th edn, Chicago University Press

Indexing

BS 6529: 1984 (1991) *Recommendation for examining documents, determining their subjects and selecting indexing terms*

Collison, R. L. (1969) *Indexes and indexing: guide to the indexing of books*, 3rd edn, E. Benn
One of several guides to indexing.

Society of Indexers
Woodbourn Business Centre, 10 Jessell Street, Sheffied S9 3HY
www.indexers.org.uk
The Society provides information about indexing, employment and training.

Biographical information
(see also BIOGRAPHIES)

British Council (1979) *British writers*, 8 vols, Scribners

Cox, M. (ed.) (2001) *Who wrote what? A dictionary of writers and their works*, Oxford University Press
25,000 works by 3000 authors; author and title listings.

International authors and writers who's who, Melrose. Bi-annual

Seymour-Smith, M. (1990) *Who's who in twentieth century literature*, Weidenfeld

St James Press produces the following annual titles:

Contemporary poets
Contemporary dramatists
Contemporary novelists

Other sources
The Society of Authors
84 Drayton Gardens, London SW10 9SB
Tel: 020 7373 6642; Fax: 020 7373 5768
E-mail: authorsoc@writers.org.org.uk
www.writers.org.uk/society
An association which campaigns for authors and gives members advice on business aspects of publishing contracts, copyright, etc. Publishes *The Author*.

Tips and pitfalls
Talking to authors can be enormously pleasurable; talking to wannabe authors usually less so. Beware of getting drawn into doing their research, passing opinions, or offering to read!

INDEX